HERITAGE OF FEAR

Illusion and Reality in the Cold War

HERITAGE OF FEAR

Illusion and Reality in the Cold War

a review by
Richard Lawrence Miller

Walker and Company   New York

Copyright © 1988 by Richard Lawrence Miller

All rights reserved. No part of this book may be reproduced or transmitted in any form or by any means, electronic or mechanical, including photocopying, recording, or by any information storage and retrieval system, without permission in writing from the Publisher.

First published in the United States of America in 1988 by the Walker Publishing Company, Inc.

Published simultaneously in Canada by Thomas Allen & Son Canada, Limited, Markham, Ontario.

Library of Congress Cataloging-in-Publication Data
  Miller, Richard L. (Richard Lawrence)
    Heritage of fear : illusion and reality in the cold war : a review / by Richard L. Miller.
    p.   cm.
  ISBN 0-8027-1021-2
  1. Communist countries—Foreign relations—History—20th century. 2. World politics—1945- 3. Communist countries—Foreign relations—History—19th century. 4. Communism—History. 5. Communist strategy. I. Title.
D847.M49   1988
327'.091717—dc19   88-10827
                                                                                       CIP

Printed in the United States of America

10 9 8 7 6 5 4 3 2 1

To
*Americans who risked their lives
defending democracy
abroad and at home*

Contents

Preface ix
Acknowledgments xi

I.	THE FIRST COMMUNISTS	1
II.	COMMUNISTS AND WORLD WAR I	6
III	EUROPE AFTER THE WAR	18
IV.	TOILERS OF THE EAST	31
V.	SOVIET-GERMAN AMITY	41
VI.	REPUBLICAN COMMUNISTS AND THE SPANISH CIVIL WAR	51
VII.	THE BALTIC REGION	61
VIII.	POLAND IN WORLD WAR II	81
IX.	THE BALKANS	91
X.	THREE GOVERNMENTS THAT FOUGHT THE FUTURE	115
XI.	COMMUNIST TRIUMPH IN CHINA	129
XII.	COMMUNIST FAILURE IN KOREA	137
XIII.	SOUTHEAST ASIA	159
XIV.	THE CHALLENGE OF INDIA	177
XV.	DECLINE OF THE STALINIST SYSTEM: POLAND AND HUNGARY, 1956	185
XVI.	CUBA: THE EMERGENCE OF CASTRO	203
XVII.	COMMUNISM ON ONE ISLAND	218
XVIII.	COMMUNIST FAILURE IN LATIN AMERICA	234
XIX.	AFRICA	253
XX.	CZECHOSLOVAKIA	264
XXI.	FRENCH INDOCHINA	279
XXII.	THE FATE OF EMPIRES	297
XXIII.	THE CHALLENGE OF ISLAM	307
XXIV.	POLAND IN THE 1980s	322
XXV.	CENTRAL AMERICA IN THE 1980s	331
XXVI.	WITH THEIR BACKS TO THE WALL	349
XXVII.	A STATE OF SIEGE FROM WITHIN	356
XVIII.	THE CHEATED GENERATION	372

Notes 379
Sources Cited 401
Index 413

Preface

Previously I have written books about the Missouri politics I know so well, about the development of national business enterprise that seems so familiar, about American beliefs that are part of my own life. In contrast, while writing the present book, I dealt with ideas so bizarre as to be nearly incomprehensible to a lover of freedom, with cultures untouched by the eighteenth-century Enlightenment, which inspired the founding of our beloved country, with minds as alien as anything encountered in science fiction, with horrors that are no more than an intellectual abstraction to most Americans.

This book surveys the Communist movement from its nineteenth-century origins to the 1980s, concentrating on the theme of military aggression. The historical record shows that most charges of Communist aggression have little to do with a concerted plan for world dominance.

This may sound provocative today. In past times physicists were provoked when someone said the speed of light in a vacuum is invariable. Biologists were provoked when someone said evolution is a result of random changes in molecules. Statesmen were provoked when someone said that black Americans should no longer wear chains. Politicians were provoked when someone said each citizen should have one vote. And yet, upon reflection, all those notions have been accepted. Their value became obvious because actions based upon those premises were more successful than acts that ignored them. As world events over the last few decades demonstrate, American actions based on the fear of Communist takeover have not been very successful. This could be true, not because the United States made some crucial error in responding to this threat, but because the threat did not exist.

Communist regimes have proliferated since World War II. This menacing growth is real, but its nature is different from what is commonly assumed. Neither the Russians nor anyone else is pulling the levers in some grand headquarters that runs Communist activities throughout the world. The Soviets have very definite desires, as do the Chinese, the Cubans, the North Koreans, and all the rest. These desires, however, are hardly centrally planned or coordinated and often have little to do with promoting Communism. Indeed the goals of various Communist regimes sometimes conflict so harshly that they go to war with one another.

Could a Keystone Cops conspiracy among deadly enemies create one Communist government after another? Or might the cause be something else? If so, should we deal with that "something else" instead of wasting our resources chasing phantoms?

If such questions seem important, reading this book may help the search for some answers.

This book follows the standard Western usage of the term *Communist* as a label for someone who resists a Western or capitalist regime, even though the label is often inadequate and sometimes technically inaccurate. Salvador Allende of Chile, for example, was a Marxist and would probably have been indignant if someone called him a Communist—or a Marxist-Leninist or a Maoist or Stalinist or Trotskyite. And Socialists and Workers and innumerable organizations have given themselves still different names to distinguish themselves from "official" Communist parties that refused them membership. Among these groups were dedicated social revolutionary conspirators who sought a totalitarian dictatorship. Other members might have cared nothing about theory and were perhaps simply seeking to own a piece of land someday or were fighting in self-defense against a foreign invader. Some of those latter individuals may not have even thought of themselves as followers in a political group, let alone as an elite subject to party discipline. No single word can encompass the spectrum of these groups and imply the occasional vague nature of their beliefs and membership, so this book simply uses *Communist* to refer to these groups in all their diversity.

This book also uses the term *American* to describe persons and policies associated with the United States of America. This is a term of convenience and is not intended as an abuse of an appellation to which the inhabitants of two entire continents are entitled.

Acknowledgments

The research and writing of this book were funded by Patricia J. Schneider and Mary Jeanne O'Halloran. Richard K. Winslow and Samuel S. Walker, Jr., had the vision to see the potential in the manuscript I submitted to Walker and Company and were willing to take a chance on my ability to produce the present book. Editors Barbara Ravage and Linda Venator had the fortitude to guide me in that process. Mary Jeanne O'Halloran and Marilyn Cannaday kindly offered additional suggestions on literary style. Sometimes writers can be hard to deal with, but each of these persons put up with delays and exasperating frustrations, providing unwavering support. I hope this book justifies the faith demonstrated by these helpers.

When you look around at the leaders people follow and take orders from unquestioningly, what do you see? For the most part, you can't say that the leaders are where they are because of any particular talent or ability, can you—most of them aren't really very bright when all's said and done. In many cases their only claim to exceptionality is their abnormal gullibility and extraordinary capacity for self-delusion. But the people don't see it. The leader-image that exists in the minds of the followers is something quite different. The person that the followers follow is a fantasy that they manufacture in their own imaginations, which they can project onto anyone who'll stand up and play the role. All that a leader needs is the gall to stand up and tell them he's got what they're looking for. They'll believe it because they need to.

They need to believe they're in capable hands. . . . Truth isn't the important thing. The important thing is to be certain.

Code of the Lifemaker

JAMES P. HOGAN

HERITAGE OF FEAR

Illusion and Reality in the Cold War

I.

The First Communists

Although today communism is often equated with violent uprisings and repression, the ideas of early communist philosophers had little to do with military activity. Communism began as an economic and political theory, devised in response to the oppression of the working class by the middle and upper classes in newly industrialized Europe. The best-known early statement of its goals was the *Communist Manifesto*, written in 1848 by Karl Marx and Friedrich Engels.

THE COMMUNIST MANIFESTO

Although Marx and Engels wrote in support of the lower classes, neither had a lower-class background. Karl Marx was not an oppressed member of the proletariat: by the time he coauthored the *Communist Manifesto*, he held a doctoral degree. Nor was Marx an underground revolutionary, writing secret tracts in favor of government overthrow. Marx was a highly visible member of European socialist groups. Moreover, his brother-in-law later served as Prussia's minister of the interior—if the Prussian government had considered Marx a threat, they could have found him. He was bankrolled by Engels so writing the multivolume book *Das Kapital* could continue. Even so, Marx at times lived in privation.

The son of a wealthy textile manufacturer, Friedrich Engels, in V. I. Lenin's words, "had come to hate autocracy and the tyranny of bureaucrats while still at high school,"[1] which he never finished. The rebelliousness of Engels continued long after adolescent hormones had passed. He was fired by a sense of injustice he saw in the incomes earned by top businessmen and their lowly employees. Drawing upon centuries of historical data and philosophical principles, Engels and Marx argued that cynical exploitation of laborers could have more to do with their poverty than merit did. Marx would eventually express their arguments in a sophisticated technical fashion in *Das Kapital*, but the two men first stated their case in the more simple pamphlet called the *Communist Manifesto*.

The *Communist Manifesto* was written just before the revolutions of 1848 swept Europe. Some may see a causal relationship between the political tract and that violence, but it is more accurate to see them both as expressing the spirit of the time. For several years Europe had been enduring a depression that caused great privation among factory workers. Even the factory owners were uncertain whether industry would flourish better under capitalism or socialism. The communists did not cause the unrest; they were as caught up in the intellectual and economic swirl as everyone else.

The manifesto has been cited as the first blueprint for Communist world conquest, but perusal of the document demonstrates that it is nothing of the sort. It is a political pamphlet written by two young men in their twenties, arguing the communist case. Marx and Engels marveled at the technological accomplishments made possible by concentration of capital but argued that the capitalist economy was now beyond the control of those who created it, as demonstrated by the boom-and-bust cycle that had begun to appear. The authors noted that the great factories had replaced individual skilled craftsmen with workers who performed minor, repetitive tasks all day. Workers had become interchangeable and could therefore be acquired cheaply. Since organizers of the capitalist economy failed to prevent depressions, which harmed everyone, and since they paid workers poorly even in good times, the bourgeoisie (bankers, employers, and managers) had forfeited any right to run society. It was time to give the proletariat (workers) a chance to run things.

Marx and Engels argued that private property made people poor. According to their logic, for instance, if the wealthy owner of a great factory refused to pay decent wages, that factory was the cause of worker poverty. Therefore, private property, the cause of oppression and poverty, would be severely limited under the dictatorship of the proletariat. Elimination of private property was an innovation that distinguished communists from other protest groups. In addition Marx and Engels viewed society as evolving toward an ultimate stage in which economic goods were distributed equitably, religion was no longer needed to pacify the downtrodden, and the need for government ceased to exist because all members of society willingly worked together for society's benefit.

To nineteenth-century readers the phrase *dictatorship of the proletariat* had a far different meaning than it does today. Then, *dictatorship* referred not to a form of government, but to the exercise of control in a society. The United States would have been called a dictatorship of the bourgeoisie because that class of people generally controlled American society. A dictatorship of the proletariat could operate through a democratic government with free elections and a bill of rights. Indeed that was the plan of many communist revolutionaries. In the 1800s most of Europe was controlled by autocratic monarchies, so overthrowing them really could move a country toward freedom.

Although the *Communist Manifesto* contained mostly theory, it did have a short action section in which communists listed their specific demands: "progressive or graduated income tax . . . a national bank . . . cultivation of waste-lands, and the improvement of the soil . . . free education for all children in public schools . . . etc."[2] Admittedly that last demand—*etc.*—had an elastic quality, but there is no reasonable way to read a plan for world conquest into the document.

In this regard it is worth considering the new preface Engels wrote for the manifesto on May 1, 1890, after Marx's death: "The European and American proletariat is reviewing its fighting forces [in holiday parades], mobilised for the first time, mobilised as *one* army, under *one* flag, for *one* immediate aim: the standard eight-hour working day, to be established by legal enactment. . . . If only Marx were still by my side to see this with his own eyes!"[3] If holiday parades advocating an eight-hour day made a communist revolutionary's heart beat faster, clearly communism began as something tame.

Nonetheless, it provoked passionate opposition from the wealthy factory and newspaper owners and from politicians. Their objection was not to the call for abolition of private property, which even communists viewed as a distant goal to be achieved when the state withered, but to such achievable demands as the establishment of free public schools and the adjustment of wages to correspond with profits. Because of such demands, European leftists were treated as scum. Ironically, the specific communist program to which the bourgeoisie objected—a national bank, soil improvement, public schools—is heartily endorsed by Main Street Republicans in the 1980s.

THE "SCIENTIFIC" BASIS OF COMMUNISM

Marx and Engels and their successors argued that communism is scientific and based on hard facts.

Engels was a cosmopolitan writer who strayed from economics and philosophy into natural science, where he found himself among the company that believed that Lamarckian evolution was correct, that dogs and horses understood human languages, that heavenly novas were most easily explained by collisions, and that "the heat radiated into cosmic space [by stars] must be able to become transformed into another form of motion, in which it can once more be stored up and rendered active. Thereby the chief difficulty in the way of the reconversion of extinct suns into incandescent vapour disappears."[4]

The point is not to ridicule Engels for errors but to establish that Engels, like everyone else, was fallible. His economic science may have had as many flaws as his natural science did. Communism is sometimes promoted as scientific, as if it should share the credibility given to scientific research and discovery. Communists in general, however, lack a scientist's alacrity for discarding venerated explanations of phenomena when faced with contradictory facts. Marx and Engels, moreover, developed their theories in the nineteenth century. The ensuing years have drastically modified scientific understanding of many fields, and there is no reason why the work of Marx and Engels should be regarded as inherently more reliable than that of other nineteenth-century scientists and thinkers whose original work has sometimes been modified beyond recognition.

DEMOCRATIC IDEALS OF EARLY COMMUNISTS

Nineteenth-century communists, including Marx and Engels, held forth the Commune of Paris as the ideal communist state. This utopian group, formed in Paris during the revolt of 1871, supported traditional democratic institutions and was ruthlessly destroyed by France's autocratic government. The Commune of Paris created the illusion that democracy and communism could flourish together, and this was the standard communist belief until World War I.

This belief was an illusion because members of the Commune of Paris shared many values, so that choosing the preferences of one group over another's was unnecessary. Such a group can get along fine with all the democratic niceties. A problem arises if a utopian group assumes control of an entire state. If most citizens do not share the utopian values, a choice must be made between democracy and the utopian values—which is more important, majority rule or a minority's vision of a perfect society?

In V. I. Lenin's 1902 pamphlet "What Is to Be Done?" he argued that if democracy stands in the way of communist revolution, democracy must fall. This shocked the world communist movement and split it into two factions: Socialists, who advocated victory through political means; and Communists, who sought power through violence. Yet neither Lenin's ascendance among communists nor his takeover of the Russian Revolution during World War I posed a threat of armed aggression against the United States, let alone to the entire West. Neither the rhetoric nor the actions of early Russian communists indicated they intended to march against the United States.

But the communists had suddenly gained legal authority to give orders to the Russian army in the middle of World War I, and those orders could decide the war's outcome. Formerly, local police departments had been able to deal adequately with communist rebels. Now the greatest military machines in Europe, on both sides of the war, were confused about their safety. This was not because communists per se were running the Russian government, but because the Russian army's role in World War I had become uncertain.

That uncertainty is where our story begins in earnest: not in nineteenth-century rhetoric, not in Bolshevik dreams of social transformation; but in the mud and snow of European battlefields and amidst the cigars and brandy of diplomats.

II.

Communists and World War I

LENIN

Like Marx and Engels, Vladimir Ilich Lenin came from an economically and socially comfortable background. He was of the Russian gentry, and his father was a judge. Like Engels, young Lenin experienced the oppression of authorities as a teenager, when he was expelled from Kazan University. His adolescent rebellion against his father was particularly bitter. Lenin's classic tract "What Is to Be Done?" used the title of a Nikolay Chernyshevsky novel about generational conflict. For young Lenin the psychological struggle was so intense that he is said to have become uneasy upon reading Anton Chekhov's "Ward No. 6," a story about borderline insanity. Indeed, one can fairly ask whether the possible irrational origins of Lenin's revolutionary fervor prompted his insistence that communism was grounded on scientific bases, whether his rebellion was motivated by psychological need rather than intellectual analysis of the state of society.[1]

By the 1890s he had joined the Russian Social Democratic Workers party. This group called for universal suffrage, free speech, separation of church and state, free and universal education, an eight-hour work day, abolition of child labor, and state-funded old-age insurance. Although there is nothing very subversive to the modern American way of life in this, such calls were regarded as dangerous to the czarist way. A revolution in 1905 resulted in the creation of a parliament and some agricultural reforms, but the outcome was far short of goals desired by Social Democrats such as Lenin.

Lenin led a faction calling itself Bolsheviks, which in 1903 broke away from the Social Democrats and became the Russian Communist party. From the beginning Lenin advocated an elite party membership. He believed the proletarian masses would participate in the revolution, but that his small core group would lead those masses in the desired direction.

THE RUSSIAN REVOLUTION

The Communists did not overthrow Czar Nicholas. World War I overthrew him. Military defeats and high casualties in the war caused a contagious lack of confidence in the czar, and on March 15, 1917, he was forced to abdicate. He was succeeded by the so-called provisional government, first headed by Prince Georgy Yevgenyevich Lvov and then by Aleksandr Kerensky. Its subsequent fall and replacement by a Communist regime has been called the first instance of Communist military aggression, in this case directed against a free government in Russia itself. How justified is that claim?

Partly because it vowed to continue Russia's involvement in the war and partly because it failed to promote a thoroughgoing reform of social conditions, Prince Lvov's provisional government rapidly lost the support of the Russian population.

Throughout the spring of 1917 the administration's authority was disintegrating. Groups of workers, peasants, and soldiers banded together to oppose the provisional government. These groups, called *soviets,* were roughly equivalent to vigilante town councils in America. In April 1917 the Communists adopted the slogan "All power to the soviets." They did not mean by this that the soviets should run every aspect of people's lives, but that the formal power of the Russian state should be transferred from the provisional government to the robust and growing soviets, who opposed the war. The result would be to transform Russia from a nation governed by a central bureaucracy into a confederation of independent city-states. This appealed to many who were suspicious of a central government and opposed the war, and it helped develop popular support for the Communists.

By summer observers were no longer wondering if the provisional government would fall, but instead were trying to discern its successor. Lenin staged an unsuccessful uprising against the government in July 1917 in Petrograd; although he failed to gain control of the government, Prince Lvov resigned and was replaced by Kerensky. Matters did not improve, however, as Kerensky vacillated about policy.

American Ambassador David Francis was appalled at the thought of ordinary citizens running the Russian government. Allowing everyone to vote for upper-class candidates was one thing, but Francis protested that if government officials were ordinary citizens they "would lose . . . the respect of the Russian people and all of the Allies as well as their own self-respect."[2] His views were seconded by U.S. Consul General Maddin Summers, a political conservative whose brother-in-law was a wealthy Russian noble.

Fortunately for those who wished to thwart the Communists, some alert quasi-independent American operatives on the scene were more practical-minded than the U.S. diplomatic corps. William Boyce Thompson, an engineering associate of Herbert Hoover, ran the American Red Cross in Russia. Also on hand was Republican businessman Raymond Robins. When the Bolsheviks arranged a "democratic congress" in early autumn, Thompson and Robins packed the meeting with anti-Bolshevik revolutionaries, who voted down all the resolutions designed to weaken the provisional government.[3]

Lenin's group decided to brazen it out with public relations and announced that the Petrograd soviet now exercised the power of the Russian state. This is analogous to opponents of the District of Columbia city government announcing that they run the federal government. The Bolshevik claim met skepticism in Western diplomatic circles, the skepticism increasing with physical distance from the scene.

Scoffing grew when results of the long-promised Constituent Assembly (national parliament) elections became known in late November 1917. The Bolsheviks had won only 175 of the 707 assembly seats, a minority "government" indeed. Yet Western diplomats failed to notice two crucial factors.

Although Lenin's group trailed nationwide, it led in most big-city totals. An axiom of revolution says that political trends in cities will later take place throughout a country. It follows, therefore, that the election results indicated that the Bolsheviks were on the cutting edge of Russian politics, destined for greater things.

The second crucial point was that the Bolsheviks had tremendous power in Petrograd, where the Constituent Assembly was to meet, and Lenin made clear that the Bolsheviks intended to eliminate the assembly. Indeed, it had scarcely convened before some Bolshevik functionaries appeared in the chamber in January 1918 and announced that parliament was adjourned until further notice. The assembly made no attempt to resist peaceful dissolution, and no public dismay was apparent.

Note that the Bolsheviks sent no armed horde storming into the parliament. They simply told members to go away, and the members did. The assemblymen themselves apparently had little interest in continuing the provisional government. In contrast, the Bolsheviks already had the support of an unofficial nationwide government in the form of soviets, which thereafter became the official government.

This was the Communist revolution in Russia. Americans today seem to think that vicious cutthroats used skulduggery to overthrow a democratic Russian regime in a bloody war. This impression is incorrect. The provisional government simply lost the support of the Russian people, and in the end its members voluntarily folded up shop. The Bolsheviks, with support of the soviets, stepped into the void. No military action was involved. The earlier November 1917 assault on the Winter Palace, glorified as the greatest battle of the revolution, had only a half dozen casualties. In this respect the Communist revolution foreshadowed the coup that brought Corazon Aquino to power in the Philippines seventy years later: scarcely a shot was fired.

THE U.S. GOVERNMENT SEEKS TO OVERTHROW THE COMMUNIST REGIME

Americans in Russia quickly perceived that the Bolsheviks were planning to stay in power. These Americans began promoting cordial relations until Ambassador Francis put a stop to that. President Woodrow Wilson and Secretary of State Robert Lansing concurred with the ambassador. Wilson refused to recognize the Bolshevik government, although not because of the manner in which it came to power. Like Francis, Wilson simply felt that a government comprising mere peasants and laborers could never be taken seriously. He found the very concept offensive, as did Lansing, who criticized the attempt "to make the ignorant and incapable mass" dominant.[4]

Lansing decided to find a strong Russian who possessed armed support and could overthrow the Bolshevik regime. The two most likely candidates to head a friendly military dictatorship in Russia were czarist generals Alexei Kaledin and Mikhail Alexeev.[5] In Petrograd American Consul General Summers (whose noble Russian in-laws were losing a fortune from Bolshevik actions) dispatched a representative to feel out Kaledin and Alexeev, even though no instructions had arrived. American officials knew what to do without waiting for orders.

Meanwhile, the Allies quickly extended the blockade against Germany to include Communist Russia, and in October 1919 the Allied Supreme Council was pressuring neutral governments to participate. The blockade continued after the war, until January 1920.

The Bolshevik regime had scarcely come to power before the United States began working to overthrow it. No one suggested that the Communists posed a military threat to America—such a claim would have been laughed away. Instead, Secretary of State Lansing called the Bolshevik government "a direct threat at existing social order"[6] (that is, at rule by a wealthy oligarchy), not a military threat. At the time the United States feared only the philosophy of the Communists, not their nonexistent military capability. Officials invented a cover story that Lenin was a German agent. The story stated that American efforts to destroy the Communist government were for self-defense against the German Kaiser. No responsible person in the American government believed the story; it was intended to mollify public opinion, which might otherwise be shocked that the United States would try to destroy a government that had done it no harm.

THE COMMUNISTS SHRINK RUSSIA'S SIZE

Far from seeking territorial expansion, the Communists immediately expedited the breakup of the old czarist empire, allowing various ethnic and national groups to declare independence from Russia and to set up their own sovereign states. The U.S. government strongly opposed Communist efforts to reduce the size of Russia; Secretary of State Lansing felt such actions would encourage anticolonial feelings in the British empire, endangering the English hold on India and Ireland. So, in addition to other reasons, the United States wanted the Communist government overthrown because American leaders opposed national self-determination of peoples and the Bolsheviks favored it. In ironic contrast, British leaders such as David Lloyd George wanted the truncated Communist Russia maintained, as a smaller and so lesser threat to the British empire.

Granted, the Communists did expect the new states to have governments friendly to Bolshevik Russia. The Allies, however, immediately threw support to anti-Bolshevik elements of these areas, enabling them to form governments in the Ukraine, White Russia, and the Baltic states. This support precipitated Red Army action against these governments.

Persons who believed in a Communist conspiracy of world conquest would later make much of this so-called Communist aggression, but the alarmists did not acknowledge that the anti-Communist regimes existed only as a result of Allied intervention. They were not formed by consent of the people in those areas, and they failed to represent the majority's desires. Not that the majority wanted Communism either. As in most places, the majority just wanted to be left alone. The point is that the anti-Communist governments had no greater claim to legitimacy than the later Communist regimes.

RUSSIA QUITS THE WAR

The British, French, and Americans were supporting various anti-Bolshevik Russians. In addition the Germans were fighting all Russians, no matter who they were. Thus, the Communists found themselves facing opposition from both sides in World War I as well as from domestic opponents.

Fortunately for the Bolsheviks, the Germans were willing to end their war against Russia—for a price. The armistice document was the Treaty of Brest-Litovsk, signed in March 1918. Because the Bolsheviks gave up large chunks of Russia to the Kaiser with this treaty, it has been cited as a classic example of both German harshness and Communist willingness to betray the interests of Russia in order to consolidate their power.

Such a view ignores several facts. Getting out of World War I was certainly in Russia's interest—the czar and the provisional government had fallen largely because of their stubbornness in continuing the war. Furthermore, the "forfeited" territory had already been seized by the victorious German army. The treaty merely acknowledged this fact. More important, the old Russian empire was rapidly breaking up as regions reasserted their national independence. The Bolsheviks consequently had never controlled the territory given up through Brest-Litovsk. They assented to the loss of something they never really had. Through the treaty negotiations, however, the Communists gained recognition from a major European power (Germany) as the legitimate successor to the provisional government.

All in all the treaty was tolerable for the Communists, particularly since they expected the Kaiser's government to fall, thus allowing Russia to get everything back after the war. And indeed, in 1919 the Treaty of Versailles forced Germany to return the territory, effectively nullifying the Treaty of Brest-Litovsk.

THE ALLIES INVADE RUSSIA

Around March 1918 U.S. officials in Russia reached agreement with the Communists to begin joint operations against Germany if the Kaiser's forces renewed their attack against Russia despite the Treaty of Brest-Litovsk. The Communists agreed to an Allied landing at Murmansk as part of the contingency planning. Unknown to the negotiators on either side, the discussions were a ruse by top American officials to camouflage plans to overthrow the Communist state.[7]

At first the United States sought to send Herbert Hoover's American Relief Administration, a humanitarian organization that was feeding continental Europe's population, into Communist Russia. Then the United States planned to invade on the pretext of protecting the relief workers. There was even talk of invading first and having the Hoover men follow, so the attack could be explained as a means of bringing food to Bolshevik territory. Secretary of War Newton Baker questioned that scenario, wondering if anyone would believe the United States was entitled "to use military force to compel the reception of our relief agencies."[8] Secretary of State Lansing agreed: "Armed intervention to protect the humanitarian work done by the [Hoover relief] Commission, would be much preferable to armed intervention before this work had begun."[9] Hoover was aghast at the idea of an attack upon Communist Russia, warning Wilson: "We should probably be involved in years of police duty, and our first act would probably in the nature of things make us a party with the Allies to re-establishing the reactionary classes. It also requires consideration as to whether or not our people at home would stand for our providing power by which such reactionaries held their position."[10] This particular plan was abandoned.

In the meantime the Brest-Litovsk treaty caused great consternation among governments fighting Germany. They had two main objections. First, the Russian army was no longer distracting Germany on an eastern front. In fact, that had been the case long before the treaty, but the Allies were appalled that the Communists had the power to order the Russian army to cease fire altogether. The second big complaint was that the Allies had delivered over 160,000 tons of war matériel to the Russian port of Archangel (Arkhangelsk) and over 800,000 tons to Vladivostok. With Russia out of the war, who was going to use the supplies and for what purpose? And who would pay for them? They had been supplied to the provisional government on credit, and the Communists had repudiated any obligation to honor their predecessor's undertakings. If the Russians refused to pay, did the Allies still own the goods?

The Allies, including the United States, responded to this situation by invading Russia. Keep in mind the Communists had attempted no military aggression against any of the attackers. Quite the contrary, the Communists were attempting to get out of World War I and to avoid fighting any country.

The Allies claimed they merely wanted to protect these supplies against German seizure. As with the fake story about Lenin being a German agent, the explanation for invasion allowed Allied attempts to overthrow the Bolshevik government to be disguised as a fight against German imperialism. This claim was ridiculous in the case of Vladivostok, 4,000 miles from the nearest German soldier. The supplies were there because no one could figure how to move them across Siberia to the scene of fighting. It seemed doubtful that the Germans could come up with a solution in midwinter or that the Communists would have cooperated if a solution had been found. Indeed the Communists were moving the Archangel goods into the interior, away from the Germans, as fast as they could. The Allies apparently objected because they had not been consulted about this action. It is difficult to understand what was objectionable in the Communists' doing something on Russian territory without consulting the Allies beforehand, particularly since the action—keeping the matériel away from the Germans—was something the Allies wanted anyway.

A more plausible explanation for Allied distress was that the supplies could be used by the new Communist Red Army to fight the anti-Communist White armies being financed by Western governments. Western support for this White effort began soon after the November 1917 revolution and was not inspired by the

Brest-Litovsk armistice between the Kaiser and the Russian Communists.

The American consul in Vladivostok, John Caldwell, called for an invasion in response to "numerous requests" from "better-class Russians for foreign intervention and protection to enable them to organize."[11] Even this American official on the scene said nothing about danger of supplies falling into the Kaiser's clutches but spoke instead of promoting a civil war.

Another factor contributing to Allied antagonism toward Bolshevik Russia was money owed to banks in England, France, and the United States. Interest on Russian bonds was paid by the banks on the assumption that they would be reimbursed by the czar's successors. As time and the provisional government passed, the banks and bond holders began to feel uneasy. A contemporary observer, Charles Edward Russell, noted, "Here, then, is a great force constantly growing greater. In the deliberate view of these interests, or most of them, there is no chance for the payment of the bonds and the interest charges except through a return of Russia to the monarchial form of government. . . . For some months these interests in England and France listened with pleasure to the dulcet murmurings of the Russian nobles and other wealthy refugees that outlined various plans by which the old régime could be restored. More than one act of more than one government was influenced in consequence; to a great extent we owe to this source the movement for intervention."[12]

The Allied invasion invigorated opponents of the Communist state, who were supposed to rid the world of Communists while installing a Russian government that would renew the war against Germany and pay debts contracted by the czar and the provisional government. The West did not propose to install a democratic government in Russia—the Whites were no more democratic than their hero, Czar Nicholas. (One reason the Communists killed the czar was to be sure Allied intervention would not reinstall him on the throne.) The Allies intended to replace one dictatorship with another.

This Western intervention, via foreign troops and financing of local Whites, was the start of the Russian civil war. Unlike the Communist revolution, which was virtually bloodless, the civil war cost millions of lives. Until the Allies intervened, anti-Bolshevik Russians, lacking local support, had been inactive. Outside support from the Allies made the civil war possible. It also transformed Communism into a patriotic cause, rallying millions of Russians who cared little about Communist goals but who cared mightily about preventing foreigners from dominating Russia. The Allies thereby transformed the Bolsheviks from subversives into patriots, generating widespread public support that had previously eluded the Communist cause.

The invasion began with the April 1918 landing of Japanese forces at Vladivostok. The British landed in Murmansk in June, and the French joined them in Archangel in August. American troops arrived that same month on the Baltic and Pacific fronts. With Allied support, White General Anton Ivanovich Denikin began operations in southern Russia. The Communist government was attacked from all sides.

Unlike the Communists, who recognized and, after a fashion, practiced the principle of national self-determination, the Whites were intent on re-establishing the old czarist empire. The West backed anti-Communist Russian aggression against newly independent countries freed from the old empire by the Bolsheviks. Azerbaijan and Georgia both feared invasion by General Denikin.

Although the Japanese ostensibly invaded to protect the Vladivostok supplies from the Kaiser, they refused to leave the area until October 1922. The United States had foreseen the Japanese reluctance to disengage once they landed on Russian territory. Later apologists for American actions claimed that the United States invaded only after the Japanese did, in order to limit Japanese expansion in Russia. This fails to explain why the United States repulsed Lenin's request for a Communist-American military alliance against Japan. The American attack upon Russia was anti-Communist, not anti-Japanese. After all, American forces on the Baltic front could have rather little effect on the Japanese.

Although the United States government opposed Japanese expansion in Russia, Washington depended on White Admiral Aleksandr Kolchak to do the anti-Japanese (and anti-Communist) job for America in Siberia. As historian William A. Williams noted years later, "Though Wilson fretted about Kolchak's extreme conservatism . . . his anti-Bolshevism was never in doubt, nor his willingness to pay Russia's old debts."[13] Upon his arrival in Siberia, Kolchak overthrew the anti-Communist governments already functioning and proclaimed himself supreme ruler of Russia, a claim recognized *de facto* by the Allies.

Historian D. F. Fleming has commented, "Until the Nazis made wholesale murder a scientific business, the campaign of Admiral Kolchak in Siberia resulted in the most gigantic tragedy of all recent times." One day his men "slaughtered fifty-two car-loads of prisoners." Terrorism was routinely used to discipline villages:

"Women were ripped open, children bayoneted, and men flayed alive."[14] Kolchak's brutality against political opponents and peasants finally forced his own forces to turn against him, collapsing Siberia's military anti-Communist struggle in early 1920.

Many decades later, defenders of American actions claimed that the United States did not send a very big invasion force and the scale of fighting was far less than that of major World War I engagements. This ignores two facts:

The scale of fighting between American forces and the Red Army may have been small, but that does not mean that American influence in the civil war was insignificant. The United States and its allies financed and supplied the Russian counterrevolutionaries who carried on a civil war that cost millions of lives. It is disingenuous to argue that the small number of U.S. troops in Russia meant the United States had little to do with the civil war.

Second, at the time the United States invaded Russia, the Communist government was in a precarious situation much like many unstable Third World regimes in the 1980s. The Communists did not control the area later comprised by the Soviet Union. They controlled only a number of cities and surrounding territory. The United States and its allies expected what was later called a brushfire war, requiring only a modest number of troops. Concluding from the numbers that the United States had an insignificant involvement is to ignore that the Allies expected to destroy the Communist regime with that modest force.

In this regard it is interesting to note the Communist reluctance to believe the United States would attack a country that had consistently sought friendly relations. The Japanese had fought Russia once, scarcely ten years earlier. Britain and France also had a recent history of war with Russia. But relations with the United States had always been friendly. The Communist regime gladly cooperated with American businessmen, exempting operations such as Singer Sewing Machine, Westinghouse Brake, and International Harvester from expropriation measures applied routinely to non-American corporations. Even after U.S. troops arrived on Russian soil, the Communists refused to intern American civilians in Russia. They believed that Woodrow Wilson would order only token participation in the invasion, simply to mollify the Allies, who were exerting intense pressure for American involvement. Not until midautumn 1918 did the Communists realize that America was a full and active partner in the military aggression.

The argument that the invasion was designed to protect the Archangel and Vladivostok supplies from Germany eroded when the war ended in November 1918 while the fighting in Russia continued. Indeed, by December 1918, the British ordered German troops into action against Russia. The military aggression was supplemented by diplomats negotiating the Treaty of Versailles, who carved sections from prewar Russia. The Allied diplomats who orchestrated the dismemberment of Russia, which had never attacked an Allied country, were the same people who had called the milder Treaty of Brest-Litovsk a horrible example of the German mailed fist.

The architects of the Treaty of Versailles represented the same governments that had signed secret treaties with the czar giving Russia large chunks of its neighbors in return for its entry into the war. These men saw no objection to their granting territory they did not control to czarist Russia, but when Communist Russia later took such territories they called it Communist villainy. If the secret czarist treaties had remained in force, the Russians would have dominated Eastern Europe after World War I as they did after World War II. The Western powers thought czarist control of Eastern Europe was acceptable but waxed indignant about Communist Russia making such gains. Communist exposure of these secret deals between the czar and the West had much to do with European outrage against the Soviet regime, and also with Wilson's demand in the Fourteen Points for open covenants openly arrived at.

It is in this context of dismemberment and invasion by Western powers that we should view the Communist calls for world revolution. Attacked on all fronts, the Communists believed the Soviet state would fall unless Western domestic difficulties forced those powers to stop. The call for world revolution was made in self-defense, not intended as aggression. As we shall see, few heeded the call.

III.

Europe after the War

Democratic governments weathered the war in fair shape, but autocratic governments fell throughout Europe. The geographical dimensions of many countries were in flux, and the nature of the new governments was also uncertain.

Many so-called bourgeois democracies were established on paper, with elections and parliaments and other trappings of democracy. Nonetheless the existence of these institutions did not mean that government officials, let alone the peasantry, had the centuries of democratic heritage that made such institutions a liberating force in America. If an autocracy and a parliamentary government are run by virtually the same people, little change will occur in the average citizen's life.

This was sensed by many in Europe. To them the Communist regime in Russia was an inspiring example of ordinary people running the state, with the potential for making a real change for the better in the average citizen's life.

The Communists showed little respect for human liberty, but neither had any of the autocratic governments that had just fallen. In those lands *freedom* was an intellectual abstraction, frightening to those who desired an ordered life. To them the Communists seemed no more oppressive than the old autocrats or the new wealthy oligarchies that ruled through elections that were an empty facade.

The Communists were different, however, in that they were attempting to distribute land to the people who worked it and industrial profit to the workers whose labor produced it. For many Europeans, Communism looked better than the new postwar governments in Germany, Hungary, and Poland, which were inaccurately called democracies.

Moreover, the ordinary European peasant or worker felt small loyalty to the new, so-called democratic regimes, which promoted the interests of the wealthy elite and lacked the power built up over the centuries by autocracies. The recent overthrow of strong autocracies made the overthrow of weak bourgeois-dominated governments look easy. This evaluation was shared both by Communists and their opponents and generated much hope or fear, depending on one's political persuasion. Much potential for unrest existed in Europe after the war, due to exhilaration prompted by the fall of powerful autocracies and the challenge from the innovative Communist program in Russia.

Given this background, let us now examine what was happening in several new governments of Europe.

GERMANY

Germany was considered the most likely country to follow Russia into Communism. The homeland of Marx and Engels, it had the kind of advanced industrial society that Communist theory targeted.

Communist confidence that Germany was next made the territorial losses in the Brest-Litovsk armistice more palatable to them. As we know, the Communists thought the Kaiser's government would fall and that all the territory could then be reacquired after the war. When the Russian diplomatic mission opened in Berlin after the Brest-Litovsk treaty, the operation avidly encouraged overthrow of the German government. This activity has been cited as an example of the Russian Communists' unscrupulous aggressive tactics, but the United States wanted the Kaiser's regime defeated anyway. Besides, there is nothing extraordinary about a government seeking the overthrow of a regime with which it has diplomatic relations.

On November 10, 1918, a group of workers and soldiers in Berlin proclaimed a provisional government, toppling the Kaiser. But expectations that soviets would form throughout Germany soon faded. Although the German public was exasperated with the war and with the Kaiser who brought it on, they were in no mood for exotic experiments. Instead of a "people's democracy," the bourgeois Weimar Republic developed.

Admittedly, in the spring of 1919, a soviet was established in Bavaria. An accurate jest said that Communists had dictatorial control throughout the Café Stephani and lesser influence for several blocks around. This so-called First Bavarian Soviet Republic lasted almost six days. Communists immediately established a Second Bavarian Soviet Republic, which lasted only twice as long.

Horror stories circulated about "Red terror" in Bavaria, but no one was killed at the hands of the Bavarian Communists. This lack of violence was in keeping with the prewar German Communist tradition, which rejected Lenin's call for abandonment of democracy. A sailor did have ten hostages shot, but he acted independently. In contrast, the victorious anti-Communist White forces overreacted and initiated an authentic terror campaign against suspected leftists. A photograph shows a soldier-laden White vehicle decorated with skull and crossbones. A White major announced, "Anyone who doesn't yet understand that there is a lot of hard work to be done here, or whose conscience bothers him, had better get out. It is a lot better to kill innocent people than to let one guilty person escape." The entrance at one prison displayed a sign saying, "This is where we make sausages of Spartacists [leftists]." Thirty members of a Roman Catholic society, meeting to put on a play, were arrested for violating a prohibition against meetings; twenty-one were killed in a basement. A chimney sweep was shot for displaying a red flag, which was simply a trademark of the profession. In Munich almost 1,000 suspects were killed during the first week of May 1919.[1]

As the home of Marx and Engels, Germany boasted a fair number of native Communists who disagreed with the Bolsheviks. Karl Kautsky, who had edited the last volume of Marx's *Das Kapital,* predicted in late 1918 that the Russian Communist government would fall in a matter of weeks. Rosa Luxemburg, a woman with a crippled body but supple mind, articulated the German potential to turn Communism into a force promoting human liberty after the expected Russian Bolshevik collapse:

> The essence of socialist society consists in the fact that the great working mass ceases to be a regimented mass and itself lives and directs in free conscious self-determination the whole political and economic life. . . . The proletarian revolution needs for its purposes no terror, it hates and abominates murder. . . . It is no desperate attempt of a minority to fashion the world after its own ideal, but

the action of the great mass of the millions of the people which is called to carry out the mission of history.[2]

German right-wingers had no more use for this kind of thinking than did the Russian Bolsheviks. In January 1919 rightists offered a private bounty for Luxemburg's capture. She went into hiding but was apprehended in Berlin on the night of January 15 and taken to a hotel used as a center of operations by rightist paramilitary forces. She was questioned and beaten in the hotel, then tossed into a waiting car. She was shot through the head, and her body pitched out. Thus did German anti-Communists eliminate one of Lenin's most powerful challengers within the Communist movement.

HUNGARY

A Hungarian republic was carved from part of Austria-Hungary at the end of World War I. Its president was Count Mihály Károlyi. In early 1919 French General Louis-Félix-Marie-François Franchet d'Esperey began reducing Hungarian territory, large portions of which had already been awarded to Czechoslovakia, Yugoslavia, and Romania at Versailles. By stripping away Hungary's economic resources via continually updated maps with new boundaries, the French actions destroyed the credibility of Károlyi's republic: a stable government would not give up substantial portions of territory and population to unfriendly neighbors.

Károlyi and France thoroughly discredited democracy in Hungary. This is especially tragic because Károlyi was not running a democracy. He did not achieve agrarian reform, never held elections, and retained the old Hapsburg bureaucrats. When the average citizen compared life during the monarchy to life in Károlyi's republic, democracy lost. In truth, though, democracy has never failed in Hungary—it has never existed.

In 1919 the average Hungarian could see that "democracy" was failing to protect the nation's interests. A group claiming to be Communists, however, proclaimed itself unafraid of standing up to Western demands against Hungary, even if that meant war. Hungarian patriots rallied around this group, and the republic teetered.

By March 1919 the Károlyi republic had degenerated so badly that General Franchet d'Esperey no longer bothered to announce personally further reductions of Hungarian territory. A mere colonel told the republic about its latest loss. The next day it fell.

A coalition of Socialists and Communists immediately declared a dictatorship of the proletariat. As already noted, in those days the term did not signify abandonment of democratic principles, but rather indicated that ordinary citizens instead of wealthy autocrats would run the state. The new Hungarian government had people's commissars instead of cabinet ministers, but that designation was merely a romantic homage to the example of national independence in the east. The new Hungarian regime was no more Communist than the Károlyi republic had been democratic. Indeed the commissariat contained only one Communist, a man named Béla Kun.

The new government was instantly in serious trouble. The Allies treated it as a dangerous enemy. Although the Hungarians intended to refuse further demands from Western powers, such refusal hardly made Hungary an enemy state. Hungary had no intention of going on the military offensive anywhere. Even if the desire had existed, Hungary had little ability to mount any significant action after losing territory, population, and productive capacity at the hands of the Allies.

Hungary was dangerous, however, if it could successfully resist Allied domination and thereby serve as an example to other nations under the Versailles yoke. For reasons of state rather than Western military security, the new Hungarian government had to be slapped down.

Harsh Allied treatment, best exemplified by a blockade, strengthened those Hungarians who looked to Russia for help in national defense. The Russian Communists were delighted because they saw Hungary as a way to divert Allied efforts concentrated against them. The tougher the Allied treatment of Hungary, the more it needed help from Russia; this necessity increased Communist influence in the Hungarian government, which in turn increased Allied pressure. Since the Hungarian government had no alternative for resistance aid, the Hungarian friends of Russia grew in power. The Allied governments, including the United States, thus inadvertently succeeded in fostering a Communist government in Hungary, a result that had eluded the best efforts of Russian Communists in the Károlyi republic.

Béla Kun became head of Communist Hungary in 1919. Rejecting the "half-hearted" example of Russia, he instantly nationalized *all* productive property, large and small. His program was harsh to the point of absurdity. Unauthorized sale of barbers' perfume became a capital offense, although such sanctions were quickly abandoned with few, if any, casualties. Nonetheless, in such an atmosphere commerce stagnated.

Having alienated the urban population, Kun turned his attention to the peasantry. In the countryside he implemented the economies of scale by preserving large feudal estates intact, with the old lords continuing to run them despite nationalization. Rumors spread that the nationalization process might put independent peasant plots under the old lords as well. The peasants may have been unable to see much practical difference between the Hapsburgs and Károlyi, but Kun was obviously a step backward.

After single-handedly devastating the national economy while alienating both urban and rural populations, Kun strove to unite the nation by picking fights with neighboring countries. In 1919 General Walter Boehm and some old Imperial officers led a foray into Czechoslovakia. A handful of Hapsburg officers leading a Communist army was as improbable as the czar's generals commanding the Red Army. What was happening had less to do with Kun's Communism than with a settling of scores between Hungarian nationalists and Czechoslovakia. The "invasion" covered territory that had been taken from Hungary by the Treaty of Versailles. The Czech defenders fought under French commanders. The Allies quickly convinced the Hungarian forces to withdraw.

In the meantime the Allies were searching for someone to stage a coup in Hungary. A key leader in this search was Herbert Hoover, director of the American Relief Administration. Hoover was less concerned about Kun's minuscule military potential than about the disruption a Communist Hungary could bring to central Europe's capitalist economy. At the same time, Hoover was exasperated by the caliber of opposition to Kun, noting with disgust that the former ruling-class Hungarians' "deliberations of late had been devoted to the question of the resumption of the right of dueling."[3]

France promoted the idea of sending American and other troops into Hungary under French command. Hoover thought this sounded suspiciously similar to the muddled Russian invasion and was determined to thwart the French this time. In keeping with his Quaker background, Hoover engineered a peaceful coup. Kun's reputedly brutal and aggressive Communist dictatorship gave up without a fight.

Hoover achieved this by capitalizing on unrest in the Hungarian army. The men were disturbed by reports that their families at home were on meager rations. Kun had retained Hapsburg bureaucrats to distribute local food supplies because they had experience with their jobs. They continued to work as they always had, ignoring peasants who lacked bribe money. While the soldiers were fighting for the glory of Hungary, their families were being starved by government workers.

Hoover's American Relief Administration was famed for its ability to deliver food where it was needed efficiently. That elementary physical need has changed more governments than political theory ever has. Hoover dropped word that without Kun's interference the ARA could quickly relieve Hungary. He also arranged for the Western powers to announce their intention to cooperate with a non-Communist government; at the same time, Hungarian trade union leaders and army troops began a coup. Matters went smoothly. In August 1919 Kun fled the country, complaining about the Hungarians' failure to appreciate him: "The proletariat of Hungary betrayed not their leaders but themselves. . . . The proletariat which was dissatisfied with our government, who, despite every kind of agitation, kept shouting 'down with the dictatorship of the proletariat' in their own factories, will be even more dissatisfied with any future government. . . . Now I see that our experiment to educate the proletarian masses of this country into class-conscious revolutionaries has been in vain."[4]

When his government rose Kun took personal credit, and when it collapsed he blamed the Hungarian people. Both the rise and fall of his government, however, were more accurately attributable to Allied efforts.

Upon Kun's departure Romania instantly invaded Hungary, taking Budapest in four days. Not until two months later did the Allied governments tell Romania to withdraw. It did so only after much plundering, described by Herbert Hoover as "medieval."

After Kun's departure his anti-Communist successors reported that his four-month government had executed 578 persons. The Communists claimed the real figure was less by half. By comparison, the victorious White forces murdered many more people without protest from the Allies. Unlike the Kun regime executions, the White killings generally were death squad operations without judicial trials. Many top Hungarian leftists and Communists were Jewish. The Whites initiated pogroms on the excuse of protecting the nation from Communism, which they viewed as a Jewish evil.

At the end of 1919 Communism had failed to make headway in Germany, had been driven from Hungary, and was fighting for survival against Allied-funded White armies in Russia. In 1920

Lenin's government faced danger from still another enemy, Poland.

POLAND

The Polish-Russian antagonism stemmed from 900 years of rivalry. Such a long-standing feud is something alien to Americans. Reviewing its highlights can help us to understand what happened in 1920, and what Germany and Russia did to Poland in 1939. This knowledge will also put Polish events after World War II into a meaningful context.

Poland and Russia were already at odds by the eleventh century, with Poland supplying military aid to a deposed head of the Kievan state who was attempting to regain power. In the 1300s Poland annexed part of southwest Russia and continued to nibble at Russia's western principalities in the 1400s. Poland held some of these territories until the latter 1700s. The intimacy of Russo-Polish relations was demonstrated in the 1600s when the Russian oligarchy elected Poland's king, Wladyslaw IV, as czar of Russia.

In the early 1700s an election was held to choose the Polish king. One candidate was promoted by France, the other by Russia. The French candidate, Stanislaw Leszczyński, had previously served as king of Poland and was the father-in-law of France's King Louis XV. When the French candidate won, Russia invaded Poland. Thereupon a pro-Russian group of noblemen elected the Russian candidate, Augustus III, king. He eventually prevailed, and Stanislaw I departed to France.

When the throne became vacant again thirty years later, the Polish diet again elected a Russian candidate, Stanislaw Poniatowski, as king. Less subservient than his predecessor, Stanislaw II proposed changes in the Polish constitution that would lessen Russia's influence. Russia then invaded on the excuse of protecting Polish freedoms, which Russia claimed were threatened by the constitutional changes. As a result the Polish government signed a treaty putting the nation under perpetual Russian protection. Civil war broke out, with the Polish government using Russian troops to fight rebels supported by France. The matter was soon settled when the Polish government agreed to give up a third of the nation to Russia, Austria, and Prussia.

A few years later, in 1791, the Polish government once again tried to institute the constitutional changes that had provoked Russia. A handful of pro-Russian Poles then organized a semilegitimate confederacy, which branded the changes as revolutionary and implored Russia to intervene on behalf of law and order in Poland. This request was promptly fulfilled by the Russian army. The Polish government thereupon yielded a big chunk of Poland to Russia and in 1793 signed a treaty of perpetual alliance. Western powers expressed dismay and sent Poland massive shipments of sympathy and good wishes. "The French Republic is actively occupied," said foreign minister Pierre Henri Lebrun-Tondu, "with the great measures that may release this interesting nation [Poland] from the odious yoke that oppresses it. . . . Courage, energy, and perseverance, and Poland will be saved."[5] England warned that if Poland were partitioned, His Majesty's government would be forced to declare its disapproval. "The King," said foreign secretary Lord William Wyndham Grenville, "would never be a party to any [such] concert or plan."[6] Nevertheless, in 1795 Russia, Austria, and Prussia seized what was left of Poland, and the nation vanished from the map.

Erasing lines on a map, of course, does not erase a nation with a thousand years of history. Indeed, in 1815 when the Congress of Vienna reordered European affairs after Napoleon's final defeat, the diplomats awarded Russian Poland considerable autonomy.

Polish nationalist agitators kept exploring for the outer limits of permissible behavior and found that boundary in 1830. That summer had seen revolutions in France and Belgium. The czar called up Polish regiments to join Russian units being sent to aid antirevolutionaries in France and Belgium. The Poles refused. The diet declared the czar deposed as ruler of Poland. For years European powers had implied they were ready to send aid if Poland acted to throw off the Russian yoke. While Poland waited a year for the aid to start, the revolt was crushed by the czar. Believing the Roman Catholic Church had rallied Polish defiance, Russia began to restrict the Church's activities in the region.

Over the next few decades, Britain and France continued their murmurs of support for a free Poland, and in 1863 the Poles revolted yet again and again waited patiently for help. The 10,000-man Polish army was a poor match for the better supplied 80,000-man Russian force sent to suppress the revolt. England and France intervened with a protest note, which the czar rejected. The United States refused even to sign the note. The czar ordered mass deportations of Polish landed gentry. The end of this revolt silenced Western suggestions that they might help Poland free itself from Russian domination, a silence maintained until the 1950s.

Even during World War I France assured Russia that its right to Poland was unquestioned.

After the czar fell, the provisional government in Russia announced that it supported a free and independent Poland, but it had to remain bound to Russia through a military pact. Polish patriots found this inadequate and rejoiced when, immediately upon accession to power in November 1917, the Bolshevik government freed Poland with no strings attached. This was in keeping with Communist tradition. Since 1865 Communists had called for an independent Poland in order to reduce Russia's role in Europe. Communists generally, and the Russian government particularly, wanted an independent Poland.

This does not mean that Poland's people or its new government forgot the centuries of rivalry and suddenly burst with goodwill toward Russia. Nor did the Allied governments forget. The world war victors all wanted a Polish state, and France wanted a strong ally on Germany's east. In 1919 the Allied Supreme War Council equipped a formidable Polish force and pointed it in the direction of the Russian Communists. Instead it conquered the Austrian and Ukrainian states of West and East Galicia and absorbed them into Poland. The council told Poland to release Galicia, but the order was ignored. Unlike the weak Communist regimes in Bavaria and Hungary, anti-Communist Poland was a strong military power that immediately demonstrated its intent to conquer neighbors. But unlike the Communists, the Polish regime did not threaten the social order, so the Allies did nothing about its aggression.

As in the Hungarian situation, the Western powers were more interested in fighting Communism than in supporting democracy. In 1919 a group of Polish democrats led by Ignacy Paderewski attempted to implement a free society. They promoted not only the forms of democracy, such as a parliament, but (in the words of Herbert Hoover) "knew well the canker of Poland was the terrible subjection and poverty of the peasants under the system of great land-holdings" along with the "exploited . . . industrial workers."[7] The Paderewski democrats pushed through agrarian reform by having the government buy great estates and sell off portions to peasants on easy terms.

Hoover watched in fascination as the Allies instead strengthened the power of General József Pilsudski, "a dictatorial person with a strange mélange of social and economic ideas," who had led Poland against the Allies in World War I and who opposed representative government.[8] With aid from the landed gentry, Pilsudski soon ejected Paderewski and the democrats from the

Polish government. Though the general was an enemy of democracy, he was also an enemy of Communism. The Allies' invasion of Russia was failing, and they were counting on Pilsudski's vigor to cause the Soviet government problems.

The Paris Peace Conference, at which Russia had no representative, failed to get Polish agreement on an eastern border for Poland. Thus the Poles were free to extend the border as far as their army could go into Russian territory. Lenin frantically sought peace negotiations in the spring of 1920 but was rebuffed. In late April Poland attacked Russia, seizing Kiev in a week and rolling through the Ukraine. Although France supported the war of conquest, other Western powers evinced a distinct embarrassment. Embarrassment turned to consternation as the Red Army not only repelled the unprovoked Polish attack but pressed deep into Polish territory. The resulting Communist leadership's uproar, however, was as big as the West's.

A pragmatic group led by Joseph Stalin wanted to halt the advance and offer terms to Poland. Stalin and his supporters felt that Polish resistance would stiffen dramatically if their nation seemed in danger. Stalin's group predicted that Red Army performance would decline as the struggle shifted from righteous defense to greedy conquest.

In opposition to Stalin was a more idealistic group led by Lenin. They viewed the operation less as national conquest than as part of the world revolution. They felt the Warsaw proletariat would be heartened by the Red Army's advance and would rise up to establish a Communist Poland. The Russo-Polish border would then become irrelevant, regardless of its location on a map, since Communist solidarity would transcend such pettiness. Lenin's group drew strength from worldwide opposition to Poland's aggression. British and German workers refused to transport munitions bound for Poland, and some English workers even formed councils of action in which hopeful Russians detected the glimmer of British soviets. Lenin's group argued that halting the advance would betray workers around the world.

Lenin's group won the policy dispute, but Stalin's perceptions were proven correct. As the Red Army prepared to take Warsaw, workers there joined the Polish national army rather than set up soviets. The Russians were pushed back as fast as they had advanced. An armistice-in-place was declared in October 1920, and those positions became the basis of borders in the 1921 Treaty of Riga. Poland had succeeded in regaining the eastern border lost in the first partition of 1772, taking a large portion of White Russia.

As during the Allied invasion of Russia, the Polish invasion rallied the Russian people around the Communist government, whose Red Army was defending the nation. The anti-Communist aspect of the Polish attack backfired in the long run by strengthening the Communist position within Russia.

The Germans also had a grudge against Poland because the Treaty of Versailles had given a sizable segment of German territory to the new state. Poland, the country that had ceased to exist in the 1700s, now encompassed parts of Germany and Russia. This inflamed some European emotions in much the same way that Israel would later inflame the Middle East. In the Polish context feelings were even stronger because the country had been created specifically as an opponent of Germany and Russia.

Thus Weimar Germany watched Soviet Russia's military action against Poland with satisfaction. There was even tentative contact between Germany and Russia about the Red Army restoring to Germany some of the territory that had been used to create Poland. These discussions were about twenty years premature.

SUBSEQUENT EVENTS IN GERMANY

Although mutual sympathy was drawing Germany and Russia closer together, contradictory forces were generated by Communist idealists who kept seeing revolution around the corner in Germany. This idealism existed mainly among members of the Comintern, a new though ultimately ineffective organization set up to coordinate world revolution. They sent the deposed Hungarian leader Béla Kun into Germany as an agitator to promote revolution there. In March 1921 miners and German police began clashing, when miners decided to resist the introduction of police reinforcements in the Mansfeld vicinity. Kun seized this moment to call a general strike, which in turn was supposed to engulf the nation in revolution. Not only did a strike fail to appear, but Kun managed to set German workers fighting one another instead of the government, as unemployed laborers invaded nonstriking factories to disrupt production.

The Communists tried another revolt, without Kun, in 1923. Secret agreements between the German army and Russia misled Moscow into imagining that the German military would do nothing to interfere, but there was no German army affection for Communism. The outcome of a revolt without popular support in a state with a strong military tradition should have been easy to predict, but despite ample experience to the contrary, Communists still believed the German proletariat would rise up when the word was given.

When the word *was* given on October 22, few volunteers for the class war appeared; the abortive revolution collapsed quickly. The Communists were not alone in misreading the public mood. A little more than two weeks later, on November 9, the Reichswehr also crushed Adolf Hitler's Munich putsch.

So ended the will-o'-the-wisp of proletarian revolution that the Bolsheviks had been pursuing in Germany since 1918. Even Communist idealists had to admit that revolution in Europe was unlikely. Three revolts in Germany had failed, Kun's Communist Hungarian government had quickly collapsed, and the masses had not risen up in Poland even when Red Army support was available. In line with Stalin's thinking, the Russian Communist leadership de-emphasized world revolution and concentrated instead on consolidating their power in Russia, a policy that Stalin called "socialism in one country."

By the mid-1920s Communists still had little muscle in Europe. Yet both they and their opponents exaggerated this strength—the Communists in order to appear strong, their opponents in order to justify military spending and harsh repression of civil liberties. Thus two diametrically opposed groups—Reds and Whites—both felt it in their interests to create and maintain a fiction of Communist power in Europe that vastly exceeded reality. In fact, the Communist menace was a swindle perpetrated on an innocent citizenry by Reds and Whites united in contempt for human liberty.

Ironically, although the call for world revolution had been ignored in Europe, it had been heard in distant China, which stood apart from the German philosophy that nurtured communist theory and which lacked the highly developed capitalist industrial base that communist theory required in order for revolution to be possible.

IV.

Toilers of the East

The first Communist successes outside Russia arose among inhabitants of lands southeast of Russia, the "toilers of the east" as they were called by the Soviets. This chapter deals with the Communist achievement in Mongolia and with the first steps toward Communism in China. Later chapters discuss developments in other parts of Asia.

MONGOLIA

The empty and inhospitable land of Mongolia provided a home for the world's longest-lived Communist regime outside Russia. As was true with Russia itself, nothing in Marxist theory predicted such a development. Marx saw Communism as happening in a highly developed industrial society, and nothing could less accurately describe Mongolia.

In modern times the desolate nature of Chinese-ruled Mongolia allowed it to serve as a buffer between the czarist and Chinese empires. Commercial interests from both countries were active there as the twentieth century opened, but the area itself was so grim that neither of the two giants wanted to defend it. The more aggressive Chinese traders gained mortgages on vast quantities of Mongol wealth and on future local governmental revenue. In 1911 the Mongol leadership was cultivating Russian goodwill in hopes that czarist help might be arranged to resist the growing Chinese control of Mongolian society. Sun Yat-sen's revolution in China provided the moment of opportunity, and Mongolia declared itself an independent state. That exceeded the bounds of Russian goodwill. The czar made a deal with China that resulted in formal Chinese sovereignty over Mongolia, with Russian administration of the government.

This displeased the Mongolians, who long ago had ruled Russia and who were now experiencing a reawakening of national consciousness. Via tireless diplomacy Mongolia reached agreements with Russia and China affirming its autonomy and crept toward increasing independence—with negotiators taking advantage of the pressures World War I brought upon the czar. After the czar's overthrow, the Japanese in early 1919 helped the Mongols to proclaim a huge, independent state, and in so doing angered China and Russia, both of which were already nursing grudges after having lost recent wars and territory to Japan.

The Communists continued the czar's work of increasing Russian influence in Mongolia. Unlike the czar, however, the Communists wanted to create a new Mongolian way of life. To do this they pressured Chinese trading companies and their agents to leave Mongolia, and also sought to break the power of the lamas, whose feudal-style ecclesiastical organization formed the basis of Mongol society and oriented it toward China rather than Russia. In this context the Communists can be seen as missionaries trying to bring their style of European civilization to a backward people, just as missionaries and businessmen from Western powers were trying to bring *their* version to Asia and Africa.

In the summer of 1919, eight years after Mongolia declared its independence, Russia indicated a desire to establish diplomatic relations with Mongolia, bluntly implying its recognition of Mongolian independence from China. The Peking (Beijing) government, for whom the possibility of Mongolian independence was intolerable, had been seeking an end to its autonomy through negotiations with Mongolia. In August the Chinese negotiator in Mongolia called for a large contingent of troops to strengthen his bargaining posture. The Mongolians thereupon agreed to give up their autonomy, but insisted on sixty-three separate conditions. China sent General Hsü Shu-tseng to handle the talks. He took the Bogda Gegen of Urga (the highest-ranking figure in Mongolia's religious/political hierarchy) hostage, cut the sixty-three points to eight, and gave the government a thirty-six-hour ultimatum to accept. Mongolia accepted Chinese sovereignty.

Mongolia quickly became a haven for White forces under Japanese command in the Russian civil war, who spent as much time fighting the Chinese in Mongolia as they did the Communists in Russia. Their presence became as much an aggravation to the Mongols as to the Communists. In 1921 leaders of Mongolian irregular troops engaged in guerrilla warfare against Japanese-supported forces asked the Red Army to cross the border and oppose the Whites.

The Bogda Gegen of Urga had already invited Communist aid the previous year. He wanted General Hsü expelled, and after the Americans and Japanese turned down his request for help, he tried the Communists. Turmoil in the Chinese government resulted in Hsü's departure before any Russian forces appeared, but China still ruled Mongolia, and the Bogda Gegen's invitation still held.

The Red Army supported the newly formed pro-Communist Mongolian People's Revolutionary Army, led by commanders of the old partisan forces who had fought the Japanese and Russian Whites, in a successful drive to eliminate the anti-Communists and Chinese while consolidating Communist control over the country. The Bogda Gegen retained glory as secular head of state until his death in 1924, while that office's powers were exercised by the Communists. After his death, the Communist Mongolian People's Republic was established.

The Mongolian People's Republic succeeded because it was backed by the Red Army. That the government required Russian military support, however, does not mean the Communists had less popular support than factions backed by Chinese armies or Japanese-led Russian White forces. Nor does this mean the Communists were more intent on having their way than was the czar. Russian Communist conduct in Mongolia was no more sinister than the actions of non-Communist groups.

In November 1921 Russia and Mongolia signed a treaty that recognized the latter's full control over its territory. In effect this meant that Russia no longer recognized China's long-time sovereignty, an implication that turned China against the Soviet Union for decades. No matter who ran things in China, all parties agreed on wanting Mongolia.

By mid-1922 the Red Army presence had dwindled to a single battalion, supposedly under orders of the Mongol government. The last contingent left in 1925. This did not mean that Soviet influence had declined in Mongolia—quite the contrary. The troops left because Russian influence had grown so great that a military presence was no longer needed. The traditional Mongol leadership quickly forgot their pleasure over Soviet aid in pushing out the Chinese and Japanese-led Russian Whites, and instead got angry as the influence of the Communists increased. A couple of sporadic revolts against the Mongol Communist government around 1930 crumpled under small-scale Soviet military response.

The Communist interest in Mongolia was secondary to revolution in China. As we shall see, in some ways the outcome there was no more satisfying to Russia than it was to the United States.

CHINA

Like Marx, Engels, and Lenin, many early Chinese Communists did not come from proletarian backgrounds, and many typically became aware of communism as university students—an elite position in China. Of his student days, Mao Tse-tung recalled, "The intellectuals were the only clean persons . . . the workers and peasants seemed rather dirty."[1] University of Peking students who founded the Chinese Communist party around 1920 were unclear about communism. A later military commander, Chu Teh said: "Our study club in Luchow could not conceive of the proletariat guiding a revolution . . . we thought of the proletariat as servants, coolies, and salt workers who could not read and write. It was confusing because Communist writers who preached Marxism were themselves high professors, students and other intellectuals and not workers."[2] Before Liu Shao-chi became China's head of state in 1959, he had also been the chief ideologue, yet he sheepishly admitted that when the party was founded, "I only knew that Socialism was good . . . but I was not clear what Socialism was."[3] Chinese Communist leaders became fluent in Communist jargon, but always remained fuzzy about content. Stalin snorted in 1944, "Communists, the Chinese Communists? They are to Communism what margarine is to butter."[4]

From the start the Chinese Communists were doing something rather different from what the Russian Communists were doing, and both groups eventually realized this. The Chinese operation cannot be accurately described as part of some worldwide conspiracy of conquest.

China was already in revolutionary turmoil when the Russian Revolution occurred in Russia. After the overthrow of the Ch'ing (Ying) dynasty in 1911, warlords were given control of the Chinese government. Sun Yat-sen, who had orchestrated the overthrow of the empire, ran a shadow government, the Kuomintang, made up of revolutionaries calling themselves nationalists. They (and many other groups) opposed the formal Chinese government, despised for its acquiescence to Western capitalist exploitation of the nation's people and resources. Weak as it was, the Chinese government participated in the Allied invasion of Communist Russia and allowed White General Grigori Semenov to use Chinese territory as a privileged sanctuary for raids against Russia. Lenin and Sun Yat-sen became friendly because they shared common enemies.

On May 4, 1919, massive student riots erupted in Peking in protest against the government's acceptance of the Treaty of Versailles grant of Shantung to Japan, which students viewed as yet another surrender to capitalist exploiters. In the course of the riots the Chinese minister to Japan was killed and the May Fourth movement was born. The movement attracted a conglomeration of dissidents, including a so-called Marxist group of professors and students (whose jargon was more orthodox than their beliefs). Chinese dissident admiration for Communist Russia was increased by the Bolshevik denunciation and abandonment of czarist treaties exploiting China and by the shared resentment of the Allied powers.

The University of Peking's chancellor aroused attention in 1922 with a speech greeting a Soviet Russian diplomat in Peking: "The Chinese revolution was a political one. Now it is tending towards the direction of a social revolution. Russia furnishes a good example to China, which thinks it advisable to learn the lessons of the Russian revolution, which started also as a political movement but later assumed the nature of a social revolution. Please accept the hearty welcome of the pupil to the teachers."[5]

Such comments from an establishment figure may have alarmed anti-Communists in the West, but the speech highlighted a controversy among Chinese revolutionaries. The nationalists simply wanted to change the government; Communists wanted to change the government *and* change the structure of Chinese society, destroying the power of the wealthy, who exploited workers and peasants, and allowing the average person to receive more of the fruits of his labor. This split would later cause bloodshed.

The speech would have been controversial also among Chinese patriots, who viewed their 1911 revolution as the model for Russia's 1917 experience. The chancellor turned things around and said the Chinese should learn from the Russians.

In the summer of 1923, nationalist Sun Yat-sen sent one of his top lieutenants, Chiang Kai-shek, to Moscow with orders to bring back Soviet arms and expertise. The Russians dispatched a senior general with full staff to create a nationalist Chinese army. Over the next few years Chiang repeatedly denounced his top enemy, British imperialism, while hailing the nationalist alliance with the U.S.S.R. and expressing gratitude for all the Russian Communists were doing to help the nationalist cause. He requested that the Kuomintang be admitted to the Comintern, the bureaucracy theoretically coordinating the world Communist revolution. Sun Yat-sen had already installed Comintern operative Mikhail Borodin as a Kuomintang political adviser, believing the Kuomintang and the Soviet Communists were working together toward the same goal.

The military angle of the alliance was moving along splendidly. The Kuomintang started a military academy in Whampoa (Huang-pu), funded by the U.S.S.R. and under the command of Chiang Kai-shek. His chief of staff was a senior Soviet general, and most instructors were Russian as well. The Chinese nationalist military college was a Russian Communist enterprise. This was recognized by press reports at the time, noting that the graduates "have been distributed all over Kwantung to preach Bolshevism and organize what they call peasant leagues among farmers of all ages, and drill young men for the farmers' corps in the Red Army."[6]

Sun Yat-sen died in March 1925. His parting words hailed the U.S.S.R. and "the heritage left to the oppressed peoples of the world by the immortal Lenin" and expressed hope that "the day will soon come when the U.S.S.R. will welcome a friend and ally in a mighty, free China, and that in the great struggle for the liberation of the oppressed peoples of the world both those allies will go forward to victory hand in hand."[7]

With Sun's successor, Chiang Kai-shek, poised to take command of the Chinese revolution in partnership with the Soviet Union and its military advisers, it would be worthwhile to turn our attention to the Chinese Communists and Mao Tse-tung.

When established in 1921, the Chinese Communist party was not a group of professional revolutionaries (as in Russia) but instead was an assortment of intellectuals leaning in one leftist direction or another. The party was more a debating society than an active and practical revolutionary organization, at least in comparison to the nationalist Kuomintang. The Soviets were glad to have more supporters but bothered little with them. Also, unlike the Kuomintang, Chinese Communists freely criticized Russia, for instance, by demanding the liberation of Mongolia. In contrast, Sun Yat-sen had pronounced "an immediate evacuation of Russian troops from Outer Mongolia" as neither "imperative [n]or in the real interest of China."[8]

Evidently on Sun Yat-sen's invitation, Chinese Communists began joining the Kuomintang, since the Kuomintang was the center of revolutionary action, functioning as something of an umbrella organization for revolutionaries of various persuasions. Moscow, however, was much displeased since, by orthodox party doctrine, a Communist can belong to no other organization that can give him orders. Russia wanted the Chinese Communists to stay out of the Kuomintang but at the same time encouraged the Kuomintang's revolutionary activity. Soviet policy thereby excluded Chinese Communists from China's revolution. Chinese Communists nevertheless were firm in their decision, planning to infiltrate Kuomintang leadership positions and eventually break up the Kuomintang from within, leaving the Communist party as China's top revolutionary organization.

Why, oddly, did Russia back the Kuomintang over the Chinese Communist party? The reasons were geopolitical, not ideological. The foreign exploiters that the Kuomintang opposed in China were the Western powers, which were also enemies of Soviet Russia. Thus, a Kuomintang success would divide the energies of these enemies, diverting them from Russia at last and toward China. For that reason crucial Russian aid went to the Kuomintang, which was seen as much stronger than the Chinese Communists and more likely to succeed in ousting the warlords, who encouraged the West.

The Soviet Union's decision to back the Kuomintang had strong geopolitical justification, but meant that in China the Russian Communists were abandoning the social revolution that communism advocates. This was well understood by all parties and left the Chinese Communists livid. In their view a Kuomintang victory would help Russia but do nothing for China. Indeed, such a victory would only strengthen the existing Chinese social order and thus be a step backward. Russian nationalism seemed to take precedence over Communist ideals. Though it would take a while for anyone to articulate it clearly, the Chinese began to feel the torch of world Communist leadership had been passed to them.

Let us reiterate, because these matters have been so misunderstood: Russian support for the Kuomintang was motivated not by the desire to promote world revolution, or even Communism in China—indeed, the Russians froze the Chinese Communists out of the deal. Rather, Soviet military backing for Chiang Kai-shek was prompted by the hope he could establish a vigorous nationalist regime in China that would cause trouble for China's capitalist exploiters. Since these happened to be Russia's enemies, the hope was that their attention would be partially diverted from overthrowing the Russian Communists. The Soviet Union was not trying to conquer China or install a Communist government there. Russia was using Chiang Kai-shek to divert the Western hostility.

In 1925 Tai Chi-t'ao, a friend of Chiang Kai-shek, put out highly publicized pamphlets filled with Marxist jargon but which nonetheless argued that social revolution had no place in Kuomintang. In other words, Communists should be eliminated from the organization.

For the illiterate a message was delivered with bullets. In solidarity with striking cotton workers, sympathy strikes had been called in various foreign-owned businesses. The Canton–Hong Kong strikers openly called for freedom of speech, an eight-hour work day, and an end to child labor—demands in which the British governor saw proof of Communist agitation. Under British leadership, the Shanghai police killed a dozen demonstrators. A month later British and French machine-gunners slaughtered many more Cantonese demonstrators. As part of all this, the foreign and Chinese mercantile class agreed to stand together against social revolution. Their voices began adding volume to the voices of anti-Communist propaganda.

More important, this agreement had support from the upper Kuomintang leadership. Chiang Kai-shek and his nationalist revolutionaries had made common cause with the foreign imperialists that the Kuomintang had been established to overthrow; they would stand together against the social revolution preached by Chinese Communists. Chiang now saw social change, not foreign capitalism, as the greater danger to his growing power. Army troops began supplementing police suppression of strikes.

In the face of these setbacks, the Comintern advised Chinese Communists to wait patiently. In the spring of 1926, Chinese Communists asked Chiang's Russian military advisors to divert 5,000 rifles from the Kuomintang to them. The Soviets refused to help arm the Chinese Communists.

Soon thereafter Chiang Kai-shek made a decisive move. He was eager to use the excellent army he had built up with Soviet aid on an expeditionary march to the north. His Russian advisors had prevented this march for months (Stalin was adamant on this point), feeling the expedition would encourage Western military action against Chiang. Chiang disagreed and in 1926 decided to proceed, dismissing some Russian advisors and expelling the Chinese Communists from the Kuomintang. As part of the expulsion, Mao Tse-tung was fired as deputy head of the Kuomintang's propaganda squad. The purge of the Kuomintang was not a consequence of the Northern Expedition, but did consolidate Chiang's control as the expedition began. The march north devastated the warlord forces that had kept China in virtual anarchy, and transformed Chiang and the Kuomintang from revolutionaries to governors.

Since 1922 Kuomintang revolutionaries had spouted Marxist propaganda and expressed fraternal regard for the Soviet Union and since 1924 had received Russian military support in developing an excellent professional army. The West could have ostracized Chiang Kai-shek and promoted an economic blockade, forcing nationalist China into closer ties with Russia. Instead, the West maintained trade relations and political contacts, cultivating Chiang rather than his enemies. When he tired of Russian interference he had somewhere else to turn.

In 1926 the Russians were reluctant to admit that Chiang had turned against them. As the architect of Soviet policy toward Chiang, Stalin was particularly reluctant. If the situation went sour, the Politburo would blame Stalin. Stalin had yet to consolidate his power; he had to feel uneasy.

He used rhetoric to deny the problems, insisting even a year later that "Chiang Kai-shek is submitting to discipline."[9] A week after Stalin made that assertion, Chiang made a clean sweep of the remaining Communist elements in the Kuomintang. By the spring of 1927, the Kuomintang had broken diplomatic relations with Russia. Stalin now abandoned Lenin's prescription of using bourgeois nationalists to lead revolution in China, instead calling for leadership by peasants and workers—by the Chinese Communist party.

For Chinese Communists the situation became grim in 1927. With Chinese Communist encouragement Shanghai workers took over the city in February and set up a soviet of sorts, expecting Chiang Kai-shek's revolutionary army to provide support. Instead, Chiang allowed warlord Chang Tso-lin's forces to return to the city and eradicate many activist workers. Finally in April Chiang's revolutionary army arrived to "liberate" Shanghai from warlord forces.

The Comintern believed that the Kuomintang was essentially in step with the Chinese Communists and, as usual, now resolutely acted as that policy dictated, telling Shanghai workers to disarm and prepare to cooperate with Chiang. As soon as workers followed Russian Communist instructions and rendered themselves defenseless, Chiang fell upon them.

Using members of Shanghai's gangster community as enforcers, squads of Chiang's army struck throughout the city against leaders and organizations of workers. When 100,000 workers staged a mass protest rally, Chiang's machine gunners coolly swept the throng in a cross fire. Those who escaped were "hunted down with fixed bayonet and broadsword. Forces from the foreign concessions participated in the reign of terror."[10] The death toll was estimated to be in the tens of thousands. Some of these were Chinese Communists, of course, but most were simply ordinary working men and women seeking better conditions from employers and government.

Such tactics guaranteed a massive retaliation from the many millions-strong Chinese peasantry—if only someone were skillful enough to organize the opposition to Chiang. And indeed Chiang would eventually be unable to withstand the upheaval. All that was years in the future, however.

As the 1920s closed, Communist Russia was almost as isolated as ever. All attempts to set up fraternal regimes in Europe had failed. Stalin's scheme to promote a nationalist Chinese revolution under Chiang Kai-shek had backfired horribly, with Chiang throwing out the Russians, massacring Chinese Communists, and accommodating the Western powers he was supposed to divert. Communists elsewhere throughout the world were easily dealt with by local police departments. No Communist military threat loomed anywhere.

Although the situation was less grim than it had been a decade earlier, the Soviet Union was still friendless and alone, surrounded by enemies who possessed strong military capability. The long-term prognosis for the Soviet state appeared dismal.

As the discouraging events of the 1920s unfolded, Stalin had a flash of brilliance, devising a policy called "socialism in one country." This policy had immediate ramifications that are discussed in the next chapter. Simultaneously, in a development incomprehensible to Comintern ideologues but easily grasped by any American precinct worker, Stalin would find a way to make common cause with a previously implacable foe—rightist Germany—raising these two countries from the ruins imposed at Versailles to the greatest powers in Europe.

V.

Soviet-German Amity

This chapter is a lesson in politics that demonstrates how diplomats worked to isolate two great nations from the world community. The plan worked splendidly—except for its outcome.

The diplomats assumed that the implacable differences between the governments of rightist Germany and Communist Russia would complement the isolation being orchestrated from chancelleries throughout Europe. They failed to consider what might happen if, badgered on every side, German and Russian enemies discovered one overwhelming common interest—survival.

With their minds concentrated on that goal, the two foes found each other useful. The manufacturing ability of one combined with the raw materials of the other to create the greatest war machine Europe had ever known, a machine ready to smite those who had fettered them.

The outcome of these machinations demonstrates what happens to those who depend on their enemies to do their work for them and to those who forget that all of their bickering enemies nevertheless have a common foe. After all, the art of politics rests in finding ways to set aside differences.

As the 1920s began, Russia and Germany were the outcasts of Europe. Russia had been militarily invaded by the Western powers, and its territory had been appropriated by Versailles diplomats. Germany too had lost territory, with millions of former citizens finding themselves under the rule of hostile neighbors. Western powers despised the one country for its social revolution and the other for its role in the First World War. Leaders of both were apprehensive about long-term survival of their nations.

The situation was complicated by Germany and the Soviet Union themselves being at odds, sharing the same hatred for each other that the Western powers felt. Nonetheless, leaders in both countries could see that they would be better off facing a hostile world together rather than struggling against each other.

The conventional wisdom was that, for the two countries to become allies, either Russia or Germany would have to conquer the other. German troops had been involved in the Allied invasion of Russia, and Moscow had been encouraging fruitless Communist revolts in Germany. While nothing had come of this except mutual ill will, Western diplomats watched the self-destructive spectacle with satisfaction.

This scenario might have continued except for a bit of brilliant insight from German general Hans von Seeckt. General von Seeckt proposed that Soviet strength be used rather than fought. He argued that cultivating a friend to the east would safeguard Germany's back if an opportunity to chastise the Western powers arose. He also maintained that such cooperation would promote that happy event by strengthening German heavy industry—supplying it with raw materials and an insatiable market. Such arguments appealed to Moscow's ascending circle of pragmatists, led by Joseph Stalin.

STALIN

Unlike his colleagues in the Bolshevik leadership, Stalin had never lived—let alone studied—in the West. He was the son of an alcoholic shoemaker who died while Stalin was a child. His mother was illiterate, but Stalin did well at a church school. Like so many other Communist leaders, he first discovered the oppression of society when he was a teenager. He was particularly offended by teachers who ran the seminary he attended. He felt they were tyrants, always snooping into students' private affairs. Repelled by all this, he became an active revolutionary.

Stalin was strangely reticent about his revolutionary exploits. We can only guess at the reason, but we do know that revolutionaries of that era and region specialized in raising money through robbery, extortion, and blackmail. "All signs indicate that it was in this dim realm where revolutionary politics merged with common criminality—in this world of fierce racial and personal hatreds, of intrigues and plots, daggers and murders, of fantastic vows and equally fantastic betrayals—that Stalin has his origins as a revolutionist."[1]

Lenin was suspicious of Stalin, making comments such as this one, on Christmas Day 1922: "Comrade Stalin, having become general secretary, has concentrated an enormous power in his hands; and I am not sure that he always knows how to use that power with sufficient caution." Just over a week later, Lenin warned his colleagues, "Stalin is too rude, and this fault, entirely supportable in relations among us communists, becomes insupportable in the office of general secretary. Therefore, I propose to the comrades to find a way to remove Stalin from that position and appoint it to another man who in all respects differs from Stalin only in superiority—namely, more patient, more loyal, more polite and more attentive to comrades, less capricious, etc."[2]

Although Stalin could be charming when meeting delegations of ordinary citizens, he was gruff among leadership colleagues, resenting their airs of intellectual superiority over him and (correctly) suspecting them of plotting against him. The intellectual acclaim he received for developing the theory of socialism in one country must have been sweet indeed.

SOCIALISM IN ONE COUNTRY

Stalin and those around him were disillusioned with the idealists' dreams of exporting world revolution. Stalin felt that strengthening the Soviet state made far more sense in both the short and long runs, preserving Communist rule in a major nation, which could then bide its time and promote world revolution by example rather than by military intervention. Stalin summarized this policy with the slogan "socialism in one country."

As the world revolution failed to materialize, Russian Communists confronted the same problem faced by early Christians when the imminent Second Coming failed to occur: how to explain the delay and fill the intervening time. Stalin's response was for the country to draw inward, changing its emphasis to protecting the revolution in Russia. In addition to answering a doctrinal question, Stalin tapped the roots of Russian patriotism, arguing that Communists could muster enough strength to protect their revolution without the help of workers anywhere else in the world.

Thus, Stalin laid the theoretical groundwork for abandoning the cause of world revolution and concentrating instead on Russia's welfare. Though controversial, his advocacy of socialism in one country met the needs of many Communists, and their enthusiasm boosted his standing as a party leader.

This inward turning provided a rigorous theoretical answer to Leon Trotsky's doctrine of permanent revolution. Trotsky was a Communist theoretician who became a leader in the Russian revolution and organized the Red Army. By permanent revolution he originally meant that the overthrow of the czar and the formation of the Kerensky provisional government were not ends in themselves but were way stations en route to a Communist Russia; the revolutionary journey would continue until the Bolsheviks prevailed. After the Bolshevik victory, Trotsky's doctrine evolved into instigation of Communist revolution in other countries, on the assumption that the Russian Communist regime would inevitably fall if it stood alone in a hostile world. As each of these foreign revolutions fizzled, Russian Communists became increasingly disquieted by the consequences predicted by theory.

Through socialism in one country Stalin presented a message of hope. He not only argued that Soviet Russia *could* stand alone; he argued that this was *desirable* for the time being. Though weak in military and industrial strength, the Soviet Union had great potential power in the wealth of its land and people. Therefore, no help was needed from foreigners who attempted to make other revolutions. Such revolutions would be welcome when they occurred, but they would come in response to the Soviet Union's example rather than in response to Russia's cries or threats. Stalin also rejected better trade relations with the West as the means of obtaining needed goods. Instead, he argued that Russia should exploit its own resources and become self-sufficient. This massive increase in the U.S.S.R.'s industrial capacity would be accomplished by following the Communist model, rather than by embracing capitalism. Thereby the Westernization of Russia, which during the czar's time had seemed an inevitable consequence of the growth of industrialization, would be halted and even reversed.

Through hostility toward the West Stalin achieved the seemingly impossible feat of providing a theoretical basis for traditional Russian conservatives to support the Communist regime. Moreover, his optimistic attitude promoted national pride. Stalin's prestige soared in Soviet leadership circles, where he was hailed as a brilliant theoretician with a bold and practical vision of the future.

SOVIET-GERMAN COOPERATION

Even before Stalin took control of the Russian Communist party, the Soviet Union had been alarmed by France's occupation of Germany's industrial Ruhr district in January 1923. Moscow protested that "The sovereignty of the German people is infringed. The right of the German people to self-determination is trodden underfoot."[3] Such sentiments struck a chord with unhappy German rightists: Hitler's 1939 alliance with Stalin had its roots in their long-standing awareness of common Russo-German interests; it was not a hasty, ramshackle agreement among thieves.

Since Poland was generally perceived as a French satellite, Germany was in effect surrounded on two sides by France and was now being sliced away in the west. France seemed to be on the verge of becoming Europe's dominant power. This made Moscow uneasy because France had already demonstrated its determination to destroy the Communist state and had moved into the Ruhr over the objections of other Western powers. Since the Western powers were unable to restrain France, Soviet security interests impelled both friendship with Germany and efforts to rebuild its military.

Moreover, as an immediate consequence of socialism in one country, the Russian leadership stopped calling for the overthrow of the German government and indeed was receptive to the cooperative program avocated by German general von Seeckt. (Stalin's doctrine denied that Russia needed foreign help but did not prohibit it.)

These actions, incidentally, were viewed with alarm by European Communists in the mid-1920s, who correctly recognized that Russia was abandoning the cause of world revolution and instead supporting German nationalism. With Russia no longer involved with revolution in Europe, local Communists realized that their cause was hopeless. Even if locals effected a successful revolt in one country, other European powers could swiftly mobilize to crush it while Russia stood aside, refusing to provide any aid. This caused much bitterness between European Communists and Russia.

Although German political leaders disagreed with General von Seeckt's call for Soviet-German cooperation, the country had no tradition of civilian control over the military. Thus, the German army (Reichswehr) was able to promote the policy through secret agreements with the Soviet state. This was highly irregular diplomacy, but both von Seeckt and Stalin were more concerned about results than methods.

Under these agreements, Germany and Russia began a cooperative rearmament project in the 1920s, employing such German firms as Krupp, Bloem und Voss, Albatrosswerke, Junkers, and Kopp and supplementing them with dummy German companies and foreign go-betweens to hide their activities from Western eyes. Aircraft, tanks, artillery, and ammunition were produced in hidden areas of the Soviet Union, with the output divided between the Russian and German armies. Plans seemed afoot to construct submarines in Russia, but instead they were apparently built in Spain, Holland, Finland, and Sweden and purchased by a "non-German" dummy company. These may have been shared with the Soviet Union.

This activity not only provided the German army with training and matériel forbidden by the Treaty of Versailles, but it also helped keep the German military-industrial complex at a state-of-the-art readiness via manufacturing experience in Russia. Moreover, the Germans provided training to the Red Army.

The rearmament became so extensive that the Reichswehr eventually set up a Moscow headquarters apart from the German embassy. The German army avoided regular diplomatic channels for communication with Berlin, instead using Russian Communist channels to keep in touch with home.

These rearmament agreements were secret in that normal diplomatic channels were ignored and the ever growing participation of German industry was hidden in plain sight, apparently unnoticed—or at least ignored—by Western observers.

Yet it was noticed by Communist opponents of German rearmament, who in 1926 observed that Germany's military budget was fully one-half the 1913 amount, which had funded the buildup permitting Germany's aggression in World War I. Germany's postwar army was supposed to be only one-seventh of its prewar size. The Communist conclusion was that "Germany is furtively and secretly maintaining strong armed forces, which cannot be counted in tens or hundreds of thousands."[4]

Because of the nature of the activity, increasing numbers of German industrialists and politicians eventually realized what was going on, and the "secret" became well known in Germany. Indeed, in December 1926 the German Social-Democrats revealed the clandestine military arrangement in an effort to hurt the Reichswehr. Few reacted to the news in Germany or among the

Western powers. The only visible effect was to irk the U.S.S.R., but military cooperation continued.

Although not cooperating with the rearmament, the German government nevertheless was beginning to realize the need for Soviet-German cooperation. In 1926 the two countries signed a friendship treaty declaring each would remain neutral if the other was attacked. The treaty was renewed in 1933. These treaties foreshadow the 1939 nonaggression pact signed by Stalin and Hitler, again demonstrating that the Stalin-Hitler pact had its roots in earlier Soviet-German diplomacy.

While Soviet-German relations remained solid into the 1930s, the nature of their cooperation was changing. European diplomats unintentionally brought the steadfast enemies Russia and Germany together in friendship, but the American government attempted to counteract the trend. The Americans devised plans to help ease Germany's burden of World War I reparations payments, plans that would simultaneously tighten relations between German commerce and American financiers. The plans failed to revitalize Europe's economy but did succeed in reducing the need Germany felt for friendship with Russia—enough that the Soviets began to notice a coolness.

Cordial relations between Russia and Germany continued despite the U.S. policy, but the relationship did undergo a drastic change in character. Instead of clinging desperately to the Soviet Union, the Germans began to use the relationship more as a diplomatic tool, casting a longing look eastward whenever a Western power provoked them. To an extent Germany began to play the West and Russia off one another, a situation that distressed the Soviets greatly but was regarded by the West as an improvement in circumstances.

Another circumstance also helped cool Germany's reliance on Russia. In early 1927 the Allies removed from Germany the observers that had been monitoring compliance with the Treaty of Versailles limits on the German military. No longer being watched, Germany did not need to hide its illegal rearmament in the Soviet Union. Thus, an important reason for close relations between the two countries ceased to exist.

Trade relations were strong between the two countries into the 1930s. Germany viewed Russia as a huge market for industrial output, and Russia viewed Germany as a welcome source of needed goods. As Hitler came to power in 1933, however, German industry began to regard the Soviet Union more as a growing competitor than a customer. Nazi government actions reflected this change in attitude. (Industrial leaders had financed Hitler's rise to power, and he in turn promoted their interests.)

Oddly some Soviet observers saw Hitler as the man to orient Germany toward the East, merely because he had declared himself an enemy of the West. They failed to see the limits of depending on an enemy's enemy. The Comintern and local Communists around Europe viewed Hitler differently. They saw the Nazi government imprisoning and killing Communists. In this case, and seemingly in all others then and later, the Soviet government was silent. It has consistently viewed such persecutions as strictly internal matters in which interference from the outside would be immoral. Thus, in later times Western complaints of human rights violations within the Soviet Union engendered righteous anger from Moscow. From the standpoint of the United States, failure to protest is immoral; from the Soviet viewpoint, American protest unethically interferes in a sovereign nation's internal affairs. On this issue the Russians are not hypocrites, although their values differ from American ideals.

Some Western optimists applauded Hitler's anti-Communism. Even Winston Churchill's early comments about Hitler have been read in that light.[5] The Marquess of Londonderry, Britain's Secretary of State for Air in the early 1930s, declared soon after leaving office, "I feel that if the Nazi régime in Germany is destroyed then the country will go Communist and we shall find a lining-up of France, Germany and Russia and the menace of Communism as the most powerful policy in the world."[6] Similar comments came from Hitler cabinet member Alfred Hugenberg's rhetoric in 1933: "War, revolution and internal disruption have found a starting-point in Russia, in the vast regions of the east. The process of destruction is still going on. The time has come to stop it."[7] The echoing sentiments in such talk naturally created disquiet in Moscow.

We tend to forget that appeasers in Britain and France viewed a reduction of Nazi power as an increase in Soviet power. To the appeasers, destruction of the Soviet Union was so important that it justified strengthening anti-Communist Nazi Germany. Today the appeasers are viewed as weaklings who were afraid to stand up to Hitler; but they viewed themselves as courageous anti-Communists, clever enough to strengthen a fanatical enemy of Communism who might be willing to war against Russia without Western aid, Western involvement, or Western casualties.

Even the start of war between Britain and Germany failed to convince the appeasers that they were wrong. Here is what British diplomat Lord Lloyd said soon after the war began, with the approval of the British Secretary for Foreign Affairs:

> However abominable [Hitler's] methods, however deceitful his diplomacy, however intolerant he might show himself of the rights of other European peoples, he still claimed to stand ultimately for something which was a common European interest, and which therefore could conceivably provide some day a basis for understanding with other nations equally determined not to sacrifice their traditional institutions and habits on the blood-stained altars of the World Revolution.[8]

Such thinking was a telling commentary about how little the eighteenth-century Enlightenment meant to Western government leaders.

Disquiet in Moscow grew with the growth of friendly diplomacy between Germany and Poland in 1934. Such friendliness indicated that Germany might eventually no longer be surrounded by enemies, that indeed a friendship with France might develop. Given the record of French and Nazi hostility toward Communist Russia and the record of Polish aggression against the Soviet Union, prudent men in the Kremlin began to wonder if danger was lurking.

The disquiet was increased by the signing of the German-Japanese Anti-Comintern Pact of 1936, in which the two countries agreed to cooperate in fighting the Comintern, which was secretly defined by the pact as the U.S.S.R. Russia had regarded Japan as a deadly enemy since the turn of the century and was now in the unenviable strategic position of having strong, hostile military forces stationed near both its eastern and western territories. Russia's concern over Japan affected European politics as well. In 1937 Hitler told his senior associates that he felt Austria and Czechoslovakia could be absorbed with no military interference from Russia, because the Soviets could not disregard potential trouble from Japan.

The Soviets had fruitlessly tried to ally with the West against Hitler, not because Stalin favored the West, but because he wanted to avoid a Nazi military attack. Western anti-Communists rejected any sort of common cause with the Soviets, seeing no gain in discouraging a fight between Germany and Russia. Stalin was willing to stand with the West against Hitler but was turned down.[9]

Stalin was thus very open to the Nazi offer of a nonaggression pact in 1939. He concluded that Hitler wanted to make the West rather than Russia the Nazis' first victim. Stalin recognized that even if Germany attacked Russia later, the already fighting West would probably stand with Russia against the Nazis. Stalin had no hesitations about taking this "insurance policy," although negotiations extended to the night of August 23, 1939. By then Hitler's timetable for the Polish invasion was so tight that the treaty was written to take effect immediately, so he would not have to wait for Nazi and Communist bureaucrats to ratify the document. Hitler believed the treaty crucial to his plans as it would guarantee a quiet Russian front. In addition to its benefit as insurance against German attack, the Soviets hoped the deal would bring German help in easing tensions with Japan.

The Nazi offer to Russia came at a particularly opportune moment, not only because Stalin had been rebuffed by the West and was disgusted with its continued compliance with demands from Germany and Italy, but because events in Spain were reaching their denouement. Those events demonstrated the deadly hostility directed toward leftist regimes from the West and from Hitler, emphasizing Russia's wisdom in accepting a truce with Germany. In addition, the Spanish civil war strengthened Stalin's contention that attempts to export Communist revolution were doomed.

VI.

Republican Communists and the Spanish Civil War

The Spanish civil war was a rehearsal for not only World War II, but for the postwar establishment of communist governments in Eastern Europe. It is therefore crucial to the study of Communist aggression.

TURMOIL IN SPAIN

The Russian Revolution of 1917 had little effect on Spain. During the 1920s Spanish dictator Miguel Primo de Rivera y Orbaneja did not even suppress Communists. They were so insignificant that he allowed them to publish whatever they wanted.

When the dictatorship collapsed in 1930, a great upsurge of democratic feeling swept through Spain. In 1931 the monarchy was replaced by a democratic republic. Throughout this turmoil local Communists staunchly supported the monarchy and called the republicans unpatriotic. This did little to enhance the already modest influence of Spanish Communism.

The republicans soon alienated the upper class, the Roman Catholic Church, the military, and rightist political factions by adopting land reform, declaring a separation of church and state, and instituting antimilitary, antiwar policies. In addition, some leftists did not believe the changes were sufficient, and so they too opposed the republicans. Toward the end of 1933, elections gave the rightist factions control of the government. Republican reforms were set aside or ignored, and leftist strikes and uprisings plagued the government. Moreover, as with the republicans, some rightist factions opposed the government for not going far enough. The rightists were thrown out in the election of February 1936, and the republicans again took control. Rightist forces consolidated against them.

Unrest of amazing extent and intensity broke out—strikes, demonstrations, arson, political murders. The country seemed to be spinning apart. The government declared a state of emergency and cracked down on civil liberties, under the illusion that freedom, rather than repression, caused the unrest.

In a well-advertised move that the government nonetheless failed to forestall, General Francisco Franco led an army revolt in Spanish Morocco in July 1936, claiming a moral duty to restore the order that civilians had been unable to restore. The army rebels, known as Nationalists, were supported by much of the Spanish police and Roman Catholic clergy, along with wealthy mercantile and landowning interests.

This was the start of the Spanish civil war, a conflict with homegrown origins.

MOTIVES OF THE PARTICIPANTS

The social unrest was not random. In disregard of the republic's government, peasants in the countryside began to organize and take over holdings of large landlords. Time and again workers won the strikes they called, at a rate of ten or twenty a day when the civil war started. If an employer tried to close down a business rather than give in, workers would simply occupy the property and run it themselves.

Ordinary people were seizing control of their society. This was a truly revolutionary situation. The republic's government was less endangered by opposition than by irrelevance. The situation was similar to that in Russia in 1917, when Kerensky's provisional government exercised power in law, but the soviets exercised power in fact.

Ignored by ordinary citizens and opposed by the wealthy elite, the democratic Spanish republic collapsed almost instantly when attacked by Franco's army rebels. The form of the republic would remain for several years, however, with officials occupying governmental posts and speaking for Spain in international diplomacy. Eventually a civilian government still called a republic would exercise a certain amount of authority and capture the imagination of progressive forces around the world before Franco and Hitler crushed it. But this republic would be very different from the Spanish democracy that collapsed in the summer of 1936.

Franco's army revolt was aimed less at the civilian regime than at the revolutionary population. Indeed, the government was reluctant to organize and arm the population against Franco lest the people replace the republicans with a new government. Without waiting for the government to act, citizens across Spain spontaneously organized and armed themselves to oppose Franco's so-called Nationalists. Some of these citizens supported the republic and were called Loyalists. Others were social revolutionaries indifferent to the government.

Although the revolutionary atmosphere was strictly a domestic product, Franco claimed that "revolutionary hordes obeying orders . . . from foreign elements" were rampant in Spain.[1] He called on Adolf Hitler and Benito Mussolini, the fascists of Germany and Italy, to help him forestall foreign domination of Spain.

In contrast to the prompt fascist aid Franco received, assistance to the Loyalists was late and inadequate. With the exception of Mexico, which was hardly in a position to do much, antifascist governments simply monitored the situation.

The West did not act primarily because of the revolutionary activity of Spanish workers and peasants. The wealthy interests that controlled the policies of Western governments saw Franco as a force to crush the leftists before their influence leaked across the Spanish border. This same prejudice against lower economic classes had prompted much of the initial opposition to the Bolshevist regime in Russia.

The Western failure to act has been ascribed to their fear of confronting Hitler's military might in Spain. But, whereas the Nazis did pretty well against poorly armed Spanish foes, the forces sent by Hitler could have been matched without undue burden on democratic government arsenals. In 1936 Hitler was hardly in a position to win a military victory against a united democratic armed force in Germany, let alone in Spain. This explanation also ignores the refusal of democratic governments to sell arms to the friendly Spanish regime. Potential French arms shipments fell through when Franco merely threatened to file lawsuits against participating French banks if he won the civil war.

Fear of Hitler did not deter the democracies—*support* of Hitler did. The appeasers thought it was crucial to do nothing that would weaken Germany's ability to threaten the Soviet Union, and they believed that staunch opposition to Nazi efforts would only strengthen Russia's hand. Because Hitler opposed Communism, Britain and France felt they had to work with him in the 1930s.

The powers of Western Europe also had no intention of fighting Hitler until after he had bloodied himself fighting the U.S.S.R. According to statesmen of the era, such a conflict was inevitable, so there was no point in fighting Hitler—Russia would have to do the fighting soon enough. This argument also rationalized Hitler's gains as only temporary. (Russia had used similar thinking when signing the Brest-Litovsk armistice with Germany in World War I, unconcerned about the Kaiser's gains because the Kaiser was doomed to fall.)

The appeasement rationale was apparent to the Soviet Union and contributed to its hesitations about aiding the Spanish government. Stalin was trying to promote the idea of a united stand against fascism and was therefore reluctant to take action in Spain that went against the desires of Britain and France. He compromised by providing barely enough aid to hold off a Franco victory, in hopes that the Spanish government would in the meantime galvanize anti-Nazi forces around the world. The galvanization never came.

Russian military advisers began arriving a few weeks after the start of the civil war. They provided professional guidance to the Loyalist militias. These militias were supplemented by volunteers who swarmed to Spain from around the world, forming brigades emphasizing particular nationalities, such as the Abraham Lincoln Brigade from the United States. Some brigade commanders later became famous in the Communist movement—the Yugoslavian Josip Broz (Tito), the German Walter Ulbricht, the Italian Palmiro Togliatti. These brigades were promoted by the Comintern, and Comintern projects were always staffed by non-Russians. Russian brigades might have had riskier diplomatic consequences than arms sales and professional military advisers. Not only were there no Russian brigades, apparently there were no Soviet citizens in any brigades although Soviet military advisers helped provide professional leadership.

Unlike the Western democracies, the Soviets were willing to sell military equipment to the Spanish government. Interestingly, the Russian tanks and aircraft outperformed Franco's Nazi equipment. Perhaps the Soviets had learned something from the years of secret rearmament cooperation with Germany.

Because the Spanish government had to rely exclusively on the Soviet Union for military aid, Russian advisers greatly influenced strategy and tactics and were able to freely disregard the Spanish government's desires. If the Spanish government complained, Soviet advisers readily offered to go home and to cut off Russian arms supplies. Although the Spanish government resented the Soviet stance, it did nothing since it had no other source of military assistance.

THE SECRET WAR

Alongside the military battles that captured headlines, another struggle was occurring in Spain. It transformed the legitimate government from a democratic republic into a Communist dictatorship. Often the Spanish civil war is called Hitler's dress rehearsal for World War II, but it was also a dress rehearsal for some of the techniques that local Communists would use to seize the governments of Eastern Europe after World War II.

When Franco's revolt began in July 1936 the handful of Communists (perhaps 200) in Catalonia merged with the Socialist party of that region. The combined party served as a Loyalist base for thousands of foreign Communists who arrived to fight fascism. These volunteers had been activists in their home countries and brought a lot of practical organizing skill to the new Catalonian political party.

The Communists believed that Spain's interests would be best served if Communists ran the country. The spontaneous revolutionary activity of the population, which had made the republican government irrelevant and prompted Franco's revolt, blocked Communist control. Ironically the Spanish soviets were neither inspired by Communists nor controlled by them. When the soviets gained power in Russia, the Communists ran the country because they ran the soviets. If, however, the Spanish soviets gained power, Spanish Communists would be left in the cold.

To seize power in Spain, the Communists had to oppose the workers' revolution that communism theoretically sought. The Communists infiltrated the organs of the Spanish government, seizing power by gaining control of the state rather than by gaining support of the people. Communists then had to defend the Spanish government against the revolutionary population and against Franco's Nationalists, because a collapse of the republic would foil the Communist bid for power.

The fight against Franco and the fascists is well known, but the fight against Spain's own people has received less publicity.

The Franco revolt began in July 1936. Around August the Republic's authority had collapsed throughout the country as local revolutionary committees (soviets) took over governmental functions ranging from the post office to the police force. The Republic's officials could issue orders, but no one felt obligated to obey.

The soviets seized or took over management of many businesses and landed estates. Real-estate records were often destroyed in an expression of contempt for wealthy owners. The rich were commonly run out of their homes, which were then taken over by the soviets. These seizures were not limited to the upper class. Various labor unions began seizing tools from tradesmen and factories of small entrepreneurs, devastating the middle class.

Peasants in the countryside also began to feel uneasy about the soviets. Getting ownership to the land that had been tilled for an absentee landlord was popular. As farm workers acquired their own land, however, the supply of farmhands declined. This labor shortage in turn hurt family farms big enough to need hired hands. Sometimes, in an expression of classic nineteenth-century communist ideals, farmers were even forbidden to have land requiring hired labor—a person could own only what he could personally cultivate. These smaller operations were now often forbidden to sell crops on the open market, required instead to sell to the local soviet at a fixed price. Such a practice could reduce the profit margin enough to cause small farms to collapse—perhaps forcing a merger with the nearby collective farm created out of a great estate.

Urban and rural middle classes thus feared the revolutionary activity that the government was unable to prevent and that Franco and Hitler were pledged to destroy. But rather than attempting to guide the working-class revolutionaries, helping them consolidate their gains in a manner that would ease middle-class fears, Spanish Communists decided to abandon the working class and champion grievances of the middle and upper classes.

Communists in Catalonia had already merged with the far more numerous Socialists to increase the respectability and appeal of Communism and soon took over leadership of the combined political party. Communist groups throughout the country soon picked up strong middle-class support by fighting to stop the social revolution while defending bourgeois values. In a development incomprehensible except in this context, even employers described as ferociously antilabor rallied to the Communist cause.

For persons frightened by the social revolution, the Communists provided an alternative to Franco's Nationalists, an alternative that supported the Spanish government. A person could oppose revolution, defend legitimate government, and stand for law and order by joining the Communists.

When Socialist Francisco Largo Caballero became premier of Spain in August 1936, he brought two Communists into the cabinet. Never before had Communists entered any government by lawful means. This was the first glimmer of challenge to the Communist dogma that revolution was necessary to gain power. This challenge would eventually split the Communist world into two camps, one supporting Nikita Khrushchev's advocacy of peaceful coexistence and one supporting Mao Tse-tung's call for wars of liberation.

Largo Caballero and the Communists desperately wanted to retain international recognition as the legitimate Spanish government. The attitudes of Britain and France toward the revolution influenced the Spanish heavily in this regard. To mollify these two powers, the Spanish government had to move decisively against the social revolution. This was also necessary merely to function as a national government, since many governmental operations had been taken over by local soviets. In order to survive, the central government had to regain those powers and eliminate the reforms achieved by the soviets. Struggle among the social revolutionaries, the Communist Loyalists, and the non-Communist Loyalists weakened their ability to fight Franco.

Establishment of a secret police corps demonstrated that, although the Spanish government was still garbed as a republic with democratic institutions, those clothes hid a dictatorial state. As Russian military aid grew along with the Soviet embassy, Russian advisers played a preeminent role in the Spanish secret police. Combining the talents of agents who were inheritors of Ivan the Terrible and the Spanish Inquisition produced methods that were crude but effective in crushing the leaders of social revolution around the country.

In addition to practicing naked terrorism, the Spanish government set out to nationalize industries. Normally such a move is considered a leftist step, but not in the context of the Spanish civil war. Factories and many other businesses had already passed into the control of local revolutionary committees (the soviets). The nationalization did not take ownership from private individuals but rather from the soviets.

Nationalization stripped a significant source of power from the soviets, and was thus a tremendous setback for them and therefore for the social revolution. It boosted the central government's power significantly. The wealthy class could view nationalization as a possible move toward eventual reprivatization, a further reason for them to support the Communists.

Around March 1937 the Spanish Communist party claimed to have almost 250,000 members, up from 40,000 before the civil war had started less than a year earlier.[2] This was phenomenal growth, especially if Communist sympathizers and fellow travelers are added in. Simultaneously other political parties were disintegrating from factional strife or were becoming paralyzed by confusion, giving the Communists a commanding position within the Spanish government.

Ambitious politicians could see where the future lay and decided to be on the winning side. Some openly joined the Communist party; others retained their nominal party identification but secretly collaborated with Communists and sabotaged rival parties from within. Premier Largo Caballero steadily lost control of the government, discovering that increasing numbers of officials whom he thought were answerable to him actually took their orders from the Communist party. Communist infiltration of the Spanish government succeeded not because of spies or bribery, but because politicians who loved power sought out the Communists.

Spanish Communists had powerful backing via military threats by the Soviet Union. Russia never suggested that the Red Army would invade, nor did anyone believe that would happen. The peril was just the opposite—Russia would threaten to halt military aid if the Spanish government refused to do its bidding. The Spanish state feared the *absence* of Soviet military power, an amazing turnaround from what causes unease about Soviet military power today.

Russian interference in the Spanish state grew quite pervasive. For instance, the Soviets demanded the dismissal of Spain's undersecretary of war if military assistance were to continue. This threat was delivered in person to Largo Caballero by the Soviet ambassador, who used Spain's foreign minister as his interpreter. The premier accepted, albeit with irritation, his foreign minister's role as assistant to the Soviet ambassador.[3]

In the spring of 1937, Spanish Communists and their political allies forced Largo Caballero from office. His replacement was Juan Negrín, a man more easily manipulated by Russia and the Spanish Communists. Such Russian use of Spanish officials, legally appointed to high office and exercising power legitimately, pioneered techniques that would be used repeatedly to achieve Communist control of governments in Eastern Europe after World War II.

The secret wars between Communists and non-Communists in Spain went unnoticed by a world watching the very public civil war that pitted Franco and the fascists against the republic's antifascists. In the end Franco achieved military victory. His success was mourned throughout progressive circles as a defeat for democracy, but as we have seen, Spanish democracy had ceased to exist years earlier. The government defeated by Franco had long ago betrayed Spain's native population and the foreign volunteers who fought for it. By the time Franco achieved victory, he merely changed a Communist dictatorship into a fascist one.

THE ABSENCE OF COMMUNIST AGGRESSION

We should pause to consider Soviet military aid to Spain in the context of Communist aggression. The republic was diplomatically recognized as the legitimate Spanish state. This Spanish government came under attack from rebel forces supported by Hitler and Mussolini. The government thereupon requested aid from foreign states maintaining friendly relations with it, offering cash for military supplies on the international arms market, but Western governments refused to help.

Then, upon explicit invitation of the Spanish state, the Soviet Union sold armaments to that state and provided advisers who guided efficient use of these supplies while helping the Loyalist militias and foreign volunteer brigades to operate with professional military expertise.

Because the Western powers refused to sell war goods to the Spanish government and also refused to hinder rebel receipt of Nazi war goods, Soviet military aid became crucial to survival of the Spanish government. The Soviets could thus gradually take over military operations in the Spanish government, also becoming highly influential in its civilian branches. This was similar to what later happened in South Vietnam when it accepted military aid from the United States.

Although Soviet influence grew great within the Spanish government and among the populace, the Soviets cannot be accused of military aggression. The Red Army did not invade Spain. Soviet military goods were bought and paid for in a strictly commercial deal between the Spanish and Russian governments. Had the Western powers been willing to send advisers or sell arms, the

Spanish state might never have turned to the U.S.S.R. There is no credible reason to believe that the Russians would have entered Spain uninvited. Indeed, there is no reason to believe they would have come if the Spanish government had not paid them to come.

Although no Communist military aggression occurred in Spain during the civil war, the legitimate government was transformed from a democratic republic to a Communist dictatorship. This process involved a complex interplay of forces: a revolution among the populace, a Hitler-supported rebellion against the already teetering government, a refusal of Western democracies to aid that regime, and its desperate solicitation of Soviet aid. The international volunteers fought for democracy, but the Spanish government merely fought for survival. The form that survival took was a Communist dictatorship in the guise of Western institutions.

VII.

The Baltic Region

We have already seen that the Hitler-Stalin nonaggression pact of 1939 had its origins in years of close military cooperation between the two countries and in Stalin's efforts to delay a German attack upon Russia. Hitler used the delay to overrun Poland, while Stalin used it to seize the Baltic states and conduct a war against Finland. Stalin's activity has been portrayed as Communist aggression. Such a portrayal ignores six centuries of conflict between these states and Russia.

LITHUANIA

Established as a state in the twelfth century, during the 1300s Lithuania annexed much of southwest Russia, located in areas later known as Byelorussia and the Ukraine. In 1386 Lithuania's leader, Wladyslaw Jagiello, married Queen Jadwiga of Poland and became the Polish king Wladyslaw II. The two countries remained tied, existing as separate states with the same rulers, from 1386 until 1569, when Lithuania voluntarily merged with Poland, primarily because of continuing territorial disputes with Russia. When Poland was partitioned in the late 1700s, Lithuania became part of Russia.

By World War I, the Lithuanian part of Russia had a population of two million, almost all of them farmers who were exploited by powerful landowners. Occupied by German forces in 1915, the area was still part of Russia after the czar fell and while the Kerensky provisional government was in power. Not until the Communist revolution of November 1917 did the Lithuanians proclaim themselves to be an independent country, albeit with intimate ties to Germany. In February 1918 the Lithuanians declared independence again, this time without any relationship to Germany. The Lithuanian declaration became a bargaining chip in Brest-Litovsk peace treaty negotiations between the Kaiser's government and the Russian Bolsheviks. The treaty practically annexed Lithuania to Germany—an indication that neither the Kaiser nor the Bolsheviks had taken Lithuanian independence very seriously.

Nor did democratic countries. Accounts of the Baltic states' struggles for independence generally make little mention of the Allied powers' refusal to grant official diplomatic recognition to Lithuania, Latvia, or Estonia after the war. In later years Bolshevik postwar military activities in the Baltic would be portrayed as aggression against these small countries. At the time, however, the West refused to recognize that the countries existed. Indeed, the West supported Russian White forces operating in those areas— forces that sought to keep the territories as part of Russia. If the weak Bolshevik regime fell, the West had no intention of accepting the pretensions of political independence made by Baltic patriots. The West considered these areas parts of Russia.

In addition to aid for Russian White forces in the Baltic, the Allied powers were concerned about Bolshevism, which led to a mischievous clause in the November 11, 1918, armistice. This clause required the German army then occupying the Baltic area of Russia to remain and fight Bolshevik forces. Thereby the war on the eastern front continued, only instead of fighting a united Russia alone, the Germans now fought a divided Russia with Allied assistance.

Mischief arose because the Germans had their own plans for the Baltic area. Germany had long influenced the region economically and socially, and the Kaiser's government had hoped to convert the territory into a colonial adjunct of Germany. These schemes remained after the Kaiser's departure, and the German Baltic army provided a means of fulfillment.

Through much of 1919 the Germans ran a sophisticated shell game, gaining Allied support by identifying native military opponents as Communist regardless of political orientation, refusing some Allied orders on plea of military necessity, and evading orders when no convenient excuse existed for outright disobedience. In autumn 1919 the Allies finally realized that Germany was simply continuing its wartime program in the Baltic. They forced the Weimar government of Germany to disband the Baltic army.

In Lithuania this situation had been complicated by ties that the non-Communist government had with Germany during World War I. Poland argued that a so-called independent Lithuania was actually a German fiction devised to cover up conquest of Baltic Russia. Unlike Lithuania, Poland had diplomatic recognition from the Allies, and maintained that the Versailles negotiators should award Lithuania to Poland.

Rather than trusting diplomacy, however, in April 1919 Poland invaded Lithuania. The German army was in Lithuania at this same time. The Western powers decided to send a friendly military mission to the area, a contingent of officers with largely administrative and advisory duties, not an assault force. The Allied officers worked to get the German army out, while at the same time trying to limit the Polish advance. The Allies repeatedly announced lines that Polish forces were forbidden to cross, and the Poles crossed them anyway. The Allies had no troops in the area to enforce their wishes.

Russian forces rolled over Lithuania in July 1920 in response to the Polish attack on Russia. When the fighting stopped, Lithuania was no longer part of Poland. Soon afterward Russia recognized an independent non-Communist government of Lithuania, two years before the United States did so. Communist entry into Lithuania was actually a prelude to the reestablishment of an independent nation.

Of course Communist Russia's motives were impure. The Bolsheviks expected an independent Lithuania to cause trouble for France's satellite, Poland. Yet the Communists had done something that no other Russian regime had done for centuries: recognized an independent Lithuania.

As hoped by the Communists, Lithuania's relations with Poland were sour throughout the 1920s. From the Soviet view this had the added benefit of complicating Lithuania's relations with other Baltic states, since Poland loomed large over them. Lithuania also managed to annoy Germany by occupying Memel (now Klaipéda), which had been Prussian from the 1600s until World War I. Lithuania was thus isolated in Europe. In contrast, its relations with the Soviet Union were good, and the two agreed to a neutrality pact in the 1920s.

During this interwar period, it is notable that Russia was willing to have a non-Communist government in neighboring Lithuania.

Indeed, by the time of the 1939 Hitler-Stalin pact, a fascist dictatorship ruled Lithuania.

LATVIA

Like Lithuania, Latvia was part of Russia when World War I began. A Bolshevist government promptly appeared in Latvia after the Russian Revolution and was just as promptly crushed by the German army. The territory then went to the Kaiser as part of the Brest-Litovsk armistice agreement with Russia.

A Bolshevist regime was quickly reestablished at war's end, and in January 1919 Russia recognized the Latvian Soviet Republic. Although the Latvian government was Communist, diplomatic recognition by Russia affirmed the principle that Latvia was independent and no longer part of Russia.

In contrast, the Western Allies still viewed Latvia as part of Russia. As was happening concurrently in Lithuania, the Allies directed the defeated German army occupying Latvia to remain in place and fight the Bolsheviks. This German army was not provisioned by the Allies, so it took whatever it wanted from the Lett population.

A grim little war developed. When the Allies put this German army to work fighting the independent Communist Latvian government, they thought they were battling Communism; but the struggle can just as easily be portrayed as a fight against Latvians who had patriotically resisted the same German army once before.

Although the Western Allies saw Latvia as a useful staging ground on which to rally Russian White support against the Bolsheviks, the Allies still considered Latvia a part of Russia. Wanting to avoid offending the Russian Whites, the Allies gave only half-hearted support to the independence-seeking Latvian anti-Communist regime established by Kārlis Ulmanis, a former high-school teacher who had lived in the United States for several years before World War I.

As was true elsewhere in the Russian civil war that erupted with the help of Allied intervention, the Latvian struggle became a fierce bloodletting between Reds and Whites. The civilian population suffered horribly. The great city of Riga became a metropolis of terror. Herbert Hoover reported to President Woodrow Wilson that "the town [is] in the hands of a starving mob, among whose actions was to drive some twenty thousand bourgeoise women and children into an island in the bay, and the results are beyond all description."[1] Hoover admitted, however, that this did not occur until after Communist military forces had been forced out of Riga. The "starving mob" was not committing a Communist atrocity.

The bourgeois class was brutalized; Hoover reported that hundreds were murdered daily. It is less certain whether this was done on orders of a central Communist government or by vengeful individuals in an anarchical situation after the Communist government lost authority. Hoover's staff reported that the city's jails had been opened and that dangerous criminals roamed at will, terrorizing the area.[2]

The Ulmanis White regime had been driven out of Riga when the civil war began. He tried to regroup in the town of Libau (Liepāja), but a rogue German-led force pounced on him and routed his government. Ulmanis escaped to Sweden. The situation was degenerating into factions of fighting warlords.

In exasperation Herbert Hoover (who had close liaison with Allied military authorities) sent word to German general Rüdiger von der Goltz to link up with White Lett forces and take Riga. This secured the city against leftist forces, but the terror described by Hoover continued, merely shifting to White perpetrators brutalizing the proletarian class. Hoover's men instantly sent a forty-car railway train of food and supplies to Riga, and he insisted with partial success that the White terror cease. As we have already seen in Hungary, in postwar Europe a group's ability to provide food gave it legitimacy among the population; thus Hoover's aid was crucial to calming the Latvian scene. Temporarily.

General von der Goltz's army then turned on the White Latvian forces loyal to Ulmanis, starting a war between the Germans and the anti-Communist Latvian government. At the same time Estonian military forces attacked von der Goltz's army. The Estonians, with good reason, feared that the German-led army intended to conquer the Baltic region. In July 1919 the Estonians attacked Riga, which was being held by von der Goltz. What was left of the city came under attack by infantry, machine gun, artillery, and poison gas.

General von der Goltz's forces were hard pressed and asked the Allies to negotiate an armistice in the same month, which was quickly arranged. Ulmanis reestablished his government in Riga with Hoover's food backing him up. Another German-Latvian flare-up occurred in the autumn of 1919, but this time the Allies gave immediate and firm support to the Ulmanis nationalists. The remnants of von der Goltz's forces were defeated on the field. Some returned to Germany, and the rest disbanded.

The four native factions—Russian Communists, Russian Whites, Latvian Communists, and anti-Communist Ulmanis Latvian nationalists—could now fight undisturbed. Despite vigorous military opposition, Latvian Communists still held Latvian territory, reflecting the great popular support the Latvians had for the Communists. Many of them did not care if they were ruled by Russia. They felt social revolution was more important than political independence and preferred the former under Russian rule to the latter under the Ulmanis regime. Latvian units of the old czarist army formed the core of the Russian Red Army. Nonetheless, the combined anti-Communist forces, with the assistance of Polish units, finally cleared Latvia of all Communist forces in early 1920.

Bolshevist Russia decided that an independent non-Communist Latvia could be a useful conduit for trade between Russia and the capitalist world and accepted the situation. In the summer of 1920, Russia granted formal diplomatic recognition to the Ulmanis regime. In contrast, the West still hoped to defeat Lenin's government and so continued to support the Russian Whites and their claims to the Baltic region. Not until July 1922 did the United States recognize a free and independent Latvia under the Ulmanis regime.

Ulmanis gained and lost power as elections and parliamentary politics shifted. He served as prime minister four times, becoming increasingly disenchanted with political bickering. As early as 1927 his opponents feared that he might attempt a coup. Soon after he became prime minister in March 1934, the parliament ordered all Nazi and fascist officials to be removed from government. Instead of complying, Ulmanis abolished the parliament and instituted martial law. In 1936 he made himself president as well as prime minister and ruled Latvia as a fascist dictator.

His dictatorship ran the country in 1939. Like Lithuania, Latvia was not a democratic state when Hitler and Stalin agreed to their nonaggression pact. But as with Lithuania, during the interwar years the Soviet Union once again tolerated an independent non-Communist country, formed from Russian territory.

ESTONIA

Estonia too was part of Russia when World War I began, and it remained so under the provisional Kerensky government after the czar fell. Under Kerensky Estonia was allowed to establish a national council to draw up regulations by which Estonia would be allowed to exercise home rule as part of the Russian empire. At the same time, soviets formed in Estonia, as elsewhere in Russia, and challenged the national council's authority. When the Communist revolution occurred in November, the soviet in Tallinn declared itself to be the government of Estonia and forced the national council to terminate, but not before the national council had declared Estonian independence from Russia. This declaration by a defunct organization had little standing.

The Balts were among the groups most hurt by the Communist government's policies. The Balts were ethnic Germans who dominated the economy in Russia's Baltic region. In December 1917 and January 1918 they invited Germany to occupy Estonia. The Brest-Litovsk armistice talks had broken down, and Germany resumed combat on the eastern front. The Kaiser's troops quickly invaded Estonia in February 1918.

The Communist regime abandoned the field. The national council then reappeared and once again proclaimed Estonia an independent country. The next day German forces seized Tallinn; Germany annexed Estonia in March as part of the Treaty of Brest-Litovsk.

Upon Germany's signing of the November 11, 1918, armistice, the national council reemerged and for a third time declared Estonia's independence. Their status as the government was challenged directly by Bolsheviks who formed the Estonian Soviet Republic, and more subtly by General von der Goltz's Allied-sanctioned German army, which conducted the same kinds of obstructions in Estonia that it had elsewhere in the Baltic region.

Although the Bolsheviks had substantial popular support in Estonia, polling almost 40 percent of the vote in elections held after the Russian Communist revolution, they did not have as much support as in Latvia. They were pushed out of Estonia by the end of February 1919 by nationalist forces and the British navy. The British played a substantial role, as the fighting was concentrated within shooting distance from the seacoast.

Estonia then became a haven for the Russian White general Nikolay Yudenich, who was planning to restore the old Russian empire after defeating Lenin's regime. Estonian nationalists did not welcome Yudenich, since success for his cause spelled doom for theirs. The nationalists were powerless to do anything about him, however. After all, Yudenich had helped push the Communists out of Estonia and his forces continued to deter a return by the Soviet Red Army. Moreover, he received supplies from France and England, and Estonian nationalists seeking international recognition as a state could not defy the desires of Europe's two great powers. The West made clear that such recognition would be impossible unless Estonian nationalists cooperated with Yudenich. The nationalists knew cooperation did not necessarily mean that diplomatic recognition would follow, but they tried to make the best of an awkward situation.

Estonia thereby became a staging ground for campaigns in the Russian civil war. This was a major reason for the British presence in Estonia. Indeed, British general Sir Hubert Gough was an adviser to the White invasion force. Yudenich's first advance toward Petrograd (Leningrad) in the spring of 1919 failed. He tried again in the autumn, established a provisional Russian government, and pushed to within twenty-five miles of Petrograd. He needed only a revolt of the populace in order to seize the city, but the rebellion never occurred. Communist forces quickly pushed Yudenich back into Estonian territory.

The Russian Bolshevik government refused to allow the Red Army to cross into Estonia. This restraint was probably prompted more by fear of British reaction than by respect for Estonia. Nonetheless, Soviet Russia refused to violate Estonian territory despite the invasion by anti-Communist forces.

In February 1920 the Soviet Union signed a peace treaty with the anti-Communist Estonian regime and formally recognized its legitimacy. The Western powers continued to withhold such recognition from the national council, which had disappeared and reappeared so often. The national council's inability to govern Estonia without substantial foreign backing diminished its credibility. Yet, if Lenin recognized the regime, could its foreign backers do less? This put the West in an awkward position, but it continued to support Russian White claims to the territory. Not until July 1922 did the United States grant official diplomatic recognition and thereby abandon the view that Estonia was simply a district of Russia.

Lenin defended his decision to recognize the anti-Communist Estonian regime by predicting a Bolshevik revolution in Estonia that would establish a friendly government, but the revolution did not come.

By 1924 some Communists were getting impatient. Uneasy Russians wondered if Britain had convinced Estonia to give the Baltic islands Oesel and Dagö (Saaremaa and Hiiumaa) to England. And Estonian Communists were upset by repression. In December perhaps 300 of them staged a brief rebellion in the capital city

Tallinn. Estonian authorities extinguished the outbreak, sometimes executing rebels without trials.

The uprising was immediately blamed on the Comintern and the Soviets. Encouragement from Russia was certainly plausible, but it is less certain whether this was an officially approved project or the unauthorized work of Soviet firebrands. Whether Russia supplied the would-be revolutionaries with anything other than advice is unclear. Either way the incident was small and probably would have been considered a minor urban riot if Communists had not been involved.

Communist involvement, however, gave the Estonian military an excuse to take over what they characterized as a negligent government, which now became an anti-Communist military dictatorship. By 1939 it was also fascist. Nonetheless, the Soviet Union again tolerated an independent government, again carved from Russian territory, during the interwar period.

FINLAND

As with its interest in the three Baltic states, Russian involvement in Finland predated Communism. Finland was a Swedish province since the sixteenth century. During the 1700s Russia acquired parts of Finland, with the remainder still Swedish. The czar coveted the Swedish province; during the Napoleonic wars Russia invaded Sweden, and in 1808 Russia proclaimed ownership of the Swedish province. The Finns disputed this claim, and a year of fighting ensued before Russian ownership was settled.

Russia made Finland a grand duchy, a Russian province to be run by a grand duke, who could run the country independently. In theory, this meant Finland would recognize Russian sovereignty but could run its own affairs. In practice the grand duke was also the czar of Russia. Nonetheless, this arrangement gave Finland an identity separate from Russia. Russian law did not prevail in the grand duchy of Finland, which had its own Swedish-based laws.

Relations between the grand duchy and Russia became friendly, and in the 1860s the czar allowed Finland to have a diet. The diet wrote a Finnish constitution, accepted by the czar, saying that the grand duke could no longer make any basic changes in Finnish law without the diet's consent. This made Finland an autonomous constitutional monarchy, even though its monarch was an absolute ruler in Russia.

The fall of the czar in 1917 raised the question of whether

Finland was still a part of the Russian empire. Legally the Finns had a good case: their only connection with Russia was the czar, who had served as grand duke. But Kerensky's provisional government refused to recognize Finnish independence. Indeed, the Kerensky regime increased the number of Russian troops in Finland. (The czar had sent Russian forces into Finland during World War I to secure Petrograd from attack.) Diplomatic bickering continued until Kerensky's government fell and the Bolsheviks took over. In December 1917 Communist Russia reluctantly accepted Finnish independence—reluctantly perhaps less because of any desire to retain Finland against its will than because the government would not be Bolshevist.

Russian Communists encouraged Finnish Communists to seize power, and in early 1918 a Communist revolution established a Bolshevist regime in Finland. About half the Finnish electorate had voted for Marxist socialism in the elections of 1916 and 1917, so the Communist government had some popular support. This was an exhilarating moment for Communists. The Russian Revolution was no longer unique. Another country had opted for Communism, and world revolution seemed ready to spread westward through Europe.

Unfortunately for the Communists, a civil war erupted between the Finnish Red Guard and the anti-Communist Civil Guard.

During the civil war leftist Finns claimed they did not want Russian help. The Finns wanted to avoid linking their struggling regime with the Russian one, because the Finns, like almost everyone else, expected the Russian Bolshevik government to sink quickly, and they wanted to avoid being brought down with it. The Finns forlornly hoped that demonstrating such independence would help establish friendly relations with the Western powers.

Although the Finnish Communists apparently accepted Russian arms, Russian troop strength in Finland steadily declined during the civil war. The Bolsheviks were pulling out the forces that the czar and Kerensky had sent in. Indeed, the speed of withdrawal increased when the civil war started. Nonetheless, Finnish Whites worried that the trend would be reversed, refusing to believe that the Bolsheviks would stand aside.

From the start, departing Russian troops just tried to keep out of harm's way. They would fight defensively against the Civil Guard but took no part in any offensives. This inaction disappointed the Finnish Communists, who had expected help from Russian forces already on the scene even if no reinforcements arrived. In March 1918, long before any decisive battles, Russia had evacuated all its soldiers. Perhaps a thousand zealots stayed behind to stand with the Finns, but even those volunteers began to disappear as word of German plans circulated. The Russian Red Army played almost no role in Finland's civil war.

The German army, however, played a crucial role. Finnish Whites requested German intervention to fight the Communist Finns. The first arrivals were Finns who had been trained in Germany, whose professional leadership immediately fortified White forces. German matériel also came, and in April 1918 General Rüdiger von der Goltz (the same general who would later dominate the Baltic states) arrived in Finland with a German army, knowing that he would meet no Russian resistance. Indeed, the Brest-Litovsk agreement had stipulated that no Russian troops would be in Finland.

The Germans quickly conquered Finland and were hailed as liberators by Finnish Whites. This attitude seemed strange: no other foreign forces were in the country for the Whites to be liberated from. The Finn parliament even proclaimed the Kaiser's brother-in-law, Prince Friedrich Karl of Hesse, as king of Finland, certainly a step backward from the national independence granted by the Russian Bolsheviks. Clearly the Whites feared foreign dominance less than a social revolution that permitted lower classes to take control of their own lives.

The victorious Whites instituted a reign of terror. Historian Franz Borkenau reported: "Tens of thousands were captured and sent to concentration camps, where many of them died of hunger and exposure. It was the first instance of that White terror which avenged a few hundred victims of the propertied classes in the blood of tens of thousands of the poor."[3]

The Hessian king had not yet arrived when Germany lost World War I, and Finland's parliament declared that it now exercised all powers formerly held by the grand duke and made Finnish general Baron Carl Gustaf Mannerheim regent. He had spent almost thirty years in the czar's army before returning to Finland and taking command of the White civil guard in January 1918. Mannerheim's mopping-up activities against leftist Finns were, in Herbert Hoover's faint praise, "positive enough, but not so inhuman as those applied by the Communists against the non-Communists in Russia."[4]

Under Mannerheim the Finns harassed the Soviet Union with border attacks, attempting to extend Finland's border eastward during the Allied invasion of Russia. Finland did not formally participate in that invasion, although it aided Estonia when Russia chased Yudenich's army back across the Estonian border.

Russo-Finnish relations included some minor squabbles in the 1920s, but the two governments generally got along. Relations were good enough that the 1939 Hitler-Stalin nonaggression pact caused no alarm in Finland.

THE WINTER WAR

At the time of the 1939 pact, as we have seen, Lithuania, Latvia, and Estonia all had pro-Nazi fascist dictatorships. Given their history of hostility toward the Soviet Union, it is easy to see how they might have created a sense of unease in Moscow. In theory the Hitler-Stalin pact should have reduced any threat to Russia from these pro-Nazi border states, but of course that assumed Hitler could be trusted.

Stalin did not make that assumption. Speaking of the treaty, Stalin said in October 1939, "One cannot rely on it." He warned, "We must be prepared in time. Others who were not ready paid the price."[5] Stalin's original view—that the pact merely bought time and that a Nazi attack against Russia was likely—had not changed.

Since spring 1938 Stalin had been trying to reach an agreement with Finland about a coordinated defense against German attack. The Finns rebuffed him with protestations of neutrality in the great struggle. Stalin's attitude seemed to be that Finland was nonetheless hostile toward Russia. Germany, of course, had been instrumental in setting up the Finnish government twenty years earlier. Germany had also helped supervise construction of the fortified Mannerheim Line from which the Finns could launch an attack across the Russian border. And for more than a century Russia had been nervous about a potential military threat against Leningrad (Petrograd) from Finland. Stalin was still concerned about this and was angered by the Finnish refusal to remove their troops from the Russian border. His concern was heightened because significant sympathy for fascism existed in Finland, and the government refused to pledge that it would not support the Germans if they attacked the Soviet Union. In November 1939, as had happened when Russia experienced such fears about national security in Napoleon's time, the Russians invaded Finland. Thus began the Winter War.

Although we can condemn this action, we must also see it as

part of the centuries-old dance between Russia and Finland, not as a Communist innovation. Indeed, we must remember that barely twenty years earlier Finland had been a Russian province, a fact that the Kremlin never forgot in its attitude toward Finland.

Although the Winter War is now commonly portrayed as a product of collusion between Hitler and Stalin, in fact the Nazis were shocked when news of the attack arrived in Berlin. The Soviets had not bothered to consult Germany before acting. The Germans were displeased at the thought of Russia halting exports of Finnish raw materials to Germany, and not just because of the loss to the Reich's war economy. The act could also be interpreted as evidence that Russia was well aware that the Hitler-Stalin pact was temporary, and that Russia was maneuvering to weaken Germany's ability to expand the war further eastward. The Nazis were also appalled at the possibility that a Western power intervention in Finland might cut off German imports of Swedish raw materials.

The United States, which had spent years merely viewing Japanese and Nazi activity with concern, took only three days to announce a "moral embargo" against supplies to Russia. German, Italian, and Spanish "volunteers" fought against Russia in Finland. (In a dictatorship the degree of voluntariness to such enlistments is questionable.) Remarkably, they were also joined by French and British volunteers. The French and British governments also sent munitions. The Nazis and British may have been at war, but they stood together against Russia in Finland. The British and French governments even readied armies to join the battle against Russia, but noncombatant countries refused permission to cross their territories and thereby allowed the Allies to avoid the folly of starting a war with Stalin while waging a desperate struggle against Hitler.

In late January 1940 the Soviet Union seemed willing to negotiate an end to the conflict, but the Finns stalled. Soviet forces then renewed their push, and the Finns began to lose badly. In March a peace agreement was signed granting Russia territory that Stalin felt would be useful to promote the security of Leningrad. Russia also got the mutual defense treaty that it had long sought with Finland, but the document would later prove to be no guarantee against attack.

The Soviet peace settlement left Finland an independent state, unlike those countries conquered by the Nazis. In keeping with the czarist heritage, Finland remained autonomous but closely linked to Russia.

We should note that when the governments of England and France sent direct military aid to Finland, Stalin still refused to join the Nazi war against them. This caused consternation in Berlin, as it was an unmistakable sign of Soviet unfriendliness to the idea of war with the West. The conflict in Finland was not a joint Hitler-Stalin operation. Indeed, we have seen that Stalin hoped to stand with the West against Hitler. Moscow worked earnestly to reduce tensions with England and France in the spring of 1940, even while their armaments were being used against Russian soldiers.

RUSSIAN ABSORPTION OF THE BALTIC STATES

Lithuania, Latvia, and Estonia were all fascist dictatorships dominated by German ruling classes at the time of the Winter War. Stalin's anxiety about their stance in a German-Russian conflict was understandable, particularly since all three had pledged neutrality if war should break out between Germany and another country. Even if they remained technically neutral, fifth-column activities would thrive in sanctuaries on the Soviet border. Hitler was already trying that tactic against the Ukraine. In 1939 Stalin began pressuring the Baltic states to sign mutual defense pacts with Russia and to lease military bases to be run by Russian personnel.

In the spring of 1940 Stalin was concerned about the fall of France and the Allied defeat at Dunkirk. This portended a defeat of Britain as well, which would terminate Hitler's war in the west and allow him to turn eastward. Feeling an urgent need to move decisively to protect the Baltic area in case of Nazi invasion, Stalin presented grievances against the German-inclined Baltic states and demanded unlimited access by Soviet military forces. He also demanded that their current governments be replaced with those more friendly to the Soviet Union. The Baltic states barely had time to react before Soviet military forces occupied all three countries in July 1940. Some fascist officials were arrested and others fled. Provisional pro-Soviet governments appeared, and parliamentary elections were held on short notice. The pro-Soviet candidates ran without opposition; in some areas the vote count exceeded 100 percent of known voters. A week later the new parliaments met in Lithuania, Latvia, and Estonia. In August 1940 each voted to forgo national independence and become part of the U.S.S.R.

As a matter of principle, takeovers of independent countries should be resisted. In evaluating how indignant we should be about the Soviet's absorption of the three Baltic states, however, it is important to keep in mind that they were not free countries. They were fascist dictatorships with no democratic heritage. Therefore it is questionable how much freedom their populations lost in the Soviet takeover.

In this instance we should also recall that historically the three Baltic states had been part of Russia until 1918. The czars had never tolerated independence for these territories. Stalin's actions may be seen not as instances of Communist aggression but as a correction to a twenty-year aberration in historically Russian borders. Stalin was merely adopting the attitude the West had held after World War I: that the Baltic States were an integral part of Russia.

None of this makes Stalin's actions less heinous, but it does demonstrate that their origins lay in Russian history and had nothing intrinsically to do with Communism or world conquest. Nor should we forget that Stalin left the Baltic states alone until he appeared to be faced with three hostile fascist governments, who would be natural allies of Germany when Hitler made his move against the Soviet Union—a move that Stalin believed to be only a matter of time.

The Baltic invasion may be seen as aggressive by some, but Stalin viewed it as a legitimate national security operation involving historically Russian territory. This does not mean the other view is incorrect, but failure to recognize the genuine and very different Soviet view could lead to an inappropriate response. Motives must always be considered when evaluating actions.

THE CONTINUATION WAR

After the Soviets absorbed the Baltic states in the summer of 1940, Finland became uneasy and began looking toward Hitler as a protector. The Finnish government was comfortable with the autumn arrival of German forces in western and northern Finland, and plainly (just as Stalin suspected) was working against Russia. When Germany began supplying war goods to the Finnish government, no one had any doubts about the likely target of such matériel.

When Hitler invaded the Soviet Union in June 1941, Russia swiftly launched air raids against Finland. Finland was then delighted to join in the Nazi attack against Russia. Indeed, one

Finnish cabinet member said that Finland would have assisted the German invasion regardless of whether the Soviet Union had fired a shot against Finland.[6] The Finnish leadership was pleased to be allied with a powerful Germany. The speaker of the Finnish parliament declared that the military should drive east to seize Soviet territory for Finland,[7] and the Finn forces began to do so, crossing the Svir River and reaching the Lake Onega towns of Petrozavodsk and Karhumaki by late autumn 1941.

Stalin's fears about an attack from Finland, fears that resulted in the Winter War, turned out to be well founded. Propaganda during the Winter War about "brave little Finland" resisting Russia was distorted. The propaganda failed to note Finland's closeness to the Nazi regime fighting the West. Indeed, part of Germany's consternation about the Winter War was that Finland was considered a friend of the Reich, and therefore the war was a Russian attack against German interests.

So, while it may be justified to abhor Stalin's 1939 invasion of Finland, it must also be recognized that history proved he was correct in considering Finland a hostile military threat. And although Finland was a Russian victim, the victim was pro-Nazi and eventually stood proudly with Hitler. Indignation about the Winter War should be tempered with the knowledge that Finland was no friend of democracy.

Indeed, even after the D-day landings in 1944, Finland formally repledged to fight with Hitler. While American soldiers were sacrificing their lives to defeat Hitler, Finland was helping him. It was not an overrun country waiting for liberation; it was an enthusiastic Nazi ally. This was the government over which anti-Communists shed so many tears, a government that opposed the United States from the moment it entered the war.

Finland finally gave up its fight for Hitler in late summer 1944 and surrendered to Russia. The Soviet Union did not try to absorb Finland, nor was it occupied by Soviet troops. It remained an independent non-Communist nation, albeit sensitive to the feelings of its powerful neighbor.

THE PARADOX OF NATIONAL SELF-DETERMINATION

The fate of the Baltic states and Finland illuminates the Communist doctrine of national self-determination. This doctrine is described by Communists with some of the same words cherished by adherents of Western democracy, leading democrats to believe that the

Communists are advocating the same practices that Western democrats intend with such words. When results are rather different than expected, democrats may feel misled and decide that the Communists are liars.

Let us therefore consider the basis of Communist calls for national self-determination, and examine how the doctrine was applied in the Baltic states and Finland. This examination may help us to evaluate current world events, facilitating a more appropriate—and therefore more effective—response.

The Bolsheviks viewed national self-determination not so much as political freedom for the various peoples of the Russian empire, but rather as a loosening of ties with these nationalities, believing that the ability to secede would overcome any fears that the Communists intended to dominate them as other Russians had. Political independence would then turn their anger from Russia and toward the gentry and bourgeoisie, thereby promoting social revolution once the national revolution had occurred. National self-determination was a means to an end—social revolution—not an end in itself.

Once a nationalist victory was achieved, the revolutionary process had to continue to the proletarian stage, in which national boundaries become irrelevant because the workers' class identity with fellow workers supersedes national identity. Thus, the state's political independence need no longer be respected. Indeed, such respect would be contrary to the goal of social revolution.

Communists are referring to this proletarian stage when they speak of the "equality of nations." They believe that nationalist dreams in the czarist empire arose because some national groups received better treatment than others. Because oppressed workers did not benefit from such unequal treatment, in a practical sense the workers had no country. The czarist state had turned its back on them. The sensible response of these mistreated peoples was to withdraw from the empire and establish their own countries—national self-determination.

Nonetheless, class inequalities would still exist, with some classes benefiting from the exploitation of others. So the revolutionary process had to continue from the political nationalist stage to the social proletarian stage, in which a Communist society would end exploitation of man by fellow man. In that society, exploitation would decline and equality of economic circumstance would increase.

At that point national boundaries would become irrelevant and even harmful. Divisive national identities such as Estonian and

Russian would be replaced by an awareness that both were fellow workers. Once again the worker would have no country, but this time it would be a positive experience.

Rather than be divided among various political states, Communists believe workers must combine their strength into one massive force that can stand against the capitalist world. The separate countries must voluntarily join together in a union of soviet socialist republics, where all nations are equal (rather than some being exploited by others). In this new voluntary federation, which could grow even larger than the old involuntary czarist empire, the states would still have a technical right of secession. But they would never need to exercise it because of the equality of nations.

To Communists, national self-determination is not the separation of peoples into political states, but unification of peoples into a proletarian whole where all nations are equal.

How did this doctrine work when applied to the Baltic states and Finland?

Lenin had long advocated the right of national self-determination in the Russian empire. Because, however, it was supposed to be simply a stage preliminary to the proletarian revolution, Lenin did not favor automatic secession by any Russian district. Instead, he supported such a step only if proletarian consciousness seemed to be developing along with national consciousness.

The fall of the czar who had exercised such strict control over the far-flung Russian empire was followed by the fall of the Kerensky provisional government that exercised looser control. The Bolshevik regime had no control whatsoever even if it wanted any, and its own collapse was considered imminent. When pent-up nationalistic forces burst forth in the Russian empire after the Communist revolution, no power could stop their drive to statehood.

The Bolshevik regime was displeased by Finland's demand for political independence because the Finns did not appear bound for proletarian revolution. The situation was more promising in Estonia, Lithuania, and Latvia. These three Baltic states were, moreover, special cases because they were under German occupation and already lost to Russia. (Finland was unoccupied when Lenin's government granted it independence.) In 1918 Communist Russia merely relinquished sovereignty over the Baltic districts, which was not the same thing as recognizing political independence—indeed, the world at large viewed this Baltic region as annexed to Germany. The Russian act, however, directed nationalist aspirations against Germany rather than against Russia and promoted goodwill toward the Bolshevik regime.

Indeed, Lenin was wise enough to ride atop the revolutionary wave of nationalism in the Baltic states and Finland, praising and welcoming it as a force that would promote revolution. As Communist social reforms such as land distribution to peasant farmers became apparent, revolutionary fervor that had been dedicated to national aspirations shifted to defense of the social revolution. This is one reason that anti-Communist forces in the Baltic states had such a hard time expelling Communist revolutionaries. The Communists' social gains were more important than political independence. The proletariat preferred to live under communism, even Russian Communism, than live in a noncommunist country. They stood with the Russian Red Army rather than with the nationalist forces of Estonia, Latvia, or Lithuania.

Moreover, the Communist willingness to accept the secession of these districts generated popular support for Lenin's government. This lessened the amount of help available to Russian White forces, because they were pledged to destroy the political independence of the new countries once the Russian Bolshevik regime was defeated.

In vindication of the Communist doctrine of national self-determination, concern about social gains became a driving force to restore the empire, since many people in the new states cared more about social gains than about political independence, and Bolshevik rule would help protect social gains. The proletariat really did unite; the new national boundaries became irrelevant and could be erased. Uniting the workers of the world was not empty rhetoric. It could be seen, actually happening, and was a heady experience for Communists.

An outside observer might have thought that Lenin was weakening his regime more and more with each piece of territory that he gave up. In reality his policy strengthened Communist Russia's military security, because those new countries had every reason to oppose the Russian Whites attacking the Bolsheviks.

But the new states of Latvia, Lithuania, and Estonia quickly became satellites of foreign powers hostile to Communist Russia. A reawakening of patriotism in a Russia fighting Western animosity reversed the initial enthusiasm for separation of the new states and eventually prompted the decision to return them to Mother Russia.

Rather than progressing to the proletarian stage in the Baltic states, national revolution regressed to fascism. From the Communist viewpoint, Stalin's absorption of the Baltic states was a correction of national self-determination gone awry. (Such an interpretation, however, need not deny that Stalin may have had less pure motives in the Baltic; he was a master at cloaking practical actions in ideological garb.)

VIII.

Poland in World War II

After World War I, the Treaty of Versailles created the state of Poland from pieces of Germany and Russia. Both were displeased. Indeed, when the Allied powers wanted to send military aid to the Poles invading Russia in 1920, Germany refused to permit the munitions to cross its territory. A couple of years later, German general Hans von Seeckt, who masterminded the secret military agreements with Russia in the 1920s, stated bluntly: "The existence of Poland is intolerable."[1]

The Treaty of Riga, which terminated the Polish invasion of Russia, gave Poland a sizable chunk of White Russian homeland. In Washington, D.C., the ambassador of the White Russian forces, which the United States stubbornly recognized as the legitimate Russian government, declared that "restored Russia will never approve a treaty of dismemberment forcibly imposed in times of adversity; nor will the peasant population, predominantly Orthodox, of the Western provinces of Russia acquiesce in the domination of Polish Catholic landlordism."[2] Leaders of anti-Communist Russia supported by the United States vowed to reclaim territory yielded to Poland and also expressed hostility toward Poland's Roman Catholic hierarchy.

The Treaty of Riga also curved Poland protectively around Lithuania. In 1921 Poland convinced Finland, Latvia, and Estonia to join a mutual assistance alliance plainly directed against Russia. The French were credited with instigating the alliance: Poland was considered a satellite of France, having been created specifically as a state friendly to France by the Treaty of Versailles. France had endorsed Poland's invasion of Russia the next year. When France occupied the Ruhr in 1923, Soviet chairman Lev Borisovich Kamenev said, "whether we become involved depends entirely on Poland" because a mobilization of that country to oppose the Reich "would in the long run be directed against us."[3]

Diplomats of the German Weimar Republic and the Soviet Union sought to agree on a defense against the common foe Poland but failed because neither country wanted to face a Polish attack if the other ally called for aid. Both Germany and the Soviet Union feared Poland in the 1920s, a fact commonly forgotten today, when the relative strengths of these nations are now so different. Indeed, when Poland annexed the predominantly Ukrainian-populated East Galicia around 1920, Russia could only sputter indignantly.

That same year Russia and Germany secretly agreed on a mutual long-range policy of pushing back the Polish frontiers. Afterwards the anti-Communist Weimar Republic fretted that the Soviet Union might someday decide to accept the status quo and abandon the goal of reducing Poland's size.

In 1926 General Józef Pilsudski, who had driven Ignacy Paderewski and the democrats from Polish government several years earlier, lost patience with civilian rule entirely and staged a coup. In their enthusiasm for revolution, many Communists joined the coup. Pilsudski was by no means friendly to them, and he jailed many after his victory. Nonetheless the fascist-leaning Pilsudski dictatorship came into power with Communist backing, a circumstance both parties quickly sought to forget. Normally, with such backing Western powers would label a revolutionary leader Communist, but apparently Pilsudski's longtime anti-Communist credentials saved his government from the harassment the West typically inflicted upon new regimes that had achieved power with Communist support.

In just a few years Pilsudski's hatred for representative government spread throughout the country. The large National Democratic party had favored Western democracy in 1918. By the 1930s it had become a reactionary organization friendly to fascism and anti-Semitism, with strong support from the powerful Polish Roman Catholic hierarchy. This "liberal" alternative to Pilsudski's style of government had much public support, demonstrating that the flame of Polish democracy had guttered and died.

The mistrust developing between Germany and the Soviet Union in the early 1930s found expression in Poland. First the Soviet Union signed nonaggression pacts with Poland and its mentor

France, intending to guarantee their refusal to participate in any German attack against Russia. A couple of years later Hitler reached a political understanding with Poland, putting Nazi support behind the fascist-leaning Polish government on Russia's border. The Polish dictatorship played a deep and dangerous game, whose rules suddenly changed in 1939.

That spring the Soviet Union offered to join England and France in a commitment to defend countries on Russia's border. The point was to deter Hitler from attacking eastward. England and France, however, wanted to encourage that very thing. They refused to stand behind the countries blocking Hitler's way. Ironically the Western powers' refusal had the support of East European governments, who perhaps feared the effect of Soviet troops on populations that had been Russian until recently. Those populations may have been less interested in their national independence than the government leaders were.

For twenty years the Polish oligarchy had ruled ten million people who regarded Russia as their home, along with many others who viewed Germany in the same way. Few of these Polish citizens would oppose recovery of their towns by these two countries. The Polish leaders realized this but failed to temper their actions. Instead, they antagonized more neighbors, intimidating Lithuania with an ultimatum in March 1938 and grabbing some of Czechoslovakia in October "like an eager and vindictive vulture"[4] after diplomats meeting in Munich accepted Hitler's desire to take over Czechoslovakia.

The Polish dictatorship did not notice that the trembling of its two large neighbors to the east and west was no longer caused by fear—they had spent over a decade cooperating in a massive mutual rearmament. In the summer of 1939, Hitler offered Stalin a nonaggression pact; after Stalin's springtime rebuff by the West, the Soviet dictator seized the pact as an opportunity to delay a Nazi attack against the Soviet Union. In the same treaty, Hitler agreed to resume the German-Russian cooperation against Poland.

With treaty in hand, the Nazis attacked and nearly defeated Polish forces in September 1939; the Soviet Union then swept in and advanced to the points Stalin and Hitler had agreed upon—roughly the Curzon Line that the Western powers had proposed as Poland's eastern border after World War I, but which Polish aggressors had disregarded in favor of invading and stealing a portion of Russia.

In one respect it is fair to say that these unwilling Polish citizens were liberated by forces of their Russian homeland after resisting

Polish assimilation for twenty years. But the ethnic Russians had a czarist heritage and found the Communists nearly as unpleasant as the Poles. At least the Polish government had tolerated Ukrainian ethnic and national aspirations and allowed Ukrainians to blow off steam in harmless activities. The Communists, however, found such behavior unacceptable.

Ukrainian political and cultural activities were quickly curtailed. The Soviet secret police went to extremes in ferreting out native Polish leaders; even stamp collectors and restaurant proprietors were included as security risks to be arrested. Such arrests customarily included family members. As Soviet fears of Nazi attack grew, from 800,000 to 2,000,000 of these Poles were relocated thousands of miles eastward under brutal conditions indistinguishable from those used by the Nazis to transport Jews.

The main idea was to shift unreliable populations far from any opportunity to help the Germans and to position Communist patriots on the border. A social motive also existed for the deportations of Poles: many locals would resist Russian-style socialism on their home territory but would gradually adopt it if uprooted and moved to Russia. Such deportation was hardly a Communist innovation; it had been used time and again by czarist governments since the 1400s.

The Soviets also captured thousands of Polish military officers and sent them to prison camps in Russia. After Poland was defeated, someone asked Stalin what to do about these camps, and reportedly he responded with one word: "Liquidate."[5] Perhaps he meant to close the camps and send the prisoners home, as was done with other Polish officers, but bureaucratic underlings interpreted the order literally. After all, in 1937 Stalin had called thousands of Polish Communists to Russia under various pretexts and had them killed. In the spring of 1940 about 8,000 Polish officers from the camps were murdered. Their bodies were dumped into mass graves, some of which were found by the Nazis in 1943 around the Katyn Forest in Russia.

The Nazis expressed shock at such an atrocity and piously called upon the International Red Cross to investigate. Poland had a government-in-exile based in London, which also joined in the call. The Russians fiercely resisted any inquiry. A generous-minded person could see ambiguity in the evidence investigators found, especially since both the Soviet Union and Germany had a motive and the ability to slaughter the Polish officer corps. Nonetheless the Russians acted guilty, judging from their resistance to

Red Cross inquiries at the time and touchiness about the subject later.

The mass murder terribly strained relations between the Soviets and the Polish exile government in London. In 1941 Polish prime minister Wladyslaw Sikorski had personally asked Stalin about the whereabouts of the officers and had been assured of their safety. In addition, the London Poles increasingly feared that a Soviet liberation of Nazi-occupied Poland would be accompanied by attempts to introduce a Communist society there, leaving the Polish exile government as a footnote in history rather than leader of a resurgent Poland.

The London exiles dreamed of a strong Poland that would be the most powerful nation of Eastern Europe, able to make neighbors tremble in fear. Both Winston Churchill and Franklin Roosevelt tried to convince the London Poles that they were overreaching, but time and again they found dreams of grandeur preferable to the reality of being a small group of men isolated from distant events out of their control.

For a while their activities, such as their "order" that the Red Army not enter Polish territory in pursuit of Nazi forces, caused only amused embarrassment. Allied amusement turned to consternation and then anger when the London Poles, under the leadership of Prime Minister Stanislaw Mikolajczyk, rejected the Curzon Line as Poland's eastern border. They were trying to keep the territory taken by Poland in its 1920 invasion of the Soviet Union, land that even anti-Communist Russians had vowed to reclaim one day.

Both Stalin and Churchill adamantly opposed the Poles' demand. "I cannot feel," Churchill told Parliament, "that the Russian demand for reassurance about her western frontier goes beyond the limit of what is reasonable or just."[6] Churchill believed it crucial to agree on borders before the Red Army marched past Russia's 1940 boundaries. He was amazed that the London Poles were so greedy as to reject a definite limit on the Soviet border, which would also definitely limit Poland's. The Poles preferred to negotiate borders after Soviet forces took all of prewar Poland. Churchill and Stalin decided to establish the border approximately on the Curzon Line and let the London Poles fume helplessly. In later years anti-Communists would condemn eventual Russian usurpation of the authority of the London exile government, but they expressed no complaint when Churchill did the same.

The Warsaw uprising against the Germans in August 1944 provided the London Poles with their last chance to establish some sort of authority in Poland itself. Because this disastrous military action wiped out the anti-Communist Polish Home Army, Stalin has often been blamed for promoting the venture. Whether or not such blame is justified, the London exiles were eager for the uprising. It was as much their idea as Stalin's.

In July 1944 Russian forces drove the Nazis back toward Warsaw. On July 29 Radio Moscow exhorted Warsaw's population to rise against Nazi occupiers. The next day another Russian radio station made the same appeal. Both strongly implied that a revolt would bring swift help from the Red Army. The Polish Home Army, a well-organized resistance group connected with the London exiles, took to the streets of Warsaw on August 1. They did this without first checking with the Allied chiefs-of-staff liaison in London.

A few days earlier a Communist-sponsored National Polish Liberation Committee had been formed in Lublin, Poland, challenging the authority of the London exiles. The London group suddenly comprehended their isolation and realized they would quickly have to do something to retain legitimacy. After all, what could command more attention—a voice on the shortwave or a local townsman lobbing gasoline bombs at the panzers? Moreover, a trained army of Poles under Russian command was helping liberate the country from Nazi occupation. This gave the Communist Lublin committee even more credibility.

At the start of August the rapid liberation of Warsaw by Soviet forces seemed assured. The London exiles felt the only way to remain in authority was to have friendly forces controlling the capital when the Russians arrived. With blessings from the London exiles the Polish Home Army conducted an insurrection in Warsaw for political reasons, not military ones, as demonstrated by its conduct, seizing positions of political significance such as the city hall while ignoring military sites such as bridges.[7]

The Red Army advance halted outside the city, and its air force disappeared. The Nazis took advantage of the situation to hammer the Polish army from the ground and the air.

On August 4 Churchill urged Stalin to air-drop arms and ammunition to help the Warsaw resistance. Stalin replied that such aid was pointless since the fighters could not possibly defeat the Nazis. After Royal Air Force supply efforts failed, Churchill asked Stalin twice more for Russian airdrops. He refused Churchill, as well as a joint appeal from Churchill and Roosevelt. The U.S. Army Air Force sent 110 bombers to make pinpoint drops of supply canisters one day, but only fifteen containers landed close enough for the Polish Home Army to retrieve them.

Churchill proposed to Roosevelt that they press Stalin and try to force him to aid the Warsaw fighters, but Roosevelt thought it a bad idea to pressure Stalin on the issue. Churchill considered proceeding on his own but decided aid to Warsaw was not worth possible destruction of the alliance against Hitler.

The Polish Home Army surrendered to the Nazis in early October. Approximately 10,000 had been killed and 12,000 wounded. Anywhere from 50,000 to 150,000 Warsaw civilians were also killed in the uprising.

In the West it is generally accepted that Stalin encouraged the Warsaw uprising and then withheld aid. The assumed purpose was to eradicate the anti-Communist Polish Home Army, thus easing a Communist takeover of the country.

There is another view: Stalin's refusal to send aid was consistent with Soviet policy throughout the war. Even Polish Communist partisans complained. Wladyslaw Gomulka said, "Before 1944, Russian arm-drops were infinitesimal."[8]

Moreover, although the sudden Russian halt outside Warsaw seems strange, it can be explained tactically. A large river and a lot of swampy territory, difficult to cross, separated the Russians from the city. In addition, the Russian tactic of surrounding the city kept Nazi forces bottled up inside and helpless. There was no military reason to attack Warsaw directly, and the Nazi garrison's inevitable surrender was then accomplished with smaller loss to Russian forces arrayed against the city.

Of course, a tactical explanation for the Russians allowing the Polish Home Army to be destroyed does not mean that political reasons were irrelevant. After all, the actions of the Polish Home Army itself were primarily politically motivated.

With their military arm in Poland destroyed in the Warsaw uprising, the London exiles split into two factions. One, headed by Mikolajczyk, who resigned from the government, wanted to compromise with the Soviet Union and the Polish Communists. The other, headed by his successor, Prime Minister Tomasz Arciszewski, sought full power in Poland through conflict between Russia and the Western Allies, in hopes that the Allies could force Russia from Poland. Military men such as General Wladyslaw Anders and former Commander-in-Chief Kazimierz Sosnkowski joined the latter faction. The London exiles had earlier rejected Churchill's urgings and decided to wait for Russia to occupy all of old Poland before discussing borders. The fruit of this folly was that the London group now was on the verge of losing any status as a Polish government regardless of borders, since the Lublin Communist committee was in place on the scene.

Churchill was irritated by the London exiles and made his exasperation plain to Stalin, reiterating that postwar Poland should certainly have a government friendly to the Soviet Union. Stalin seems to have concluded that Churchill would do nothing to interfere with establishment of a Communist government in Poland, especially since the West was preoccupied with the Battle of the Bulge. In January 1945 a Communist government derived from the Lublin committee appeared in Poland, competing with the London exiles.

Unlike the London group, the Communist Poles accepted the Curzon Line as Poland's eastern border—but in return they received a big piece of Germany from the Russian liberators. At the Yalta Conference in February 1945, Stalin, Churchill, and Roosevelt agreed to postpone deciding the exact size, but all agreed that part of Germany should go to Poland. They also concurred that the Communist government in Poland would be recognized as the legitimate provisional government, with the understanding that some non-Communists would enter the government and that free elections would be held. The London Poles had finally lost all standing in the eyes of Stalin, Roosevelt, and Churchill. The London group fell victim not to Communist aggression, but to their own greed.

Soon after the European war ended, several non-Communist Poles from the London group entered the pro-Soviet government; Stanislaw Mikolajczyk even became deputy prime minister. The free elections (which Communists define as meaning everyone is free to vote, not that there will be much choice on the ballot) were postponed. Since after the Yalta conference the Western powers had once again reiterated in April that they desired a Polish government friendly to Russia, Stalin appeared to wonder about the point of elections—after all, everyone had agreed on a pro-Soviet government in Poland. Moscow seemed genuinely puzzled by the West's irritation when no elections took place in Poland.

The puzzlement contained an element of suspicion because Western policy had promoted a Polish government hostile to the Soviet Union for the past twenty-five years. Since quick elections could provide an edge to great landlords and the Roman Catholic hierarchy, doubt arose in Moscow about the West's pledge to reverse its traditional policy.

U.S. secretary of war Henry Stimson and White House–Joint Chiefs liaison Admiral William Leahy shared Moscow's bewilderment. Historian D. F. Fleming noted that Stimson believed "the Russian conception of freedom, democracy and voting was quite different from ours, and he 'thought that the Russians perhaps were being more realistic than we were in regard to their own security.' " Leahy "recalled that 'he had left Yalta with the impression that the Soviet government had no intention of permitting a free Poland, and that he would have been surprised had the Soviet government behaved any differently than it had.' "[9]

When the European war ended in May 1945, Russia had freed all of Poland from Nazi domination. The campaign had been virtually an all-Communist effort, giving credibility in Poland to the pro-Communist government. Additional strength came from its administration of the German land given to Poland by Russia when Polish borders were shifted westward.

The peasantry wanted to be left alone. Their attitudes toward the Communist government ranged from indifference to mild support—the latter attitude assisted by land reforms that distributed parcels of huge estates.

The old landlords were furious. They had always controlled Poland's government. Some had preferred Hitler to Russia. Indeed, some had supported the 1920 invasion of Russia. In addition, the new Polish boundaries included the estates of the old Prussian Junkers, the German aristocracy that had composed the core of German fascist militarism. For all these landlords a Communist government in Poland meant an end to the feudal life-style they had enjoyed on their estates.

They supported vigorous anti-Communist guerrilla warfare against the government. These partisans were fighting the Polish government that the Western powers recognized as legitimate. A veritable civil war was fought in some places. The guerrilla conflict killed hundreds of Russian soldiers in 1945.

Although the conflict was fierce, the pro-Soviet government had the edge. It had the military and civil servant apparatus behind it, along with the invaluable support of Russia. With dwindling support in the countryside as land reform proceeded, the guerrilla campaign for the old order ceased.

Not only was Stalin determined that Poland would never again be ruled by an unfriendly government, he was determined that the friendly regime would be strong enough to prevent invasions of Russia like those that had come via Poland twice in twenty-five years. Stalin bluntly responded to Churchill's concerns about the nature of Poland's postwar government: "Poland borders on the

Soviet Union, which cannot be said about [the proximity of Poland to] Great Britain and the U.S.A."[10]

In 1953 Churchill acknowledged the point: "Russia has a right to feel assured as far as human arrangements can reach, that the terrible events of the Hitler invasion will never be repeated and that Poland will remain a friendly power and a buffer."[11]

IX.

The Balkans

Romania, Bulgaria, Yugoslavia, Greece—all but one became Communist as World War II ended. While this development resulted partly from the region's history, it also fulfilled an agreement Winston Churchill had made with Joseph Stalin.

In mid-1944 Churchill had unsuccessfully tried to convince the London Polish government in exile of the importance of making a deal with Stalin before the advancing Red Army was in a position to dictate terms. The London Poles disregarded Churchill's advice, and little was heard of them afterward.

Heeding his own advice, in October 1944 Churchill met with Stalin in Moscow. Franklin Roosevelt had already given Churchill the authority to negotiate for American interests in Eastern Europe. On a piece of paper Churchill wrote out the following formula for three powers' predominance in Eastern Europe:

Romania : Russia 90%
  The Others 10%
Greece : Great Britain in accord with USA 90%
  Russia 10%
Yugoslavia : 50/50%
Hungary : 50/50%
Bulgaria : Russia 75%
  The Others 25%

Churchill passed the paper to Stalin, who looked it over, made a blue pencil check mark in the upper right corner to signify his acceptance, and handed it back. The deed took scarcely longer than this description.¹

Thus was the fate of Eastern Europe planned. Note that the agreement gave 0 percent influence to the native peoples.

GREECE

During the First World War King Constantine I of Greece was pro-German, but Great Britain and its allies forced the Greek government to join them. Chagrined when Greece lost a war with Turkey in 1922, in 1923 some Greek colonels overthrew King George II and a republic was established. Violent political unrest ensued for the next twelve years, with different factions struggling to control the government. In 1935 the monarchy under George II was restored; the king soon became a figurehead for a country ruled by a fascist military dictatorship.

The dictator was Ioannis Metaxas, who had viewed what he called "notorious parliamentary institutions" with contempt since the 1890s, writing in December 1899, "I shall do something myself in order·to drink some parliamentary blood. . . . There will be opportunities for that."² He had studied at the war academy in Berlin and returned to Greece determined to infuse the country with the "German spirit." For years he was something of a political joke; yet he ingratiated himself with the monarchy and made good connections, biding his time. In an astonishing two-month period in 1936 he moved upward from one governmental post to another, becoming premier with the assent of King George II.

Metaxas maintained cordial relations with both Germany and England. He was able to stay on good terms with England while instituting a fascist dictatorship for several reasons. His regime supported commercial interests, sometimes forcibly. For instance, Metaxas called striking workers into military service and assigned them to their civilian jobs—if the strike continued the "deserters" would be subject to military penalty. Conservative elements of the British elite admired such tactics. In addition, England had a long-standing interest in Greek affairs that transcended any particular government. And there was King George II himself, whose love for England was as open as Metaxas's admiration for Germany. The king's detractors called him the "British High Commissioner."

England recognized that Metaxas ran a fascist state friendly to Germany but that he was not a German military ally. Quite the contrary. Metaxas knew that fascist Italy had designs on Greek territory and that Italy could rely on German assistance if fighting broke out. As a result, in April 1939 British prime minister Neville Chamberlain guaranteed military aid to Greece if it were attacked.

Italy did invade Greece in October 1940, and England honored its commitment. In so doing, Britain became military allies with the fascist Metaxas dictatorship against fascist Italy. Although England was pressed by the Battle of Britain and unable to offer much help, Greece managed to repel the Italian attack. This deeply impressed Churchill, who resolved that the government of Greece was worthy of all the support England could muster.

In early 1941 Hitler's intention to invade Greece had become obvious. The British Mideast command sent the Army of the Nile to Greece, along with other Commonwealth and Allied units. Germany invaded in April and, in sharp contrast to the outcome of the Italian invasion, Greek resistance collapsed. The British had to conduct another Dunkirk-style emergency evacuation to save what they could. In part the Greek collapse can be explained by the more powerful German thrust; in part it can be explained by the death of Metaxas in January. The "strong" state he created fell apart immediately upon his demise, and a coherent resistance to Hitler became impossible.

Rather than staying in Greece to rally his people in a time of adversity, King George II and a group of Metaxas followers fled first to Crete, then moved to Cairo and South Africa, and finally settled in London, where they became the government in exile under Churchill's sponsorship. George II and his officials did nothing without Churchill's prior permission.

Greece was occupied by Germany and by Hitler's allies Italy and Bulgaria. Each ran its own districts of occupation, though they had joint control over Athens. Since the Metaxas fascist government had ruled under the royal patronage of King George II, collaboration with fascist occupiers became fashionable among the Greek upper class. They served the Nazis and thrived, while the majority of Greeks suffered terribly—the Nazis treated them no differently than they treated other conquered peoples. Since Greek royalists were identified with Hitler's tyranny, most of the population despised them.

After the king's departure, demands arose for him to pledge he would never return unless he were invited back by the Greek people. The demands came from across the political spectrum, ranging from Communist revolutionaries to a wide consensus of well-known and respected Greek politicians from left to right. Objective observers, including British and American officials who investigated the situation, concurred that basically only two people favored the king's return—the king himself and Winston Churchill. The stubbornness of those two men promoted chaos.

The most blatant evidence of the chaos could be seen in Cairo. The Greek government in exile established a branch in that Egyptian city, to which the defeated Greek army and the escaping British forces had been evacuated in the spring of 1941. Instead of being used in combat, the Greek forces in Egypt simply sat and stewed. With little else to do than discuss politics, they routinely engaged in mutinous churning.

Some officers were royalists. Many others were republicans, as were many of the men. As time went by, the army took in increasing numbers of refugees from Greece, who tended to be leftist. Although all these men were willing to help liberate Greece from Hitler, many of them were unwilling to help reestablish the monarchy. Military discontent grew when plans were announced to merge the units and put them under a single royalist commander with officers who had been Metaxists. The assumption was that the command consolidation was the first step in making the army into a force for restoring the monarchy. Both the king and Churchill were insisting that George II would return to Greece at the head of his army.

The discontent in Cairo climaxed in the great mutiny of April 1944; it involved not only the Greek army but elements of the navy as well. Churchill ordered the British military to put down the mutiny in the Greek forces, an effort that took three weeks. Despite light casualities, the incident destroyed the Greek military. The British spent months interviewing men who had not joined the mutiny and weeded out everyone who was not a staunch anti-Communist. This rightist group was then organized into the Third Brigade, to be sent to Athens when the Nazis left the city.

Chaos was not limited to the Greek government in exile, but also developed in the British government as it dealt with Greek matters. Churchill directed that full support be given to King George II and to Greek guerrillas fighting the Nazis. The guerrillas had feuding factions, but most were united in opposition to the monarchy. Thus, Britain was working to strengthen the king's enemies in Greece while purging them in Cairo. England supplied Greek leftist guerrillas with millions of dollars and with thousands of tons of supplies during the German occupation. British officers infiltrated the country and assisted leftist partisan operations.

The Greek partisan situation was one of deadly enemies temporarily allied against a common foreign foe. The surrender of

Italy in 1943 raised the possibility of a Nazi evacuation from Greece. An end to the anti-Nazi struggle would start the postponed civil war among native Greeks. The participants were basically divided into three factions—royalists, republicans, and leftists.

The leftist group, which operated independently from Moscow, was already so dominant that its victory in a civil war seemed certain. It had three main components: the KKE (Kommunistikon Komma Ellados—Communist Party of Greece); a Communist-dominated coalition of political groups called EAM (Ethnikon Apeleftherotikon Metopon—National Liberation Front); and the Communist guerrillas called ELAS (Ethnikos Laikos Apeleftherotikos Stratos—National Popular Liberation Army). The acronym ELAS cleverly played upon patriotism because it mimicked Ellás, the Greek's name for their country.

ELAS received the godsend of surrendered Italian arms, freeing the Communists from dependence on English military aid. Thus, Britain lost much of its leverage in the situation. A Greek civil war was under way in earnest by October 1943. None of the factions was able to prevail, and in February 1944 American mediators helped the English to restore cooperation among the partisan camps. They agreed to stop fighting each other and fight the common German enemy; factional conflict merely simmered until the autumn of 1944, when the Nazis evacuated Greece. A London *Times* special correspondent estimated that probably 80 percent of the Greek population opposed the return of King George II. Nevertheless, Churchill decided to reinstall the king. No election was held to ratify this action. Instead, Churchill used military force to impose this government on Greece, dispatching British units to Athens as soon as the Nazis withdrew.

In October 1944 the king's prime minister, Georgios Papandreou, arrived in Athens accompanied by other members of the royalist government (no longer the government in exile) and by British and American diplomats. King George II was absent because Papandreou had warned that the government would be toppled by an EAM-led revolution if the king returned at this point. Even the king's prime minister recognized the monarchy's unpopularity.

Collaborators with the Nazis, including officials of the Nazi puppet government, were left undisturbed by the returning monarchy. The monarchy's credibility was so low that a majority of Greek officers organizing the new national guard had to be recruited from officers of the vicious Nazi security battalions. The battalions had been a Greek police arm of the puppet Nazi government and had attempted to preserve law and order primarily by eradicating ELAS.

Leftist partisans had done the bulk of fighting against the Nazi occupiers. An English general frankly admitted in October 1944, "We should never have been able to set foot on Greece had it not been for the magnificent efforts of the Resistance Movements of EAM and ELAS."[3] And now the British military repaid those "magnificent efforts" by backing the discredited royalists who had supported a fascist dictatorship.

Churchill's fame as leader of the anti-Nazi crusade may make his Greek policy seem inexplicable. Yet several explanations exist. One is that Churchill remained loyal to the Greek regime that had fought the Italian invasion so well. Another factor was Churchill's occasional romantic turn of mind—he admired the Greek heritage and also admired monarchies. But the main and overriding reason was Churchill's imperialistic bent; he wanted Britain to dominate Greece. A British puppet regime such as George II's, which could not exist without English support, was far more reliable for this purpose than any Greek government with an independent base of support would be, let alone the leftist regime that would probably take power if the Greek people had their way.

The leftists tried to operate constitutionally, joining the royalist government and working within the system to change things. Despite massive British effort, provincial areas of Greece remained outside the monarchy's authority, and partisans controlled the countryside. In December 1944 England ordered all leftist partisans to disarm. Rather than call for a revolt, leftist ministers resigned from the Greek cabinet. Normally such a breakup of a coalition is the first step to a change in government policy.

The breakup was supplemented by the normal democratic procedure of a public rally of supporters on December 3. The enthusiastic crowd was well disciplined, not a hostile mob. Police fired into the throng, creating instant martyrs. Members of the crowd then attacked police. A general labor strike took place the next day, and uniformed and armed leftist partisans surfaced on the outskirts of Athens. Serious fighting began there. Papandreou, who had been appalled by the suffering of his nation during the war, offered to resign and thereby prevent more bloodshed. Such an offer is normal in a parliamentary democracy when a government's conduct rouses unrest. Indeed, the leftist ministers had resigned to force the formation of a new government. Their mission appeared accomplished.

Churchill, however, refused to permit Papandreou to resign, a telling commentary on how much of an English puppet the royalist Greek government was. With Churchill's decision, the focus shifted from politics to the military realm.

The leftists seemed to lack any plan of action. A Russian officer scoffed at the situation, calling the Greek leftists "just a rabble of armed men, not worth supporting."[4] They improvised a formidable campaign nonetheless.

Although the English military contingent in Greece held its own as the new phase of civil war started in December 1944, the battle seemed sure to turn against them unless reinforcements arrived. Because World War II was still in progress, Churchill had to balance the importance of crushing leftists in noncombatant Greece against fighting Nazis elsewhere in Europe. In mid-December 1944 the British Fourth Division was en route to Italy, but the destination was changed to Greece.

Even when the Battle of the Bulge erupted and seemed to threaten the Allied hold on Europe, Churchill refused to divert British forces from Greece. They could have swiftly stressed the Nazis by intensifying the Italian campaign. Instead, he continued to send English forces from Italy to Greece and called on Stalin to press harder on the eastern front so the advancing Nazis could be weakened without threatening the drive in Greece. Stalin instantly agreed to speed up the date for a new offensive, which began just five days after Churchill's request, so Churchill would not have to lessen the English forces hunting leftists in Greece.

Even though ordinary Greeks opposed the British-supported king, they tried to proclaim their faith in Western democracies. "Demonstrating crowds of the left-wing, antifascist resistance were heard chanting 'Long live Roosevelt! Long live Churchill! No King!' even as they were shot down by British troops who had been sent (in American planes) to crush them, and to reimpose the hated rightist monarchy."[5]

During the Athens street fighting, British forces took the offensive in lower-class districts, turning homes into rubble. In contrast, they protected upper-class areas populated by wealthy royalists. The Greek population drew its own conclusions from these deeds.

The Soviet Union refused any help to the leftist forces. At a meeting in Athens with Churchill and local Communists, a Soviet representative confirmed that British troops were in Greece with Stalin's approval.

It would be wrong, however, to view the Greek fighting solely as a left–right or Red–White struggle. As happened in other Balkan countries, once the locals no longer had to fight their common Nazi enemy, they began a bloodletting based on old rivalries, unrelated to communism or capitalism. BBC correspondent Kenneth Matthews was on the scene in Greece. "What we saw was the consequence . . . of vendetta, fratricidal crime." He continued, "The victims of revolution were not the standard-bearers of a dying order. They were not the discredited politicians, the war profiteers, the exploiters of the economy. They were the people themselves, in all their ordinariness and semi-innocence, caught on the rim of a maelstrom of blind violence and sucked under." The terror described by Matthews operated as all the others described in this book: "Some [victims], no doubt, the policemen and soldiers, had a symbolic status, as the guardians of existing law; their wives and children, their sweethearts, friends and neighbors, suffered by a contagion as random as the plague . . . or because they were on somebody's list."[6]

A cease-fire was reached in January 1945, and the six-week-old hostilities ended. Under pressure from both Churchill and Stalin, leftist partisans agreed to disarm, just as the British had originally demanded.

Although Stalin had impeccably abided by his October 1944 agreement with Churchill, Bulgaria and Yugoslavia were not obligated by the deal. In December 1945 they decided to help organize a Communist Greek rebel army. Reportedly Stalin approved of this effort, but no Russian aid was provided.

Tito's interest was partly philosophical as a fraternal Communist. But he was also interested in splitting the northern region of Macedonia from Greece, to be associated with Yugoslavia. The Greek Communists agreed to this territorial split in return for Tito's aid. Macedonian politics had long been a powerful influence in Bulgaria and probably had prompted that country's interest in the Greek Communist army as well. Bulgaria, and Albania too, extracted promise of Greek territory in the future in return for a pittance of military aid.

The Greek Communists apparently intended to ignore the territorial agreements if they took power. Perhaps Tito suspected this. At any rate his help was mainly passive, allowing the Greek Communists to cross the well-defended Yugoslav border when pursued by Greek government forces.

In the retrospect of defeat, Greek Communists saw this new civil war from 1946 to 1949 as a mistake. Despite the strong appeal of leftists in Greece, the Communist party itself was small. Likely this was why it boycotted the first postwar elections in March 1946.

The very fact of those elections illustrated that the rightist regime was not yet a dictatorship. Many leftists (as opposed to Communists) still preferred to seek power through democratic politics rather than revolution.

Nonetheless, the two elections of 1946, held amid growing violence, tended to bring victories for rightists. The September 1946 plebiscite even supported reestablishment of the monarchy. Such results may have reflected the custom that whoever controlled the election machinery controlled the results.

By definition revolutionaries do not abide by election results. The low electoral support for Greek Communists and the repression they suffered from royalists convinced the native Communists that armed struggle was the only way to achieve power.

In November 1946 the royalist prime minister Constantine Tsaldaris threw all opposition political parties out of the government. Even the British now became uneasy that the Greek monarchy was eliminating any base of popular support, and with it any possibility of governing via ballots instead of bullets. The civil war worsened.

In February 1947, England, with Churchill no longer prime minister, gave up and left the scene. In March 1947 U.S. president Harry Truman immediately stepped in with hundreds of millions of dollars of American military aid to the rightist Greek government. Even with this massive support, the Greek army remained on the defensive in 1947. This was the start of the Truman Doctrine that imagined a pattern of Soviet aggression in the brush fire wars that erupted in the turmoil after World War II. The doctrine supported American military intervention in all of them and would be embraced by later presidents, becoming an unquestioned linchpin of U.S. foreign policy. The doctrine also expressed Truman's repudiation of the October 1944 Churchill-Stalin deal.

Stalin had consistently refused to aid the Greek Communist insurgency. For many years he had been skeptical about the possibility of foreign Communist revolutions and had argued against Kremlin intervention. In Greece Stalin's natural inclinations were reinforced by his old deal with Churchill. In 1948 Stalin went a step further. No longer staying aloof from the battle, he demanded that Tito stop helping the Greek Communist rebellion. In defiance of Stalin, Tito continued. This was an early example of the limits of Moscow's control over Communist rebellions.

Then, in an astounding move illustrating how little they knew about Stalin or their best interests, the Greek Communist leadership decided to back Russia in the great contest of will between Stalin and Tito.

The insurgents' situation quickly declined. Tito, angered by the Greeks' support of Stalin, as well as by the recent Greek decision to honor Bulgaria's demand for the Macedonian territory he wanted, cut off Yugoslav aid to the Greek Communists and, more important, closed the border. Albania closed its borders as well. A safe haven no longer existed for Greek Communist partisans, and Stalin maintained his consistent hostility to the rebellion. Moreover, this was not a popular uprising. Unlike the 1944 spontaneous popular revolt, the later guerrilla campaign had been advanced by a core of militants encouraged by Yugoslavia. Greek Communists declared no noble aims, provided no great calls that galvanized the people. Greek Communists were just a political faction that wanted to run the country. Few Greeks found this a goal worth fighting for. The Communists had no bases in the countryside. They roamed continuously and dragooned conscripts from villages—a tactic that further eroded support. Greek Communist fighters apparently were well equipped, despite the lack of cooperation from Russia and Yugoslavia, but were simply unable to enlist converts to the cause.

Reflecting upon Truman Doctrine aid to Greece, an American observer later wrote: "The army was galvanized into action. Its manpower was not increased, its training was not greatly improved, and there was no significant increase in its equipment. The army was simply made to do what it was capable of doing, and no more than this was needed to gain the victory."[7]

Although matériel is hardly irrelevant to military success, such supplies seemed secondary in the Greek conflict. Neither side was wanting in physical support. A fighting spirit and the will of the people made the difference. We (or planners of covert operations) may hear claims that some amount of goods will make the difference in a brushfire war, but such claims should be viewed with caution.

In 1944, had Stalin ordered it to do so, the Red Army could easily have continued its advance and crossed the Greek border, supporting the popular leftist resistance forces seeking to establish a government there. Instead he abided by his agreement with Churchill and watched as leftist forces in Greece were annihilated while an oppressive rightist regime was imposed on an unwilling people. At Churchill's request Stalin even used Russian troops to relieve pressures caused by the Battle of the Bulge, lest British forces be diverted from the antileftist campaign in Greece.

In 1945, therefore, the Soviets considered the Stalin-Churchill accord sealed in blood. The February Yalta Conference would be a mere formality at which Roosevelt would ratify the actions of his two allies. Russia had demonstrated its good faith in Greece and now believed it was time to collect on its side of the agreement, in Romania.

ROMANIA

The Soviet Union and Romania have a history of unfriendly interaction predating the advent of communism. For centuries Russian czars and Turkish sultans had decided the fate of Romania. The land of Bessarabia had been a particularly sensitive issue for centuries. The area had been under Turkish rule from the early 1500s until the Russo-Turkish War of 1806 to 1812, when Russia acquired it. After the Crimean War, in 1856, Romania gained south Bessarabia, which the Russians took back in 1878 with the Treaty of Berlin. The Romanians were particularly angered by this because they had just assisted the czar in his war with Turkey. Karl Marx harshly criticized the czar's action, and Friedrich Engels later wrote to Romanian leftists that "you have suffered much as a result of . . . the twice repeated annexation of Bessarabia, not to mention the innumerable Russian invasions of your country, situated as it is on the route to the Bosphorus."[9]

Russian interest in Romania clearly began long before communism. And Romania has a history of both anti-Russian and pro-German orientation. In 1883 Romania had joined the Triple Alliance of Germany, Italy, and Austria-Hungary, who had pledged to defend one another if Russia attacked.

Romania was not, however, an innocent victim. It coveted its neighbors' territory, seizing part of Bulgaria in the Balkan Wars just before World War I. Romania then agreed to betray the Triple Alliance and enter the war on the side of the Triple Entente—England, France, and Russia—but only at the price of receiving yet another portion of Bulgaria and the entire Transylvania region of Austria-Hungary.

This plan went awry when Romania was soundly beaten by Germany, Austria-Hungary, and Bulgaria. In the surrender to Germany in February 1918, Romania accepted what historian

Hugh Seton-Watson called "oppressive economic conditions" in return for receipt of Bessarabia, which had been part of Russia for the past forty years and which declared independence from Russia after the Communist revolution. Just before the November armistice, Romania briefly declared war against the Central powers again and thus technically became a victor. Romania then received Transylvania from the Austro-Hungarian empire, which had defeated Romania. In an odd turnabout from the ordinary outcome of wars, Romania lost and yet wound up with territory from friend and foe alike.

Geographically Romania was now twice the size it had been before the war, but this gain must be set against an economic loss described by Herbert Hoover: "The German, Hungarian, and Bulgarian armies unmercifully plundered the country, not only during their invasion and occupation, but especially in their retreat at the Armistice. Their loot included all the food they could find, 80 percent of Romania's animals, most of the agricultural implements, and even much household furniture. Never in all history had there been such gigantic theft of railway rolling stock."[10]

Romania expropriated the Hungarian landlord estates of Transylvania, liberally distributing them to Romanian peasants. These land reforms were an extension of the desperate attempt to strengthen peasant fighters during the war through a limited land distribution scheme affecting holdings of the Romanian aristocracy. The land reforms did much to deter the growth of bolshevism in Romania, where traditionally "peasants starved amidst the richest cornfields of Europe."[11]

After World War I, the Romanian government pursued a policy of autarky, or self-sufficiency: economic isolation seeking to eliminate imports and to produce everything a country needs. As part of this goal, the government nationalized many private companies, particularly those owned by Hungarians. Normally such a move would paint a regime red and bring the wrath of the West, but Romania was anti-Communist by definition, since it was part of the arrangements France had devised in the 1920s to surround and contain the Soviet Union. Romania's interregnum economic policies stirred no protest in the West, even though those policies were hard to distinguish from those of the Communist regime after World War II.

The Romanian monarchy easily rode the wave of democratic feeling that swept across Europe after World War I. Although a fine-sounding constitution was adopted, the kings and their associates used its provisions to pervert democracy, appointing and dismissing cabinets at will and controlling the electoral process as thoroughly as the later Communists would.

Debate in Romania's parliament mocked democracy as much as the fraudulent elections did. A leader of the old ruling elite explained to an American reporter, "In our country a parliamentary debate works like this: First they disagree with you. Then they call you names. Then they shoot you."[12]

In some ways the transformation of Romanian politics resembled the Polish situation. Romania's National Liberal party advocated bourgeois-dominated democracy in the 1920s but became a reactionary group in the 1930s. They served as a front for the dictatorship headed by King Carol II, which moved toward fascism. Romania in no way could be considered a democratic country before World War II. Describing a government notorious for its brutal racism and corrupt bureaucracy, journalist C. L. Sulzberger wrote, "If ever a land deserved revolution it was Romania. King Carol was later to assure me Romanians were truly democratic because the peasants uncovered their heads and clutched their forelocks when he passed! He was an immoral, selfish man."[13]

Part of the enticement Hitler offered to Stalin for his signature on the 1939 nonaggression pact was an expression of Nazi disinterest in the fate of Bessarabia. The Soviet government had broken diplomatic relations with Romania in 1918 over its seizure of the territory, and diplomatic relations had not been resumed until 1934. Some persons in Russia had then talked of regaining Bessarabia via military force while pessimists considered formally accepting Romanian ownership. Little had been resolved up to 1939.

Russian preoccupation with that problem resulted in orders from the Comintern to the handful of Romanian Communists, apparently directing them to seek the return of Bessarabia to the Soviet Union. Years later Romanian Communist dictator Nicolae Ceauşescu bitterly rebuked the Soviets for this. This arguing among Communists over Bessarabia's status indicates the irrelevance of Communism to the question—and also illustrates the divisions behind the fraternal facade linking Communist regimes.

In June 1940 the Soviet Union seized not only Bessarabia but northern Bukovina as well. Seething Romania enthusiastically contributed more than twenty divisions to Hitler's attack on Russia a year later. Romanian forces moved past Bessarabia and into Russian territory, taking Odessa and setting up Romanian administration over part of Russia. Their reign was characterized by atrocities against Soviet citizens in the area. The Soviet Union claimed that 200,000 Odessa residents died by Romanian hands.

In a move reminiscent of its conduct during World War I, in 1944 Romania surrendered to Russia and then, at the last minute, switched sides and declared war on Germany. So Romania finished fighting the war on Russia's side.

The Soviets saw the opportunistic character of these actions and pushed for a pro-Russian government in Romania after the war. In a few years the Romanian Communist party rose from a membership and influence of nearly zero to become the dominant force in government. This transformation was remarkable given that Communists traditionally had been considered enemies of the nation.

This sudden change was undoubtedly promoted by the large Red Army contingent in postwar Romania. Nonetheless, the change had more than naked force behind it. The conduct of Romania's old Nazi leaders was exposed in war crimes trials, and those revelations seriously undermined the respect that such persons had enjoyed. Romanians interested in politics wanted a leadership untainted by association with the discredited old regime, and the Communists certainly had no such connections.

Recognizing the traditional Romanian interest in real estate, the Soviet Union gave the impression of supporting Romania's title to an area of Transylvania that the Nazis had given to Hungary. This Soviet position gave local Communists some influence. They also let women vote in elections and lowered the voting age to eighteen. These elections were inadequate by democratic standards, but were no worse than the elections under previous Romanian dictatorships. American journalist Edgar Snow found that "under the Red Army labor was no longer persecuted by the police, and local leaders asserted that the Russians did not interfere in employer-employee disputes, 'except that the Red Army is not used against labor.' "[14] Snow noted that this was a "very big" change in labor relations. Many Romanians may have felt less oppressed under Communism than under the royal and republican dictatorships.

Nonetheless, immediate elections with general suffrage would probably have brought in a right-wing government. The old ruling elite had weathered the democratic storm after World War I very nicely, and by 1945 had years of election-rigging experience. Such manipulations may even have been unnecessary in 1945, since the peasantry still professed loyalty to the monarchy. Communism was an alien idea, and local adherents were almost nonexistent.

The Communists began a long-term program to generate popular support before elections were held.

Romanian Communists thought this goal was backed by the Soviet Union and by the United States and Britain as well. Since the spring of 1944, England had sought a deal giving it and the United States a free hand in Greece, with Russia having its way in Romania. Churchill and Stalin formally agreed to this in November 1944, and Britain immediately crushed strong leftist forces in Greece without a word of protest from Russia. Instead, the United States was the country that complained about British conduct in Greece, although American aircraft aided the operation and the United States recognized the British-installed right-wing dictatorship as legitimate.

Now, after Russia had fulfilled its side of the bargain by standing aside during events in Greece, England and the Truman White House began complaining about Russian influence in Romania and insisted on immediate elections. It is easy to see how Stalin might have viewed this as violating his 1944 agreement with Churchill. The Yalta Conference had affirmed that postwar governments of Eastern Europe should be friendly to Russia, in contrast to the prewar hostility. Immediate elections would stymie this change in Romania, a country with a historical record of hostility toward the Soviet Union. England was apparently repudiating its Greece-Romania trade-off, and the United States was apparently repudiating the Yalta accords. The Russians felt betrayed.

In February 1945 Soviet deputy foreign minister Andrey Vyshinsky told Romania's King Michael to appoint a government more friendly to Russia. When King Michael demurred, the Soviet official gave him until noon the next day to obey or face the consequences.

The king stalled briefly, but the Communist government was in power under his reign by early March 1945. American journalist Howard K. Smith admitted at the time that it was "very hard to think of any constructive alternative" to Communism and that he viewed elections at that point as "an invitation to Fascism here more than elsewhere."[15] The king's staunch anti-Communism led to his forced abdication in 1947, and the Communist People's Republic came into existence.

Although the United States protested the absence of democracy in postwar Romania—a concern that had never surfaced before the war—advice to Truman indicated that money was at the core of American hostility to the Communist regime. In September 1946 White House adviser Clark Clifford complained to Truman that

Russians who had been collecting reparations in Romania two years earlier had confiscated American-owned oil equipment. Such an incident was likely because more than 85 percent of Romania's petroleum was in American hands before the war. The State Department urged that diplomatic recognition be withheld from the Communist regime unless it reopened Romanian markets to American business and respected American ownership of various properties.

Eastern Europe was the Third World of that era, economically exploited by generations of Western capitalists. For example, rich mineral sources were owned by American, British, and French interests. Sometimes these sites were left undeveloped in order to protect prices. Therefore, East Europeans had to pay high prices for imported materials that would otherwise be readily available at home. This policy was also designed to keep Eastern Europe from becoming an industrialized competitor to the West. Instead, the region served as an agricultural breadbasket.

The change from subservient capitalist governments to independent Communist governments in Eastern Europe had a tremendous effect on the international economy. Not only were East European markets less open to imports, but these countries were now free to develop their resources and industrial potential. This meant the West faced price competition in raw materials and market competition for finished goods. The sudden Western concern about Communism in Eastern Europe was almost surely caused more by altered financial advantages than by the largely unchanged civil liberties situation.

The concern also had a social aspect. The diplomatic corps of non-Communist states was recruited mainly from upper-class patricians. Diplomats from the fallen capitalist governments of Eastern Europe were losing vast estates to Communist land reform measures and losing their private companies to Communist nationalization. They found ready sympathizers in wealthy colleagues of the Western diplomatic corps.

Class loyalty generated indignation over Communist activities, a resentment never generated by the vicious economic exploitation and brutal suppression of civil liberties practiced by the old capitalist regimes. This personal indignation in the diplomatic corps combined with pressure from business institutions whose profits were challenged by the new order in Eastern Europe. The resulting opposition to Communism in that region had little to do with concern for human liberty.

BULGARIA

Before World War II Bulgaria was an aggressor country whose leaders were known as "the Prussians of the Balkans," stealing territory from neighbors by means of a military that cultivated savage behavior. Memories of such conduct still colored relations with neighbors after the war.

Postwar Bulgaria has been called virtually a republic of the Soviet Union, but its intimate relations with Russia have a longer history. In the 1800s Bulgarian army officers higher in rank than lieutenant were Russians. Toward the end of the century Bulgaria was ruled by Czar Alexander II's nephew, Prince Alexander Joseph of Battenberg. By 1910 Bulgarian socialists copied even the vernacular of Russian socialists.

Simultaneously, Bulgaria admired Germany. When World War I began, the German King Ferdinand I presided over Bulgaria's harsh dictatorship. Bulgaria sided with Germany. As the war went badly for those countries in the summer of 1918, many Bulgarian peasants deserted the army and returned to the land they farmed. No pursuit or punishment occurred. Quietly, the remaining troops reached a consensus that they would serve only until September 15, 1918. When on that date the French launched a major assault against Bulgarian positions, the Bulgars just went home, leaving the French bewildered.

Just before World War I many Macedonian refugees fled to Bulgaria as the Serbs pushed them out of the Macedonian homeland. They formed a fiery and destabilizing element of Bulgarian society, similar to the effect that Palestinian activists would later have in Middle Eastern countries. The Macedonian refugees actively influenced Bulgar politics, and in 1918 they helped quell a revolt against the Bulgarian dictatorship.

A republic was proclaimed at the end of World War I, run by the so-called Peasant Union. This government's good relations with Yugoslavia thwarted the Macedonian expatriates' hopes to retake their homeland. They became so infuriated that they helped in a 1923 military coup led by Aleksandŭr Tsankov, which overthrew the Bulgarian government, and instituted a dictatorship.

The Bulgarian Communists, who had recently polled around 20 percent in a national election, might have provided enough support to foil the takeover if they had been willing to join with other leftists and the peasant leaders. But, exhibiting the doctrinaire approach of Communist ideologues, they decided to sit out the fight because it was irrelevant to Lenin's promised world revolution. The fight, however, turned out to be highly relevant to the survival of individual Communists, as they learned when the government began hunting them down. They then attempted an uprising, which quickly failed. It was followed by a White terror that practically exterminated the Bulgarian Communist party, along with quite a few Bulgarians who had probably never heard of Communism.

In the spring of 1925 a Bulgarian general was murdered, apparently as part of a Communist plot designed to culminate at his funeral two days later: the dictatorship's officials gathered for the services in a Sofia cathedral, where a bomb planted by left-wing terrorists exploded. It claimed more than a hundred lives, with hundreds more wounded, but all the government officials survived.

In the 1980s such terrorist incidents have become so commonplace as to produce only a momentary shock value, but the world of the 1920s recoiled in horror. Local Bulgarian Communists had apparently planned the bombing on their own without seeking guidance, for even Stalin joined in the condemnation: "Communists had not, have not, and cannot have, anything to do with the theory and practice of individual terror."[16] His statement was probably sincere, although he hedged with the word *individual*, meaning that such acts might be acceptable if performed on Communist party orders. Yet even Paul Lendvai, an unsympathetic chronicler of Communist activity, found the Sofia bombing to be "an act of terrorism without precedent in Communist history."[17]

Bulgaria entered World War II as a Nazi ally, declaring war on Great Britain and the United States, but not on the Soviet Union. England was viewed as traditionally hostile to Bulgarian aspirations in the Balkans, so war with England had some popularity. Bulgarians were indifferent to the United States despite their government's willingness to follow the Nazi lead. Their old ties with Russia, however, would have made a war to the east unpopular. Moreover, Russia had the potential to inflict immediate harm, whereas Britain and the United States seemed far away. Indeed, the Bulgarian government hoped to finesse matters and profit as a Nazi ally without suffering any military costs. Even before Bulgaria's December 1941 war declaration against the United States and Britain, Hitler had helped Bulgaria acquire parts of Yugoslavia, Greece, and Romania. In September 1940 he forced Romania to sign the Craiova agreement, which gave southern Dobruja to Bulgaria. In February 1941 Bulgaria signed a military agreement with Germany. In return Hitler promised Bulgaria the Greek

Aegean seacoast, a promise that was kept after Germany invaded Greece and Yugoslavia. After that invasion, in which Bulgaria participated, Hitler also gave part of Yugoslavian Macedonia to Bulgaria. After World War II, Bulgaria managed to retain the Romanian territory awarded by the Nazis, an outcome that strained relations between the two Communist states.

When Germany invaded the Soviet Union in June 1941, Bulgarian Communists decided to fight against Germany's interests within Bulgaria. Pitched battles were avoided; there were slim odds of winning against the large contingent of the Reich's soldiers in Bulgaria. Instead the Communists used sabotage, along with work stoppages and the placement of sympathizers in the Nazi-allied Bulgarian army. This activity was opposed in a beastly fashion by the Bulgarian police and military. Entire villages were terrorized in punishment for partisan activity, and captured insurgents were tortured. The Bulgarian dictatorship worked industriously for Hitler while native Communists worked against him, with scant popular support.

In the spring of 1944, as the Red Army approached through Romania, Bulgarian Communists sought an arrangement with bourgeois opponents of the Bulgarian regime, hoping to assure Communist participation in a new government. Although anti-Communists would later say that Russia obviously intended to take over Bulgaria, this plan was not apparent to local Communists at the time. Bulgar Communists did not realize that Romania was on the verge of switching sides in the war, freeing the Red Army for a swift advance. And even so, Nazi-allied Bulgaria was at peace with Russia. A Russian occupation therefore did not seem inevitable. Because Bulgar Communists were not anticipating any help from the Soviet military and had always been considered an unpatriotic element, they were uncertain whether they could join any new Bulgarian government.

In August 1944 the Soviet Union declared war on Bulgaria. A couple of weeks later the Bulgar dictatorship collapsed, and a coalition of political groups allied themselves as the Fatherland Front. They participated in a coup and formed a government. Communists held few positions, but those they did hold were crucial, controlling the police and the courts. Thousands of citizens were killed or imprisoned on orders of the Communist-controlled justice system.

Two days before the new Bulgarian premier Georgi Dimitrov took office, he had been a Russian citizen. This citizenship has been used as evidence that the Bulgarian government was a Moscow puppet. Dimitrov, however, was a native Bulgarian who was extradited to Russia after trial in Germany for his alleged role in the 1933 Reichstag fire; it would seem he became a Soviet citizen then. His authentic Bulgarian background notwithstanding, he had firm Communist credentials, having served as secretary general of the Comintern.

Yet it would be incorrect to label the Fatherland Front as a Moscow puppet organization. A key Fatherland Front figure, Colonel Damyan Velchev, had helped organize both the 1923 coup that overthrew the Peasant Union government, and the 1934 coup that created the Nazi-allied government. Now he helped the Fatherland Front's seizure of power through yet another military coup. The Fatherland Front had strong native Bulgarian elements with long ties to national politics, even if those men had murky ideological loyalties.

Ironically the presence of men such as Velchev prompted a mass extinction of the Bulgarian officer corps. The record of coups mounted by the Bulgarian military concerned the Communists, who did not intend to be the next victims. Communist unease heightened when the Greek officer corps, albeit with Winston Churchill's aid, destroyed the leftists of Greece. At the climax of that Greek action at Christmas 1944, Bulgarian courts initiated trials that "cut down the Bulgarian army officers as with a scythe."[18]

The Bulgar heritage, not Communist ideology, prompted the terror conducted by the Fatherland Front. Journalist C. L. Sulzberger once described Bulgarians as "Europe's finest murderers."[19] This reputation proved itself well earned, as the Fatherland Front initiated the worst killing spree of any new Eastern European government. Vengeance delayed from the White terrors of the 1920s was clothed in juridicial garb, with leftists paying back old enemies. As author J. F. Brown said, "If many innocent people got in the way during the process, the new Bulgarian leaders were hardly squeamish enough to be concerned."[20]

The Fatherland Front won over 85 percent of the November 1945 vote. Foreign observers reported that the election seemed calm. Nonetheless, the vote total was less a popular endorsement for the regime than an example of the traditional skill possessed by Balkan governments in rigging elections.

The elections of October 1947 saw the last non-Communist challengers on the ballot. Their showing approached 30 percent of the vote—bleak by free election standards, but pretty good for a balloting characterized by blatant intimidation and probably a dishonest count.

Disappointing as the installation of Communist rule in Bulgaria might be, still it is well to remember that democracy had never existed there *before* Communist rule. Opponents of Bulgar Communists were not necessarily prodemocratic. Communism did not win against democracy in Bulgaria. Democracy never competed.

Officials in the capitalist West expressed outrage at the Communist domination of Bulgaria. No such expressions occurred about previous Bulgar dictatorships with their vicious disregard for human rights. Under those regimes in the 1920s and 1930s, however, Western governments and banks had been able to dictate restrictive monetary policies. Although this action hindered growth in the Bulgarian economy, it prevented the inflation of Bulgarian currency used to pay debts to the West. Bulgaria was forced to turn over its customs revenues to repay such debts. The resulting pressure to keep high tariffs hurt the country's ability to compete against the West in foreign markets. The West forced Bulgaria's national bank to curtail commercial lending, and Western banks then picked up that business. Westerners even controlled the policies of native Bulgarian banks, and those banks in turn controlled entire networks of businesses, including sugar refining, food processing, cement works, and tobacco sales. Mining operations were owned directly by Westerners. Labor unions were illegal, and in 1933 a member of parliament who advocated an eight-hour work day was murdered.

Protests about lack of democracy in Bulgaria began only when the Communist takeover extinguished the lucrative economic exploitation by the West.

YUGOSLAVIA

The remaining Balkan country in the Churchill-Stalin deal was Yugoslavia, another state where democracy was unknown. Created after World War I from remnants of the Austro-Hungarian empire plus two independent states, Yugoslavia held free elections only once in its history, in 1920. The Communist takeover did not extinguish a democracy.

After World War I, native Yugoslavian Communists were a minority but nonetheless influential in politics. In the Yugoslav parliament only two political parties, the Serbian Radical party and the Democratic party, had more representatives than the Communists. The Communist party was not a small group of fanatics without popular support. It had a tremendous student contingent, some from pampered backgrounds: "Few Communist parties can boast of having organized street riots in which a participant arrived in a chauffeur-driven Cadillac."[21] The students were enthusiastic but brought the germ of generational conflict that poisons political movements dependent on students. Extremists assassinated one politician and tried to kill the monarchy's regent.

Communists were expelled from parliament forthwith, and party membership declined from a high point of around 60,000 in 1920 to about 6,000 by the start of World War II. The decline was assisted by murderous involvement in international party disputes of the 1930s: "Stalin succeeded in killing more [Yugoslav] Central Committee members than either the Yugoslav police in the interwar period or the Axis during the war."[22] Some surviving Yugoslav Communists no longer wished to be too involved with Moscow, including an ex-mechanic who once called himself Josip Broz but came to be known as Tito.

Tito's World War II partisans had a reported strength of 800,000. In contrast, the Russian partisans who carried on highly touted exploits against Nazi invaders had a top strength of 250,000. Tito led a formidable force, operating in formidable terrain; he was not the sort to be intimidated by anyone.

Allied representatives first appeared in Tito's headquarters in 1942. England and the United States poured in military aid. "The Russians provided advice of doubtful value, but nothing else."[23] The West's interest, along with Russia's disinterest, demonstrates a general lack of concern on all sides about whether Tito's Communists took over Yugoslavia.

Remarkably, Moscow even told Tito to avoid any action against the Yugoslavian monarchy. As with Poland and Greece, Yugoslavia had a London government in exile supported by the Allies. One message from Moscow advised: "Do not consider your fight only from your own national point of view, but also from the international standpoint of the British-American-Soviet coalition."[24]

Stalin was enraged when Tito coolly ignored such admonitions in late 1943 and established a provisional government designed to replace the exiles. The locals declared the monarchy ended and told the king, Peter II, never to set foot in Yugoslavia again. The extraordinary spectacle of Stalin steadfastly supporting an anti-Communist monarchy and opposing Communist revolutionaries must raise question about his eagerness to take over Yugoslavia. The situation was typical of Stalin's coolness toward Communist revolution in other countries. While denying Russian supplies to Tito's partisans, Stalin was willing to aid the non-Communist *chetnik* partisans of Serbia, who opposed Tito. It was the United States and Britain that took the lead in coming to terms with Tito's provisional government. Only after their example did the Soviet Union abandon its unwavering support of the Yugoslav monarchy.

Because of Western concern over Communist persecution of religious clergy, it may be worthwhile to briefly note the actions of the Roman Catholic hierarchy in Yugoslavia during World War II. When the Nazis gave fascist terrorists free reign in an Orthodox Serb region, Archbishop Stepinac praised "the splendid opportunity of furthering the Croat and the Holy Catholic cause in Bosnia."[25] His sentiments were echoed by various bishops and lower clergy. While some were disturbed by "methods of 'conversion' through wholesale massacres and the threat of annihilation,"[26] they were not disturbed enough to forthrightly condemn the brutal fascist regime. When the fascists lost the war, Communist victors descended upon the Roman Catholic Church, imprisoning some clergy on charges of fascist collaboration and some others apparently for mere association with an institution tied to the West. This was not a matter of atheistic Marxism versus Christianity, but rather friends of victims versus friends of oppressors. When Pope Pius XII made Stepinac cardinal in 1952, Yugoslavia broke diplomatic relations with the Vatican until the mid-1960s.

Not all Roman Catholic clergy collaborated with the Nazis in Yugoslavia—the record demonstrates otherwise. And Communist persecution of religious clergy is not justified. But such persecution sometimes has causes irrelevant to ideology or religion.

Fellow Communists soon branded Yugoslav Communists as "leftist deviants" after the war. The Yugoslavs promoted continual military provocation against the West, deviating from Russia's approach of progress through political negotiations. Yugoslavia and the Soviet Union split when Stalin kept trying to discourage Tito's proposals for military action in Greece, Italy, and Austria.

Stalin was so angered by Yugoslavia's war-threatening conduct that he plotted an unsuccessful coup against Tito, which further harmed their relations. Border skirmishes broke out between Yugoslavia and its Communist neighbors who were faithful to Soviet policy.

In later years some elements in the West would praise Tito for standing up to the Soviet Union. They seemed to forget that it was Tito who pushed for war and Stalin who pushed for peace. In the early 1950s, the United States actually sent Tito over half a billion dollars of military aid, a move that had to be regarded as hostile by the Soviet Union. The same imprudence could be seen in American talk of military aid to the People's Republic of China in the 1980s, talk promoted by China's defiance of the Soviet Union. American leaders seemed so enthusiastic about China's post-Mao stance that they disregarded the origins of the Sino-Soviet split, which developed largely because the Russians advocated peaceful coexistence with the West whereas China demanded war. Of course, hostile relations are not desirable with Yugoslavia, China, or any other Communist state. But the West should recognize that Russia's enemies are not necessarily friends of the West and that cordial relations are not the same as friendship.

The Russo-Yugoslav split demonstrates that the Communist bloc is not some single well-oiled machine efficiently grinding away at the West. Rather, some Communist regimes have long been deadly enemies of one another, far more hostile to fraternal states than to the West. Failure to recognize this reality has limited the effectiveness of efforts to deal with the Communist challenge.

Although Yugoslavia became a Communist country, it is hard to demonstrate that Stalin violated his deal with Churchill, in which they agreed on a fifty-fifty split of influence in Yugoslavia. Neither had counted on Tito.

Yugoslavia became the first Communist state to ignore instructions from the Soviet Union, to reject the notion that what was good for Russia was good for Communism. This was the start of a growing trend. Although the number of Communist governments would increase over the years, these countries did not constitute a new Russian empire. Other states would also go their own course, much to the frustration of the Soviet Union. By the 1980s the Soviet Union was a powerful country but no longer the dictator of the Communist world.

X.

Three Governments That Fought the Future

This chapter discusses the means by which Albania, Hungary, and East Germany turned to Communism. In the years leading to World War II, all three had been ruled by regimes that attempted to avoid the future. Their efforts to achieve that impossible goal eventually led to Communist control, providing a common link among the experiences of industrial Germany, feudal Hungary, and the one Balkan country outside the Churchill-Stalin deal—Albania.

ALBANIA

Albania is a land known for violence. An old Albanian song begins, "Let us fight as it is our custom." In the 1930s a sign on the parliament building instructed: "Deputies will please check their guns." American journalist C. L. Sulzberger reported, "A doctor told me 30 percent of the cases in [the capital city] Tirana's hospital were knife and gunshot wounds."[1]

Albania largely stayed out of combat in the Balkan War of 1912, which ejected Turkish power from the Balkans after half a millennium. Albania then took advantage of the outcome to proclaim its independence from the Ottoman Empire in 1912. Serbia, Greece, and Italy quickly divided Albania among themselves in World War I. During the war's turmoil, Albania once again declared independence, which was confirmed by a diplomatic conference in 1918 and by a treaty with Italy in 1920, in which Italy gave up possession of the unruly territory in return for dominance over the Albanian government. Albania's borders were guaranteed in a 1921 agreement involving Italy, France, England, Japan, and the League of Nations.

In 1922 Ahmed Zogu made himself Albania's dictator under the country's four regents (one Roman Catholic, one Orthodox, and two Muslim). His manipulations cancelled election results and offended elements who thought they had won. The army overthrew him in 1924, but he and the two Muslim regents found haven in neighboring Yugoslavia, which had a large Albanian minority and competed with Italy for influence in Albania. The next year Zogu staged a coup of his own with help from Yugoslavia, the Anglo-Persian Oil Company, and remnants of General Pyotr Nikolayevich Wrangel's White Russian army, which had made its way to Yugoslavia after losing to the Bolsheviks during the Russian civil war. With this coup Zogu overthrew Monsignor Fan Noli, the Harvard-educated Orthodox bishop of Durazzo (Durrës), who had been appointed prime minister by the Orthodox regent. Zogu abolished the regency and set up a republic with himself as president. His tough police corps was supervised by English officers, and Britain controlled much of Albania's oil resources through the Anglo-Persian Oil Company.

In 1928, midway through his presidential term, Zogu appointed himself King Zog of Albania. "Open criticism or any sign of disloyalty to the King was 'treason,' punished . . . by execution. The executions were carried out without undue formality."[2] King Zog depended on wealthy landowners for his support.

"Free" Albania was not a democracy. Indeed, it could hardly be said to have been free from other countries. Aside from his obligations to Yugoslavia and Great Britain, Zog leaned toward Italy, which furnished so much economic aid that Albania became firmly entwined with its benefactor. For example, through loans, Italy provided half the Albanian government's revenue, and Albania agreed to let Italy influence any proposals that would reduce native Albanian revenue. Italian banks achieved great influence in the Albanian economy. Italian Railways had exclusive rights to some Albanian oil production. Thousands of Italian settlers arrived. If any threats to Albanian sovereignty arose, Italy was authorized to act as the League of Nations's agent to intervene as Albania's protector. Italy's fascist dictator Benito Mussolini finally became dissatisfied with Albania's technical independence and conquered it in April 1939.

Albanian Communists made their headquarters at a cigar store in the capital of Tiranë. The store was run by a former high-school teacher named Enver Hoxha, a man once described as "the bandit who made his revolution stick."[3] When he died in 1985, an editorial in the *Manchester Guardian Weekly* noted that "any mention of the word 'diplomacy' seems to have had the . . . effect on Enver Hoxha" of "immediate recourse to a revolver."[4]

Despite Hoxha's toughness, in Stalinist circles he was always suspect because he had gone to a French university and had lived in Paris in the 1930s, a cosmopolitan sojourn made possible by a scholarship awarded to him. "The East European comrades have never been quite happy about those six years in the West—Stalin, for example, never trusted Hoxha."[5]

During World War II Albania was occupied by Germans as well as Italians. If later stories about brave exploits of Albanian Communist partisans were true, their activities were, curiously, never noticed by the Nazis, who never sent anyone looking for Albanian guerrillas.

Although Hoxha may have merely dabbled at harassing the German forces occupying Albania, he was diligent about exterminating nationalist guerrillas who were fighting the Nazis. During World War II, Albania, like other Balkan nations, suffered through a civil war between anti-Nazi partisans who were Communists and those who were anti-Communist nationalists. In this struggle for wartime supremacy, Hoxha was assisted by the United States and England, who aided the Communists but refused to support the nationalist fighters. The Western tilt toward the Communist anti-Nazi forces was so strong that, by the spring of 1944, "the British, who were celebrating the Communists' victories, sent scores of nationalists and non-collaborators who had fled to Italy back to their death before firing squads in order 'not to embarrass our relations with Hoxha.' "[6]

The Allies supported the Albanian Communists because of Albania's close political and territorial ties with Yugoslavia. Indeed, a particular geographical spot might be Albanian one day and Yugoslavian the next. Admiration for the excellent work of Tito's Communist partisans apparently influenced Allied dealings with Albania's left, with the military need to help Hitler's enemies clouding ideological judgment.

In 1944, with Yugoslav assistance the Albanian Communists formed a provisional government that achieved authority throughout the country. No Russian soldiers were involved, and Stalin seems to have had nothing to do with the outcome in Albania.

118 ■ HERITAGE OF FEAR

Indeed, Hoxha had never traveled to Moscow and seemed to have no dealings whatsoever with Russia until *after* the Communists achieved power in Albania.

Albania's postwar relations with Yugoslavia were as close as their prewar relations with Italy. The Albanians eagerly accepted Yugoslav money and expert advisers but fretted over the growing Yugoslav influence in Albanian affairs. The Yugoslavs began moving military units into Albania, and they even represented Albania at international Communist meetings because the Albanian party was a subunit of the Yugoslavian Communist party.

All these factors had much to do with Albania's decision in 1948 to support Stalin in his dispute with Tito. Yugoslavia broke off relations with Albania, but Russia and other Communist states quickly replaced the help Yugoslavia had given. Because Russia had no historic desire for Albania, this aid had fewer and weaker strings than Yugoslavia's. For the time being, Albania was pleased. In 1960, however, Hoxha objected to Nikita Khrushchev's insistence that Communism could prevail by peaceful means. Instead, Albania supported Communist China's call for wars of liberation. In late 1961 the Soviet Union severed its ties with Albania and cut off all economic aid. China then supported Albania economically, but once again Albania turned on its benefactors, attacking Chinese policies after Mao Tse-tung's death in 1978. China, too, cut off aid. The Albanians then followed their natural inclination to turn inward, spurning the rest of the world. Into the 1980s Albania remained isolated by choice, behind an iron curtain covered with poison ivy, a land alien to the West and inscrutable to most Communist regimes.

HUNGARY

Hungary was the one country outside the Balkans that Churchill and Stalin bargained for: they agreed to a 50/50 split of influence.

As in the Balkans, democracy was unfamiliar to Hungary before World War II. There were political parties, but those who advocated democracy were fringe elements on the political scene. In the 1930s the government passed from the oligarchic tyranny so familiar to Eastern Europe and adopted the innovative oppression of fascism. In 1941 Hungary joined the Axis powers, declaring war first against Russia and then against the United States.

The arrival of the Red Army in Hungary in 1944 was accompanied by brutality and thievery. While the Hungarians hated and feared Russians because of their harshness, they nevertheless also welcomed them with admiration and gratitude. Nazi rule had been as harsh: the Russian liberation interrupted Nazi plans to kill another 250,000 Hungarian Jews. So there was a divided feeling in Hungary: Much resentment existed over the Red Army's behavior, yet there was also thankfulness for its arrival.

In December 1944 a provisional government appeared in Budapest even before Soviet forces arrived in the city. As might be expected, Hungarian Communists had some influence in it. But to almost everyone's surprise, key positions were held by notorious Nazi collaborators, which considerably weakened the moral force the government would otherwise have enjoyed.

The top Hungarian Communist was Mátyás Rákosi. He had been an aide to Béla Kun, the leader of Hungary's short-lived Communist government after World War I. Rákosi's enthusiasm for remaking Hungary from feudalism to communism was strong, but he spurned such concepts as decency, loyalty, and honesty.

The November 1945 elections were fair by Hungarian standards, even allowing universal suffrage. Everyone knew the results the Soviets wanted, but the Red Army appeared to exert no intimidation. Communists received only 17 percent of the vote but gained control of the new coalition government's police. The power of arrest certainly gave the Communists an edge in promoting their power, but their increasing influence in government was based on more than fear.

As elsewhere in Eastern Europe, Hungarian land ownership was dominated by holders of large estates. One man owned almost 570,000 acres. A Roman Catholic bishop controlled about 266,000 acres. Feudal-type estates had been a foundation of both Hapsburg and fascist rule. The peasants who worked these estates led miserable lives. Indeed, the landlords had the peasantry drafted into the army to fight for Hitler.

Land reform followed the Red Army across Hungary. By 1947 more than a half million persons had received enough acreage to live on; many now owned land for the first time in their lives. Historian Hugh Seton-Watson noted, "This reform indeed transformed Hungarian agriculture, and was an event of great political as well as economic importance."[7]

The resulting good will toward the Communists and ill will from the Roman Catholic Church, which lost enormous estates, had political importance. Although the Roman Catholic Church retained schools devoted exclusively to religious studies, the government nationalized those Church schools that had taught secular studies. Even some Roman Catholic members of parliament voted for this takeover, leading to threats against them from Cardinal Archbishop (and Prince Primate) József Mindszenty. In addition to the school and land reform measures, he also condemned new laws making divorce possible, warning that "men forgetting decency and chivalry will break with wild passion upon defenceless women to satisfy their passion."[8]

Hungarian Communist concern for some types of social justice did not extend to all the democratic ideals cherished by Americans. Because he refused to permit secularization of the schools, Cardinal Mindszenty was accused of treason and, after a sensational, quite possibly unfair trial, received a life prison term. His imprisonment caused an uproar in the West.

Communists seized firm control of the Hungarian government in early 1947. In their eyes it was an act of self-defense in response to the moral encouragement that Hungarian rightists took from the Truman Doctrine. Remembering the fall of Béla Kun's Communist government, the Communists feared they would be massacred if they were expelled from government by rightist forces. Indeed, the old landlord class was incompetently plotting to seize the government. The Communists subsequently outlawed one political party after another, though few members of opposition parties were dragged off in chains. This Communist seizure of power was virtually bloodless.

The coup lacked violence because the opposition parties had long been rejected by the Hungarian people. Although the old-guard politicians could manufacture a sizable vote total when they controlled the electoral process, as could any East European government, such totals did not necessarily reflect true support. These men represented the interests that had oppressed the Hungarian population for a thousand years.

Although the Communists pushed, the rightists contributed to their own fall by conduct that journalist Joseph Harsch characterized as "staggering political sterility, absence of wise leadership, and incorrigible inclinations toward nepotism and corruption."[9] Historian D. F. Fleming summarized the situation thus: "When invited to produce three-year plans for Hungary's [postwar] reconstruction the other parties had not bothered to do so. The conservatives contented themselves with dreaming of the restoration of the great landed estates and the return of the common man to his 'suitable' place. The result was that an astonishing number of anti-communists accepted the communist claim to represent the people, regardless of elections, admitting that the communists were the motive power for rebuilding and revitalizing Hungary."[10]

Unfortunately for the people of Hungary, the Communist leader Rákosi was as authoritarian as any of the country's previous leaders, and his schemes of economic development failed to achieve promised results. Whereas an able and self-confident leader might have faced reality and modified his behavior accordingly, Rákosi suppressed even fellow Communists and left their queries unanswered. As pressures grew, he closed all safety valves. The resulting explosion will be examined in a later chapter.

GERMANY

The Nazi regime in Germany had fought the future, loosing a terrible war in a futile attempt to preserve standards of economic, social, and ethical conduct that Western civilization was rejecting. Unlike other defeated countries that became Communist in similar circumstances, however, only part of Germany would become Communist.

The postwar situation in Germany was different from that in most other countries where the Soviet Red Army had fought the Nazis. The army had advanced only across northeast Germany. British and American forces had taken the south and west of the country. The pattern of occupation had partly a military basis, partly a political one. Three districts of military occupation were drawn up by the three allies during the war. When Germany surrendered, the armies took their respective places as previously agreed, with the addition of a French army zone in the British-American areas. A joint commission of the victorious Allies would rule Germany.

The physical division of Germany into occupation zones differed from the Churchill-Stalin deal for Eastern Europe, which had established percentages of influence for Russia and the other Allies to be implemented throughout the whole of each country. In Germany arrangements for influence had specific geographical boundaries. Not only did Truman accept Soviet occupation of eastern Germany; he even agreed that part of German East Prussia could be formally incorporated into the Soviet Union.

The Russian-occupied zone did not turn Communist simply because of the presence of Soviet troops, however. A substantial Russian contingent occupied Austria, but no part of that country became Communist, despite the fact that the Soviets had helped foster the provisional Austrian government, in which a Communist was minister of the interior. The Soviet Union signed an agreement to remove its troops from Austria and abided by it.

Unlike Austria, Germany had a long Communist heritage. Karl Marx and Friedrich Engels were both German. A powerful leftist political element existed until Hitler suppressed it. In Germany Communism was not considered foreign, and its supporters were true believers rather than coerced skeptics.

Presented with an already fertile ground, the Russians had the foresight to arrive with seed. The Western powers had recognized various governments in exile for countries overrun by the Nazis, but Germany's Nazi government, obviously, never had to go into exile, and the West did not think to organize the freedom-loving Germans who had risked their lives opposing Hitler into a government in preparation for Hitler's fall. When the Western powers occupied Germany, they had no democratic German government waiting to replace the Nazi regime.

The Soviets, however, had carefully cultivated leftist exiles during the war. Remember that the Russians had enjoyed close relations with the German republic before the war. Many ties had existed with responsible German leaders. The Russians could therefore enter Germany with a formidable group of native Germans who knew their hometowns and were ready to promote Communism.

Political parties became active once again in Germany soon after the Nazi surrender. They could operate in all occupation zones and thereby provided a symbol of national unity. The parties had real ideological differences, however, which led to the Communists being nurtured by the military occupier in the eastern zone, while their political opponents were encouraged by Western occupiers in the western zone. Thus, although the parties were all-German, they became a force promoting political division.

In July 1945 four political parties, the Socialist Unity (Communist), Social Democrat, Liberal Democrat, and Christian Democrat parties, formed a coalition in the Russian occupation zone. The Social Democrats soon offered to merge with the Communists, but at first the offer was rejected. The proposal was accepted in April 1946, but by that time the Social Democrats no longer wanted a merger. The party split into eastern and western factions, with the leadership in the Russian zone agreeing to combine the eastern faction with the Communist party. In autumn 1946 elections in the Russian zone, the combination party failed to get a majority even though the other two parties were hampered by measures such as exclusion of some candidates and limitations on rallies. This was the last time opposition candidates appeared on the ballot there.

Naturally enough the cold war disputes that arose in the late 1940s among the United States, Britain, France, and Russia were reflected in the Allied Control Council, the joint commission that was supposed to be coordinating the administration of German affairs. As disagreements grew intractable, the council tended to allow each country to act as it wished in its own occupation zone. Because, by definition, the commission was supposed to be resolving issues that affected the entire country, such unilateral actions often left the dissenters disgruntled.

The Soviets reached the end of their patience in 1948. The occupying powers were arguing about a new currency. On March 30 General Lucius Clay, military governor of the American occupation zone, announced that the new money would be introduced in the western zones regardless of Russian objections. Because of the intertwining of politics with money, two separate currency systems would encourage Germany to divide into two separate political states. When General Clay made his announcement, a diplomatic conference was taking place in London. At this meeting—from which the Russians had been excluded—a decision would be made to form a West German state, intended to be a Western ally hostile to the Soviet Union. One can imagine the reaction if the Soviet Union had at that time excluded Western representatives from a conference establishing an East German state intended as a military ally against France.

The Soviets placed General Clay's statement in the context of the on-going London conference and saw the proposed currency change as a threatening act. They vehemently protested both the currency plan and the work of the diplomatic conference. On March 31, the day after General Clay's announcement, the Russians returned the pressure, apparently in an attempt to change the decisions. The Russians retaliated in a sphere where they had some control—transportation.

They began by harassing passenger and freight traffic bound to and from Berlin. The city was in a unique position—deep within the Soviet occupation zone, yet administered by all four powers. Survival of the Western enclave in Berlin depended on Soviet good will for the basics of existence—food, coal, electricity. The good will had begun to evaporate.

Britain, France, and the United States quickly responded by boycotting surface transport and switching to an airlift. (A firm understanding existed among all four powers that certain air lanes would always remain open.) There was no blockade in April 1948. Food shipments came in by rail as before, and highway traffic was unimpeded if drivers had the new passes demanded by the Russians. Indeed the airlift was quickly abandoned because it served no economic need, evidently intended merely to demonstrate a theoretical alternate supply route for Berlin.

Tension seemed to be easing in May, when England was allowed to resume its river transit to Berlin. Then, on May 20, the United States blocked Russian traffic wanting to enter the American zone of occupation. A couple weeks later the London diplomatic conference ended with a formal announcement that a West German government was to be created, thus dividing Germany into two countries. This was a drastic change of plans the Russians had agreed to since the war ended. Previously the idea was for a single united Germany to emerge from the four-power occupation.

Up to this point, despite the foreign military occupation, Germany had been considered one country by its citizens and by the world diplomatic community. Perhaps the creation of West Germany was merely a recognition of how 1948 differed from 1945. But the Western Allies' formal repudiation of the previous agreement had repercussions on Berlin, whose status had been created as part of that plan. The assumption had been that a united Germany would be ruled from Berlin; thus, the city was administered by all four powers even though it was deep inside the Soviet zone of occupation. If a united Germany had been abandoned, should the four-power occupation of Berlin be abandoned as well? If the situation had been reversed and a major Soviet military presence had existed in a German city near the French border, would the West have wanted the status quo to continue after its raison d'être ceased?

In a time of calm and goodwill, the issue might have been successfully negotiated, much as an end to the British occupation of Hong Kong was settled forty years later. But 1948 was not a time of calm and goodwill between the United States and the Soviet Union, so a confrontation developed instead.

The final straw was when the new Western currency appeared at the end of June. The Soviets saw this as proof that the creation of a hostile West Germany was underway. They clamped a surface transportation blockade on Berlin to force the Western enclave out of the city and out of the eastern occupation zone.

For a year the West mounted a heroic airlift to supply West Berlin residents with the physical necessities of life. The continuing success of this effort, and the Soviet unwillingness to risk war by escalating the pressure, led the Russians to end the blockade in May 1949.

Having failed to change Western determination to create a West Germany, Russia sought to weaken the perceived threat by creating an East Germany allied with the Communist bloc. This division of the country split its resources and industry between two uncooperative regimes, weakening Germany's ability to repeat the military aggressions it had conducted in Europe during the first half of the twentieth century. This boon to world peace was forgotten as Germany and Berlin became the stages for conflict instead of actors playing main roles.

WHY EASTERN EUROPE WENT COMMUNIST

With the exception of Czechoslovakia, whose story we shall examine later, we have now seen how the Communist advance occurred in Europe after World War II. Perhaps we can draw some conclusions.

The Soviet Union demonstrated no interest in forcing Western Europe to turn Communist. In Austria, the single West European nation where Russia had troops, no effort was made to set up a Communist provisional government. Moreover, the Russians agreed to pull out their troops and followed through on that commitment. Elsewhere in Western Europe, Moscow advised Communist parties to cooperate with governments rather than challenge them.

The East European nations that went Communist had no democratic heritage. A claim that these countries lost their freedom is accurate only in that the postwar governments became more compliant to Russian wishes than the pre–World War II, largely fascist, regimes had been. The peoples of those countries lost few, if any, freedoms. Those who complain about the Communist election record fail to consider the crooked non-Communist elections before the war, if elections were held at all. The prewar anti-Communist governments had a civil liberties record no better than the postwar Communist regimes.

Land reform, not civil liberties, was crucial in legitimating Communist regimes in the eyes of the citizenry. When World War II began, most East Europeans were peasants. (The important demographic exception was in Czechoslovakia, where the peasantry constituted only a third of the population.) Most peasants did not own enough land to live on. The Communist land distributions generated much popular support—and a small, but influential, amount of bitter hatred from the landlord class, which moved in international diplomatic circles.

The major explanation for Soviet influence in postwar Eastern Europe derives from World War II, not from any plan of world conquest. Stalin repeatedly approached the West about a united stand against Hitler to prevent war but was continually rebuffed. The West wanted to stand aside in hopes that Hitler would attack Russia. Instead, he struck in the other direction. The West now needed Russia on its side and had to be willing to compromise in order to guarantee good will from the Soviets. Thus, the West lost its first chance to prevent a Communist Eastern Europe when it decided that a Nazi war against Russia was preferable to peace. By attacking the West first and weakening it, Hitler, not Stalin nor Churchill nor Roosevelt, made a Communist Eastern Europe possible.

The West lost its second chance as delays continued in the Allied effort to open a second front in Europe. "For each Londoner killed in the Blitz, twenty Russian civilians were killed in the siege of Leningrad."[11] Every week that Russia had to absorb the full force of Hitler's onslaught gave Stalin that much more leverage in concessions from Roosevelt and Churchill regarding Eastern Europe.

These concessions were not prompted solely by a sense of sympathy. Roosevelt and Churchill were worried that Stalin might make a separate peace with Hitler unless the Allies made continuation worthwhile. The Soviet Union made a crucial, perhaps the decisive, contribution to the war against Hitler, which Churchill and Roosevelt recognized at the time. Military needs in World War II dictated generosity toward Russia's postwar desires.

And those desires were far from unreasonable. The West had rearranged Europe after World War I, sometimes carving countries from Russia, to create regimes hostile to the Soviet Union. In some cases, as with Poland, the armies of these nations attacked the Soviet Union and seized territory. Some of the countries joined with Hitler to attack Russia again. Experience had demonstrated the result of active and belligerent neighbors in Eastern Europe. Stalin was determined that those neighbors would be docile and friendly in the postwar world. This was a legitimate national security interest, supported by the facts of history. It was not the expression of a Soviet desire to rule the world. Indeed, similar concessions about a friendly Eastern Europe had been made to

Czar Nicholas to keep Russia fighting in World War I. No charges were leveled that the czar intended to conquer the world.

American journalist Edgar Snow traveled in Eastern Europe during the initial Soviet wartime occupation and understood the essence of the situation:

> In the liberated lands beyond Soviet borders one saw no proletarian uprisings of the conventional pattern. There were no open exhortations to workers to overthrow the bourgeoisie; no demands for a "workers and peasants dictatorship"; no open denunciations of capitalism; no extravagant prophecies of an early Communist or socialist Europe. . . . If the Kremlin was fostering revolution it was doing so with a hand heavily gloved in velvet, and it was pointing rather than pushing.
> . . . The way it looked from Moscow, all those nations and the many peoples within their changing boundaries were, without the violence and internal bloodshed of class war, going to realize a number of revolutionary reforms in common, more than they ever shared before. They would do so in a quiet, orderly manner, with excellent and stable police power, under the occupying forces, backing up the decrees of their own governments. There would be little barricade fighting to win this reformed new world. The fighting was done on the Volga and on the Don, the Dnieper, the Danube, the Vistula, the Oder and the Bug.[12]

An elderly Stalinist told Snow, "It is the people of those countries themselves who are getting rid of fascism and turning to the only possible form of government left to them."[13]

And, in the end, it was not Soviet troops nor Russian agents nor diplomatic deals that cost the old regimes the support of their peoples. Rather, the conduct of the landlord-warrior class and their servants in government doomed them. Had the old regimes at least behaved civilly toward the Soviet Union instead of attacking, had the old regimes possessed the creativity to accommodate the economic and social demands of a changing world, had the old regimes represented the interests of the vast majority of the populations, then Eastern Europe might never have adopted Communism.

But the old regimes had no answers to the demands of a world that had just gone to war against the ideals they represented. Just as Communism did not win against democracy in Eastern Europe, because democracy was never in the competition, neither did Communism really win against the old regimes. These reactionary governments offered no alternative to the way things had always been. And since times had changed, the Communists won by default.

And that is the tragedy of Eastern Europe: not that it adopted Communism, but that it was never offered democracy.

XI.

Communist Triumph in China

The survival of Mao Tse-tung and the activists around him during the 1930s and their eventual victory in the next decade is a tale of triumph normally found in classical mythology rather than history. One might think Mao would have received hearty congratulations from the Soviet Union, but instead the Soviets found fault: "poor Mao had always been mistaken, had engaged in either right- or left-wing deviations; the general line had somehow always eluded him."[1]

The ideological dispute between Russia and China would later become more acute, but that element of the Sino-Soviet conflict was an overlay hiding deeper disputes having nothing to do with arcane arguments about Communist political theory.

SINO-SOVIET RIVALRY IN MONGOLIA

Control of Mongolia, the oldest Communist state outside Russia, had been a long-standing source of dispute between China and Russia. Russian czars and Chinese emperors had argued over domination of Mongolia for centuries. Joseph Stalin was adamant that the issue be decided in Russia's favor. In 1941 he convinced the Japanese invaders of China to agree that Mongolia would remain untouched. At the Yalta Conference in early 1945, he persuaded the United States to agree as well, as part of the price for a Russian declaration of war against Japan. He even convinced

Chiang Kai-shek to agree in August 1945, in return for reaffirmation that Russia recognized Chiang's regime as the legitimate government of China. But Mao Tse-tung refused to accept Stalin's demand; as early as 1936 Mao had publicly declared that Mongolia should be absorbed by China, and he restated his views during the war. This territorial dispute, which had nothing to do with ideology, created tension between China and the Soviet Union.

CHIANG, GERMANY, AND JAPAN

In the 1930s Russia behaved as though Chinese Communists did not exist. The 1930 Shanghai convention held by Chinese Communists was barely acknowledged by the Soviet Union. The most prominent mention of Mao in the Soviet press that year was a premature obituary. Even the Comintern retreated from the idea of social revolution in China, drastically reducing the work force and money formerly devoted to that purpose.

It is perhaps coincidence, but perhaps a meaningful one, that German general Hans von Seeckt led Chiang's forces in their fifth great "annihilation drive" against the Chinese Communists in 1934. It was von Seeckt who masterminded the military cooperation between rightist Germany and Communist Russia in the 1920s. Although the Prussian general was staunchly anti-Communist, which could explain his support of Chiang, von Seeckt's position with Chiang could, perhaps, also have been related to his ties with Russia, indicating a continuing Soviet tilt toward Chiang. Chiang did, however, maintain close Nazi contacts in the 1930s, getting continual advice and expert aid from the hundred German officers assigned to him.

In contrast to the effective military advice given to Chiang, the Chinese Communists received disastrous guidance from Otto Braun, the general sent by the Comintern to organize Mao's forces. Braun directed the outgunned Chinese Communists to abandon guerrilla warfare, convincing them instead to adopt a traditional battlefield strategy, which quickly devastated their forces. In October 1934 the shattered remnants then fled on the famous Long March, a desperate year-long trek of about 6,000 miles by foot over difficult terrain to a new home in northern China.

Mao and his associates had smart and skeptical minds. It is reasonable to assume that they could see how this military setback dovetailed with the friendship Moscow had sought with Chiang for years. Mao was willing to view the bad advice from Braun as coincidence. But like Tito in Yugoslavia, Mao viewed the Soviet Union with suspicion.

In his fifth annihilation drive, Chiang was undistracted by the need to fight against Japanese invaders, who had just seized Manchuria in 1931. He had reached a truce with Japan early in 1932, in which they agreed to leave each other alone so he could face his Communist opponents.[2] Chiang regarded the Communists as a more pressing threat to his authority than the Japanese, and he was right: the Japanese were satisfied with dividing China with him, whereas Mao's Communists wanted everything.

Chiang's government continued these friendly relations with Japan through the 1930s and into World War II. By agreement reached in June 1940, Japan would, for the remainder of the war, leave his forces alone and concentrate on fighting Mao's.[3] Earlier, at Japan's request, Chiang suppressed anti-Japanese agitation in areas he controlled, arresting prominent citizens who opposed Japanese exploitation, suppressing magazines, and breaking strikes. He even punished Chinese industrialists who tried to avoid cooperating with the Japanese invaders. Chiang's reluctance to help armed resistance against the Japanese in Manchuria resulted in a mutiny by officers and men who called on him to fight Japan. In 1938 the president of the Kuomintang, Chiang's chief assistant Wang Ching-wei, joined the Japanese invaders outright and in 1940 became premier of a puppet Chinese government established by Japan.

Although the Japanese became notorious for torturous crimes, the scale of fighting in China was nothing like that in the European theater. Around 1940 the Japanese army in China, holding a territory bigger than Western Europe, consisted of around 400,000 men. So did Mao's army. Given that only a fourth of the Japanese strength in China was devoted to dealing with the Communists (the bulk of the Japanese either serving on garrison duty or concentrating on siege tactics to cut off supplies to nationalist Chinese), Mao's forces clearly had a distinct numerical edge in the contest despite their inferior supplies. Indeed, the edge was so great that Mao devoted most of his resources to fighting Chiang's army, just as Chiang applied most of his energies against Mao. To the leaders of both Chinese military forces, the Japanese were merely a distraction from the main business of civil war, an attitude never quite grasped by American decision makers far from the scene.

MANCHURIA

At the Yalta Conference held toward the end of World War II, the United States accepted Russia's interests in Port Arthur and Manchuria. Franklin Roosevelt recognized Russia's historical involvement in the area and China's past and present inability to keep Japanese aggressors out of the area. Behind that recognition was not a fear of confrontation with Stalin but a certainty that few Americans desired a massive United States military presence in the area to prevent further Japanese aggression. Unfortunately for Stalin, his understandings with Chiang and the United States were not regarded as binding by the Chinese Communists once Mao assumed power. They forced him to compromise on various aspects of the agreement regarding Manchuria, Dairen, and Port Arthur, evidence that, from the very beginning, Russia did not dictate to Communist China.

The Yalta agreement on Manchuria specified that China would regain ultimate sovereignty even though Soviet troops would liberate the territory from the Japanese. Although the Russians did stall in evacuating Manchuria after the war, the United States also delayed pulling its military units from China. The Russians said they would not leave until the Americans did. In fact, the Soviets were invited to stay by Chiang, who twice asked them to delay their departure in order to give him more time to move his forces into the area.

The Soviets had no desire to overstay their welcome in Manchuria, lest they give offense to the Chinese. On the contrary, Russia sought friendship with China and with Chiang. The two countries shared a long border; good relations could also promote the status quo in Mongolia and could protect Russia's interest in the Chinese Eastern Railway across Manchuria, a transportation link important to eastern portions of the Soviet Union. Lenin had established friendly relations with Sun Yat-sen, just as Stalin had done with Chiang. These relations became strained in the late 1920s when Chiang ordered Russians out of the country, but the quarrel was soon patched up. In late 1932 Russia had recognized Chiang as the legitimate ruler of all China and arranged an exchange of ambassadors. Russia's cultivation of Chiang demonstrated once again that treatment of native Communists was irrelevant to the Soviet Union in determining its relations with other states.

Except during the quarrel in the latter 1920s, Chiang kept encouraging the Soviets, suggesting that he was ready to intensify relations as soon as problems dividing the Kuomintang and Mao were resolved. Chiang even suggested that the Comintern accept his Kuomintang party as a member, a point ignored by those who later firmly believed Chiang to be staunchly anti-Communist. A Sino-Soviet trade treaty was signed in 1939, and in August 1945 Russia signed a treaty of friendship with Chiang's regime. A Soviet ambassador stayed with Chiang right up to Mao's victory in 1949.

All this notwithstanding, if the Russians wanted any sort of friendly relationship with China, they had to get out of Manchuria. In 1946 the Russians not only left Manchuria, but passed control of its cities to Chiang's forces, not to Mao's. Peaceably surrendering this area to anti-Communist fighters backed by the United States certainly conflicts with later charges that the Soviet Union wanted to conquer the territory.

American indignation about the temporary Soviet presence in Manchuria should have been tempered by recognition of the United States military presence in northern China, for, morally, the American position was no better. By December 1945 the United States had 100,000 American servicemen fighting Mao's forces. Bewildered American GI's sent letters to relatives and congressional representatives, pleading to go home, and the impatient soldiers even staged demonstrations in China. They had no desire to fight a Chinese civil war. The United States even told the remnants of Japanese invaders to keep their weapons and used the Japanese soldiers as allies in the war against Mao's army. The United States allowed the Japanese to continue fighting Mao's forces, just as if V-J Day had never occurred.

American journalist Edgar Snow, who spent years in China during the civil war, was convinced that Chiang never planned to retake Communist-held territory unless U.S. pilots, sailors, and troops attacked and weakened the Communists first. Chiang's reluctance to risk his own forces should be remembered when evaluating his many calls for America to take the military offensive in China.

American interference in the Chinese civil war, like participation in the Russian civil war a quarter-century earlier, served only to inflame anti-American sentiment and to justify the acclaim Communist forces received as patriots fighting foreigners.

Strange as it may seem to Americans today, the Russians suspected that Mao would establish friendly ties with the United States.[4] After all, Mao had had a good military relationship with the United States in the 1940s. The Chinese Communists even offered to put their army under American command during World War II, but the United States refused when Chiang protested. (He realized it would be awkward for him to attack the Communist army if it were under American orders.) The Soviet Union acted as if its old ties with Chiang might provide leverage in China, supporting the generalissimo in hopes of countering the feared American alliance with Mao's Communists.

Nothing in the Soviets' behavior indicated that they expected Mao to prevail over Chiang. At best, the Russians seemed to have hoped that the Communists would become powerful enough to force occasional concessions from Chiang. The Soviet attitude was already known to American policy makers in 1944. Patrick Hurley, Roosevelt's special emissary to China, reported that Mao's forces were operating independently of Russia and that Russia's attitude toward them was no more than lukewarm.

Indeed, at the end of World War II, Stalin told the Chinese Communists that a successful revolution in China was impossible and advised Mao instead to try to form a coalition government with Chiang. The Russians also advised Mao to disband his armed forces.

Certainly a look at the numbers supported such advice. In the summer of 1946 Chiang had virtually unlimited access to the U.S. treasury and had thousands of American experts on the scene, including pilots for his 500-plane air force, which was unchallenged by any Communist aircraft. In contrast Mao had foot soldiers scavenging food and supplies from the land, with no significant Soviet aid, let alone Russian troops. If technology could make the difference, Mao did not have a chance.

Ironically the American aid to Chiang provided a substantial part of the Communist armament, partly through capture, partly through black market sales by corrupt nationalist officials. Such was the character of the staunch anti-Communists. Whenever Mao's forces staged a victory parade, American weapons were in evidence. On the other hand, Russian arms supplies to Mao remained modest. Chiang's forces never displayed many captured Soviet weapons, and skeptics wondered if the few that were displayed were merely samples from the large quantities that Stalin had given Chiang prior to World War II.

At the end of World War II Chiang's defense of the old social order in China could no longer draw popular support by playing on the patriotic feelings against Japanese invaders. The Chinese people had a clear choice between Chiang's promise of life under the same conditions as always, or Mao's promise of liberation from exploitation by landlords and other capitalists. It did not take long for the peasantry to choose sides. Mao even received support from many of the more privileged classes crucial to postwar reconstruction and development.

By 1949 Chiang's Kuomintang organization was isolated politically; a coalition of opposition parties had joined with the Communists. The deficit spending policies of his government devastated China's economy. In a six-month period during 1948, the inflation rate was 8,500,000 percent. Under such conditions national productivity simply ceased. This heightened the suffering and unrest in cities, alienating the urban population from Chiang.

Having no other basis for retaining power, Chiang attempted to use sheer military force. On paper he began with a three-to-one advantage over Mao in numbers of troops, but by the middle of 1948 the numbers had evened out. The end was hastened by Chiang's decision to make a major stand in Manchuria. There, for the first time, Mao's forces had access to major supplies of modern matériel—Soviet-captured Japanese equipment left from World War II, given to Mao's forces by Stalin (the only noteworthy Soviet contribution to the Chinese Communists in over two decades of fighting). In October 1948 Chiang's Manchurian forces surrendered.

Now began a triumphal Communist march southward and across the Chinese mainland, with Communist ranks swelling as some of Chiang's surrendering forces changed sides, with each surrender providing more captured American-made weapons and supplies. The progress was not peaceful, but the bloodshed was tempered by the growing realization of what the inevitable outcome would be. In 1949 Chiang fled to the island of Formosa (Taiwan), where for many years he would hurl invective at the Communists who now ruled the mainland People's Republic of China.

The Chinese Communists won without Russia's help, and they have never forgotten it.

The crucial difference between Chiang's Kuomintang and Mao's Communists had nothing to do with freedom, but rather, was based on economic, and so, political policy. The Kuomintang sought power by keeping peasants out of the political process, instead currying favor with corporate interests and the rural gentry, who based their wealth on exploitation of ordinary people. Chiang opposed land reform, supported taxation by landlords, prohibited farmer organizations, executed labor union leaders, outlawed strikes, and called for work days exceeding twelve hours. During World War II men were left imprisoned for debt rather than released to fight, a telling comment on national priorities under

Chiang. He also sought to keep the citizenry disarmed, lest weapons be turned against the interests he defended. The country was governed from the top down; the central Kuomintang bureaucracy appointed local government officials. The Kuomintang was the only legal political party.

In contrast Mao's Communists sought power by cultivating support among the peasantry. They gave peasants the land of absentee landlords, limited rents charged by resident landlords, encouraged the restoration of wasteland into production, used progressive taxation, put a moratorium on debt collection, ended usury, penalized speculators, armed the citizenry, and organized the illiterate population to meet war needs even though people might transfer such organizational experience into political channels. American journalist Edgar Snow reported that even Chiang's Kuomintang believed that an honest poll would have put Mao into power.[5] Chiang had the guns, but Mao had the people.

It is also important to remember that, just as with Eastern Europe, China was a country that had never known democracy. Civil liberties had never existed there. The Communist triumph did not overthrow a democratic government; it replaced a long line of harsh and repressive regimes.

After the Communist victory in China, angry Americans were determined to discover who "lost" China and to punish them. But the Americans never had China. Nor did the Russians. Although the fight may have eventually been between American-supported Chinese and Soviet-supported Chinese, the contestants were Chinese all along. No foreigner "lost" the country.

China once again belonged to the Chinese. In the 1940s this development was called a boon to Russia; in the 1980s it was called a boon to the United States. The thrust of Chinese history in the twentieth century, however, has been to end domination by foreigners and to reassert ancient power and greatness. One global power or another may benefit temporarily from Chinese actions, but those actions will be intended to promote the interests of China.

XII.

Communist Failure in Korea

The Korean War was a gloomy experience for all participants. The United States grew frustrated as soldiers died while military victory became elusive and seemingly irrelevant. Korea's land, cities, and people were devastated—every day of war meant there was less worth fighting for in the country. And the Communists lost as much as anyone. When the armistice was signed, they had not only failed to gain an inch of territory, but they faced the largest military machine the world had ever known, a force that would be increased rather than reduced as peace ascended. The prospects for Communist military success were never lower than at the end of the Korean War.

ANTECEDENTS

The path toward that exasperating conflict can be seen in events that began in the nineteenth century when the strength of the Chinese empire was declining, when the United States was a regional power of little concern to anyone but immediate neighbors, and when Russia's czar was one of the mightiest men on Earth.

By 1784 Russia had expanded all the way across Asia, had jumped the Pacific Ocean at the Bering Sea, and had established Alaska as Russian territory. During the nineteenth century, observers of the situation could see that the expanding United States would inevitably bump into Russian North America. Should the czar take any actions necessary to defend his Alaskan realm? Responsible Russian observers said no. In 1860 one of them expressed such sentiment by saying that American acquisition of Alaska "is inevitable. It cannot be prevented; and it would be better to yield with good grace and cede the territory."[1] Fort Ross, the old czarist settlement near San Francisco, had already been sold to the Americans in 1841. In 1867 Alaska, the New World's last Russian possession, was sold as well.

Instead of pursuing a North American empire, Russia looked south along Asia's Pacific coast. By 1860 the czar's rule extended to the Amur River, which became the Russo-Chinese border. In that year, one Russian said that his nation "has a manifest destiny on the Amur, and further south, even in Korea."[2]

In the 1890s Russian capitalist A. M. Bezobrazov acquired a timber interest in Korea and told the czar that expanding the empire in that direction would be profitable. The czar vacillated, with some advisers arguing that the empire had plenty to cope with already and others arguing that further expansion would be financially lucrative, for businessmen and for the czar himself. The czar opted for profit over caution. In 1900 the Boxer Rebellion in Peking gave Russia an excuse to move toward the area. The Boxers, so-called because of their mailed fist symbol, were Chinese fighting against European exploitation of their country. Russia and other countries, including the United States, sent military expeditions to suppress the rebellion in China. After defeating the Boxers in 1900, foreign military contingents remained in China. Their presence helped expand European economic penetration. This aided Russian business operations in Korea, which geographically was virtually cut off from Russia by China.

Korea was nominally an independent state in the latter nineteenth century, though strongly tied to China. By the 1870s, however, Japan was pursuing a vigorous economic penetration of Korea. Similar Russian activity in the peninsula ran up against the Japanese. The Russo-Japanese competition became so fierce that a war broke out in 1904, which the Russians lost.

The defeat in 1905 proved that the czarist regime was no longer invincible and promoted a series of revolutionary rebellions that year. The outbreaks in Russia were stamped down, but the unleashed revolutionary fervor eventually led to the czar's 1917 overthrow after the regime had been weakened by World War I.

Following the Russo-Japanese War, Japan moved into Korea and in 1910 formally annexed it; many Korean refugees fled to Russia.

A few Korean refugees went to the United States. One of them was Syngman Rhee, who received a Ph.D. from Princeton in 1910, and became a friend of university president Woodrow Wilson and his family. As the head of a Korean independence movement operating from the United States, Rhee encouraged a Korean rebellion in 1919, but it was swiftly crushed by the Japanese. The Versailles peace conference made no change in the *status quo* of Korea, and Rhee's group dissipated.

At the same time Korean exiles in Russia sought Communist support for a revolution to liberate Korea from Japan and to change the social order. Comintern leaders, however, were so skeptical about the prospects in Korea that the Korean situation was used as a punishment assignment for Comintern personnel who fell into disfavor. In fact, little action occurred in Korea itself, and native Communists in Korea became caught up in intraparty feuding so disruptive that they were expelled from the Comintern.

Around 1930 the disorganized Korean Communists closed up shop and integrated themselves into the Chinese Communist party. Their base of operations was China, particularly in Manchuria to the northeast, which bordered Korea. Consequently very few native Communists were still in Korea to meet the Soviet Red Army when it advanced against the Japanese in Korea during the final days of World War II. Instead, power passed to Korean exiles returning from Russia, Manchuria, and China. They formed the Korean Workers party, which became the ruling Communist party in North Korea. Unlike the Communist situation elsewhere in Asia, the Korean Communist party lacked roots in the native population. The exiles had become outsiders without any local standing.

KOREA IS DIVIDED AFTER WORLD WAR II

The Russians entered Korea at the request of the United States, which feared that liberating Korea would be harder than conquering the Japanese home islands. In view of the potential for casualties, the Pentagon was delighted when in 1945 Stalin agreed to invade Korea. Delight turned to consternation when Japanese resistance melted away as the Russian offensive began in August 1945. No one had expected the offensive to coincide with the Japanese surrender that came a few days later.

Korea was a low priority for the United States, as demonstrated by the low rank of personnel in charge of devising government policy on the situation. Nonetheless these underlings began scrambling for a way to prevent Russia from occupying all of Korea. Two colonels were ordered to draw up a plan on the spur of the moment, and a few hours later they suggested that Korea be divided arbitrarily at the 38th parallel to provide two zones of military occupation. The Soviet Union, which had liberated the north during the war, was to occupy territory above that line; the south was to be occupied by American forces, none of which would arrive until after the war. The proposal was rushed to the Soviets, who agreed. Thus was Korea divided, in a plan hastily thrown together by two American colonels. One of them, Colonel Dean Rusk, would later, as U.S. secretary of state, be as responsible as anyone for the American war in Vietnam.

The Russians adhered strictly to their part of the 1945 Korean agreement; Soviet units already south of the parallel withdrew immediately when the line became the occupation zone border. Thereafter the Russians made no effort to go south of the parallel even though they could easily have done so in the month before United States forces arrived in Korea after World War II.

Koreans were abashed to find out that liberation from decades of Japanese rule in 1945 did not mean independence. Instead, under the terms of agreements made in Cairo in 1943 and Yalta in 1945, neither of which Korea was party to, Korea was still to be under foreign rule, governed as a trusteeship by the United States, the Soviet Union, Great Britain, and China under Chiang Kai-shek. As with the partition of Germany, there had been some expectation that the two zones of military occupation would be jointly administered by the four allies, but in practice Russia and the United States ran their respective zones. The trusteeship was never implemented, but it caused resentment among Koreans.

When American general John Hodge arrived on September 8, 1945, he was welcomed to Korea by representatives of the newly formed Korean People's Republic, a coalition of nationalists and Communists. General Hodge promptly proclaimed the native government illegal. In its place an American military government was established to administer Korea south of the 38th parallel, with the assistance of former Japanese occupiers and their collaborators. Regarding the latter, Colonel William Maglin explained, "We felt that if they did a good job for the Japanese, they would do a good job for us."[3] Maglin's implication that Korea was a conquered country rather than a liberated one was typical of American officials. This ambiguous attitude created confusion among U.S. personnel and resentment among the Korean people. Eventually strikes and riots brought a declaration of martial law by the American military regime.

RHEE TAKES COMMAND IN SOUTH KOREA

The ambitious Syngman Rhee, who from an exile based in the United States had spent almost four decades in fruitless attempts to find support for his dream of leading a Korean revolution, recognized that the turmoil after the war could be used to gain personal power.

The American government considered Rhee a nonentity. He had a well-earned reputation for intolerance of questions about his aims and for imagining Communists everywhere. In 1945 he had complained of alleged pressure from Chiang Kai-shek's regime to give Communists more power in Korea. Later Rhee claimed that General Hodge was trying to promote Communism. Rhee's high profile helped reinforce Western notions that the country would need to be governed as a trusteeship until Koreans developed responsible leaders. In 1942 Stanley Hornbeck, chief of the State Department's Office of Far Eastern Affairs, bluntly told Rhee that his so-called provisional government was merely a small club of expatriates; that same year the club ousted Rhee, ending his credibility as self-proclaimed spokesman for Korean independence. The American attitude was hardly unique: in 1945 "the longest-lived government-in-exile in modern world history . . . died out without being recognized by any government in the world."[4]

Rhee then abandoned the goal of a free and united Korea that had rallied other exiles around him after World War I and in 1945 called for immediate independence of a truncated South Korea. He was astute enough to see that the Truman administration would welcome this opportunity to confound the Soviet Union with an anti-Communist Korean state. Traditional nationalists were appalled at the prospect of splitting Korea for the foreseeable future.[5] Rhee was able to manipulate American fear of Communism to achieve his goal even though he was opposed by other anti-Communist Korean patriots. He was a pioneer in demonstrating how ambitious Third World politicians are able to piggyback to power astride the United States, exploiting anxiety about Communism, despite opposition from native populations.

In June 1945 Truman had dismissed Rhee's provisional government as unrepresentative of the Korean people's desires. Nonetheless, Truman soon decided that no other Korean leader was suitable for American support: "We had no choice but to support Rhee."[6] The reason for Truman's change of mind is unclear, but probably had to do with hopes that Rhee's dependence on American support would make him a reliable puppet. The United States brought Rhee to Korea in October as a private citizen. Korean politics traditionally centered around individuals more than governmental institutions, and private citizen Rhee began acquiring power by currying favor with wealthy rightists. This influence increased when General Hodge made him a political adviser to the American military government. The State Department had warned that Rhee was an extreme right-winger, but such a warning was not a matter of concern to General Hodge, who once complained that the *Christian Science Monitor* was printing Communist-inspired material about Korea and on another occasion griped that he had been "handicapped by a lot of false and misleading information put out by the Communist, pinko, and idealist liberal press of the United States."[7]

Hodge began to change his mind about Rhee, however, when Rhee and those around him started complaining about "conditions of slavery under the Military Government."[8] Hodge objected to Rhee's "God complex, carrying with it the fixed idea that he and he alone should dictate to his people without advice from anyone. . . . Many of his attacks [on me] have followed the best Communist vein—so much so that many well-informed Americans here are prone to believe that he has sold out to the Russians."[9] Hodge threatened Rhee, telling him to act in concert with American wishes or face destruction,[10] but by then Rhee had developed a personal political machine throughout South Korea "ranging from women's clubs to terrorist bands."[11] Unless the United States was prepared to fight a war against Rhee in Korea, his power was unassailable.[12]

Rhee's ascendancy was confirmed in a May 10, 1948, election. Truman called this "the first free election in Korean history"[13] and noted that it was held under United Nations observation. In fact, the balloting was not *run* by the United Nations; it was merely watched by thirty observers who were responsible for the entire country. Rhee's political machine won control of the National Assembly, which proceeded to name Rhee the first president of the Republic of Korea.

Rhee established a rightist regime in which landlord and capitalist interests so predominated that prominent Korean liberals stayed out of the government in protest. Tremendous conflict broke out between Korean nationalists, who had risked their lives for their country during decades of Japanese oppression and who sought to help the average Korean, and those politicians who had curried favor with the American military occupiers to gain personal power and who served the interests of landlords and businessmen exploiting average Koreans. Political murders by extremists of left and right either eliminated or drove off talented public servants, leaving the untalented in charge.

KIM IL-SUNG TAKES COMMAND IN NORTH KOREA

While Rhee consolidated his hold on South Korea, a similar process was occurring among Communists in North Korea. Old-time native Communists, survivors of the big chill from the Comintern, assumed that a united Korea would be governed from the country's capital of Seoul, in the south. Therefore, they made Seoul their base of operations, so they could be close to the center of the nation's political activity, ready to act when Korea became a free and united nation.

Their ineffective work against the nationalists had little impact on events in South Korea in the years before the republic was created. The American military government and Rhee eliminated Communist activity in the south, the Americans using arrests and Rhee's supporters using terrorism. But the congregation of top Communist talent in South Korea had a big effect on events in North Korea, where the Soviet Union nurtured Communist activity. There, by default, the less competent Communists were thrust into increasingly higher positions of importance and authority in the north.[14] The real Communist action was happening all over North Korea, unbeknownst to the old hands closely monitoring political debates in Seoul and waiting for their chance, which never came. When eventually they fled north, they found themselves shut out of the Communist regime.

Kim Il-sung had risen to the top position in that regime. "Kim Il-sung" was a patriotic name adopted by many Korean revolutionaries of various political stripes. The original "Kim Il-sung" was active in the early twentieth century, but it is unclear whether he was one person or a legend credited with the deeds of many. Reportedly the eventual leader of North Korea was born with the name Kim Song Ju.

Notwithstanding Kim's Korean heritage, he was a product of China. He was educated in Manchuria, where he attended Chinese schools despite the availability of Korean ones. He was not part of the Korean Communist exile community in China. He joined the Chinese Communist party in 1931 and during World War II was active with Chinese Communist guerrillas. Until he appeared in North Korea at the end of World War II he had been uninvolved with any Korean revolutionaries.

In 1945 and 1946 Kim sought to usurp the influence of that exile group and gain power in Korea for himself. Unlike most Korean exiles, he chose to reject closeness with Mao Tse-tung's Chinese Communists and instead opportunistically allied himself with the Soviet Red Army occupying Korea. Since the Soviets were unenthusiastic about Mao's revolutionary activity in China, they were delighted to back a Korean with a bona fide Chinese background who would work to reduce Mao's influence in Korea. Soviet advisers soon permeated the North Korean regime.

As was the case in Eastern Europe, the Communist regime immediately gained popular support through land reform. Distribution of land in the North to nearly three-quarters of a million peasants began in March 1946. Not until two years later did the United States military government in the south begin similar efforts, which were first moderated and then halted by the incoming Rhee government. Rhee's attempts at land reform ultimately took a different slant from the reforms of the Communists: South Korean peasants were given a choice of either harsh purchase contracts from their landlords or eviction.

It is important to remember that both Syngman Rhee and Kim Il-sung had spent little time in Korea, having lived much of their lives in exile from their homeland. Each achieved power through strong foreign backing. Significantly, neither regime was run by the patriots who had spent generations struggling for a free and united Korea. Cold war bickering between Russia and the United States had caught Korea in the middle and drastically changed its politics.

PREPARATION FOR WAR

By 1950 the two hostile Korean regimes were snorting at each other across the 38th parallel. Border incidents were frequent, with both sides making forays into the other's territory. General Douglas MacArthur, U.S. commander-in-chief in the Far East, thought it feasible that Rhee would initiate a war against North Korea,[15] and Secretary of State George Marshall was concerned about the possibility as well.[16] Indeed, in October 1949, Rhee publicly griped that the Americans were trying to prevent him from attacking North Korea.[17] This was true.

Moreover, the United States was doing its best to avoid any possibility of being drawn into a war on the Korean peninsula. In 1947 George Kennan's State Department Policy Planning Staff recommended that the United States "cut our losses and get out of there as gracefully but promptly as possible."[18] The Defense Department buttressed State's recommendation with a finding that an American military presence in Korea was unnecessary for national security and would actually be a liability if hostilities broke out in that region.[19] In April 1948 the National Security Council warned that the United States should be careful to avoid any commitments that could be used as a pretext for involving America in a Korean war.[20] The Joint Chiefs of Staff agreed.[21] So did General Douglas MacArthur, who said the United States should leave Korea because it could not be defended.[22] As supreme commander of American forces in Japan, MacArthur would likely be responsible for military activity if the United States were ever drawn into a Korean war. In 1948 Truman said that the United States would stand aloof from any fighting between North and South Korea, regardless of who started it.[23] In March 1949 Truman and the National Security Council decided that all U.S. forces should be pulled from the peninsula.[24] This process was completed in June. Also in March 1949, MacArthur publicly defined the U.S. Pacific defense perimeter as bounded roughly by the Aleutian Islands, Japan, the Ryukyu Islands, and the Philippines—a boundary that pointedly excluded Korea.[25] In January 1950 Secretary of State Dean Acheson publicly agreed with MacArthur's definition.[26] In May 1950 Senate Foreign Relations Committee Chairman Tom Connally downplayed the significance of Korea so much that he even predicted the United States would make no attempt to thwart a Russian attack on the peninsula, let alone a conflict involving the Koreans and no one else.[27]

The Soviet Union was also trying to stay clear of a war in Korea. The U.S.S.R. had removed its occupation forces from Korea in 1949. The Soviets had no mutual military assistance pact with North Korea. Nikita Khrushchev remembered that when Kim said he wanted to invade South Korea, Stalin removed Russian military advisers from North Korea, leaving Kim on his own to plan strategy and tactics.[28] When the war began, the Soviets, who were boycotting United Nations proceedings in protest over China's being represented there by Taiwan, rather than Peking, declined to veto the Security Council resolution that sent troops to fight North Korea. "It's Kim Il-sung's affair," Stalin had told Khrushchev.[29] Later, when Kim ran short on supplies during the war, Russia did not replenish them and indeed stood aside even as the Communist Korean regime appeared to be in danger of annihilation.

Both Truman and Stalin had done everything feasible to stay out of a Korean war, yet Truman would find himself drawn in almost immediately.

THE KILLING BEGINS

The long-expected war started on June 25, 1950. The question of which side fired the first shot has been debated ever since. Kim had planned an attack, but Rhee had a motive for provoking an attack in hopes of rallying support around his unpopular regime. Rhee's political machine had managed to lose a May 30 parliamentary election and was on the verge of collapse, opening the possibility that Rhee would soon be replaced. Both Kim and Rhee had reason to be pleased about the outbreak of hostilities, so assessing blame is needless.

Since a carefully considered consensus existed among every responsible U.S. government agency that American involvement in a Korean war had to be avoided, it seems odd in retrospect that the United States entered the conflict with such alacrity. Perhaps the explanation is to be found in the spirit of the times. In the United States, a misunderstanding of events in Eastern Europe had promoted a feeling that Russia was attempting to conquer the world. The Korean conflict was immediately blamed on Stalin. The Korean War had to be fought to resist this "Russian aggression," because Hitler types must never be appeased again.

In addition, the American view of Korea had changed. In 1945 the world considered Korea one country. This opinion was still held by the Communists, who regarded the Korean conflict as a native civil war. By 1950, however, the United States regarded Korea as two countries and viewed the war as aggression by one state against another.

In the United States, the Korean conflict was being called the Greece of Asia. In Greece an American-supported government had recently defeated the Communist insurgency, which had begun in

World War II. So optimism existed that such a success could be repeated in Korea.

There was also fear in America, the mightiest nation on earth in 1950. The Communist revolution had triumphed in China the previous year, and the idea of that enormous country being Communist sobered many Americans. There were recriminations about "who lost China," fanned by the rhetoric of Republican senator Joseph McCarthy, who claimed to have proof of wide penetration of the Democratic Truman administration by Communist traitors. McCarthy never revealed the proof, but many Americans could not believe that a U.S. senator would make such serious charges without foundation. It was widely believed that secrets stolen by Communist spies had taught Russia how to make atomic bombs, and many Americans feared that Truman and the Democrats were no longer able to protect the country. And 1950 was a Congressional election year.

Truman prided himself on being able to make quick decisions, and he took little time to discard all the reasons that had been given in past years for staying clear of a war in Korea. No one stood up to him and said no. Not the secretary of state, not the secretary of defense, not the Joint Chiefs of Staff, not Congress, no one.

Since his days in the U.S. Senate, Truman had a pet idea that an international police force should enforce law in the world. He directed that the United Nations be asked to provide police protection to South Korea. The United Nations agreed quickly; in those days of generous foreign aid and insatiable American markets, the United Nations did whatever America asked. Thus began what Truman liked to call the Korean police action, a convenient term that allowed him to involve the United States in a major military action without a congressional declaration of war.

The personnel would mainly be American. Indeed, even before the United Nations voted, Truman had already ordered MacArthur to defend South Korea. Although eventually about fifteen members of the United Nations would become militarily involved in the Korean War and the campaign was authorized by the United Nations, the whole operation was controlled by the United States. The United Nations provided a piece of paper saying that action was justified, but it was an American action. Truman became the agent of the United Nations, and the chain of command went from him to the secretary of defense to the Joint Chiefs to MacArthur. The United Nations had no authority over the American military.

THE GENERAL

Douglas MacArthur was one of America's most distinguished generals, credited by the public as the architect and engineer of victory over Japan in World War II. He had a reputation as a maverick willing to take bold gambles. These traits had caused unease among Washington officials who dealt with him in World War II.

Before that war he had been responsible for developing the Philippines defense plan against Japan, but "armed struggle . . . totally disproved important military theories previously championed by him in the face of severe criticism."[30] Rather than admit he was mistaken, MacArthur blamed Washington for the desperate situation of the Philippines under Japanese attack. As the defensive situation worsened, MacArthur's headquarters issued over a hundred communiqués proclaiming his brilliance under great odds: "They were also frequently inaccurate; for example, they mentioned glorious victories in several battles that never occurred."[31] In fact, throughout World War II MacArthur routinely filed inaccurate battle reports inflating his accomplishments: claiming to have sunk the battleship *Haruna,* alleging that the battle for Davao had been won when weeks of hard fighting remained, proclaiming all quiet at Buna when American forces were hard-pressed in vigorous combat, exaggerating enemy setbacks—Japanese shipping losses were less than 5 percent of MacArthur's claim in a report on action around Rabaul. Some communiqués falsely portrayed MacArthur as being at the front lines when he was actually 500 miles away from the fighting. In 1944 he even had photos taken of himself at a jungle warfare exercise; they were then sent to the press as pictures of MacArthur in combat at the front.[32] With such false information MacArthur craftily generated public pressure on Washington officials to agree to his demands. His superiors were outraged by the tactic but allowed the general's reports to go unchallenged lest public morale be undermined.

While MacArthur was careful to avoid outright insubordination in World War II, he made little effort to clear his actions with superiors. He made and implemented major decisions about allocation of military resources in the Pacific, taking gambles such as removing the Eighth Army from the Luzon liberation campaign when the Sixth Army was in trouble there. He even told an associate that he planned to disregard a Joint Chiefs directive and invade Java, but in the end he pulled back from that scheme.[33]

Another element of his maverick reputation came from his

willingness to participate in partisan politics while on active duty. He sought the Republican presidential nomination in 1944, with his intelligence-staff chief General Charles Willoughby serving as go-between for communications with senior Republican leaders. MacArthur won the Illinois primary, but the effort faded when he refused to return home to campaign.[34] He sought the Republican nomination again in 1948 but, after again refusing to return to campaign, quit the race after losing in the primaries. Some Democrats then approached him in hopes of dumping Truman, and MacArthur toyed with the idea of running as a national unity candidate of both parties—evidence of both his self-esteem and his lack of political savvy. After the Republican convention chose Thomas Dewey as their candidate, MacArthur asked the hopeful Democrats to drop the idea.[35]

When Truman told MacArthur to defend South Korea, it should have been clear that trouble would arise. All one had to do was assume that MacArthur would behave as he had in World War II—and few seventy-year-old men change their ways. Moreover, when the Korean War began, an additional factor, little recognized but of great importance to the military hierarchy, complicated the situation: the highest-ranking general on the Joint Chiefs of Staff had four stars; MacArthur had five. He outranked his superiors.

Keeping this self-starter under control was indeed going to be tough.

THE DOUBLE WAR

The military action of the Korean War can be outlined in one paragraph. The North Koreans nearly defeated Rhee and took over much of South Korea, only to be pushed back across the 38th parallel and then nearly destroyed as MacArthur rallied the United Nations forces, sending them through North Korea and up to the border of China. Communist China then intervened in the war, pushing the United Nations forces back into South Korea. An armistice was signed in 1953 virtually restoring the territorial status quo that existed when the war began. The straight border along the 38th parallel was replaced by one that tilted—North and South Korea traded some land. North Korea was thwarted and gained nothing, and the South Korean state was strengthened by a continuing American military presence.

MacArthur accepted the command of forces to defend South Korea even though he believed the country's defeat would pose no military threat to the United States. He had stated this in public the year before the war. He had once again excluded Korea from America's Pacific defense line in a memo dated June 14, 1950, and presented to secretary of defense Louis Johnson and Joint Chiefs chairman General Omar Bradley hours before the war began.[36] After touring the battlefront on June 29, his view remained unchanged.[37]

MacArthur took command in Korea because he viewed the war as an opportunity to achieve a larger personal goal—the military destruction of Communist China. He knew his superiors in Washington would be aghast at such a project, but he was confident he could do it despite their opposition. After all, he would be in charge of combat in a country bordering China, and his combat orders had never been countermanded. Moreover, he was a master at manipulating American public opinion to pressure Washington officials into granting his demands.

So the general fought a double war in Korea, one against the Communists, and one against his lawful superiors. He was shrewd in both theaters of operation.

The anti-Communist credentials of President Truman and his advisers were sterling. Their eagerness to push back Communism was second to none. They were anxious, however, not to take on too much at one time. When the Korean War began, the U.S. Army could muster only "less than half the number [of men] it had had on Pearl Harbor Day. The Navy had been reduced in strength as drastically as the Army."[38] Washington therefore wanted to keep the war limited to Korea.

In pursuit of that objective, secretary of defense Louis Johnson cautioned MacArthur to be sure that Chiang Kai-shek attempted no adventures against Communist China during the Korean crisis. MacArthur said not to worry, he realized that Truman wanted "to protect the Communist mainland."[39] While not quite insubordinate, such verbal barbs outraged the Truman administration. This particular one came about the same time as a public statement to the Veterans of Foreign Wars in which MacArthur emphasized the importance of defending Chiang Kai-shek's Formosa government. While no one could point to any particular sentence at variance with Truman administration policy, Truman and his advisers instantly saw the overall thrust of the statement as contrary to the president's low-key policy in Formosa. Truman ordered MacArthur to withdraw the statement, which the general did, albeit under protest.

The VFW controversy of August 1950 was inherently of small

importance, but it portended great events. General Omar Bradley saw the incident as the first of a series leading to MacArthur's dismissal the next year. More significant at the time, this public reprimand was probably MacArthur's first. He was stunned and decided that he had formidable enemies in Washington. But he was undeterred from his goal of war against Communist China.

Within days of MacArthur's start of combat operations in June, officials in Washington noted that MacArthur was violating his orders to operate only below the 38th parallel. Instead, he was widening the war by ordering air attacks against North Korea's capital, P'yŏngyang. Truman quickly authorized such attacks, making disciplinary action against MacArthur moot.

In mid-August MacArthur began air strikes along the border North Korea shared with China. On two occasions United States bombers drew antiaircraft fire from Chinese territory but sustained no damage. MacArthur later characterized this antiaircraft fire as Chinese aggression. On August 27, American airplanes attacked Antung (Tan-tung), China. China merely issued a diplomatic protest, which the United States refused to accept.

By October 1950 MacArthur had pretty well run North Korean forces back across the 38th parallel, successfully completing the United Nations mission of repelling the Communist army from South Korea. That should have been the sensible end of the affair, but pressures existed for conquering North Korea and thereby ending Korea's political division. Rhee had been pushing this option before the war started. In addition, the military option now seemed the *only* way to achieve a united non-Communist Korea, since the United States believed that Koreans would vote a Communist government into power if free elections were held.[40] Capitalist countries, particularly Japan, added pressure because they wanted to reopen the North Korean markets. And there was MacArthur's desire to move against Communist China.

On September 27, 1950, the United States government ordered MacArthur to exceed the United Nations directive and move into North Korea while demanding unconditional surrender. MacArthur unleashed Rhee's forces, which had been eager to move north for at least a year. By October 3, they had penetrated fifty miles into North Korea, apparently under U.S. air and sea cover. At the same time, American bombers struck just south of the Chinese border. American ground units "officially" entered North Korea on October 7. Several hours later the United Nations authorized operations north of the 38th parallel.

The goal no longer was to repel North Korean forces from South

Korea. Now the aim was to conquer North Korea, a rather different proposition.

On October 8, immediately after receiving United Nations authorization to operate north of the 38th parallel, MacArthur exceeded that directive by bombing an airport sixty miles within the border of the Soviet Union. Although the Soviets had reacted mildly when American forces shot down a Russian bomber flying about eighty-five miles from the Korean coast in September, they were firmer in their protest when MacArthur began bombing their country. This act was a direct violation of orders from the Joint Chiefs prohibiting flights over Russian and Chinese territory. The day after the bombing incident, the Soviet Union asked Truman for assurance that no repetition would occur. The very next day the White House said Truman was flying to Wake Island to discuss the war with MacArthur. It has been assumed that at Wake Island Truman told MacArthur to avoid attacking Russia.[41] A record of such a warning has never been found, but no more strikes against the Soviet Union occurred.

When the Joint Chiefs had told MacArthur to invade North Korea in September, they had forbidden use of non–South Korean troops in provinces bordering China. The point was to avoid provoking Chinese entry into the war. On October 24 an Army spokesman in Korea stated that this buffer zone extended forty miles south of the Manchurian border. The same day, however, MacArthur ordered American soldiers to enter the buffer zone. On October 26, Truman said he understood that a buffer zone stretched all across the northern border of Korea, but MacArthur headquarters corrected the President with an announcement that United Nations forces would join South Korean units in going all the way to the Yalu River bordering China if necessary to eliminate the Communist threat in Korea. The U.S. congressional election campaigns were peaking. Many votes would be decided by perceptions of the Democrats' vigor in pursuing the war. Truman issued no rebuke to the popular general.

Despite orders to keep American bombers well away from the Manchurian border, MacArthur continued to send aircraft close enough to draw Chinese antiaircraft fire. He again cited this as evidence of Chinese aggression.

Four days before the congressional elections MacArthur sent American units against the Changjin Reservoir, a target of marginal importance to victory in Korea but of intense interest to Communist China. Two days before the election, reports surfaced that mainland China's electricity-generating facilities on the Yalu might be destroyed if China increased its forces opposing the United Nations in Korea. Chinese forces had pressed American soldiers harshly for several days.

The day before the elections, MacArthur indicated that he might soon receive authorization to attack Manchuria. He was incensed when, on that same day, the Joint Chiefs attempted to restrain him by ordering cancellation of all bombing missions closer than five miles to Manchuria. MacArthur declared that such bombing was vital and demanded that the question be put to Truman for a decision. Truman, who surely did not relish the thought of election day headlines proclaiming that he would not allow the steps MacArthur deemed necessary for the protection of American troops, overruled the Joint Chiefs and told MacArthur to go ahead.

By election day, November 7, North Korea had been virtually conquered by United Nations forces. The Chinese Communists had pulled back. Advancing United Nations forces made little contact with Communist troops. An armistice and a non-Communist political unification of the country were in sight. The United Nations planned to discuss the situation on November 8.

On November 7, however, MacArthur's command announced that border flights were no longer banned and that targets along the Yalu would now be attacked. American voters went to the polls, and American bombers went to the city of Sinŭiju and destroyed it with 630 tons of bombs. Sinŭiju was at the mouth of the Yalu, across from Antung, and regarded as sensitive by Communist China (U.S. airplanes had drawn antiaircraft fire from across the border there before). The American raid included Yalu River bridges at Sinŭiju. Two days later MacArthur hit them again, along with another span near a hydroelectric facility. The next day American bombers struck another Yalu River city. U.S. air crews repeatedly crossed several miles into Chinese air space, directly violating orders issued to MacArthur, orders that reflected not only the desire of his superiors in Washington but the unanimous insistence of all United Nations members that had forces under MacArthur's command.

I. F. Stone described the situation aptly: "Let Americans think for a moment how they would react if the armies of another great power from across the seas were crushing a Mexican government friendly to the U.S.A., strafing Texas border towns, and operating under a general who threatened war against the U.S.A. itself."[42] Add to that Truman's November 30 statement that the general, who had a reputation for exceeding orders, could use atomic bombs at his discretion.

MacArthur twice scheduled a major offensive to start on the days that peace talks were to begin. He first planned to open an attack on November 15, which had been set for weeks as the opening of talks with Communist China at the United Nations. The Chinese delegation, however, postponed its arrival until November 24. MacArthur postponed his offensive until then.

Although the military rationale for this offensive was unclear, MacArthur may have intended to provoke a Chinese response in order to receive permission to expand operations into China. This prospect was viewed with excitement by Chiang Kai-shek's supporters, a group that certainly included MacArthur.

Although this permission never came, the Chinese Communists did. In December 1950 MacArthur's thrust to the Yalu was stopped and reversed by the Chinese. MacArthur refused to admit his offensive had failed. Instead, he made the astonishing claim that an offensive had never been intended, that he had merely sent his entire army to the Yalu on a reconnaissance mission, and the mission was being pulled back after succeeding in locating the Chinese.[43] To the press he complained that his reconnaissance mission had been halted and turned around by the Chinese Communists because Washington officials had restricted his military actions.[44]

Soon after Christmas 1950, the Pentagon asked MacArthur what steps he recommended. He replied that the choices were either to devastate Communist China or to abandon the Korean peninsula. He said that if he were not allowed to take the war to China, the United Nations forces in Korea would be destroyed.

Two members of the Joint Chiefs, generals Hoyt Vandenberg and J. Lawton Collins, immediately flew to Tokyo to confer with MacArthur and then went on to Korea for a personal inspection. In Korea they were astonished to find that, contrary to MacArthur's reports, the United Nations forces were secure and in no danger of being run out of Korea. This discovery was heartening but flabbergasting. It meant MacArthur either did not know what he was talking about or was lying. Either way, the Joint Chiefs now realized his judgment could no longer be trusted.

And that meant MacArthur would be dismissed, perhaps not immediately, but inevitably. His vexing behavior had been tolerated because he was considered a military genius, and his antics were the price of getting his battle skill. With the realization in Washington that MacArthur's military ability could no longer be trusted, he became just a querulous old man. The next time he caused trouble, none of his superiors would argue that his services were still required.

Truman was astounded in mid-March to receive intercepts of messages by Spanish and Portuguese diplomats reporting conversations with MacArthur in which he virtually vowed to widen the Korean War, with the intention of destroying the Chinese Communist regime via atomic weapons—even if that brought the Soviet Union into the war.[45]

Then, in late March, the Joint Chiefs recommended to MacArthur that he make no advance north of the 38th parallel because Truman was about to announce a diplomatic peace initiative. On March 24, 1951, MacArthur publicly declared that China was incapable of defeating United Nations forces and that his command could defeat China if the United Nations chose to do so. MacArthur offered to meet the enemy commander-in-chief to arrange an armistice. MacArthur's announcement soured the diplomatic atmosphere so badly that Truman abandoned his peace initiative.

Truman's ire was much the greater because MacArthur's statement was made in contradiction of a standing order—directed specifically at MacArthur—that all government personnel obtain advance clearance from the Defense or State departments on public statements relating to military operations or diplomatic matters. Following MacArthur's challenge to China, Joint Chiefs chairman General Omar Bradley repeated the standing order.

At the start of April MacArthur publicly charged that Washington had prevented him from arming more South Koreans and that Washington was allowing political considerations to interfere with his military prerogatives. In response to U.S. House minority leader Joseph Martin's cry "If we are not in Korea to win, then this Truman administration should be indicted for the murder of thousands of American boys,"[46] MacArthur told Martin, "It seems strangely difficult for some to realize that here in Asia is where the Communist conspirators have elected to make their play for global conquest, and that we have joined the issue thus raised on the battlefield; that here we fight Europe's war with arms while the diplomats there still fight it with words. . . . As you point out, we must win. There is no substitute for victory."[47] Martin released MacArthur's comment on April 5, 1951.

A stream of foreign diplomats descended on the State Department to express alarm, while Americans frustrated with Truman were galvanized by the phrase "No substitute for victory." Those Americans, like Joseph Martin, were typically Republicans. Truman was well aware of MacArthur's Republican partisanship and presidential ambition—the two men had discussed the subject at their Wake Island conference—and this had to color Truman's perception of MacArthur's conduct. In the spring of 1951, the general privately admitted to General Edward Almond, "I have become politically involved," and said "I may be relieved by the President."[48]

Truman asked his senior advisers if the time had come to dismiss MacArthur. They all instantly answered yes. They had no hesitation because they had intimate knowledge of MacArthur's conduct, which involved more than his war against Truman administration policies. There were military grievances against him as well. He had withheld vital information requested by the Joint Chiefs, such as plans for the Inch'ŏn landing.[49] He had avoided insubordination only by twisting his orders almost beyond recognition, as in sending American troops toward the Yalu on the day of U.S. congressional elections. He had refused to accept responsibility when his campaign plans failed, as when he alleged that his failed November offensive was merely a reconnaissance mission. He took credit for the successes of his subordinates, such as General Matthew Ridgway's February 1951 offensive.[50] He had tried to force the Joint Chiefs to decide between the false alternatives of attacking Communist China or accepting defeat in Korea. Rather than making careful and objective reports of military developments, he had exaggerated and deceived to promote his desires. By April 1951 General of the Army Douglas MacArthur had proved himself wholly unworthy of public trust.

On April 11, 1951, President Truman relieved MacArthur as commander of United Nations forces in Korea and stripped him of all other authority—removing him as head of the military occupation of Japan and commander of the army's Far East forces as well. An uproar ensued. The public did not know what senior Washington officials had known about him since World War II. MacArthur's decade of manufacturing publicity for himself had made him a national hero. He returned to the continental United States for the first time since he had departed fourteen years earlier. He rode in parades and gave a triumphal speech to the U.S. Congress. To oppose MacArthur became unpatriotic: "The happiest group in the country," said Senator Richard Nixon, "will be the Communists and their stooges. . . . The President has given them what they have always wanted—MacArthur's scalp."[51] Always there was the slogan, "No substitute for victory, no substitute for victory."

By any rational standpoint, the Korean War was an American victory. The North Koreans had been repelled. The South Korean state had been preserved. Russia had not dared to intervene, and the Chinese had been pushed back. Yet Americans believed it was a defeat because MacArthur said it was. He said victory in Korea could not come without the destruction of Communist China, and Communist China still existed. MacArthur said victory had been prevented by politicians (that is, Democratic politicians) who had allowed the death and suffering to be for nought. The Republicans took up MacArthur's cry: the Democrats had prevented victory. The volume grew louder and louder as the 1952 presidential elections approached, and the people elected a Republican general, Dwight Eisenhower, who promised to go to Korea. The implication was that this general, the architect of victory in Western Europe during World War II, would at last win the Korean War.

In reality, when Eisenhower took office in 1953, he was determined to get United Nations forces out of Korea regardless of whether the result was called victory. Rhee's stubbornness in rejecting U.S. peace plans, opposition that occasionally seemed to express itself in attempts to sabotage peace talks, soon put the United States at loggerheads with South Korea. In June Rhee declared that his troops might leave the United Nations forces if a truce were signed. Skepticism thus arose about the ability of the United Nations to enforce a truce. Rhee also called for a formal military alliance between South Korea and the United States, an alliance requiring the United States to help conquer North Korea in ninety days unless Communist behavior satisfied Rhee. Four days before the armistice was signed, Rhee said that he would renew the war in ninety days even without American help.

U.S. secretary of state John Foster Dulles scrambled to convince the Communists that no double cross was intended. Both he and Eisenhower sent angry messages to Rhee, and General Maxwell Taylor, commander of the Eighth Army in Korea, dusted off Truman administration plans to overthrow Rhee by fomenting a coup.[52] The Communists decided to take a chance on American good faith and signed the armistice in July 1953. The war was over.

Traditionally the Korean War has been labeled a costly stalemate. That bitter evaluation, however, can be justified only if the purpose of war is viewed as the acquisition of real estate. If we examine it with a broader perspective, however, we can see a tremendous victory for Western cold warriors and a devastating loss for Communism.

All thought of dumping the odious Rhee and Chiang regimes disappeared. Instead massive American military support was pledged to defending the governments of South Korea and Formosa, and no skepticism existed about willingness to use that force. Any Chinese Communist dreams of consolidating Formosa with the mainland evaporated indefinitely. Not only the United States, but the United Nations, now stood behind Rhee.

Any movement toward American withdrawal from military bases in Japan now ceased. American bombers would remain poised on Japanese runways for swift strikes against the Soviet Union, and large numbers of American infantry would remain in Japan, ready for quick Asian deployment.

The Korean War helped push through a Japanese peace treaty allowing Japan to have guns and certifying it as an opponent of Communist China and the Soviet Union. In Europe the Korean situation was used to promote the rearmament of West Germany, a prospect dreaded by Russia.

In the United States, industry geared up for permanent wartime production, which would provide America with overwhelming matériel supremacy for decades. The Defense Department was further strengthened by enormous increases in budget and manpower, consolidating its position as a dominant factor in the national economy. Military aid to foreign states became routine American policy.

Thus, the Korean War ended with Communists in a weaker position around the world and provided a sweeping victory for American leaders who advocated harsh cold war policies. Few influential voices would question those policies any more. With opponents silenced, cold warriors would have free reign, unchecked by any need to defend their actions.

The Korean War was no stalemate. It was a triumph for those who sought conflict with the Communist world; a war fueled not by the Soviet Union and not by any threat to America's military security, but by Douglas MacArthur's dreams of martial conquest in Asia and by the cowardice of Washington officials who hesitated to tell him no.

XIII.

Southeast Asia

Below Korea is Southeast Asia, a vast region with natural resources that have brought wealth to Western corporations for many years. Its importance can be measured by the Dutch determination to hold onto their colony of Indonesia after World War II, when Holland's world empire had disappeared centuries before into history textbooks. The British flag still flew over the colonies of Burma and Malaya, and at the close of World War II the Philippines passed from Japanese hands back to the Americans, who had held the islands ever since taking them from Spanish control in the 1890s.

After World War II, each of these four lands experienced so-called Communist rebellions that had been nurtured by long histories of resentment against colonial exploitation. This chapter is about those rebellions—which the Communists lost every time. Additionally, in the case of Burma, we shall see how Cold War intrigues affected its relations with China.

PHILIPPINES

When the United States triumphed over Spain in the Spanish-American War of 1898, Spain turned over its colony in the Philippines to the Americans. After years of broken promises of Filipino independence, in 1932, the U.S. Congress passed a bill granting independence to the colony in 1946. The transition timetable was proceeding as planned until December 1941, when it was suddenly overturned by the Japanese invasion and occupation of the islands during World War II. In many Western colonies throughout Asia, the Japanese posed as liberators from European oppression and thus gained native support. This pose did not work as well in the Philippines, where the United States had demonstrated every intention of leaving and the Japanese demonstrated none whatsoever. Remnants of American military forces still on the islands after the defeat of General Douglas MacArthur were therefore able to ally with Filipinos in organizing guerrilla resistance against Japan.

Among the most effective was a guerrilla group known as the Hukbalahap (People's Anti-Japanese Army), more commonly called the Huks. They managed to wrest a number of districts from Japanese dominance, controlling them well enough to collect taxes.

The Huks were Communist inspired, the Filipino party having been founded with encouragement from Indonesian Communists in 1930. Although two of the party founders had received training in Moscow, the Huks were distinct from the Phillippine Communist party and were not a military arm of the party. Nonetheless the Huks are often characterized as Communists. The Huks got along poorly with American guerrillas and demonstrated a Balkan-like enthusiasm for fighting Filipino opponents during the war. After the war the Huks formed a political party, and in 1946 seven of their candidates were elected to the parliament. That body refused to seat the Huk members. Denied the opportunity to press their case democratically, the Huks began an armed struggle against the government.

In 1946 the United States granted independence to the Philippines as promised, leaving behind enormous supplies of military goods. These rapidly disappeared, some used as graft for officials, and some taken by the Huks. Ironically, the U.S. Army, not the Soviets, armed the Huks for a nearly successful Communist takeover of the Philippines. The Huk revolt was strictly a domestic phenomenon.

The postwar Filipino governments headed by Manuel Roxas and Elpidio Quirino rapidly earned the hatred of citizens. Soldiers who had fought against the Japanese were denied lawful back pay unless they gave a portion of it to assorted bureaucrats or agreed to promote ambitious politicians by working in their election campaigns. Many police officers were holdovers from Japanese rule and were resented. Government forces became notorious for harsh treatment of the peasantry. The rural population was alienated by military terror tactics aimed at eradicating the Huks, such as destruction of entire villages where Huks had found shelter. Such government conduct gained the Huks converts and sympathizers. Unlike ordinary citizens, the Huks, with their American arms, had the firepower to resist.

But the growing Huk strength was not simply the result of the people's anger at being victimized by the government's terrorist tactics. The Huks seemed to champion peasant rights against wealthy landlords. Citizens who needed simple types of help and received no response from corrupt bureaucrats were aided by the Huks. So the Huks received support not only as the government's opponents but as the people's proponents.

The dishonest national elections of 1948 indicated that Quirino feared he could not win an honest contest, and lessened his government's prestige among the populace. The Huks, however, were also losing popularity. As the government imposed harsh penalties on those helping the Huks, civilians withdrew their support. The guerrillas then resorted to terrorist tactics to coerce aid from the population. The Huks' brutality cost them the moral support of the people.

Anti-Huk efforts received a stunning boost in 1950 with the appointment of Ramón Magsaysay to the post of secretary of defense. He revitalized and cleaned up the government's military forces. He had earned solid credentials as an anti-Japanese guerrilla in World War II and used that knowledge to organize a military campaign that snuffed out the Huk movement in just four years. He also traced and arrested top Huk executives operating in Manila. The Huks never regained central leadership, and their units fell apart as coordinated effort disintegrated into random ineffective actions.

Magsaysay combined harsh military pressure with a generous rehabilitation program for Huks who surrendered. In effect, an amnesty existed for any Huk who gave up. The lack of penalty for previous Huk activity was made even more attractive by the opportunity to resettle on virgin land. The former guerrillas were accompanied by non-Huk settlers to create a diverse community of small landowners.

In protest against the Quirino government's corruption, Magsaysay resigned as secretary of defense in 1953. Later that year he was elected president. He then strengthened the Huk rehabilitation program and instituted land redistribution through government purchase of large estates that were then resold as smaller tracts. His land reforms eliminated the key Huk appeal: the Huks promised land redistribution if they gained power, but Magsaysay had already provided the land. The movement died out.

The resettlement program was accompanied by low-interest government loans to ease the burden of debt and to break the power of local private moneylenders. Magsaysay also encouraged farmers' cooperatives, developed roads for access to towns and markets, and promoted electricity and irrigation projects. His death in 1957 was a serious blow to the Filipino morale. He is remembered for his personal incorruptibility and passionate concern for his fellow citizens.

Ferdinand Marcos was the next Filipino president of importance to the story of Communism in the Philippines. He was elected in 1965 and turned out to be more like Quirino than Magsaysay. Marcos built a network of relatives, cronies, and allies for the distribution of political and economic favors. In the 1970s he abolished free and honest elections and joined the ranks of Third World dictators that we shall encounter in this book. The United States not only tolerated but encouraged the Marcos regime. One reason for American support was strategic—Marcos was willing to let the United States have large military bases in the Philippines, regarded as crucial for Pacific and Asian operations. In addition he was a militant anti-Communist and an equally enthusiastic promoter of American business enterprise in the Philippines.

Those latter two traits all too often find expression in policies designed to boost profits by monopolizing markets and exploiting laborers and consumers. Such policies under Marcos, combined with his disregard of political and human rights, ironically provoked the sort of Communist military threat that Marcos and the United States sought to deter. The Huks were gone, as was the Communist party of that era. But the oppression engendered by the corrupt Marcos regime encouraged the growth of the Communist New People's Army. Like the Huks, this new Communist organization was a domestic phenomenon, having no direct involvement with the Soviet or Chinese Communist parties.

The New People's Army (NPA) lacked foreign support and had a strength in 1985 of only about 12,000, less than 1 percent of the Filipino population. Yet it posed a serious challenge to the Philippine government. This was particularly striking considering the gross advantage the Philippine army had in numbers and weapons. The explanation must be found in the sentiments of the population.

The Communists pushed for social reform mainly in the countryside, where inequities were starker than in the cities. Workers were typically held in peonage by plantation owners—private security patrols monitored activity on plantation land and commonly controlled access to villages. Wages were low. A French journalist told the story of a wealthy planter's conduct. After a plantation hand died of starvation, several others asked for rice. The planter thereupon fired them.[1] Nor did workers dare seek higher wages. Throughout the Philippine countryside paramilitary death squads tracked down persons suspected of agitation against the status quo. Landlords and private warlords held sway. The Communists sought to break the power of those groups, called for people to have a right to control their own labor, and for the land of great estates to be distributed to peasants who could then become independent farmers. In the 1980s a sugar-cane worker said, "We just hope for bosses who are more honest, soldiers who don't point their guns at us and don't burst into our homes at dead of night. A plot of land for growing food. That's all."[2] Those are goals that Americans believe the United States represents. Yet in the Philippines of the 1980s, that is what communism was all about.

A Roman Catholic priest in the Philippines pointed to a key aspect in the rebellion: "Village people see no basic difference between Communists and Christians."[3] An Irish missionary in a Philippine Communist district agreed about the peasantry: "They'd like to live decently, but they know nothing of the class struggle."[4] Such observations are significant for two reasons. They illustrate a theme we shall often encounter, of oppressed persons who seek the benefits promised by democracy but support Communists because they seem to offer such promises. The churchmen's remarks also illustrate a related phenomenon that began to grow in the 1970s, an attempt by devout Third World Christians to reconcile their religious faith with communism. Until then Christianity and communism had been seen as enemies. The attempt to unite the appeal of Christianity and communism and to combine their power is a phenomenon hardly recognized, let alone understood, by makers of Western foreign policy. The impact, however, could become enormous in Third World countries with Christian populations.

By 1985 the Marcos regime was crumbling. Part of his decline can be attributed to the growing Communist rebellion that ranged from labor unrest to guerrilla warfare. A more important factor was the alienation of politicians and businessmen whom Marcos had excluded from his largess. In 1985 they called a truce to their intramural bickering and united on a single candidate, Corazon

Aquino, to represent them in presidential elections Marcos had called for early 1986. Like many other dictators, Marcos occasionally ran rigged elections to veneer his regime with legitimacy. Previously he had been able to count on a divided opposition handing him easy victories. To defeat his united opponents in 1986, however, Marcos had to resort to such blatant and raw electoral fraud that the nation exploded in protest, insisting that Aquino was the rightful election victor. The mass protest had backing from respected leaders in business, the judiciary, the Roman Catholic hierarchy, and—not unimportantly—the military. The switch of allegiance by key military leaders not only cost Marcos the ultimate tool of government authority but helped to keep the protests peaceful. There were no machine-gunnings or bombings of unarmed throngs.

Perhaps most importantly of all, the United States withdrew its support from Marcos. He had been a tyrant, but he had received American backing because there had been no non-Communist alternative to his regime. Now Corazon Aquino provided such an alternative, and she clearly had wide support in the nation. Soon after the United States announced that it opposed any use of force by Marcos against Aquino, Aquino became president of the Philippines through a peaceful coup in February 1986.

The advent of the Aquino government held no guarantee of an end to the Communist military activity. The NPA had been fighting against Marcos, but it was also fighting for a radical restructuring of power in Filipino society. Problems of social injustice were brought to Aquino's personal attention by delegations of activists, but they found her unresponsive. Neither she nor her officials challenged the social system that had created their personal wealth. Most members of her cabinet had declared annual incomes of over $100,000 and none had peasant or laborer origins. Corazon Aquino herself came from a wealthy landlord family—their Hacienda Luisita had 30,000 people living there, under the rule of a private security force. Upon taking office she said of leftist social reformers, "Thank God, they didn't help [the Aquino election and coup]. Now I don't owe them anything."[5]

Realizing that Aquino showed scant sympathy for the radical social transformation sought by the NPA, the guerrilla leadership demanded progress in this direction before agreeing to Aquino's call to end the insurgency. She replied that the NPA had no grounds to continue fighting now that Marcos was gone, and she vowed to use all the military force at her disposal if they refused to give up.

Unlike Magsaysay, however, Aquino offered the Communists nothing in return for ending their struggle—no land to farm, no place to live, no job to earn a living. When Communist representatives asked for at least a guarantee of personal safety if they surrendered, she told them to look to the insubordinate and harshly anti-Communist Philippine army for protection. Yet the military refused to disband the undisciplined Civilian Home Defense Forces and private warlord armies that fought the NPA and their civilian sympathizers.

Land reform even for non-Communists remained stalled under Aquino, with increasing complaints about favoritism toward big landowners allied with her regime. One chronicler of her government reported, "In South Cotabato, Mindanao, twenty-five corn-growing tenants who had gotten land on an estate were harassed, one shot to death, another injured, and ten ejected forcibly by armed goons hired by the owner. Witnesses identified the killers, but no arrests were made, nor did the government attempt to reinstate or protect the tenants."[6]

The initial Filipino exuberance prompted by the fall of Marcos became muted as the reality of Corazon Aquino became more apparent. She was, at best, lukewarm to reforming the social injustice that had helped undermine Marcos. She showed a dislike for unsolicited advice, and a streak of arrogance became evident in her—a political opponent meeting with her said he needed to consult with his associates, and Aquino thereupon broke off the meeting with the declaration, "I am the leader of my people, and I never consult."[7] A press report in 1988 spoke of her growing use of nepotism and her favoritism toward some of the same families who had allied themselves with Marcos when he ran the government. Senate president Jovito Salonga said in disgust, "We did not suffer fourteen years of the Marcos dictatorship only to see the return of the same practices."[8]

If the Aquino government seeks to base its power on the strength of wealthy businessmen rather than the power of the people, the appeal of Philippine Communism is unlikely to decline.

U.S. secretary of state George Shultz and others hailed Corazon Aquino's accession to power as a victory of the democratic process. Perhaps it was a victory for freedom, but a national insurrection and military revolt are hardly democratic. Shultz and others confused freedom with democracy, a common error. Even the democratic process is not enough to promote democracy; in some societies the majority of citizens oppose democracy and would defeat it in a referendum. The core of democracy involves acceptance that each person has an equal right to happiness, and this acceptance is shown by the effort to give people more power over their lives.

BURMA

For many years Burma was the easternmost province of British India; it became a separate crown colony in 1937. England freed the colony in 1948, and Burma became an independent state squeezed between India and China.

Since Burma shares a border of several hundred miles with China, it is not surprising that the Chinese Communist revolution leaked into Burma. Although the Burmese Communists' military activity began with a flash in 1947, it disappeared in the 1950s. The Burmese government's army handled the job by itself, and no masses of volunteers from Communist China arrived in support of the quarreling Burmese Communists. It was a native Burmese operation from start to finish, though participants on both sides included residents of Burma who considered themselves Chinese.

A far greater threat to Burmese national security came from Chiang Kai-shek's Nationalist Chinese. About 10,000 of them fled to northern Burma in 1948 and 1949 as the Communists overran China. Chiang's men in Burma mounted guerrilla operations against Communist China for many years, apparently with American help. (Although published accounts explaining American aid to the Nationalists are ambiguous, there is no other logical reason for the CIA to have continually supplied the Nationalists with arms. If Chiang's forces were simply there to discourage Burmese rebellion or accommodation with Communist China, constant resupply would not have been necessary. Moreover, the Burmese would not have worried about retaliation from the Communist Chinese if Chiang's men were minding their own business within Burmese borders.) The Burmese government repeatedly demanded a halt to these military activities, which threatened to provoke Chinese Communist attacks on Burma or, perhaps worse, Chinese aid to Burmese Communist rebels, but Chiang and the United States disregarded Burmese sovereignty over its territory. Burma was also provoked by the banditry of Chiang's troops when they were not harassing Communist China, which resulted in combat between Chiang's forces and the Burmese national army.

In contrast, combat between the armies of Burma and Communist China was limited to minor action within a disputed border area in northern Burma along an extension of the McMahon Line from India. This was an old quarrel that arose long before any Communists arrived. Chiang Kai-shek's maps of China also showed the disputed area as Chinese. In 1960 the dispute was finally resolved when Communist China agreed to accept the McMahon Line as the border. This agreement was doubly important because the same line was a proposed border between China and India, but Communist China did not accept it as the Indian boundary. The Burmese had achieved a settlement that remained elusive to India. Burma was outraged that its diplomatic triumph might be swept away by Chinese Communist reaction to Chiang's American-supplied forces in northern Burma.

After the Burmese appealed to the United Nations to resolve the problem in 1953, most of Chiang's men were transported from Burma, but several thousand remained. They continued to be supplied by the United States for operations against Communist China. In the end Burma and Communist China mounted a joint action in 1961 that drove the Nationalists out of Burma and into Thailand and Laos. How ironic that Burma should have to join with Communist China in repulsing the forces of Chiang Kai-shek, which (according to Chiang) were protecting Burma from Communist China.

In the 1960s the United States paid the price for its high-handed behavior when the Burmese government under Ne Win moved away from neutralism and toward the left. Communist Chinese advisers and aid became more welcome than American, which was seen as a threat to Burmese independence.

Trouble eventually arose with China. Under the strict rules of Ne Win's police state, wearing Mao badges was illegal. Riots broke out when college students defied the ban in 1967, and the businesses of Chinese merchants in Rangoon were looted. Dozens of persons were killed. Burma's relations with Communist China soured as a result, but the situation was rectified by late 1970. Nonetheless an intermittent Communist insurgency developed along Burma's border with China and simmered into the 1980s.

After years of coolness toward the United States, including rejection of American military aid, Burma showed some receptiveness to the possibility of better relations with the United States in the 1980s, including talk of an agricultural aid program. Ne Win retired from government in 1981 but remained the real ruling power in the country as the 1980s progressed. Despite a willingness to listen to friendly overtures from the United States, Burma was hardly a friend of America.

MALAYA

Down the Malay Peninsula a few hundred miles south of Burma is Malaya. European colonial powers contended for dominance here, not only because of the natural resources, but because of Malaya's strategic command of the Strait of Malacca, through which much of the world's maritime commerce passed. Britain took control of Malaya in the nineteenth century and the area remained part of the British empire until it joined with Singapore and two Borneo states in 1963 to form Malaysia.

In the 1930s the Malayan Communist party was prominent in agitating against British colonialism. When World War II broke out, Malayan Communists continued to cause problems for the British but abandoned efforts to harm the British war effort. Although Communist parties in some countries promoted aid to Britain because of its alliance with Russia, the change in Malayan Communist policy occurred long before the two European countries allied. It was prompted by the Chinese Communists in response to the Japanese invasion of China. Then, as later, the core of Communist support in Malaya was from expatriate Chinese. Moscow had little say, let alone control, over Malayan Communist activity.

By the late 1940s Malayan Communists had gained prestige as opponents of both the British and of the Japanese, who had occupied the peninsula during the war. The Malayan Communists' experience in political agitation and military combat, combined with strong popular support, gave them a marvelous opportunity to take over the government in 1945, before the English came back. Yet for no clear reason the Communists refrained from doing so, a restraint inconsistent with any Communist plan for world conquest.

Instead, three years later Malayan Communists began an armed rebellion. It has been suggested that they did this on orders from Stalin. If Malayan Communists were taking orders from any outside element, however, it was more likely from their Chinese brethren, who had a demonstrated record of independence from Moscow.

Regardless of whether Malayan Communists took orders from the outside, the revolt itself was prompted by local activists and fought only by native guerrillas. Throughout the next twelve years of fighting, the Malayan Communists remained self-sufficient, with Communist bloc help limited to rhetoric.

The Communist rebellion in Malaya has been aptly described as "a relentlessly waged contest of guns, knives, bows and arrows, wits, endurance, and patience."[9] Even where the Communists had little popular support, whole divisions of British Commonwealth soldiers were needed to put down the revolt (in stark contrast to the situation in Burma).

Perhaps the most effective anti-Communist military tactic was the destruction of villages where Communist guerrillas had found friendly aid. Residents were relocated at gunpoint into so-called new villages bearing a remarkable resemblance to concentration camps, complete with guards and barbed wire. These security measures were used both to keep residents in and keep guerrillas out, so that the villagers would not help the insurgents.

British-led forces took twelve years to put down the Malayan Communist rebellion, completing the job around 1960. Their success was not, however, testimony to the use of determined military measures to prevail over such an insurgency. The West won in Malaya with a three-pronged approach that can be summarized as security, offensive, and victory.[10]

The security prong had both civil and military aspects. Local officials received motivation and support to enforce decisions of the central government. The accompanying military strategy was to break up large insurgent commands into smaller units, rendering the guerrillas more inefficient because they lacked coordination as well as concentrated manpower and firepower.

The offensive prong exploited the fact that trained military units can defeat guerrillas in battle if the military knows when and where to find them. To obtain this information, intelligence sources were cultivated among persons from whom the insurgents extorted aid. Sometimes the government cultivated such sources with negative techniques, such as threatening a villager with prosecution if cooperation were not forthcoming. Other times positive methods were used, with individuals and entire tribes receiving monetary rewards for betraying the guerrillas.[11]

The victory prong consisted of competent honest civil government to meet the needs of the people. If such needs are met, an insurgency will fail.

Tough military pressure against the guerrillas was accompanied by bribery. The Malayan government literally paid the Communist rebels to stop, one at a time, until nearly the whole guerrilla force had been bought off with amnesty, money, and food. Such generosity gave the insurgents every reason to abandon their harsh lives as hunted prey in the jungle. Guerrillas who surrendered would tour areas where they had been active, extolling their new lives and serving as living proof of lenient treatment.[12]

The success of bribery—one of the oldest known political solutions—demonstrates the lack of idealistic zeal in the Malayan Communist guerrilla rank and file. They were motivated by self-interest—one of the most powerful motivating forces—in search of a few basic necessities. Once those were provided, enthusiasm for fighting evaporated.

This important lesson has been repeatedly proved and ignored. The average Communist revolutionary fighter cares little about ideology. He or she is fighting for something easily comprehended by Americans—food, shelter, the right to receive the fruits of labor. More attention to these elementary human necessities could substantially reduce the apparent necessity for massive American military power around the world.

INDONESIA

The Communist experience in Indonesia was unusual. Although Communists were a revolutionary force, the head of state eventually embraced and encouraged them. Then, despite their officially sanctioned status, a status that allowed them to grow and become one of the largest Communist parties in the world, the movement suddenly collapsed almost overnight. Nothing like the Indonesian experience has happened elsewhere.

As the twentieth century began, Indonesia was a Dutch colony called the Dutch East Indies. The Communists who appeared there after World War I were social reform activists, a small splinter group that emerged from the Sarekat Islam (Islamic association) of Muslim nationalists defending small businessmen. Such origins must have seemed strange indeed in Moscow, which promptly labeled the Dutch East Indies Communists heretics after a small revolt failed.[13] These local Communists had no help from the outside.

Indeed, although they used the name Communist, they had virtually no interest in what we think of as communism. Instead they were simply one of several groups agitating against Dutch colonial rule. The brief Communist revolt that the Dutch crushed in 1926 should be viewed in the context of numerous native rebellions that the Dutch smothered over a period of centuries, rather than as an example of Communist struggle for world domination.

During World War II, General Douglas MacArthur's headquarters in Australia transported Communists from New Guinea to fight underground against the Japanese in the Dutch East Indies. MacArthur, not Moscow, sent Communist agents to the Dutch East Indies. There, they found themselves facing a canny nationalist named Sukarno, who urged the defeat of the United States and Britain in World War II and who helped the Japanese round up slave labor. In 1945 Sukarno declared Indonesia's independence. Though the Communist Party was legalized, it was different and distinct from Sukarno's nationalists.

Sukarno's Indonesian republic faced harsh military opposition from Holland, which viewed Indonesia as covetously as Hitler had viewed Holland. In autumn 1948 the Netherlands had Sukarno's forces hard pressed. Suddenly the Indonesian Communists attacked Sukarno's forces as well, hoping to take over the rebel government and thus be the leaders of Indonesia if the war for independence succeeded. The Communists, however, began with little popular support and lost what little they had by their atrocities.

Sukarno's army defeated the Communists in a couple of weeks. Nonetheless, the challenge had come at a very serious moment and could have led to a Dutch victory. After Indonesia won the war for independence in 1949, the officer corps never forgot the Communist betrayal. The Indonesian military thus became and remained a powerful opponent of Indonesian Communists.

Although the Communists would grow politically powerful in the Sukarno regime, they realized that the Indonesian armed forces would never allow a Communist government. This background conflict may not have been apparent to Western observers who emphasized Sukarno's Communist sympathies, but it was a crucial aspect of Indonesian politics.

Right after Indonesia became independent, the Kremlin attacked Sukarno as one of the "Nehrus . . . and other feeble-minded bourgeoisie of the East."[14] Sukarno had just led a revolution overthrowing an oppressor who had held sway over Indonesia for centuries, but the Soviet message was that he ought to leave the anti-imperialist struggle to Communists, who understood how to do it.

Sukarno was statesman enough to ignore the insult if magnanimity would be profitable. In 1956 Indonesia signed a big Soviet trade deal that yielded imports of Russian military goods. This alarmed the U.S. Central Intelligence Agency and State Department, which seemed unaware of the Indonesian army's hostility toward Communists. Within a couple of years, the CIA began working to overthrow Sukarno.[15] He knew about these attempts, which further alienated him from the West. A key CIA operative in these efforts was Benigno Aquino, who allowed his family's gigantic Hacienda Luisita plantation to be used as a Philippines training base for anti-Sukarno rebels. Apparently Benigno Aquino also acted as a go-between in American efforts to instigate an army coup against Sukarno.[16] Aquino's widow, Corazon Aquino, later became president of the Philippines.

The U.S. State Department began portraying Indonesia as a state leaning toward Communism under Sukarno, a portrayal that helped promote that very result. For instance, in 1958 Indonesia attempted to make a multimillion dollar purchase of weapons from the United States but was turned down. Indonesia then found eager vendors behind the Iron Curtain. The U.S. State Department responded thus: "We regret that Indonesia turned to the Communist bloc to buy arms for possible use in killing Indonesians who openly opposed the growing influence of Communism in Indonesia."[17] Of course, the weapons *possibly* had any number of other purposes. Indeed U.S. secretary of state John Foster Dulles soon explained that the military goods were more likely intended to fight the Dutch in West Irian, an operation conducted by the *anti*-Communist Indonesian army. But the American people were left with the impression that the Communist bloc was Indonesia's first choice for military aid, when in fact America had been the first choice. And the American government gave its people a misleading reason for why Indonesia wanted the weapons. Nor were Americans told that Indonesians who openly opposed Communism included CIA-supported rebels attempting to topple the government. With duplicity and the cold shoulder, the United States managed to push Sukarno ever more leftward, creating a self-fulfilling prophecy of growing Communist influence in Indonesia.

The State Department comment about the alleged purpose of the arms deal failed to point out a second crucial fact: the Communists appeared to be Indonesia's biggest political party, and they appeared likely to win the 1959 general elections. They would form the government, becoming the world's first freely elected Communist regime. In Indonesia, the Communist party appeared to be the people's choice.

The Indonesian officer corps, remembering the betrayal of 1948, was adamantly opposed to a Communist government. The army demanded postponement of the elections, and Sukarno acceded to this demand with alacrity. In 1959 Sukarno, backed by the army, abolished parliamentary democracy and replaced it with an authoritarian state.

The next year Sukarno made a gesture toward dealing with a problem chronic to countries in which Communists find support—land reform. But it was a gesture only, and breaking up large land holdings into small parcels for peasants was intentionally slow. The peasants, impatient with the situation, organized into groups and began implementing the reform themselves, bypassing the government officials in charge.

This peasant-led land redistribution was in opposition to the Indonesian Communist party, which was cooperating closely with the Sukarno government. Thus Indonesian Communists compromised a classic Communist goal in order to maintain influence in the government.

Their willingness to compromise had more to do with the weakness of the party than with anything else. On the surface, the Communist party in Indonesia was very strong. Its huge membership was in the millions, the biggest party outside Russia and China. Russian armaments were flowing into the country. Sukarno had virtually anointed the party's chief, Dipa Nusantara Aidit, as his successor and addressed mass Communist rallies with the cry, "Go ahead! Onward, onward, onward, never retreat."[18]

But although the Indonesian Communists were certainly in a comfortable situation, they were not in a commanding position. The Indonesian party apparently did not limit itself to active militants. Many members, perhaps a great majority, joined for access to social activities and intellectual discussions—in other words, to have a good time.[19] Membership did not necessarily signify interest in party goals.

Moreover, the Russian arms were not going to Indonesian Communists, but to the staunchly anti-Communist Indonesian army. The Communists had been pushing for a Communist militia, but the army had stymied that effort. Thus, the arms, contrary to U.S. State Department implications, were not going to Indonesian Communists nor was the Sukarno government using them mainly to fight anti-Communists. Indeed, the Indonesian army would use its Russian arms to destroy the Indonesian Communist party and its hapless nonpolitical members.

The party was well aware that its massive membership was no indication of revolutionary strength and that an appeal to the people would therefore fail if a showdown with Sukarno ever occurred. The party was also well aware of the army's hostility. Given these factors, Sukarno became the key to Communist power. The Communists were willing to risk alienating the people by compromise on central goals such as land reform in order to curry Sukarno's favor, in hopes of gradually taking over the government from within.

Ironically, then, despite the outward appearance of overwhelming strength, the Communist position in Indonesia was really dependent on the caprice of one man—Sukarno.

Like most dictators Sukarno did not welcome opposition. Although the Indonesian army was hardly an adversary, it was a powerful independent force that failed to support him unconditionally. Determined to forge a more compliant military, Sukarno in 1965 plotted with the Communist leadership for a violent purge of the officer corps.

Once again, desire and necessity prompted the Communist leaders to do Sukarno's bidding. They wanted to eliminate the main anti-Communist force in Indonesian government anyway, and since the Communists' power in government depended on maintaining Sukarno's favor, they could hardly afford to turn him down. If offended, he could just as easily plot with the military against the Communists, as he had in 1958 when he cancelled the elections that the Communists seemed sure to win the next year.

When the Communists made their move, they were not trying to overthrow the Sukarno government. They were trying to strengthen the Sukarno government by eliminating his enemies. This was not an attempt at revolution—quite the opposite.

It was a bloody botch. Militant Communists killed several generals in a carefully coordinated plan, but enough senior officers survived to rally the military and fight the Communists. The surviving officers included men who had fought the Communist coup attempt in 1948, men with bitter memories and harsh tempers who did not apply themselves gently this time.

A low estimate of Communist deaths is 70,000; other estimates reach 2,000,000. It seems unlikely that the military could have killed as many as 2,000,000 people in the short time required to suppress the rebellion. Nevertheless, by the time the Indonesian army was done, the Communists no longer exerted much influence on Indonesian government.

We must remember that "Communist deaths" refer to many of the nominal nonactivist members in addition to the smaller number of true militants. This is not to say the slaughter was arbitrary, however. Typical victims were rural peasants who had gained plots of land during the period of agrarian reform. Now the army killed them and gave the land back to the previous owners.

How ironic the Indonesian situation was. The world's third largest Communist party had only casual support from its largely nonpolitical members. It tried to slow attainment of classic Communist goals such as land reform and labor organizing. "Communist" peasants (and their families) died because they participated in a program that the party was hesitant about. The "Communists" were killed because of their "anti-Communist" land reform activity. The party sought power not by cultivating the strength of the people, but by cultivating the favor of one man, a dictator who frustrated the Russians as much as he frustrated the Americans. The influx of Russian arms went to the *anti*-Communist military, which used them to destroy the Communists who battled in support of the Sukarno government.

And what of Sukarno? The army let him live but removed him from office the next year. His replacement was Lieutenant General Suharto, who had fought for the Dutch and for the Japanese. Suharto's military regime remained in power during the 1980s.

The Suharto regime was anti-Communist but hardly a good neighbor. In 1975 Indonesia conquered East Timor (formerly under Portuguese control), reportedly killing nearly one-third of the 650,000 residents. In the years after the seizure, Suharto kept journalists out of the area. In the mid-1980s Indonesian military operations against Papuans resisting Indonesian control in Irian Barat (West Irian) created thousands of refugees who fled to Papua, New Guinea.

Yet Suharto, this conqueror who fought for the Japanese in World War II and who presided over hundreds of thousands of deaths after he became Indonesia's leader, was lauded by British prime minister Margaret Thatcher and U.S. president Ronald Reagan, as if a mere anti-Communist, by definition, is praiseworthy regardless of his behavior.

We have examined the situation in two of the great countries of Southeast Asia and two of the smaller ones. In no case did we find a world Communist conspiracy operating. But there was much evidence of American support of anti-Communist dictatorships, no matter how corrupt. We will again examine the question of a world Communist conspiracy in later chapters covering other Southeast Asian countries, such as Vietnam. First, however, we shall examine the situation in a nation that produced a great Communist theoretician, a land that became filled with revolutionary turmoil, and yet found a middle way of existence that confounded both the capitalist and Communist worlds.

XIV.

The Challenge of India

Three of the most important men in modern Indian history were Mohandas (Mahatma) Gandhi, Jawaharlal Nehru, and M. N. Roy. The first two names are well known in the West. Rather few Americans, however, have heard of Roy. Yet he was an important figure not only in Indian history, but in international communism.

M. N. ROY

Born in 1887, Manabendra Nath Roy led an exotic life; he was a terrorist and arms smuggler with a taste for high living, wanted by women and major police agencies around the world. British Intelligence described him as "a dangerous enemy of capitalism, landlordism, and imperialism."[1] Nonetheless, he possessed a powerful intellect and educated himself well enough to one day challenge Lenin in complex arguments of communist theory.

Roy's journey from Bengal to Moscow included many months spent in California and Mexico City, where he enthralled leftist intellectuals and wealthy persons who were fascinated by Indian culture. As the 1920s began he organized a six-member Communist party of Mexico in order to become a delegate to the Comintern in Moscow.

During his years in Russia in that decade, he debated revolutionary doctrine with Lenin. Lenin urged that Communists should support bourgeois nationalist independence movements in the

Third World, such as China's Kuomintang. Roy disagreed, arguing that such movements might favor political independence, but they failed to advocate social change. Therefore, if they achieved power, the result would merely be a change in governmental personnel rather than a revolutionary transformation of society. Roy lost the argument in international Communist leadership circles, but the ill-fated Russian cultivation of Chiang Kai-shek and the Kuomintang in the 1920s soon proved Roy right.

Lenin also claimed that no significant proletarian groups existed in the Third World, so Communists had no choice but to support bourgeois nationalists in the struggle against European colonial powers. Roy again disagreed, believing that such groups indeed existed and should be nurtured and strengthened. Again events in China, this time involving Mao Tse-tung, soon proved Roy right.

The core of Roy's challenge to Lenin was the argument that world revolution had to spread from colonial lands to their European oppressors; therefore, Communists should concentrate on liberating the Third World. Lenin believed the opposite, that the workers of Europe must rise first and overthrow their governments; freedom for colonies would then follow. In this case, later historical experience seemed to favor Roy to the extent that Communist regimes established themselves in the Third World without significant help from European workers.

Roy articulated the theoretical basis that Chinese Communists would later use to claim leadership of the world Communist movement. His persistent challenge to Soviet Communist dogma played a role in his 1929 expulsion from the Comintern despite his unlikely, but apparently genuine, close personal friendship with Joseph Stalin.

In 1927 Roy made contact in Moscow with Jawaharlal Nehru. Nehru was a top official of the Communist-front organization, the international Congress of Oppressed Nationalities (not to be confused with the non-Communist India National Congress), but was not a Communist himself. Unlike the expatriate Roy, Nehru worked on the scene in India against British rule, and he was in Moscow merely on a brief visit. Although Nehru's father once claimed that the main distinction between the Congress party and the Indian Communist party was that the former renounced violence, there was a more crucial dissimilarity.

Jawaharlal Nehru argued that political independence was the main goal, with social reform to follow afterward. This was the very point on which Roy had challenged Lenin himself; Roy and Nehru soon became opponents. Roy and Gandhi, Nehru's mentor, therefore clashed as well—indeed, Gandhi regarded Roy as his toughest enemy. The conflict was fought amidst the harsh Indian political scene after Roy returned to his native land. Expelled from the international Communist bureaucracy and eliminated from Indian politics (in the 1930s and 1940s, Gandhi and Nehru and the Congress party—not the Communists—led the revolution against Britain), Roy retired from battle but remained prominent on the Indian intellectual scene.

REVOLUTION IN INDIA

Since czarist times Russia and England had been rivals in this part of the world, challenging each other in Iran, Afghanistan, and India. Governments came and went in both imperial powers, but the great game remained.

In the 1920s Russian diplomats in Afghanistan were funding Indian agitators such as Ghulam Hussain, who started the Indian Communist newspaper *Inquilab*. This Soviet activity was simply for harassment value, with no grand plan in mind. Historian E. H. Carr found that the situation in 1921 showed "no organized campaign against [the British control of] India was within the scope of Soviet policy."[2] In 1927 Indian revolutionary Shaukat Usmani learned that Soviet Politburo member and Comintern chief Nikolay Ivanovich Bukharin "did not at all favor the idea of giving any aid to the Indian revolutionaries. . . . I knew it was no use seeing Stalin on military aid to India."[3]

World War II brought a truce to the old British-Russian rivalry. Unlike Nehru's Congress party or the Muslim League, the Indian Communist party vigorously supported the British effort to drive Japanese forces from India. This, of course, reflected Russia's desire to cooperate with England during the war. The spirit of cooperation continued after the war. In stark contrast to traditional Soviet policy, which called for liberation of European colonies, Russia avoided opportunities to inflame the Indian independence movement.

The Indian Communist party, however, soon resumed agitation when the war ended. At times the Communists seemed more intent on terrorist attacks against Nehru's Congress party than against the British, who freed the colony in 1947. Nehru became the country's first prime minister.

COMMUNISTS AS WARRIORS AND POLITICIANS

In the next year, several districts of India passed under Communist control. As so often happened elsewhere, in India one of the most powerful Communist incentives was to distribute land to peasants, thus pleasing the population and giving them a personal stake in defending Communist control of the region.

The Communists then made a big mistake. If, in 1948 they had concentrated on liberating the countryside from control of native aristocrats, the Communists might have been able to build considerable momentum. Instead, they supported the nizam of Hyderabad, the state's aristocratic sovereign, who opposed unifying his semifeudal princely state with Nehru's India. The nizam, reputedly one of the world's wealthiest men, achieved an odd alliance with the Communists, who were fellow opponents of the Nehru regime and who mounted a local guerrilla war against the national government. Nehru had an army, however, and his talk of peace and brotherhood did not preclude him from defending his position with bullets. His forces promptly took control of Hyderabad, and the region was united with his national government. Nehru's military sharply reduced, but did not extinguish, the Communist guerrilla insurgency there.

Forces of social justice generated whatever popular support the Communists enjoyed. Thus, although Nehru's troops severely limited Communist power, the challenge was never eliminated, even though the Communists frittered away much of their support with aimless violence. They did retain some popular support, enough to win the Kerala state elections in 1957. Their election dismayed both the West and the Communists.

The West was stunned that Communists could win a fair election in a democratic country. The Communists' success diminished the claim that Communists were so unpopular that they had to rely on force to achieve and keep power. It was unsettling to realize that Communists could compete on the West's own terms in free elections and win, thereby demonstrating that Communists stood for something that reasonable men could believe in.

The Communists found themselves in a peculiar position. They had to abandon a lot of standard antigovernment rhetoric because they now ran a major subdivision of the government, one of India's most densely populated states. In addition, the chronic protestors now were responsible for solving the problems they had protested. Sadly for the Communists, their government soon demonstrated it could be as corrupt and incompetent as any other kind.

Opponents immediately exerted pressures to bring down Kerala's Communist government. Riots erupted. The state's economy worsened. Finally India's president Rajendra Prasad, citing a loss of law and order, dissolved the Kerala government in 1959. New elections were held the next year amid condemnation of Communist misrule, with anti-Communist parties united in a victorious campaign. Despite losing the election to a united opposition, however, the Communists received a higher vote total in 1960 than they did in 1957. They were even more popular with the people. They did not gain control of the state government, however. Control depended on the outcome of elections for seats in parliament, so it was possible to win the popular vote, yet not have a parliamentary majority (just as a person with the popular majority in a U.S. presidential election does not necessarily become the victor, depending on the vote of the electoral college).

The political situation then turned against Indian Communists in 1962 because of events that had been developing on the country's northern border for a dozen years.

STRUGGLE WITH CHINA

For centuries China had ruled Tibet, a mountainous region to the northeast of India. This relationship was formally recognized in the nineteenth century by Great Britain. Tibet served as a buffer state between British India and the Chinese empire.

The situation began to change at the start of the twentieth century when the Dalai Lama, who ruled in Tibet under Chinese sovereignty, established friendly relations with Czar Nicholas II. Britain became alarmed that Tibet might be transformed from a buffer state into a wedge of the Russian empire driven between India and China. The alarm, however, soon became moot when the czar lost the Russo-Japanese War in 1905. Russia's influence declined in the Orient and disappeared in Tibet.

Such European probing around Tibet disturbed China, which soon moved to take a stronger role in the area. Perhaps influenced by the revolutionary forces growing in China itself, the Chinese government embarked on reforming the feudal society of Tibet, attacking the power of lamas and monasteries.

The turmoil of Sun Yat-sen's 1911 revolution in China reduced Chinese power in Tibet. In a couple of years the Dalai Lama declared Tibet's independence. Although independence was recognized by Britain, China never accepted it. Both Chiang Kai-shek's nationalists and Mao Tse-tung's Communists continued to claim Tibet as part of China. As late as World War II, the United States government agreed that Tibet was an integral part of China.

When the Communist Chinese military occupied Tibet in October 1950, however, the Korean War was in progress. The act was viewed in the context of a supposed Communist plot to seize the rest of Asia, and America forgot its previous acceptance of centuries of Chinese rule over Tibet.

India's government felt that it had inherited assorted privileges granted to Britain in Tibet over the years, and therefore was disturbed by the renewal of *de facto* Chinese control in Tibet. India was not, however, distressed enough to support Tibet's request for United Nations action on the matter. Indeed, in 1954 India and China formally agreed that the latter could have sway over Tibet.

The Chinese Communists then pressed for a social transformation in Tibet, seeking to break the power of the nobles and lamas. The Communists viewed the smashing of a feudal society as a social duty, but Tibetans were unappreciative. A large revolt broke out in 1959. It was put down with dispatch, and the Dalai Lama fled to India. He was granted refuge, but the Nehru government forbade him from establishing a government in exile.

This diplomatic caution failed to mollify the Chinese, who accused India of having promoted the rebellion. China proceeded to take pieces of India's northern territory, with the Chinese Red Army directing light fire toward Indian forces in the area.

As in Burma, the controversy swirled around the so-called McMahon Line. And, as in Burma, this was inherently a Chinese (rather than Communist) concern. The Chinese under Chiang Kai-shek claimed the same territories for China (including Tibet) that Mao did. Although Taiwan rebuked Mao's methods, Chiang uncharacteristically made no complaints about Mao's goals in upper India. China was not encroaching on India's northern border because a Communist regime ruled from Peking; China was acting because at last it was again powerful enough to do so.[4]

In October 1962 China invaded northern India to settle the dispute by force. After about a month of vigorous conflict with Nehru's troops, the Chinese pulled back. Ironically, the only thing settled by the attack was a long-standing border dispute between India and Pakistan over the Kashmir region. Each feared the other would use the Chinese activity to gain untoward benefit in Kashmir, so India and Pakistan agreed on a border.

STRUGGLE AMONG COMMUNISTS

The Communist party of India operated mainly at the state level. Rather than having a tradition of tight control from a central national office, Indian Communists had a heritage of responding to local needs. This tended to fragment the party even in normal times, and the stress of invasion by a Communist state (China) nearly wrecked the party.

Indian Communists were already split ideologically between advocates of the Russian policy of peaceful coexistence and supporters of the Chinese call for military warfare against capitalists. This split was exacerbated by the party's November 1962 resolution condemning the Chinese invasion as aggression. The party's Chinese faction was not only incensed by the resolution, but was equally outraged when the resolution was followed by massive arrests of their members by the Nehru government—while members of the Russian faction were left alone. This favored treatment did the Russian faction little good, however, since India's other political parties mounted such an effective attack on the Communists that they virtually disappeared from the national political scene by early 1963.

In February 1963 the Communist party passed resolutions supporting the Russians in the Sino-Soviet ideological competition and reaffirming that the Chinese invasion of India had been aggression. This tore the party apart. It split in 1964, and afterwards India had two Communist parties, each claiming to be authentic. The Russian-oriented party was called the Communist Party of India, or CPI. The Chinese-oriented party called itself the Communist Party of India (Marxist), or CPI-M.

Despite the Communists' near demise after the 1962 Chinese invasion, and despite the 1964 split, subsequent election results showed that a core of support for Indian Communists remained. Around 1965 Communists once again did well in the Kerala state elections, becoming the largest bloc in the parliament. Opponents quickly acted to block Communist participation in the government by convincing India's president Sarvepalli Radhakrishnan to dissolve the parliament and proclaim so-called President's rule to govern the state, on the grounds that no single party had a parliamentary majority.

The two Communist parties together won about 9 percent of the vote in the 1967 national elections. Communists entered coalition governments in Kerala, Bihar, Punjab, Uttar Pradesh, and West

Bengal. In Kerala a Communist headed the government, and Communists became the largest bloc in the government of West Bengal.

In 1967 West Bengal's land revenue minister was a CPI-M Communist who promoted the traditional Communist goal of land reform. Unfortunately for him, that same year a Communist faction called the Naxalites, adhering to the Chinese doctrine of promoting violent conflict (in contrast to the Russian doctrine of peaceful coexistence with opponents), began a vicious guerrilla campaign against property owners in West Bengal. The killings soon broadened to include anyone in the Maoists' way, including CPI Communists who adhered to the Russian theory and were winning power through elections.

This situation of course made things awkward for Communist members of the West Bengal government. The state governor dismissed the government late in 1967—a blow to the influence of Communists who advocated a democratic path to power.

The West Bengali Naxalites, who were already a Communist splinter group, broke into eight more factions. This fragmentation hindered the guerrillas' effectiveness. As the 1970s began, thousands of these Maoists and their supporters were residing in jail. And, until the 1980s, no further armed Communist threats arose in India. Then, in the spring of 1987 the Naxalites made a dramatic reappearance, organizing an uprising of landless peasants in the state of Bihar. That situation was still unsettled when this book was written. Nonetheless, its origins appeared domestic rather than a product of foreign intervention. The fighting was in the form of riot by mob rather than ambush by small numbers of guerrillas, and the strife erupted after landlord agents killed several peasants.

India provided a challenge to both the Communist and non-Communist worlds. It produced one of the most articulate of Communist theorists, M. N. Roy, who disputed the basic strategies of Lenin. The nonviolent doctrines of Gandhi challenged revolutionaries around the world. And the neutralism of Nehru challenged the premises of the cold war. Communist China called him an imperialist puppet. Russia called him a lackey of British and American imperialism. The United States vilified him as immoral for advocating a middle way to peace and democracy, without taking sides. Judging from the vigor of denunciation from both East and West, maybe Nehru was on to something.

XV.

Decline of the Stalinist System: Poland and Hungary, 1956

Autumn 1956 saw major signs of East European discontent with the Stalinist system. Over the span of a few days Russia had to face major unrest in Poland and Hungary. This was a moment awaited by Western anti-Communists since the close of World War II. Russia realized this and took decisive action to preclude any opportunity for Western intervention. The West, in turn, demonstrated acceptance of Soviet interest in Poland and Hungary. The events occurred during a peak of international tension, however, and at the time no one knew whether the situation might escalate into world war.

HUNGARIAN RESTIVENESS

Problems in Hungary had already become acute a few years earlier, in 1953 after Joseph Stalin died. In June of that year strikes and civil disorders swept East Germany, overwhelming that government's ability to deal with the problem. Russian tanks were used to restore order. At virtually the same time, a series of major strikes broke out at industrial plants in various Hungarian cities, including Ózd, Diosgyőr, and in the Csepel suburb of Budapest. Peasant unrest also appeared. In June a Russian study concluded that Hungarian premier and Communist party chairman Mátyás Rákosi had devastated the Hungarian economy by imposing a pace of industrialization unrelated to the country's needs. For example, steel mills were constructed even though Hungary lacked deposits of iron and coking coal. The diversion of resources into such projects choked enterprises that had previously thrived under market demand: the manufacture of textiles, chemicals, optics, and precision instruments. Resentment developed when Rákosi decided to impose Russian-style collective farming. This program forced peasants, who had received land distributed from great estates in 1945, to give up their farms. Agricultural productivity declined as thousands of farmers abandoned their occupation. In 1953 the Russians found that fully 10 percent of Hungary's farmland lay abandoned. Food shortages contributed to the industrial unrest. In addition, the Russians concluded that Rákosi acted arbitrarily in the administration of justice, abusing blameless citizens.

If this is what the Soviets admitted to be the case in Hungary, one can imagine the full depth of the situation. Indeed, the Kremlin confronted Rákosi and other members of the Hungarian leadership and told them that a major revolt was imminent in Hungary. "They will chase you with pitchforks," Nikita Khrushchev said.[1]

When the disturbances spread to the countryside, Russia feared the situation would not respond to repression as it had in East Germany. Instead, at Soviet instigation, the Hungarian government gave workers a raise and gave the country a new premier, Imre Nagy.

Nagy's brilliant career inspired Communists around the world. He had solid Communist credentials, having served a loyal apprenticeship under Lenin, Béla Kun, and Stalin. Yet, somehow, through all these decades, Imre Nagy had not lost the idealistic vision that sometimes attracts young people to Communism. Most of those idealists either abandon Communism or abandon their vision, but Nagy was a stunning exception—a Communist leader with a compassionate heart.

Nagy acted decisively. He freed political prisoners, closed the labor camps, and put through various reform measures. And, as an expert in Communist theoretical writings, he continually disarmed critics by quoting Stalin and criticizing opponents as anti-Stalinist. Hungary led the way for a general, though uneven, diminution of the police state atmosphere in Eastern Europe.

By the spring of 1955, Nagy had delighted the people of Hungary and had enraged orthodox party leaders in Budapest and Moscow. Despite his agility at finding authority for his actions in the words of Stalin, Nagy's actions promoting governmental responsiveness to the people were not like Stalin's savage repression of popular sentiment. In 1955 Nagy was thrown out of the government, stripped of all party offices, and expelled from the party. Nagy was officially an ex-Communist, defrocked for heresy.

The new premier was Andras Hegedus, but in case the Hungarian people failed to get the message, party chairman Rákosi, the man who provoked the near-rebellion that Nagy had calmed, resumed his old power. He had remained party chairman in the Nagy period, eclipsed by the premier. Rákosi and his circle had schemed against Nagy all that time and had exploited Kremlin bickering to improve their position. One of Rákosi's key Russian opponents, Lavrenty Beria, had been killed in the Moscow power scuffle after Stalin's death. Nikita Khrushchev, the man who would eventually take Stalin's place in the power structure, had not yet solidified his victory in 1955. He had supported Nagy in 1953 but apparently could not afford to defend the Hungarian reformer when questions grew about Nagy's orthodoxy, lest it cost support in Kremlin intrigues.

Details of Kremlin politics are not well known, but they seem to have determined the changes in Hungarian leadership during 1955 and 1956. The subsequent actions of Rákosi and Nagy would be strongly influenced by their perceptions of Kremlin politics.

Assured of renewed Soviet support, Rákosi resumed his style of rule. The disastrous industrialization program was renewed. The standard of living, which had risen under Nagy, began to decline under Rákosi. The peasants whom Nagy had allowed to leave collective farming were forced to return by Rákosi. Harsh police repression was reinstituted, and even Communist party critics of Rákosi were silenced.

This oppressive way of life had caused much resentment once before. Now it was worse, because people had tasted a liberating alternative under Nagy and realized they were now losing something vital. By 1956 open talk of rebellion circulated among the populace. Police were seen selling an underground weekly newspaper harshly criticizing the government. Even the army became restive about obeying orders. People within the government itself considered challenging Rákosi's authority. In a July 1956 public meeting one person yelled at Rákosi, "You are guilty! You should resign!"[2] Such a rebuke to the head of a police state, known for his arbitrary actions against opponents real and imagined, was astounding. It reflected not only the depth of passion by July 1956, but also the government's growing impotence as its personnel and the population itself withheld support from a regime "neither feared nor loved."[3]

Russian concern about the discontent forced Rákosi from office in July, and he was replaced as party chairman by Ernő Gerő. Nagy remained in retirement, but a growing faction within the Hungarian Communist party called for his return to power. The situation became virtually a de facto two-party system. The Rákosi and Nagy factions agreed on many things and were not diametrically opposed in philosophy or goals, yet they strongly disagreed about the means by which communism should be promoted in Hungary.

Hungarian extremist reformers proposed illegal agitation, including the formation of independent trade unions, to press for the reinstatement of Nagy. Writers begain advocating freedom of the press. In September the official Writers' Association rejected the party candidates for leadership of the organization and chose non-Communists instead. In October students abandoned the Communist student organization and established a group independent of the party.

To Americans who are familiar with hundreds of professional and social groups, the establishment of a few in Hungary may seem unremarkable. But it was a grave situation for the government. It demonstrated not only that the Communist party was rapidly losing control of society, but that viable competitors existed. By definition, this meant that the authoritarian state was ending, which meant that Communist control of Hungary was ending. The Soviet Union was highly alarmed.

POLAND

As the events in Hungary were developing, the Soviet Union also faced a growing unrest in Poland, which was every bit as serious.

In October 1953, several months after Stalin's death, the Polish Communist party admitted that industrialization had been overemphasized to the detriment of consumer goods. The party promised the Polish people a rise in the general standard of living. Moreover, in the ensuing year the police state environment eased, with writers and intellectuals openly voicing discontent about the Communist regime. In 1955 the party began discussing the possibility of a Polish path to Communism separate from the Soviet example; this discussion was encouraged by a February 1956 Soviet Communist party endorsement of separate paths. An amnesty followed for tens of thousands of political prisoners in Poland—a happy event that was nonetheless a horrifying comment on life in Poland since World War II.

In June 1956 industrial workers at several enterprises in the city of Poznań became bold enough to stage a strike. Normally this would be portrayed as criminal and antisocial because in theory the workers already controlled business. Strikers would be considered malcontents and deviants to be shunned by all correct-thinking members of society. In a Communist state, a routine Western-style industrial action is an incredible act of defiance.

The Polish government failed in its attempt to label the strikers as selfish criminals. Working conditions in Poznań were similar to those elsewhere in the country, and the population readily recognized that legitimate grievances existed over wages and hours, in addition to other factors (such as food and housing) that were tied into the Poznań strike because of the pervasive government influence on the economy. Moreover, the Poznań events coincided with an international trade fair in the city. Western observers monitored the whole affair, from complaints underlying the protests to the violent suppression of the strike. At least 150 workers were arrested, accompanied by dozens of injuries and deaths on both sides.

Similar strikes erupted elsewhere in Poland. Rather than the nationwide crackdown that one might expect, the government instead made grudging efforts to remedy some of the grievances and to improve communication between labor and management. The men arrested in Poznań received light sentences, and the government admitted that the strikers had legitimate grievances.

Although the country was not in severe turmoil, there was much agitation as the Polish Communist party's Central Committee met in July 1956. This meeting demonstrated that two factions had developed in Poland, a group of hard-line Stalinists led by Zenon Nowak and reformers led by prime minister Józef Cyrankiewicz and party chairman Edward Ochab. Harsh debate erupted about whether reforms had gone too far or not far enough.

This debate was of particular interest to the Soviet Union, involving the same kinds of issues as in Hungary but with an added twist. If the reformers won in Hungary, everyone knew that power would go to Imre Nagy, a man with a sterling record of promoting friendship with the Soviet Union. In Poland a different sort of man waited in the shadows, Wladyslaw Gomulka.

Gomulka had been an active Communist during the Pilsudski dictatorship. In 1932 the police shot him while he was trying to avoid arrest, and the wound crippled him for life. He received a seven-year prison sentence in 1936. This incarceration saved him from being swept up in the Russian dragnet of Polish Communist activists in 1937 and 1938. Most, if not all, of these party loyalists were murdered on Stalin's orders, apparently to assure Russian control of any Communist activity in Poland. Gomulka got out of prison upon the 1939 German invasion and became an anti-Nazi underground leader. In 1943 he became first secretary of the Polish Communist party, and later he headed the postwar Communist regime.

In 1947 Gomulka became a prominent advocate of a Polish communism different from Russia's. He opposed collective farming, expressed doubts about Soviet plans to coordinate Eastern Europe's economy, tolerated Tito, and even tolerated the Roman Catholic Church. Gomulka repeatedly demonstrated a judgment independent from Stalin's. Unable to make Gomulka compliant, in 1948 and 1949 the Stalinists of the Polish Communist party stripped Gomulka of all government and party posts. Despite his official fall, his continued stature in the party and in Poland was demonstrated by the regime's hesitation to put him on trial for his offenses against Russia. Not until 1951 was he arrested, and even then he was spared brutal treatment in prison. He was released sometime between September 1954 and April 1955. He had never been brought to trial. He had never repudiated his advocacy of a Polish path to Communism. And now the government itself was talking about implementing Gomulka's policy.

The Kremlin sent two of its top men, prime minister Nikolay Bulganin and defense minister Georgy Zhukov, to observe and advise the July 1956 meeting of the Polish Communist party's Central Committee. Despite blatant Soviet opposition, the reformers won the debates. Poland would seek its own style of communism, apart from Russia's. With that basic decision made, everyone knew who would be called upon to lead the nation's effort. Cyrankiewicz began appointing Gomulka's allies to influential posts, and Ochab was ready to give his office to Gomulka. When leaders of a dictatorship are willing to turn over their power to a private citizen, that citizen is a remarkable person.

The call would not come for several months. As in Hungary, the pace of events in Poland increased. In September Polish workers set up independent councils that competed with the regime's official labor unions. These councils began to take part in management decisions. In September and October, the government reduced collective farming and increased efforts to produce more food, housing, and consumer goods. Workers, intellectuals, and youths called for free speech, a bigger role for parliament, and a decentralized economy. And, as in Hungary, more and more they demanded that a particular private citizen be brought out of retirement.

To the Kremlin, the world seemed to be falling apart. Was Poland reverting to its traditional hostile status? Was Hungary ready to join a new Little Entente, preparing to form a new *cordon sanitaire* around the Soviet Union? The West had been behind such a development in the interwar period—did incendiary broadcasts from Western radio stations mean it was happening again? Was Eastern Europe to become Russia's enemy once more?

This the Soviet Union could never permit as long as it had the strength to intervene. The history of the Soviet state demonstrated the hazard of enemies in Eastern Europe. The bottom line of victory in World War II had been to assure that these nations would be run by friends. For that purpose Stalin had struck deals with Churchill and Roosevelt. Soviet party chairman Nikita Khrushchev had to act—not only because the interests of the Soviet state required it, but because his own survival required it.

To some observers in the West, the Kremlin appeared to be a monolith that efficiently carried out orders from the all-powerful dictator at the top. But in reality it was riven with factions challenging one another for power. Some in the Kremlin noted that Eastern Europe had never rebelled in Stalin's time. Khrushchev's opponents and competitors would be eager to hold him responsible for this new trouble. Moreover, he appeared to be under heavy pressure from the military, with whom his relations were occasionally testy—Khrushchev seemed to have a peasant's skepticism about the army's interest in his welfare. As we shall see, there is evidence that the Red Army was ready to act without his orders. And that would have meant that the Communist party in Russia was losing control of the country, just what appeared to be happening to the Communist parties in Poland and Hungary.

The events of October 1956 were therefore the gravest challenge the Soviet state had faced since Hitler advanced toward Moscow in 1941, and the gravest challenge the Russian Communist party had faced since the civil war in the 1920s. The nation's fate now depended on the decisions Khrushchev made while his own fate teetered.

In Poland armed citizens were surfacing—some apparently armed as an emergency militia with government approval. The Soviet fleet was visible off the coast at Gdynia, Russian army units stationed in Poland were taking positions to encircle Warsaw, and other Soviet units were appearing in Russian and East German territory bordering Poland. There was every reason to believe the Polish army would resist invasion. Poland and Russia appeared ready to do battle again, as they had so often in the past.

In the face of this crisis, Khrushchev suddenly made a grand gesture: he went to Poland. On October 19 he arrived in the seething capital of Warsaw just as the Polish politburo at last called Gomulka out of retirement. Khrushchev was accompanied by other senior members of the Soviet politburo (or presidium): his enemies Vyacheslav Molotov and Lazar Kaganovich, his ally Anastas Mikoyan, and General Ivan Konev, commander of the Warsaw Pact forces and perhaps the most prominent member of the so-called Stalingrad group of military officers cultivated by Khrushchev.

The Russians met in seclusion with Gomulka and top Polish officials. The atmosphere was tense. Introducing himself, Gomulka reportedly told Khrushchev, "I am Gomulka, and because of you I have just spent three years in prison."[4] Khrushchev behaved in a blustery manner, partly because he had that sort of personality and partly to demonstrate his firmness to Russian colleagues—several blamed his de-Stalinization policy for unrest in Poland and Hungary.

The Russians opposed Gomulka's accession to power. When the Polish determination became obvious, Khrushchev rumbled darkly about the possibility of using military force to assure a friendly regime in Poland. Gomulka coolly proposed to go on the radio and tell the Polish people about Khrushchev's threats. This proposal was a formidable counterthreat since the Russian leadership would be in Polish hands during any disturbances.

The Russian and Polish leaders laid out their requirements, what each would have to permit and accept in order to resolve the situation peacefully. Happily, the demands and trade-offs were tolerable to both sides. Gomulka affirmed that Poland would continue as a Soviet ally in the Warsaw Pact (though he dared to demand reduction of Soviet military presence in Poland), and Khrushchev assented to Gomulka's domestic reforms: the workers' councils were to be recognized and strikes would be permitted, economic planning was to be decentralized, more private enterprise and private farms would be allowed, controls on free speech and travel to the West were to be loosened. Gomulka's liberalizations have been called a revolution by cold war historian John Lukacs and by Gomulka's biographer Nicholas Bethell, although the term seems to be an exaggeration. Nonetheless, the changes were significant enough that Roman Catholic Cardinal Stefan Wyszyński called for support of Gomulka. This extraordinary endorsement of a Communist government by a church prelate was indicative of how the Polish nation came together in this time of crisis, standing once again as Poles against Russians, as had happened throughout history.

Things did not work out quite so well for Hungary.

HUNGARY: THE FIRST SOVIET INTERVENTION

Popular agitation and support for Nagy prompted his reinstatement as a party member in October. The Rákosi faction hoped this action would satisfy and quiet the people. The Polish situation climaxed soon afterward, however, and Hungarian reformers were ecstatic about the outcome in Poland, where dissidents had forced the return of Gomulka. The turbulence in Hungary became unmanageable. An armed insurrection broke out in Budapest on October 23, and Gerő was unable to contain it. The army and the police began to defy government orders. Members of the military even helped arm and direct the revolt. The situation was more serious than the Polish problem had ever become.

There is a question, however, about whether the decision on Soviet military intervention was made at the proper level in either government. On the Hungarian side, the Russian troops were actually requested by the party chief, Gerő, not by the premier or cabinet. On the Soviet side, the request was accepted and implemented by General Tikhonov, not by any military or civilian authority in Moscow. Indeed, two members of the Soviet Communist party's presidium immediately stormed into Budapest to find out who was responsible for involving Russian troops in the Hungarian situation.

On the night of October 23/24, the political situation was as confused as the military one. Nagy had been biding his time in retirement, confident that his moment would come. His confidence was bolstered by his friendly contact with Soviet presidium member Anastas Mikoyan in recent weeks, demonstrating that Nagy was once again acceptable to Russia. In a confused all-night meeting of top Hungarian government and party officials, held against a background of street fighting and approaching Soviet military units, Nagy was named premier, with Gerő continuing as party chief.

Nagy refused to request Soviet military aid, leaving Gerő to take the blame for that action. The party leadership's anger over Russian intervention contributed to Gerő's expulsion from the party chairmanship the next day. His replacement was János Kádár.

The Russian intervention of October 24 has been called an invasion. This characterization is incorrect. Although Gerő's request may have deviated from correct channels, he was a legitimate authority figure in Hungary. And in the confusion during the changeover of Hungarian leadership in the early hours of October 24, the government made some type of official request for Soviet help (announced on the radio after daybreak) even though Nagy stood aloof. There can be no question that the internationally recognized sovereign power in Hungary asked for military aid from a friendly state. It was no invasion.

Moreover, Russian forces involved in this intervention were already in Hungary and had been for years. Two Russian divisions were garrisoned in Hungary under provisions of both the Potsdam Declaration and the Warsaw Pact. These forces were soon supplemented by additional Soviet units brought in from Romania and Russia, but the crossings were conducted as a normal peacetime transportation operation and were drastically hindered by Hungarian railroad personnel. The Soviets did not come across the borders with guns blazing.

Another important and often neglected point is that the Soviet troops were under Hungarian command. Russian officers took their orders from the Hungarian authorities who had requested their aid. Consequently, the level of fighting was light. In provincial areas, the Russians showed their presence but did nothing unless they were attacked first. In Budapest insurgents could simply keep out of the way as Russian tanks roared up and down the streets. No Soviet infantry arrived to do battle. The Soviet units were available for duty as designated by the Hungarian authorities, and Nagy, who had opposed intervention, designated no duties.

Consequently, members of the Russian forces spent a lot of time standing around, wondering what they were supposed to do. In Budapest quite a bit of fraternization went on between the Hungarian population and the Russian soldiers, many of whom had already developed friendly feelings toward Hungary while on garrison duty.

By October 25 the street fighting in Budapest had diminished so much that the Nagy government expected it to end that day. The government radio requested that people go to work as they normally would. Nonetheless, some peaceful throngs milled about the city. One of them formed into a march and headed for the parliament building to call for the removal of Gerő (who, unknown to the crowd, had already been replaced by Kádár). The mood was so genial that participants talked a few idle Russian tank crews into coming along. Persons on rooftops at parliament square witnessed the incongruous spectacle of two or three Russian tanks bedecked with Hungarian flags as they rumbled into the square, surrounded by hundreds of citizens chatting amiably with the crews standing in open hatches.

The persons on rooftops were members of the AVH, the notorious and hated secret police. The AVH and not the Russians or the Hungarian army had caused most of the casualties in the revolt thus far.

True to their reputation, the AVH began machine-gunning the throng from the roofs. The Russians thought it was an ambush by anti-Communist militants.[5] The tanks opened fire on the secret police as some members of the crowd huddled behind the Soviet armor for protection. Unsure of the situation, as hundreds of screaming people ran about with gunfire echoing from all directions, some of the Russians fired into the crowd as well. The massacre swiftly halted when the tanks silenced the AVH machine gunners, but not before scores were killed. Fatalities were estimated at between 100 and 200.

In the ensuing confusion, it was unclear that the Russian tanks had halted the killing. Instead, they were blamed for starting it. Moreover, the sight of Russian forces around the country inflamed native Hungarian patriotism more than it promoted socialist brotherhood. The Soviets had intervened only at the request of Hungarian authorities, and Nagy wanted the Russians to withdraw. They began evacuating the country on October 30.

The next day Nagy and Kádár met with Soviet presidium members Anastas Mikoyan and Mikhail Suslov in Budapest. The Hungarians reiterated the necessity of removing Russian forces in order to calm the situation. To reduce public antagonism against Russia, at this meeting Nagy also announced that Hungary was leaving the European Communist military alliance known as the Warsaw Pact. This would eliminate any legal pretext for Soviet forces to cross back into Hungary. Nagy emphasized that these moves lacked any hostility toward Russia. Quite the contrary, he was known for his lifelong advocacy of Hungarian-Russian friendship. Nagy believed that most Hungarians shared his feelings. In the early postwar years, coercion had been needed to back up the Hungarian regime while it replaced the old order, but in Nagy's view most Hungarians now believed in the social revolution. He was so sure of this that he took yet another radical step by abolishing the one-party state, although the Hungarian Communist party would remain preeminent.

For their part, Mikoyan and Suslov brought an official statement from the Soviet presidium acknowledging that mistakes had been made in Hungary and saying that Hungary was free to follow its own Communist path. Mikoyan and Suslov agreed that the program of Nagy and Kádár was sensible, and the two Soviet presidium members gave their assent on behalf of the Kremlin leadership. Already Khrushchev publicly talked of Hungary henceforth having the neutral status of Finland. Messages of support and congratulations came from Tito of Yugoslavia and Gomulka of Poland.

As Mikoyan and Suslov departed Budapest, Nagy appeared to have achieved a triumph. He had come to power during an armed revolt against Stalinist policies and had safely carried the Communist state into a new era of trust and openness. A bright future of peace and prosperity beckoned.

THE DECISION TO CRUSH THE NAGY REGIME

Support for Nagy was by no means unanimous in the Communist world. East German premier Otto Grotewohl, East German general secretary Walter Ulbricht, Czech premier Antonín Zápotocký, Romanian general secretary Gheorghe Gheorghiu-Dej, and Bulgarian first secretary Todor Zhivkov all opposed Nagy.[6] They saw Khrushchev back down when challenged by reformers in Poland. This encouraged reformers who toppled the Stalinist regime in Hungary. If Nagy were allowed to succeed, his example might in turn energize the challengers within Stalinist regimes elsewhere in Eastern Europe. More dictators might fall.

In public the official radio broadcasts from these Stalinist countries harshly criticized developments in Hungary. In private the fearful rulers of other East European states exploited the same types of Kremlin contacts used by Rákosi and Nagy.[7] The private messages flowing into Moscow indicated that if Khrushchev retreated in Hungary as in Poland, communism would be threatened throughout Eastern Europe. These messages were incorrect; it was arbitrary and repressive Stalinism, not communism itself, that was threatened. Nonetheless the incorrect argument came from highly placed Communists and was a godsend to Khrushchev's opponents.

In October 1956 Khrushchev was party chairman but was by no means omnipotent in Russia. He was not yet premier, and within a year the presidium would dismiss him as party chairman. He would foil that move, but in October 1956 he was well aware of his precarious position.

His opponents were aligned with presidium members Vyacheslav Molotov and Lazar Kaganovich,[8] hard-line Stalinists who argued that Khrushchev had brought on the restiveness in Poland and Hungary by abandoning Stalin's style of governance. This Kremlin group questioned whether Khrushchev's policies would now promote similar unrest in Latvia, Lithuania, Estonia, the Ukraine, Georgia, and Byelorussia.

Since February Stalin's policies had been under attack by Khrushchev and Mikoyan. The hard-liners viewed this as virtual regicide, and the sides drawn up in that struggle had a direct bearing on events in Hungary. Khrushchev had helped bring Nagy to power in 1953, and Mikoyan had helped do the same in 1956. Nagy had become a personification of Khrushchev's anti-Stalinist drive. This made Nagy a target of Kremlin leaders who opposed that crusade.

Yet the Moscow struggle was not as simple as Stalinists versus Khrushchev. Former presidium member Lavrenty Beria had been a harsh Stalinist and chief of the Russian secret police. Nonetheless, after Stalin's death Beria had advocated a loosening of control over Eastern Europe. Khrushchev's enemy Georgy Malenkov was another presidium member known to have supported such a change. By 1956 both Beria and Malenkov had been removed from power in disgrace. Their call for a lighter touch in Eastern Europe may not have been the only reason for their fall, but such an attitude was associated with men whose policies had been condemned by other Kremlin leaders.

In addition, a military-civilian power struggle was emerging. These two groups had been suspicious of each other since the founding of the Soviet state. The military was supposed to be answerable to the party, and over the years the party had built a complex network of supervision. Khrushchev had been part of this network in World War II, acting as a spy for Stalin, with power to make or break the careers of officers in the Stalingrad area. Khrushchev skillfully ingratiated himself with these officers, taking their side in policy disputes with Marshal Georgy Zhukov, who was essentially Stalin's right-hand man at Moscow headquarters.

The simmering military-civilian tension broke into the open after Stalin's death. Premier Malenkov alienated the military by emphasizing civilian priorities in government budgeting and planning. Malenkov's enemy Khrushchev was apparently the sole Kremlin party leader with a base of support in the military, formed by the Stalingrad group of officers whose careers he had promoted. This support contributed to Malenkov's fall and Khrushchev's rise. Whatever his thinking might be on the merits of the Hungarian situation, Khrushchev had to be attentive to the army's desires in order to bolster his own power base in Kremlin intrigues. Moreover, this support was not unanimous. In autumn 1956 the Stalingrad group headed by Warsaw Pact commander Konev was quarreling viciously with another faction headed by Defense Minister Zhukov, whom Khrushchev would later remove from power.

Roman Kolkowicz, author of a RAND Corporation study on Soviet military-civilian government relations, concluded that those relations were at a peak of tension in the autumn of 1956, a peak roughly equivalent to the period in 1937 that resulted in a wholesale purge of the officer corps.[9] In autumn 1956 the Russian military was incensed that Kremlin civilians had negotiated away the Soviet strategic presence in Hungary. This loss would handicap the maneuverability of Russian ground forces in Europe. Moreover, this loss accompanied the botched intervention that had failed to quell the revolt in Hungary. The military was being ordered to end that intervention in circumstances that made the Red Army appear defeated when it had not even fought any significant action. Money was an additional factor encouraging a Soviet military desire to deal with Hungary. When discussing national security matters with the party, the military habitually gave bleak portrayals of potential threats in order to assure a hefty defense budget.

The Soviet military seemed much more enthusiastic about a Hungarian intervention than the Soviet Communist party did. Indeed, the Red Army was already heading for Hungary on October 21. This was two days before any fighting had broken out in Hungary, and it was also two days after Khrushchev had agreed to a peaceful Polish settlement. The army's action can be viewed as prudence or as evidence that some generals were restive and ready to act without orders. The Hungarian intervention had bypassed the normal chain of command. If the Communist party was no longer in full control of the Soviet Red Army, the party's control of the Soviet regime was threatened.

Khrushchev was apparently under attack from some generals and from hard-line civilians in the party. In later discussions with a Yugoslav diplomat, Khrushchev alluded to accusations made against him during the Hungarian crisis.[10] His memoirs reveal that he was bewildered by the situation, continually changing his mind about what to do. He had to act, for the same reasons as in the Polish crisis and under even greater pressures.

Under challenge from hard-liners, he now presented himself as the toughest of the tough. His memoirs suggest the bombast that he must have delivered on this occasion: "Imre Nagy used deceit and intimidation to draw people into mutiny and a fratricidal war. He shoved prominent citizens in front of microphones and forced them to endorse his leadership and to denounce the Rákosi regime. . . . We certainly had no intention of doing what the leader of a putsch told us to do. From our viewpoint, a small clique, taking advantage of the blunders committed by the Rákosi regime, had overthrown the legitimate government of Hungary. From a strictly legal viewpoint, Nagy's demands had no parliamentary backing and therefore did not have the force of law."[11]

On October 31, the same day that Mikoyan and Suslov in Budapest had given the presidium's assent to Nagy's program, their colleagues in Moscow decided just the opposite. A neutral Hungarian government would be prevented. Hungary would be kept in the Warsaw Pact. And the dictatorship of the Hungarian proletariat would be guaranteed by preservation of a one-party state.

THE SECOND SOVIET INTERVENTION

After Mikoyan and Suslov left Budapest, the Hungarian leadership was perplexed by reports that Russian military units had halted their withdrawal and seemed to be returning in greater force than before. On November 1 Nagy and Kádár summoned Soviet ambassador Yury Andropov. Andropov, who years later would become the chairman of the Russian Communist party, had been a supporter of Rákosi.

The Hungarian leaders expressed their distress about the Russian military activity and demanded an explanation. Nagy and Kádár said that if good reasons were not forthcoming, Hungary would declare itself neutral in the cold war and would ask the United Nations to enforce the neutral status. This was done forthwith when Andropov failed to justify his government's actions.

Thirty years later such an appeal to the United Nations appears naive. At the time, however, the United Nations had recently completed a successful military defense of South Korea. The U.S. State Department had indicated that the Hungarian situation might be referred to the United Nations, and American-sponsored radio broadcasts urged the Hungarian population to overthrow communism. The United Nations Security Council, which had ordered the Korean intervention, began discussing the Hungarian situation on October 28. So Nagy's appeal was not made in a vacuum. And many Hungarians believed that the strong statements of support from Security Council delegates were a prelude to positive action. A reporter accredited by the United Nations drove through Budapest with its insignia on his car's windshield and was greeted by a joyous Hungarian soldier who asked if United Nations forces had arrived.

None ever would. None had ever been intended. The words of encouragement pouring forth from the United Nations and from American-sponsored radio were as much as the West ever planned to do for Hungary.

The Hungarian declaration of neutrality was intended to express the government's displeasure about movements of the Soviet Red Army but was not intended as a provocative act against Russia. On the contrary, Nagy felt this move would assure Russia that no Western base would be established in Hungary. He was simply expressing a friend's displeasure at the action of another friend.[12] He made clear that he wanted the United Nations guarantee enforced by several powers, including Russia.

Perhaps the Soviet Union interpreted the November 1 neutrality declaration as a threat rather than a reassurance. The decision to crush Nagy, however, had already been made the day before. Nothing he did afterward made any difference.

The Russian attack began on November 4. This second intervention, unlike the first, really was an invasion. The Russians said they came in at the request of the Hungarian government, but this request came from a rump regime formed by János Kádár, who had suddenly deserted Nagy. Instead of remaining a fierce codefender of Hungarian sovereignty, Kádár had become a meek Russian servant. The reason for this switch is unclear but is frequently ascribed to an inadequate amount of personal courage and integrity.

Disregarding protests from the internationally recognized Nagy government, Soviet military units crossed the border in force. The invading armies were not garrison troops with affection for the land they monitored. Instead, some invaders were from the eastern reaches of the Soviet Union, many nearly finished with their military service and resentful about going into combat. Most were both angry and fearful, and they behaved that way. Tank and artillery fire demolished buildings. Soldiers raped and plundered.

The Hungarian army put up what resistance it could, but the fight lasted for only about two weeks. Hundreds of thousands of Hungarians fled into Austria. The new Russian-sponsored regime headed by Kádár put the Hungarian death toll at 2,700 for both interventions. Historian D. F. Fleming says the second intervention cost the lives of 30,000 Hungarians and 7,000 Soviets.

Afterwards both Khrushchev and the docile Kádár government claimed that Russian intervention had been necessary to halt an on-going massacre of Communists by rightists. Yet the Kádár government's own tally for this "massacre" listed 234 victims throughout the entire country. Of these, 164 were military personnel who died during the two weeks of combat. Even if these figures were correct, and they may well have been exaggerated, clearly rather few Communists died in the insurrection. So this excuse for Russian intervention was groundless.

The new Hungarian regime hanged hundreds of army personnel who had obeyed the orders of the legitimate Nagy government. Their crime was failure to abandon their posts and join the Soviet attack against the country they were sworn to defend. These executions may have been intended to weaken the Hungarian armed forces.

Imre Nagy was brought to trial for his conduct as premier of Hungary. He was executed in 1958.

The Soviet invasion of Hungary was the first—but not the last—war between Communist states. The conflict ended any pretense that a monolithic Communist bloc existed.

Why did things work out so well for Poland and so badly for Hungary in 1956?

In Poland the government kept up with events. Reforms in the economy, labor relations, and personal freedoms were initiated when the needs became obvious. Admittedly, citizens called for still more liberalization, but the steps already taken were adequate to keep those calls civilized and confined to normal or at least unthreatening channels. By responding to pressures for reform, the Polish regime controlled the pressures. No surging crowds roamed the streets, no armed insurrections occurred, and normal commerce continued uninterrupted. The regime asserted its independence from Russia in a negative manner by simply rejecting advice and demands, rather than taking positive steps such as withdrawing from the Warsaw Pact. The Soviet Union was displeased about much that happened in Poland, but the Polish regime demonstrated that it was in charge.

In Hungary everything happened too late. Had Nagy become premier two weeks earlier, the Kremlin hard-liners might have rallied against Gomulka instead. Had Nagy become premier two weeks earlier, armed insurrection might never have broken out. Reforms that Nagy announced day by day might have heartened the Hungarian people two weeks earlier but seemed pale once the gunfire erupted. Even then, had his government made and announced decisions more quickly, the situation might have calmed (for example, the crowd that was machine-gunned in front of the parliament building had come to demand the replacement of Gerö—an act already taken but not announced). Just a little sooner. Just a little faster.

Instead, the old Hungarian regime procrastinated so long that it was outrun by events. Then Nagy gave the impression of attempting to retain leadership by running ever faster at the head of a mob in order to avoid being trampled. When Gomulka made an agreement with the Russians, there was no question that he could carry it out. In contrast Nagy gave the impression of being unable to do so. This impression may have been incorrect, but it may have been decisive for Kremlin hard-liners watching the armed revolt.

There is plenty of blame to go around for the outcome in Hungary but at least some of it must be accepted by the United States. American-sponsored radio broadcasts encouraged the armed insurrection. The Voice of America contributed somewhat to this, but Radio Free Europe did more. Announcers urged the Hungarian people to continue the initial street fighting that brought Nagy to power, promoted armed resistance against the Nagy government and against the Russians, gave the impression that help would arrive if only the Hungarian people showed themselves worthy of it via combat, and presented reports exaggerating the extent of the insurrection. Hungarians took these broadcasts seriously. So did the Soviets, who interpreted these broadcasts as signs that Western military intervention might be possible. The American-sponsored radio transmissions helped galvanize the Kremlin hard-liners into action.

It is notable that both the United States and the USSR felt that Nagy should be overthrown. The United States dismissed him as a defender of communism, and Russia felt he threatened communism.

XVI.

Cuba: The Emergence of Castro

Fidel Castro's revolution in Cuba generated a fury in the United States that has showed no signs of abating even after thirty years. The intensity of emotion is all the more remarkable if one considers the negligible amount of harm Castro has caused the average American. A Communist regime in Cuba may be a cause for unease, but the circumstances of its birth indicate that Americans would better direct their anger toward government and corporation offices in the United States.

CUBA BEFORE CASTRO

The United States has meddled in Caribbean government since Jefferson's time and has had a particular interest in Cuba, regarding it as a possession by right if not by law. Intimate and lucrative ties between American corporations and Cuba grew during the nineteenth century, becoming ever stronger in the twentieth. Cuba was a source of raw materials for the sugar and tobacco industries, with plantations typically owned by Americans. American companies owned mineral rights, mining companies, railroads that shipped ores, processing plants, and factories that made finished goods. Americans even owned public utilities. The Cuban people received little of the wealth produced by the land and those who worked it. Ordinary Cubans who complained discovered that sometimes the police, the courts, and other government officials were owned by Americans as well.

Until the Castro revolution, the United States freely sent its troops to quell disturbances whenever Cubans became restive about the conditions under which they lived. Woodrow Wilson's secretary of state Robert Lansing frankly stated that if any Cubans disrupted the efficiency of American-dominated sugar operations, the United States would become their foe. Labor strikes were considered intolerable, and U.S. troops were dispatched to put them down.

Gerardo Machado y Morales became dictator of Cuba in 1925. He boasted that he could break any labor strike within twenty-four hours. Machado's ruthless secret police terrorized the population and killed thousands of citizens. Cuban and incoming U.S. newspapers were censored. The government closed the University of Havana. U.S. President Calvin Coolidge expressed the American government's indifference about such events in Cuba: "Her people are independent, free, prosperous, peaceful, and enjoying all the advantages of self-government."[1]

Machado's support from the U.S. government wavered after Franklin Roosevelt became president, and the dictator was overthrown in August 1933. Throngs of angry Cubans meted out mob justice—murdering the old secret police chief along with his henchmen and informers, wrecking the homes of persons who grew wealthy under Machado's favor, occupying American-owned sugar mills.

Carlos Manuel de Céspedes, who replaced Machado as president, was overthrown in September by Fulgencio Batista y Zaldívar and Havana university students. Students appointed Ramón Grau San Martín president of Cuba and were prominent in his regime. One participant later described it as government by teenagers. They made guns the basis for their authority. Student leaders executed a fellow student on the first day of Grau's regime, and the University of Havana became a gangland realm that continued for years after the Grau regime ended. Castro later said that he was in greater danger as a college student than as a guerrilla.

Grau repudiated debts that the Machado regime had run up with Chase National Bank, and the new government took over the Cuban-American Sugar Company's mills. Grau proclaimed an eight-hour work day, a minimum wage, and ended the issuance of company scrip that forced sugar workers to rely upon company stores. When American firms tried to evade taxes by selling property at unreasonably low prices to sham buyers, Grau changed the law to permit the Cuban government to buy the property at those bargain prices. In January 1934 he instituted government management of the American-owned Cuban Electric Company. Cuban interior secretary Antonio Guiteras Holmes announced, "Foreign companies who have illegally acquired vast possessions that belong to the Cuban state are going to be deprived of them," and "the government will inaugurate a socialist policy."[2] Despite such rhetoric and behavior, the Cuban Communist party denounced the Grau government because Communists had little influence, let alone control over student radicals or anyone else in the regime.

The United States refused to recognize Grau's government, although American ambassadors remained in Havana. They supported Batista, who forced Grau to resign in January 1934. The alliance of student radicals with Batista's military colleagues ended bitterly. Student leaders considered assassinating Batista but decided to let him live. Carlos Hevia served briefly as provisional president of Cuba, but submitted his resignation to Batista within a few days. Batista's junta then proclaimed Carlos Mendieta provisional president, and the United States quickly granted diplomatic recognition.

Batista's forces cooperated with United States government and business interests, using harsh measures to pacify the population whenever it acted discontented. "Army trucks plunged into every town, and the soldiery fired right and left to terrorize the inhabitants. Every night in the streets of Havana, men were dragged from their homes by soldiers and Batista's police and shot down without trial, without mercy, and left dying in the streets."[3] In 1935 union organizing and labor strikes became punishable by death.

Batista himself was elected president in 1940 as the candidate of several groups, including the Communist party. He appointed Communists Carlos Rafael Rodríguez and Juan Marinello to his cabinet. Never before had a Latin American regime had a Communist cabinet member. Ten Communists won parliamentary seats in the same election, and Communists were elected as mayors in two cities. The balloting put Communists into city councils across the island as well.

On the surface Batista's alliance with the Communists was as startling as the Hitler-Stalin pact. In Latin America, however, Communist parties operate differently from those in the rest of the world. Latin American Communists do not hesitate to make expedient deals with opponents just like mainline political parties in the United States or Great Britain. In Cuba the Communists were willing to overlook Batista's previous suppression of them in return for a foothold in the government. Batista wanted their electoral support in 1940 and was willing to let them enter the government—where he intended to prevent them from exercising any influence.

Despite the open Communist support for Batista and despite the Communist participation in government from national to municipal levels, American business interests in Cuba continued to operate undisturbed. Neither the U.S. government nor the business community seemed concerned about Communist penetration of the Batista regime, and he was never considered a Communist threat.

Batista left office peacefully when his elected term expired in 1944. The consensus is that he wanted to retire in order to enjoy without distraction the wealth he had acquired as Cuba's strong man. He continued to exercise power behind the scenes.

His successor was the man he had forced from office a decade earlier, Ramón Grau. Grau served until 1948 and was succeeded by Carlos Prío Socarrás, who had been a student leader in the 1933 revolution. Their Partido Revolucionario Cubano, better known as the Auténtico political party, was the inheritor of the social ideals of 1933 but failed to practice them. The Auténticos became notoriously corrupt.

In 1946 Eduardo Chibas broke from the Auténticos and established the rival Partido del Pueblo Cubano, commonly known as the Ortodoxo party. It drew heavy support through its calls for honest government and for return to the ideals of 1933. The popularity of Chibas grew as the 1952 presidential elections approached, and he was seen as a major candidate. The Auténticos ran Carlos Hevia, who had served briefly as the president installed by Batista in 1934. A third candidate was Batista himself. But instead of going through the political process, Batista overthrew the legitimate government in a coup and assumed dictatorial powers in March 1952. This generated little protest from the United States. Batista made clear that he would promote American business interests.

Regarding Communists, Batista managed to be all things to all men. He outlawed the Communist party but allowed Communist leaders to go about their affairs undisturbed. He once again had Communists as officials in his government, but he also managed to assume the role of militant anti-Communist, receiving much U.S. weaponry to enable Cuba to fight communism in the Western hemisphere. Actually the weapons were used to resist his own countrymen who were attempting to overthrow him. Few of them were Communists; indeed, the Communist party opposed Castro's guerrilla campaign.

Batista instituted a repeat of the Machado dictatorship, ranging from censorship of incoming U.S. newspapers to assassins and secret police terror complete with torture chambers. Unlike some dictators, Batista publicized mutilations and murders with relish, putting photos of victims on wide display. His attacks were not limited to the poor and anonymous—machine-gun fire riddled the residences of three jurists whose decisions displeased the regime. In October 1956 Batista police even broke into the Haitian embassy and killed ten Cuban refugees found there. In September 1957 a Batista attack on opponents in the city of Cienfuegos left so many dead that the count was never completed. The bodies were simply bulldozed into pits.

CASTRO'S RISE TO POWER

Such conduct generated support in the latter 1950s for a group of revolutionaries headed by Fidel Castro Ruz. He came from a wealthy landowning family that was well connected with the Batista dictatorship. Castro married into a family with equally good connections—his wife's brother was a member of Batista's cabinet. Castro was no ignorant proletarian. He was from a refined and moneyed background.

He became involved in student politics while studying law at the University of Havana in the 1940s. The university was still rife with violence. Castro armed himself. "I was," he later recalled, "always the target of cudgel blows and gunfire."[4] In 1948 he was in the Cuban student delegation to a conference in Bogotá, Colombia, when rioting broke out. He may have mingled with the crowds but eventually fled from his hotel to the Cuban embassy. The riots were falsely blamed on Communists, and Castro's dash through the streets was later called proof that he was Communist oriented from the beginning. People who knew him scoffed at such a claim. Fellow students Enrique Ovares, who became an opponent of the Castro regime, and Alfredo Guevara, who became Castro's ambassador to UNESCO, both agreed that Communists had no control over him then.

After receiving his law degree, Castro devoted more time to Ortodoxo party politics than to jurisprudence. These politicians called for a return to the radical social reforms of 1933. Batista's

1952 coup squelched the Ortodoxo party, and Castro became a violent opponent of Batista.

On July 26, 1953, he led an inept attack on a barracks in hopes of capturing weapons and galvanizing the people to rise against Batista. The dictator's forces quickly captured Castro and his followers. Castro twice escaped summary execution. Once was through luck, when his captor, Lieutenant Pedro Sarria, turned out to be a classmate from the University of Havana, who spared Castro for old time's sake. The other time a Roman Catholic archbishop interceded for this young man with good family connections. Instead of being executed, Castro was put on trial, in the course of which he gave a spellbinding speech indicting the current and previous governments. He received a fifteen-year sentence, but the men imprisoned for the barracks attack received amnesty in 1955. Castro went to Mexico.

In December 1956 Castro left Mexico and began guerrilla activity in Cuba. One of his first acts was to set fire to his family's sugar plantation.

At that time Cuba's standard of living was one of the highest in the Western Hemisphere, and Castro's support came mainly from middle-class white-collar workers, not from the urban proletariat or rural poor. The Roman Catholic Church and disgusted members of the upper class also assisted Castro. Cuba's ex-president Carlos Prío, who had been overthrown in Batista's 1952 coup, helped finance the guerrilla war. Prío's support brought other help as well—one businessman contributed $750,000 to promote Castro's revolution. These were not the sort of men who would support a Communist takeover of Cuba. Instead, their support indicated that they saw Castro playing a role in the context of Cuban history rather than the Cold War.

Despite Batista's overwhelming superiority in number of soldiers and American-supplied matériel, Castro's guerrillas overthrew Batista on January 1, 1959. His success was quite remarkable given that only about 300 guerrillas were involved until the last moment, when everyone recognized that his triumph was imminent. The victory cannot be attributed to superior skill in military tactics. Battles had been unusual events in this revolution. Indeed, corruption permeated the Batista regime so deeply that Castro could sometimes use bribes rather than bullets to defeat Batista's troops. It was this rot, this utter abandonment by lackeys and the population, that defeated Batista. Castro was more a beneficiary than a victor.

U.S. HOSTILITY TOWARD CASTRO

Soon after Castro took over, false stories began appearing in the American press about trials by mob in Cuba, in which accused persons were brought to arenas and condemned to death in an atmosphere that made Hitler's courts look like models of probity. But this is not what was happening at all.

The Batista secret police had carried out gruesome crimes against citizens for years.[5] Specific perpetrators could be identified. To prevent a recurrence of the frenzy of lynching that followed Machado's fall from power in 1933, Castro promised that his government would examine accusations and bring suspects to trial. The tribunals operated in a normal judicial atmosphere. Accused persons did not enjoy every guarantee of the U.S. legal system, but neither had they under Batista. Cuba's Roman Catholic Church hierarchy, hardly known for pro-Communist leanings, heartily endorsed the trials. Protestant leaders concurred.[6] The sensationalized stories about mob justice under Castro should be compared with the lack of American concern about tortures and murders conducted by secret police under Batista.[7]

In 1960 the U.S. government claimed that Castro was stifling freedom of the press in Cuba, and noted that five opposition newspapers had been seized when Castro took power in 1959. At the time those seizures occurred, however, the U.S. government had not protested—the newspapers in question had all been Batista mouthpieces. In the ensuing year, the number of newspapers declined further, partly because some were losing money. The same phenomenon happens in the United States without cries of dictatorial suppression. Ownership of other papers changed hands, sometimes in unfriendly takeovers by employees, but this hardly meant that free speech was being curbed.

Indeed, at this point in the Cuban revolution, plenty of opposition was openly expressed in print and electronic media without any arrests. Notably, most opposition seemed to come from conservative moneyed interests. American journalists talking with average Cuban citizens found strong support for Castro's actions. The revolution was not being imposed on a resisting people.

In April 1959 Castro visited the United States, where he met many business and government leaders. During this trip he pledged to help defend the hemisphere against aggression, a policy previously agreed to by Cuba in the 1947 Rio Pact. He tried to make a good impression wherever he went, but that effort suffered one notable failure—when Castro met Vice-President

Richard Nixon. After that meeting Nixon secretly began urging other U.S. officials to organize an invasion force of Cuban exiles to overthrow Castro. In April 1959 no one had fled Cuba because of communism; the Cuban government had yet to enact its first agrarian reform law. The only exiles were Batista supporters. The issue in Cuba then was not communism versus democracy, but nationalism versus subservience to the United States. Both Castro and Nixon had made their choices.

CASTRO AND COMMUNISM

Unlike Batista, who came into power with Communist support and brought Communists into high government positions, Castro explicitly declared he opposed that ideology. An associate recalled that when Castro left his Mexican haven to start his revolution in Cuba, "I met only one Marxist, besides Guevara, among the expeditionaries, and he was the constant butt of his companions' jokes."[8] CIA Deputy Director C. P. Cabell confirmed Castro's anti-Communist credentials. In November 1959, after nearly a year's experience observing the Castro government, Cabell gave this testimony to the U.S. Senate:

> Cuban Communists do not consider him [Castro] a Communist Party member, or even a pro-Communist. . . . The Communists consider Castro as a representative of the bourgeoisie, and were unable to gain public recognition or commitments from him during the course of the revolution. . . . The Communists were concerned, when, at the time of his trip to the United States [in April 1959], he showed evidence of a friendly attitude toward the United States. . . . Within the 26th of July movement [Castro's followers] there is considerable evidence of opposition to communism. . . . We believe that Castro is not a member of the Communist Party, and does not consider himself to be a Communist.[9]

The CIA's top authority on Latin American communism, Frank Droller, concurred, as did President Dwight Eisenhower's ambassador to Cuba, Philip Bonsal.

Castro's antipathy for the Communists was reciprocated. They had opposed his anti-Batista guerrilla campaign. Their resistance to Castro's calls for general labor strikes helped lengthen Batista's reign. Even in the summer of 1959, when Castro was consolidating his power, Communists demonstrated against him in Havana.

Given the historical record of Batista's closeness with the Communists and Castro's hostility toward them, the U.S. government had no cold-war grounds to withhold support from the new revolutionary regime. Castro announced that Cuba would abide by treaties of previous Cuban governments, including the treaty permitting a U.S. Navy base in Cuba.

Although Castro had little, if any, affection for communism, he was absolutely dedicated to a social transformation in Cuba that would improve living conditions for average citizens. For Castro this was the core purpose of the revolution. Interestingly, many of his social reforms were mandated by the 1940 Cuban constitution, but previous governments had disregarded the provisions. American officials, including President Eisenhower, Vice-President Nixon, and CIA Director Allen Dulles viewed Castro's actions as communist, but the Cuban people saw his behavior as merely the fulfillment of promises the Cuban government had long been obligated to fulfill. In the context of Cuban history, Castro was the first leader to enforce certain aspects of the country's laws.

In June 1959 the Castro government enacted an agrarian reform law authorizing later expropriation of holdings owned by some U.S. corporations. *Expropriation* means that the property is purchased by the government, somewhat like eminent domain proceedings, in which a government typically tears down whatever is on the land and converts it to another use. In expropriation the government preserves the present use of the property but places it under public ownership. Expropriation is by no means destructive, nor does it mean that the property is confiscated without compensation. The procedure is normally considered a legitimate power of a national sovereignty. Former Cuban president Prío supported Castro's agrarian reform law wholeheartedly.

Trouble arose in part because Castro used tax records to determine fair compensation. Earlier, his government had given owners a chance at reassessment, but they had indicated they were satisfied with the old valuations. They were satisfied because the valuations had failed to keep up with the land's value and were thus lower than they should have been. Now Castro turned the tables on them, basing compensation on the figures they had just approved. The owners complained to the U.S. government that Castro was cheating them. Their appeal went to Washington rather than Havana because previous Cuban governments had done whatever the United States had asked. The Eisenhower administration formally protested the proposed compensations, and consternation was great when Castro seemed unmoved. In the end, as

Cuban-American relations soured, Castro gave no compensation at all.

He proceeded with other social and economic reforms, such as lowering rates charged by the Cuban Electric Company and taking over the management of the Cuban Telephone Company (while allowing the company's private owners to continue receiving the profits). These actions were opposed by vested interests, who accused Castro of practicing communism.

At some point in this process, the Cuban Communists' perception of Castro changed from doctrinaire, ideologically based opposition to pragmatic support for reforms benefiting the population. As Communist support and U.S. government opposition became more vocal, Castro began to view the Communists as friends and the Americans as enemies.

This feeling grew when Cuban failure to heed U.S. government protests was followed in autumn 1959 by military attacks from U.S. territory by private adventurers who had access to a B-25 bomber. Light planes from Florida also flew missions against Cuba. Bombing targets included the streets of Havana and rural sugar mills. Cane fields came under incendiary air raids that burned thousands of tons of sugar cane. As an attorney, Castro was sophisticated enough to hold the U.S. government blameless for this activity, but he realized that the American government was unperturbed by the situation and seemed willing to promote it through malign neglect. Castro declared, "I would ask myself if the U.S. authorities would be so careless as to permit Russian emigrés to carry out bombing excursions over Russian cities and villages from Alaska."[10]

Castro claimed that American sabotage was behind the explosion of a French freighter unloading munitions in Havana harbor on March 4, 1960. The circumstances of that incident are unclear, but in that same month, the CIA began supporting anti-Castro mountain bands composed of mercenaries and Batista supporters. They received airdrops of weapons. Small American-led boat landings of fighters had already begun in 1959 and continued the next year. Arson and small bomb detonations were routine in Cuban cities by the end of 1960. From interrogation of suspects, the Cuban government concluded that the U.S. government was encouraging such activities.

As attacks increased from bases in the United States and the Dominican Republic, Cuba attempted to buy defensive weapons from the United States. The Eisenhower administration refused to permit such sales, a distinct message of hostility.

In this atmosphere the Castro government began its first expropriations of Cuban property owned by U.S. citizens in late October 1959: a couple of ranches and some mineral lands, including holdings of Bethlehem Steel. An International Harvester operation was also included. The scale of expropriation was minor compared to those of lands owned by Cuban citizens. The action was part of the agrarian reform program, well advertised by Castro from the start of his guerrilla career.

The American government protested this action as a "denial of the basic rights of ownership of United States citizens in Cuba."[11] The Eisenhower administration argued that property of U.S. corporations should be immune from seizure in Cuba because their interests superseded those of the Cuban people. It is doubtful that any court in the United States would accept such an argument from someone objecting to eminent domain proceedings. Nonetheless, several bills were submitted in Congress to cut the U.S. quota of Cuban sugar imports in retaliation for the expropriations.

The U.S. government was also concerned that, if it accepted the Cuban action without protest, efforts to expand American business activity in other Third World countries would be harmed. Thus, Castro was regarded as a threat to private corporate profits around the world. In 1960 aerial bombings of Cuba increased from private planes based in the United States. And CIA Director Allen Dulles set in motion Vice President Nixon's scheme for Cuban exiles to invade and conquer the island.

The United States and its European allies began closing the normal lines of financial credit that Cuba had always used. In order to keep the nation's economy functioning, Castro had to find some other source of credit. The Soviet Union appeared with a smile and a hand outstretched in friendship. In early 1960 Castro signed a big sugar trade agreement with the Russians, causing a furor in the United States.

Such American indignation is hard to justify. Castro turned to Russia only after the United States reduced its quota for Cuban sugar imports and orchestrated a shutdown of the financing that fed Cuba's economy. His only other alternative was to allow Cuba to be economically destroyed. American protests were particularly odd because Cuban trade links with the Soviet Union were not new: for years, Batista had maintained an annual sugar trade with Russia that averaged higher than that during Castro's first year in power.

As U.S. hostility toward Castro grew, Soviet support blossomed. In midsummer 1960 Russian crude oil shipments arrived and were delivered to Texaco, Standard, and Shell refineries in Cuba. Managers refused to process the Russian crude, so the Cuban government took over management while continuing to allow profits to flow to the U.S. corporations. In retaliation the Eisenhower administration stopped Cuban access to the U.S. sugar market.

With no more American dollars coming into Cuba, the Castro government acted to reduce the northward flow of pesos. Up to that point, rather few American-owned properties had been expropriated, and all those were real estate. In the summer of 1960, however, physical plants were seized and expropriated. The process continued through the autumn. Castro made plain that these actions were intended to punish the United States for its hostility.

Castro's delaration of Cuban independence from U.S. economic domination and his promotion of Cuban social welfare made him highly popular among Cubans. As in 1959, throughout 1960 independent observers reported deep public satisfaction with Castro's rule. His actions apparently reflected the will of the people. To Americans, Castro was a dictator; to Cubans, he was the least oppressive and most caring leader in their history.

Cuban freedom of the press still existed in 1960. Newspapers by no means took an unthinking Communist slant. For instance, they strongly criticized Nikita Khrushchev's conduct in the U-2 affair of May 1960. Although some newspaper editors had left the country, protesting Castro's actions, these same free-press advocates had operated comfortably under Batista's censorship and financial patronage. One of them had even editorially supported Hitler. Despite complaints from such sources about Castro's limitations of free speech, U.S. magazines and newspapers were openly available in Cuba; such had not been the case under Batista.

In August 1960, in an attempt to further isolate Cuba, the Eisenhower administration presented so-called proof of Castro's communism to the Organization of American States, a regional United Nations limited to the Western Hemisphere. The document was carefully examined by Maurice Zeitlin and Robert Scheer,[12] and some highlights of that examination are worth noting.

One proof cited by the Eisenhower administration was a quotation from a Castro associate during a Moscow visit: "The Communist Party of Cuba, which is called the Popular Socialist Party, is basically a party made up of very poor classes. There are no big capitalists in it, no imperialists, no big landowners whose land can be expropriated, no war criminals. That is, it is the Party whose members are receiving the benefits of the revolution."[13]

Such a quotation merely says that poor people were the beneficiaries of Castro's rule, not that Communists were running Cuba. Apparently even the Eisenhower administration read it that way, because the report's introduction condensed the quotation with an ellipsis: "The Communist Party of Cuba . . . is the party whose members are receiving the benefits of the Revolution."[14]

To prove that Castro was a totalitarian, the report to the OAS quoted from a Castro speech: "Democracy is that which guarantees to man not the right to freedom of thought, but rather the right to know how to think, the right to know how to write what he thinks, the right to know how to read what he or others think."[15]

Castro never uttered those words. What he actually said was: "Democracy is that form of government that guarantees to man not only the right to think freely but also the right to know how to think, the right to know how to write what he thinks, the right to know how to read what is thought by others. Democracy guarantees not only the right to bread and the right to work but also the right to culture and the right to be taken into account within society."[16]

In the report the American government also complained about Cuban efforts to correct a balance of trade deficit with the United States by restricting such trade, and said that Cuba's policy had "long been discarded by reputable economists and such trade has greatly been reduced by free world countries in recent years. This is of course the trade philosophy of the Soviet Union and Communist China, designed to destroy multilateral trade upon which the strength of the free world depends."[17] Even the Eisenhower administration's accusation admitted that the so-called Communist trade policy was used by capitalist countries.

The Eisenhower administration's allegations of Castro's communism relied upon distorted quotations, false quotations, inaccurate testimony, misstatements of fact, and questionable characterizations of behavior. U.S. officials failed to make a believable case that Castro was a Communist in 1960. After due consideration the OAS declined to endorse the report.

In 1961 Eisenhower was succeeded by John F. Kennedy, a man driven by a desire to destroy Castro. Perhaps this was colored by Castro's nationalization of various U.S. businesses in Cuba. Kennedy's father had been prominent in Hayden, Stone, an investment company with many dealings in Cuba. Allen Dulles (Kennedy's first CIA director) also had connections with U.S. business operations in Cuba.

In the first week of April 1961, the U.S. State Department released a white paper on Cuba, prepared by historian Arthur

Schlesinger, Jr., working closely with Kennedy.[18] Maurice Zeitlin and Robert Scheer have demonstrated that the white paper's tone and inaccuracy were reminiscent of the 1960 Eisenhower administration's misleading report to the OAS.[19]

The white paper cited Cuban President Dr. Osvaldo Dorticos Torrado as an example of Communist penetration of the government, since he had been a Communist organizer as a university student. As an adult, however, he had been an attorney representing wealthy corporations and had moved in Cuba's high society. Moreover, Dorticos was uneasy about Castro's anti-Americanism and publicly called for friendlier policies toward the United States. In 1959 the Associated Press named Dorticos as one who objected to legalizing the Communist party.

The white paper also noted that foreign minister Raul Roa's previous criticism of the Soviet Union had changed to praise, but failed to note that his tone had changed only after repeated attacks upon Cuba from private adventurers based in the United States. In contrast, the Soviets vigorously supported his government.

The white paper said, "In the presence of Dr. Castro, Faure Chomón, the Cuban Ambassador to Moscow, told an audience [in Cuba] on March 13, 1961, 'We Communists together will continue forward with our truth . . . and the students of today and the students of tomorrow will be greatly interested in seeing how a whole people made itself Communist, how even the children, deceived by religious schools, have become Communists, and how this is to follow that truth which unites the Cuban people. Very soon we shall see all the peoples of Latin America become Communists.' "[20] (Foregoing ellipsis as published in white paper.)

But, as with the Eisenhower administration's report to the OAS, Maurice Zeitlin and Robert Scheer found that the Kennedy administration's white paper made its argument with misquotation. They noted that Chomón's original Spanish used the term *Communist* sarcastically: "The fact is that we are close to the truth, the truth that is finding its way on earth and in space, the truth that has gotten for us the name of Communists given to us by the lackeys and their masters, the imperialists. We! the Communists, will continue forward with our truth! We! the Communists, will continue honoring the martyrs of our land, the Cuban martyrs, Catholics or atheists, socialists or nationalists, honoring ourselves with the truth that has gotten for us the name Communists!"[21]

Perhaps the most arguable contention of the white paper is its allegation that Castro's actions had forced the Cuban people into bondage: "The result has been to corrupt the social achievements and make them the means, not of liberation, but of bondage."[22] The supposed slaves certainly felt satisfied despite discontent among the wealthier classes of Cuba and among exiles who had left. American journalists who visited the island in the spring of 1961 came back with the same reports that independent observers had consistently found: despite newly instituted restrictions on civil liberties, Castro was immensely popular in Cuba and could handily win a fair election.

A couple weeks after the white paper was released, after months of insisting that Castro had no respect for international law, the United States backed a military attack against Cuba on April 17, 1961. The affair is remembered as the Bay of Pigs invasion. The idea was for the invaders to inspire the Cuban people to rise against Castro. In reality he had tremendous public support. The invaders waded ashore only to be shot or turned in by the people they came to liberate. The attack had been a CIA project, and the agency's misreading of the Cuban mood damaged the CIA's credibility for decades. Unlike previous smaller and more discreet CIA actions, American participation in the Bay of Pigs operation was so extensive that former president Eisenhower and President Kennedy had to admit their personal involvement in the planning.[23] This surprise attack against a nation at peace with the United States devastated America's moral standing around the world.

After nearly two years of continual harassment by the United States, in December 1961 Castro declared himself a Communist. To some this was triumphant confirmation of what they had all along claimed. To others, more knowledgeable about the history of Cuba and Castro's rise to power, his announcement prompted by U.S. harassment and Soviet goodwill was more a cause for sorrow than exultation. Thenceforward his domestic policy would take on a more communistic appearance but, as we shall see, Castro would bend Cuban communism to reflect his personal will.

XVII.

Communism on One Island

THE CUBAN MISSILE CRISIS

In 1962, Soviet premier Nikita Khrushchev sent missiles to Cuba. On October 22, American President John F. Kennedy announced the American discovery of this operation and called it a hostile military act against the United States, threatening the nation's existence. He announced a U.S. Navy quarantine of Cuba to prevent the arrival of more such matériel. He demanded that the missiles be removed from Cuba immediately and made clear that he was prepared to launch an air strike and invasion to eliminate them if Khrushchev failed to do so. Several days of considerable drama ensued as the world wondered what consequences might follow the sinking of a Russian ship on the high seas or an attack upon Russian military units in Cuba. The United States was unquestionably willing to do both and came very close to doing the latter before Khrushchev agreed to Kennedy's demands. Both men, along with the entire world, recognized that such actions could unleash passions that might quickly escalate into a nuclear war.

Although the Cuban missile crisis has been called Kennedy's finest hour, a number of important aspects are generally ignored. Because of the incident's importance to American relations with both the Soviet Union and Cuba, those aspects deserve mention.

The Bay of Pigs invasion convinced both Cuban prime minister Fidel Castro and the Soviet Union that Castro needed a major military deterrent to discourage a second and more formidable attack from the north. Small harassing raids from Florida continued in 1962, accompanied by Republican calls for a harsher stance against Cuba (Kennedy was a Democrat). American forces conducted large amphibious maneuvers in the Caribbean; the goal of the war games was to overthrow the "mythical" dictator Ortsac (spell it backwards). Kennedy convinced Congress to authorize the calling of 150,000 reservists to active duty. There was no evidence that he had abandoned a military option.

In 1962 the Soviet Union had many problems, including food shortages and economic-policy failures. Communist expansion had slowed, a fact that mainland China was exploiting in arguments among Communist bloc nations. Strategically the Soviet Union was weak in nuclear weapons. Russia apparently hoped that the grand gesture of sending strategic missiles to Cuba would mask these problems. If Khrushchev had simply been interested in maintaining Cuban security, a handful of short-range Russian-controlled rockets able to reach Miami with high-explosive warheads would have been sufficient. Such a force would obviously have been defensive. It could not have destroyed Florida, let alone the whole United States, but the potential loss of Miami would have been a sobering deterrent to another American-backed invasion. Instead, Khrushchev dispatched dozens of apparently armed nuclear missiles capable of reaching the American Southeast. They would give the Soviet Union a much more credible strategic capability without having to spend any money on new weapons; that money could then be devoted to the lagging civilian economy. If the Cuban project worked, it would be a political triumph for Khrushchev; it would weaken his Kremlin critics and distract attention from his failures. It would show China and its sympathizers that Russia was willing to defend Communist gains anywhere in the world. Moreover, in 1962 it was not apparent that the United States would tolerate a Communist Cuba much longer. If, as a consequence of the missile project, the United States stopped encouraging the overthrow of Castro and accepted a Communist regime just ninety miles from Florida, this would imply American willingness to accept Communist gains anywhere; and that would be a great stroke indeed.

All these factors indicate that the project was apparently inspired by the Soviets, not the Cubans. Khrushchev claimed it was his idea;[1] and Castro said that the Cubans accepted the missiles reluctantly, out of obligation for all the economic aid the island had received from the Soviets.² Castro's uneasiness proved well founded.

Whether Khrushchev and other Kremlin leaders carefully thought through the goals, options, and possible consequences of the project is unknown. There is, however, evidence of strong debate and objections to Khrushchev's idea. The commander of the Soviet Union's strategic rocket troops, General K. S. Moskalenko, lost his post in April 1962 when the presidium apparently approved the Cuban project. He was also fired as deputy minister of defense. General F. I. Golikov, director of the armed forces' Main Political Administration, would have been in charge of explaining the Cuban project to the military. He was shifted from his job at about the same time that Moskalenko was assigned new duties. After the Cuban project failed, the two men were restored to positions of influence in November 1962.³

That Khrushchev persuaded the Kremlin leadership to approve the Cuban project does not mean sound reasoning supported his thinking. Diplomats and historians spend much time in assigning logical motives to actions, but such motives do not always exist. Such actions are not necessarily irrational, but few decisions of any government follow the rules of Aristotelian logic. Analysts searching for logical motives sometimes construct elaborate rationales imputing extraordinary suppleness and foresight to government decision-makers, who were simply blundering along. The Cuban missile crisis, like the 1941 Japanese attack on Pearl Harbor, was full of circumstances supporting elaborate conspiracy theories. In examining these circumstances, however, we should remember that government leaders do not always realize what they are getting into.

The Soviets did not go so far as to announce the missile project to the press, but they were no more secretive about it than the United States had been about preparations for the Bay of Pigs invasion. The distinctive crates of Ilyushin-28 bombers were shipped across the oceans above deck. In addition, each launching site for medium-range ballistic missiles could have been constructed in a few days, but the Soviets instead took leisurely weeks, working only in daylight and without camouflage. It can be plausibly argued that such virtual advertising was intended to flaunt Soviet power while ensuring that the United States would be well aware of developments and therefore not react rashly. Or perhaps, like the U.S. Navy at Pearl Harbor, the Soviet military was simply following standard operating procedures because they had received no orders to deviate. In Russia missile sites were not camouflaged while under construction, so they were not in Cuba either. Maybe the Kremlin leadership in 1962, like the Washington leadership in 1941, wrongly assumed that field commanders would take the necessary initiative.

At any rate, the United States was not caught by surprise in October and not required to make a hasty response to a sudden military challenge. The situation is often portrayed as a virtual sneak attack by the Soviet Union against the United States, and indeed was so portrayed at the time, but the Kennedy administration knew about the situation weeks before the crisis was announced on October 22, 1962. CIA Director John McCone realized that new antiaircraft emplacements in Cuba were practical only for protecting missile bases. He warned Kennedy about this on August 22.[4] By September 21 Ray Cline, CIA deputy chief of intelligence, had a trustworthy report of Cuban missiles. This information was not gossip from refugees but came from a CIA agent who saw the rear of a missile and sketched it.[5] By September 27 the Pentagon had noted that the new antiaircraft emplacements in Cuba had the same configuration as those used at Soviet missile sites.[6] According to Congressman Robert Wilson, in September Kennedy administration officials told the House Armed Services' CIA subcommittee that strategic missiles were in Cuba.[7] On September 28 the U.S. government had photos of the Ilyushin-28 crates, confirming the bomber shipment that American intelligence had been expecting for six months.[8] The October 1 edition of the respected industry publication *Aviation Week and Space Technology* stated: "Pentagon strategists consider the present arms buildup in Cuba the first step toward eventual construction of intermediate-range ballistic missile emplacements. They point out that the defensive nature of armaments arriving from Soviet Russia is aimed at preventing aerial photographic reconnaissance. . . . If this information source is shut off, then the construction of missile sites could begin in secrecy."[9]

The bombers and missile bases were not an overnight surprise, although President Kennedy claimed otherwise to justify his response. Nor were they a military threat to the United States.

The bombers were slow-flying craft with a maximum action radius of less than 700 miles. They were already so obsolete that their main value was in training aircraft crews. In 1971 the United States described similar American airplanes in Europe as strictly defensive. The Kennedy administration felt little concern about the IL-28 bombers. After seeing photos of the IL-28 crates bound for Cuba, National Security Adviser McGeorge Bundy publicly stated on October 14 that the United States had no objection to Cuba receiving the type of military aid that the Soviet Union had sent to Egypt and Indonesia. That aid included IL-28s.[10] Roger Hilsman, director of the State Department's Intelligence and Research office, later admitted that the Kennedy administration knew "the range and pay load of these planes were too small to be a real threat to the United States."[11] During the crisis the editor of *Aviation Week and Space Technology* was hard-pressed to find anything dangerous about the obsolete bombers, noting that they provided "a reconnaissance capability over the entire Caribbean area" and "the capability for air dropping agents and arms to foment Communist revolt."[12]

The missiles were also seen as militarily insignificant. Upon first hearing the news, Secretary of Defense Robert McNamara believed that the rockets in Cuba had little military value. Deputy Defense Secretary Roswell Gilpatric agreed and held to that same view even when the crisis was over.[13] There was not even direct evidence that the warheads were nuclear rather than conventional.[14] The medium-range missiles had a distance rating of about 500 miles but were unable to go farther than Miami with accuracy. During the crisis the Kennedy administration exaggerated their range as 1,000 miles.[15] Although the intermediate-range rockets could fly about 1,200 miles, during the crisis the U.S. government exaggerated the range as 2,200 miles,[16] which falsely made the missiles appear capable of striking most of the United States. The government also downplayed its knowledge that the intermediate-range missile bases were far from complete. The Kennedy administration estimated that the facilities could not be ready until December 16 even if construction continued twenty-four hours a day.[17] Moreover, all forty-two Russian missiles in Cuba were medium-range. No intermediate-range vehicles were in Cuba.[18] So there was no threat whatsoever from the nonexistent intermediate-range capability. The Kennedy administration's contrary claim increased public hysteria and heightened support for a stern military response.

It should also be remembered that the rockets were not Cuban missiles. They were Soviet missiles *in* Cuba, controlled by Soviet personnel.[19] There was no danger of Castro lighting them off on a whim, although this fear greatly alarmed the public at the time and helped generate support for Kennedy's decision to force their removal. The Kennedy administration made no effort to correct this public misapprehension.

Soon after the crisis, Kennedy himself admitted that the missiles in Cuba were a mere propaganda stunt that posed no urgent military threat to the United States: "They [the Russians] were planning in November to open to the world the fact that they had these missiles so close to the United States; not that they were intending to fire them, because if they were going to get into a nuclear struggle, they have their own missiles in the Soviet Union. But it would have politically changed the balance of power. It would have appeared to, and appearances contribute to reality."[20]

Although the events in Cuba had little or no military significance, they provoked a nuclear crisis, for reasons of geopolitics, U.S. domestic politics, and Kennedy's personal pique.

John Kennedy was personally offended by the Russian's conduct. He had told them not to move such equipment into Cuba, and yet the Soviets did not obey him. Kennedy regarded this as a challenge to his manliness, and his manliness was something he took very seriously indeed.[21] His ire, however, was greater than the facts warranted. He was justifiably angered by false statements that Khrushchev and other Russian officials had made about activity in Cuba, but lies were nothing new in diplomacy. Kennedy's September warnings against putting missiles in Cuba were forceful: September 4, "The gravest issues would arise;"[22] September 13, "This country will do whatever must be done to protect its own security and that of its allies."[23] Yet the stern language was ambiguous, and objectionable weapons were defined in a fuzzy manner: "offensive ground-to-ground missiles"[24] were intolerable, but what about ground-to-ground missiles intended for defensive purposes? The United States considered its warnings stiff and specific, but Moscow could have viewed them as elastic bluster that the Cuban project could stretch. After all, on October 14 McGeorge Bundy indicated that the United States would tolerate IL-28 bombers in Cuba. The previous year, in an atmosphere unpolluted by the climax of Kennedy's autumn 1962 election rhetoric, Senator J. William Fulbright stated that missile bases in Cuba would be unpleasant but acceptable.[25] He was known to be close to the administration's views on foreign policy.

Moreover, when the project started in April, the Russians were not arrogantly disregarding America's September admonishments. Missile maintenance equipment may already have reached Cuba in May,[26] and the operation was in its final stages when Kennedy issued his first warning. On the basis of the mixed signals from Washington, it would have been very hard for Khrushchev to abort the project in September and admit that his critics had been right in April, when the signals had been just as mixed. His opponents could have made a case that he was too fickle to be party chairman, insisting on approval for a questionable enterprise and then lacking the nerve to finish the job once it was begun.

Geopolitically, top U.S. officials had realized for about five years that the world situation was going against Russia, despite alarmist talk to the contrary. The United States began looking for a showdown with Russia that would cripple the Soviets for years. Berlin appeared to be the choice for a while. The Berlin Wall had just been erected in August 1961, and Khrushchev was talking about signing a treaty with East Germany that would invalidate the legal grounds for the Western sector in Berlin. Kennedy and some later analysts even suspected that the missiles in Cuba were somehow tied to the Berlin situation, although Khrushchev's memoirs scoff at the idea of Berlin being worth a war. Be that as it may, the United States was determined to maintain the existence of West Berlin and was willing to turn this issue into the great showdown. A drawback, however, was the overwhelming geographical advantage the Communists would have in a confrontation there. In that regard the missiles in Cuba were a godsend for Kennedy. For all practical purposes, the Caribbean was an American lake. The United States had a massive advantage in any military contest with Russia in Cuba's vicinity.

Military standing, however, had nothing to do with the crisis. The American goal was to humiliate the Soviets so badly that they would be reluctant to make any expansionist moves for years to come.

Destroying possible Soviet dreams of expansion may have been a worthy goal, but neither the American public nor world opinion could be expected to support a challenge to a nuclear war just for this. So President Kennedy and his associates lied. Insisting that U.S. military security was in jeopardy, they claimed America's very survival was at stake.

Kennedy's handling of the crisis showed that the true U.S. goal was much broader than ensuring military security. Up to the last moment before his speech on October 22, his associates feared that Russia might announce the missiles before he did. Kennedy's men thought a Russian announcement would make the Communists look strong—the United States would appear to be reacting to events rather than controlling them. Who appeared tougher would not affect the fact of missiles in Cuba, but it would affect the perception of who won the crisis. And Kennedy's goal was not just to resolve the crisis, but to win it.

His concern over the cosmetics of toughness became crucial as the crisis deepened. On October 26 Khrushchev sent a secret letter to Kennedy offering to remove the missiles if Kennedy would lift the naval quarantine and pledge never to invade Cuba again. An unofficial "deniable" feeler that arrived almost simultaneously from a Russian embassy official in Washington did not even ask that the quarantine be terminated if the missiles were removed. Khrushchev had capitulated almost unconditionally. On October 27, however, he publicly asked for a face-saving gesture. Khrushchev suggested that he remove the missiles from Cuba and Kennedy remove obsolete American Jupiter intermediate-range rockets from Turkey. Before the crisis Kennedy had already decided to remove the Jupiters; thus, if Khrushchev's proposal were accepted, the United States would suffer no military loss in Turkey while achieving a military gain in Cuba.

Kennedy ignored Khrushchev's plea for a deal and publicly offered only a promise that the United States would not invade Cuba after the missiles left. Khrushchev had to realize what would happen to him if he agreed to a Soviet humiliation—analysts later attributed his fall from power to his backdown in Cuba.[27] But Khrushchev remembered the devastation in Russia during World War II, a devastation that Soviet generals could not prevent in 1962 if the United States attacked.[28] Khrushchev felt Cuba was not worth a war involving the Soviet Union.[29]

Yet the Soviet Union was not a one-man dictatorship. Khrushchev could be overruled by top Communist party officials. He was already having serious political problems with the Kremlin leadership, problems that climaxed in his downfall two years later. Given the difference in tone between his letters of October 26 and October 27, American officials wondered if Khrushchev was still in charge. Analysts at the time believed he had written the first, but believed the second was a committee product from the collective Kremlin leadership.[30] The Cubans later claimed the majority of the presidium opposed Khrushchev, but this is not certain.[31]

If Krushchev fell, the United States might have to negotiate with someone less concerned about peace. Several days of chaos in the Kremlin might even leave no one with authority to remove the missiles from Cuba before the United States felt impelled to strike the sites. Apparently recognizing the perils of Khrushchev's predicament, Attorney General Robert Kennedy secretly told Soviet ambassador Anatoly Dobrynin that the United States would quietly withdraw the Jupiter missiles from Turkey if Khrushchev publicly backed down in Cuba.[32] Thus, Khrushchev could portray the secret deal to his colleagues as an even trade—eliminating American missiles in Turkey in return for eliminating weapons in

Cuba. This deal was secret, however, so the Soviet Union publicly had to grovel at Kennedy's feet with nothing to show for the withdrawal other than Kennedy's statement that the United States would not invade Cuba. Khrushchev surely knew this could end his career[33] but put world peace above personal ambition. He agreed to remove the missiles, and the crisis ended on October 28.

Kennedy nonetheless continued the quarantine and insisted that his pledge to refrain from invading Cuba was invalid until the IL-28 bombers were also removed. Only seven had been assembled, and the remaining thirty-five were still strewn about in unassembled pieces. Moreover, several of the seven operational airplanes were trainers incapable of performing any combat task.[34] The aircraft had been virtually ignored during the crisis, and even American officials were unsure that the missile negotiations had also covered the bombers.[35] Kennedy's stance was especially awkward for the Russians because unlike the missiles, the IL-28s had been given to Cuba. The Soviets had no authority to remove them; that decision had to be made by Castro. Castro was already enraged by Khrushchev's capitulation on the missiles and was adamant about keeping the bombers. Kennedy continually stepped up the pressure on Khrushchev; finally Kennedy said that if the Soviets were unable to remove the IL-28s, he would destroy them by aerial attack. On November 20 Khrushchev announced that the bombers were returning to Russia. Exactly what he did to force Castro to relinquish the aircraft is unknown. But the result was to ruin Soviet credibility even in Cuba, just as the missile affair had devastated Soviet credibility elsewhere in the world. Kennedy now lifted the quarantine and promised not to invade Cuba, after accomplishing a geopolitical triumph.

Kennedy also achieved a domestic political victory. Indeed, partisan advantage was never far from his mind during the crisis. Roger Hilsman, director of the State Department's Office of Intelligence and Research, later said, "The United States might not be in mortal danger but the administration most certainly was." He said Kennedy insisted on removal of the IL-28s "for domestic political reasons."[36] When Kennedy learned of the missile photos, his first comments to aide Kenneth O'Donnell were, "We've just elected Capehart in Indiana, and Ken Keating will probably be the next President of the United States."[37] Homer Capehart and Kenneth Keating were Republican senators who made Cuba a big issue in 1962.

Kennedy later told aide Theodore Sorensen that the crisis was necessary lest Democrats be portrayed as soft on Castro.[38] During one of the meetings at which the crisis strategy was planned, Treasury Secretary Douglas Dillon pointed out that the Cuban missiles could throw the House of Representatives to the GOP in the upcoming elections.[39] Former secretary of state Dean Acheson warned Secretary of State Dean Rusk of enormous political consequences unless Kennedy acted.[40] Although these concerns were unmentioned in public at the time, observers as divergent as Khrushchev and former president Eisenhower were correct when they suspected the November elections helped prompt the crisis.[41]

Later events support the theory that Kennedy's actions had a political, rather than military, basis. In 1978 the Soviet Union supplied Cuba with MIG 23/27 jet bombers, which had far better capabilities than the IL-28s. No thunder came from Washington. The next year Cuba received SA-2 antiaircraft rockets, which could be adapted to extend their range to Florida ground targets. No protests came from the U.S. government. The Soviet "combat brigade" in Cuba, publicized in the 1980 U.S. presidential election, included elements used to guard nuclear weapons in Eastern Europe. Some observers felt the components played a similar role in Cuba, perhaps being used as security for nuclear weapons on Soviet submarines. No public questions, let alone military action, came from the United States under presidents Jimmy Carter or Ronald Reagan.

One aspect of the missile crisis was little noted by the public, which viewed it as a nuclear confrontation. The crisis certainly had the potential of becoming nuclear, but the matter was settled by U.S. supremacy in *conventional* weapons, used in a geographical area where it had tremendous strategic advantage. For the United States, the question of using nuclear weapons to settle the crisis never came up. America could use naval vessels in a quarantine and could easily destroy the rocket sites with conventional forces. In contrast, the only way the Soviets could resist a conventional attack upon Cuba was with a nuclear attack upon the United States. Since they were unwilling to go to such an extreme, they had no alternative except capitulation. Reliance on nuclear weapons as a primary deterrent can put a country in a weaker position when dealing with a sturdy conventional force. The Cuban missile crisis did not prove the need for a strong nuclear arsenal; it proved that strong conventional forces are needed.

And is there any lesson to be drawn from the extraordinary conduct of American leaders who freely admitted risking a nuclear war over an issue with little or no military significance? They seem to have been trapped by their own rhetoric on the eve of a national election. When the Republicans charged that the Soviets were planning to base missiles in Cuba, the Kennedy administration could have encouraged debate on the military significance of such a step. Instead, Kennedy and the men around him decided to raise the political stakes. They publicly accepted the Republican contention that such a move threatened the United States, warned Khrushchev not to put "offensive" missiles in Cuba, and claimed that the United States would do whatever was necessary to prevent the situation from occurring. This rhetoric made the Democrats appear tougher than the Republicans. And it was cheap rhetoric, because the Kennedy administration plainly thought that Khrushchev would never base rockets in Cuba. The administration never thought it would have to make good on its words. When the weapons were discovered, Kennedy's men were trapped. If they failed to take the promised military action, their credibility would be destroyed among the domestic electorate and the international diplomatic community. The administration could not face the humiliation of admitting it had been blustering and so instead decided to risk a nuclear war.

This decision was not as diabolical as it sounds. The accounts left by participants seem authentic, and none put the matter in such terms. In reading the memoirs, however, one is struck by the participants' knowledge of what they were doing and their unwillingness to face it honestly. Psychologically this is understandable. Who could admit he preferred to chance a nuclear war rather than confess he had been playing politics with the issue at hand? So Kennedy and his associates deluded themselves into thinking they really had been telling the truth all along, that the weapons in Cuba must be a threat, just as their rhetoric had claimed. The IL-28 bombers that had been acceptable on October 14 now became a peril. The medium-range rockets that could barely reach northern Florida were transformed into weapons that could devastate America's heartland. Nonexistent intermediate-range missiles with no launch facilities were given an exaggerated ability to strike much of the Western Hemisphere. The more Kennedy's men talked among themselves, the more they convinced themselves that a clear and present danger existed. If they failed to throw down a nuclear challenge, they would betray their country. They had to act—it was not just politics. When they looked in the mirror, they saw brave statesmen responding to a sneak attack, not craven cowards unwilling to eat their ill-considered words.

Only after the missiles were discovered did Kennedy's men pause to consider whether the weapons posed the military danger that Kennedy had warned of so confidently. How ironic that the president and his men could then conclude that no such peril existed, but nonetheless felt impelled to keep their promises to act if missiles were found—promises based on the assumption of a military threat that they now knew to be unfounded.

The peril of cheap rhetoric is, therefore, perhaps the most important lesson of the Cuban missile crisis. Chest-thumping can be emotionally satisfying and can garner many votes. Yet it discourages careful examination of reality. Truth, however unpleasant it might be, has survival value.

CUBA SINCE THE MISSILE CRISIS

A sobered Kennedy and Khrushchev sought to reduce tensions after the Cuban missile crisis. In 1963 Kennedy terminated American support for the Cuban exiles opposing Castro, and the U.S. Navy began preventing private raids against Cuba. The Soviet Union began urging Castro to reach accommodation with the United States. This displeased Castro, and questions must have grown in his mind about whether the Soviets could any longer be depended on to protect Cuba. Moreover, the missile affair had humiliated him because it revealed he had compromised Cuban independence, trading domination by the United States for domination by the Soviet Union. Castro had accepted the missiles under duress, but when the business went sour, Russia removed the rockets and bombers against his wishes. Khrushchev had even agreed to on-site inspections in Cuba to verify the removal, a stark violation of Cuban sovereignty that Castro bitterly protested. Ten years later he told a reporter, "Yes, I was furious. Our relations with Russia started on the downgrade after that for some years."[42] He was particularly irked about Russia's trade and foreign-aid ties with rightist dictatorships in Latin America, which made him question how seriously the Soviet Union could be promoting revolution in Latin America. This excellent point was ignored by U.S. policy makers, who continued to fear Soviet-supported Communist takeovers in Latin America.

Castro's distance from the Soviet Union resulted in his organization of a new Cuban Communist party. The old party, formed in 1925, had collaborated with Batista and had always considered Soviet Communists to be role models. Castro downgraded this party in 1961 when he formed the Organizaciónes Revolucionarias Integradas (ORI), an umbrella organization comprising three groups: the Cuban Communist party, the Movement of July 26th (Castro's followers), and the Directorio Estudiantil (an anti-Communist group that had also fought Batista). In July 1961 he began to transform ORI into the Partido Unido de la Revolucion Socialista (PURS). Neither ORI nor PURS had any policy-making functions. Their role was to administer Castro's decisions. It was only after the Cuban Communist party had been transformed into Castro's servant that he declared he was a Communist. At that point the Cuban Communist party took its orders from Castro, not Russia. Castro's declaration can therefore be seen as an assertion that he, not the Soviets, ran Cuba, though his announcement received a contrary interpretation in the United States.

In October 1965 Castro converted PURS into the Communist party of Cuba. The old Russian-oriented party ceased to exist. Castro's action was a declaration of independence from the Soviet Union, which fully realized his intent. Soviet aid would resume and surpass old levels, but Castro would no more tolerate pressure from the Soviets than he would from the Americans. Essentially Castro's Communist party was the old Movement of July 26th under a new name and without the two old rival factions. This identity can be demonstrated by the party's relationship to the Castro regime. In other Communist countries, the government follows party orders. In Cuba, the party follows Castro's orders.

By the late 1960s Castro had become convinced that peaceful revolution through political agitation was impossible. He began to believe that force was needed to promote and protect revolutionary movements. Castro thus began promoting Latin American revolution through guerrilla warfare. This was in part an idealistic attempt to promote social justice through communism, but it was mainly an effort to end Cuba's isolation by creating friendly states in the region. Like the Soviets before Stalin instituted socialism in one country, Castro worried that the Cuban revolution could not survive indefinitely while surrounded by hostile neighbors. As with Russia in the mid-1920s, Cuba's problem in the late 1960s was less military attack than a West taking advantage of any opportunity to weaken Castro, such as trade barriers designed to cripple the Cuban economy and thereby promote collapse of the regime. Castro's promotion of guerrilla campaigns was not intended as aggression for conquest, but rather was motivated by concern for Cuban national security. Since years of active hostility from the United States and its allies were required to drive Castro to this desperate move, there is every reason to suspect he would never have done it had Cuba been left alone.

Cuba's promotion of Latin America guerrilla warfare was highly publicized by friend and foe alike, but the campaign failed. The failure resulted partly because Castro's support was primarily rhetorical and partly because the populations to be liberated were not seeking Castro's style of liberation. Instead of joining the revolution, peasants turned in guerrillas for reward money. But Castro's grand campaign for Latin American revolution failed primarily because a revolution is hard to achieve—much harder than most people seem to realize. If U.S. Congressmen had a realistic idea of the problems facing would-be revolutionaries, perhaps fewer tax dollars would go to friendly tyrants and friendly freedom fighters. Most regimes are so stable that revolution is impossible. Instability is something that revolutionaries exploit, rather than cause.

Around 1970, as Castro's guerrilla liberation effort in Latin America was failing, his relations with Russia improved. He had already received Latin America's best air force from the Soviets. Since 1963 they had supplied excellent defensive aircraft and occasionally updated the stock as technical improvements occurred. (In 1972 U.S. intelligence concluded that Cuba's jets and air defense system were powerful defensive weapons but had no offensive capability.) With Soviet encouragement Castro began trying to find practical accommodations with his neighbors. Cuba even began establishing trade ties with regimes it once found loathsome, such as Juan Perón's Argentina. Such compromises were once the reasons for Castro's bitter condemnation of the Soviet Union, and now Communist guerrilla leaders elsewhere in Latin America similarly fumed at Castro. He even grew quiet about repression of Communists abroad, much as the Soviets had learned to keep silent about other governments' treatment of native Communists. Castro was learning to live in the real world.

The real world, however, contained some revolutionary activity that had developed without Castro's instigation. Helping an ongoing struggle was far different from attempting to provoke it. During the 1970s Castro sent foreign aid to a couple dozen countries to help strengthen their leftist regimes. In addition, he sent military contingents to Angola and southern Africa at the request of Communists fighting there. He even sent a few dozen men to fight with the Syrians against Israel in the October 1973 war. Such tangible activity began to make Cuba a power among Third World nations. The effect this Cuban activity had on Africa will be examined later in this book.

The effect on Cuba was mixed. Cuba did gain friends among

leftist revolutionary regimes around the world, opening trade opportunities. On the other hand, the Cuban economy was hurt because highly skilled persons were using their military talents in Africa rather than their civilian talents at home.

Castro may have felt the price was worth it. Cuba's isolation lessened in the 1970s. Some Caribbean nations, including Barbados, Guyana, Jamaica, and Trinidad and Tobago granted Cuba diplomatic recognition, and OAS sanctions prohibiting trade with Cuba were lifted. Foreign subsidiaries of Ford, General Motors, and Chrysler began selling to Cuba as the U.S. government chose to ignore its own trade embargo.

On the fifteenth anniversary of his revolution Castro received congratulations from Britain's Queen Elizabeth II along with messages from Pope Paul VI, French president Georges Pompidou, and Spanish Generalissimo Francisco Franco. The growing climate of toleration for Cuba had isolated the United States, not Castro.[43]

Ironically, cordial greetings from across the political spectrum were withheld until Cuba began to take on the totalitarian characteristics the United States had inaccurately attributed to it when the revolutionary regime began. Castro shut down the Associated Press and United Press International bureaus in Havana in the late 1960s. Only two Western news organizations remained in 1975, and the Cuban press had degenerated to Batista-era quality.

Castro's military assistance program in Africa indicated how secure he felt against U.S. attack in the 1970s. This sense of ease changed in the 1980s. Ronald Reagan's administration seemed to call for destruction of leftists in El Salvador and Nicaragua to clear the way for a final solution to the problem of Castro. Castro felt pressure to fortify Communists in those two countries in hopes of keeping the fighting away from Cuba. The U.S. government characterized Castro's policy as meddling, but such conduct could be viewed as vital to Cuba's national security. Cuban support for these Communists would naturally be more intense than support from other Communist countries: to them, Latin America was a matter of interest; to Castro, it was a matter of survival.

Even so, Communist rebels in El Salvador received mainly rhetorical aid from Havana. It is debatable whether significant tangible assistance to the Sandinistas materialized before they gained control of the Nicaraguan government. Such restraint may have had less to do with Castro's natural inclination than with fear of provoking Reagan into accelerating any timetable for dealing with Cuba.

In the 1980s Castro perhaps fitted the 1960 U.S. government

portrayal of him. And that is a tragedy. Because Castro began his revolutionary career seeking to implement the promises that Cuba's 1940 constitution made for equality of all citizens before the law, for free speech, for the eight-hour working day, for the banning of child labor, for women's rights, for land reform, for exploitation of national resources in the national interest. By making a genuine attempt to enforce the 1940 constitution—a document that the U.S. government approved—Castro was labeled a Communist.

The United States refused to tolerate a leader who attempted to implement many of the ideals hailed in Fourth of July orations. Castro's regime was then harassed by the United States and befriended by the Communists. Gradually, as the Free World rejected Castro, he in turn rejected the democratic beliefs that it claimed to protect. Although Castro would never have been subservient to the United States, an American policy sensitive to the history of Cuba and the aspirations of its people might have prevented him from becoming an enemy.

XVIII.

Communist Failure in Latin America

Fidel Castro's Cuba was neither the first nor the last leftist Latin American regime to feel the wrath of the United States. Neither the government of Guatemala in 1954 nor that of Chile in 1973 could withstand the pressure placed on it by the United States.

GUATEMALA

Guatemala's heritage of oppression stretches back through centuries of exploitation as a Spanish colony. After throwing off Spanish rule in 1821 Guatemala became part of Mexico and then part of a larger country known as the United Provinces of Central America before achieving independent statehood in 1839.

These political changes, however, had little effect on the average person. The writings of the liberal Pedro Molina, published in 1827, have themes still familiar a century and a half later: "The nobility of Guatemala, more tyrannical than the kings of Spain, used the lower classes as beings sprung from nature only to serve them; they held all the positions in Administration which the European Spaniards did not hold. . . . They sold justice and those from the provinces, never, never won a suit against them. They purchased the fruits of the country at the lowest possible price; being the only buyers they purchased at their whim, because as trade was not free it was not licit to sell to others."[1] Indians were particularly victimized. Although Spain ordered them freed from slavery in 1542, the order had little effect in distant Guatemala. Although the Indians constituted the vast majority of the country's people, four centuries would pass before they would be allowed to participate in Guatemala's political process.

In the decades following Pedro Molina's complaints, the presidents of Guatemala were notorious for cruel oppression. In the 1920s a series of presidents held power with army support, and in 1931 General Jorge Ubico won election to that office. He is described as "thorough, efficient, intelligent, and heartless"; in his regime, "spies, informers and brutal police abounded. . . . It was worth your life to commit a petty crime."[2] Ubico eventually declared, "I am like Hitler, I execute first and give trial afterwards."[3]

A revolt overthrew Ubico in June 1944, and a military junta took power under the leadership of General Federico Ponce Vaides. He was toppled by another military coup in October, led by Jorge Toriello, Colonel Francisco J. Arana, and Major Jacobo Arbenz Guzmán. They shepherded in a new constitution, and an election held in accordance with its provisions made Juan José Arévalo president. He became a dictatorial tyrant, and his finance minister Jorge Toriello was feared even more. Toriello eventually was sent out of the country to a diplomatic post. Armed forces chief Arana was then viewed as the main power in the regime until he was murdered in 1949. Responsibility for the crime was never proven, but witnesses identified the gunmen as associates of Arbenz's wife. Arana's death left Arbenz as the most likely successor to Arévalo, and indeed Arbenz was the regime's candidate in the 1950 presidential election. Opposition candidates and their supporters were intimidated by thugs, and the government provided transportation for voters casting repeat ballots that helped assure Arbenz's victory. Regardless of the election's fraudulent nature, he had the backing of labor unions, the military, and the bureaucracy. His political base was strong, and his future bright with hope.

Jacobo Arbenz Guzmán was a pharmacist's son who was graduated from Guatemala's national military academy and became a career officer. He married into a well-to-do planter family. He was snubbed by the Guatemalan upper class, who felt he had married above himself. Since he was an army officer and wealthy landowner, it was assumed his government would lean to the right. People were in for a surprise.

His rhetoric was not at all what one might expect from a military man: "I firmly believe that no idea is dangerous for a true democracy, sufficiently strong for itself when democracy means government of the people and for the people."[4] That March 1953 statement indicated that he staunchly believed in the American ideal of the free marketplace of ideas, confident that error would be dissipated by the force of truth. Without fear, his government soon legalized the Communist party.

Arbenz's attitude was noteworthy because, although a professional military background can promote antipathy toward Communists, such a background can also generate contempt for the ordinary politician who specializes in cutting deals and dividing the pie. Even some senior U.S. military officers feel contempt for their civilian superiors, who are viewed as leeches sucking vitality from the nation to which the officers have dedicated their lives. General Dwight Eisenhower, General Douglas MacArthur, and the head of the Manhattan Project, General Leslie Groves, all held President Harry Truman in contempt for this reason. The same kind of sentiments can be found among the military of other countries.[5]

In Guatemala Arbenz was offended by politicians who seemed to love power or who served as lackeys for interests that shunned scrutiny.[6] He was particularly skeptical of the so-called anti-Communist politicians because typically they had no program other than opposition to Communism. They made no proposals for promoting public health, education, transportation, or land reform. In contrast, the native Communists did have such programs, accompanied by supporting data about conditions in the country. The Communists did not suppress or conquer their opponents in Guatemala. The opponents left a vacuum into which the Communists rushed.

But during the Arbenz regime, from 1951 to 1954, Communists did not enter the Guatemalan government in great numbers. No members of his cabinet were Communists, and only four of the fifty-six congressmen were. These four did, however, hold important committee posts in the legislature. Political alliances with government officials of other parties also gave the Communists influence.

When fellow army officers urged that the Communists be kept out of the government, Arbenz said that such a ban would be undemocratic. He was adamant about keeping Communists in the National Agrarian Department (the government agency helping to administer the breakup and distribution of large landed estates), calling them "precisely the most effective and those who do not sell out to the landlords".[7]

A *Time/Life* magazine correspondent asked Arbenz if anti-Communism was dangerous for Guatemala. He replied, "While it defends only the particular interests of those who visibly direct it, no. As soon as it tries to break lances in the name and defense of foreign and anti-national interests, my reply is affirmative."[8] Arbenz scoffed at those who hid behind cries of patriotism and national security while promoting their self-interest.

Just a few months into his term, Arbenz grew to like Guatemalan Communists because they acted as if they genuinely cared about their country, treating government service as a civic duty rather than an opportunity to grow rich. Because they also supported his social reforms, he began to look upon them as dependable allies.

His promotion of social reform was uncommon in a military man. The military normally sees its job as defense of the status quo; Arbenz instead wanted to change it. Perhaps his middle-class background made him sensitive to the economic exploitation that was the basis of upper-class prosperity in Guatemala. He married a woman of radical political tendencies, who was friendly with prominent Communists of Guatemala, El Salvador, and Chile before Arbenz became president. Whatever the origins of his sense of social justice, apparently it was not based on political expediency after he became president.

For centuries the Guatemalan government had been a servant of the domestic upper class and, more recently, of great corporations based in the United States. Arbenz quickly attacked the bases of ruling-class power. He pushed agrarian reform to distribute land to peasants, liberating them from having to work for great landlords. Arbenz was also the first Guatemalan ruler to open the political process to Indians. Giving them the right to vote portended an enormous change in the government's orientation. The Indians constituted 70 percent of the nation's population and could now easily control the outcome of any future election. The cruel exploitation of this labor pool seemed destined to end.

Wealthy individuals and corporations feared that their prosperity would be reduced by higher wages. Their anxiety increased as Arbenz pushed economic reforms that would force corporations to use their capital productively. He wanted to promote the economic development of Guatemala through private enterprise, but corporations did not like being told what to do with their assets. Arbenz also tried to break lucrative monopolies held by some companies, and he diminished the privileged treatment they formerly received from the government. The companies seem to have thrived during the Arbenz presidency, but they nonetheless worried that Arbenz intended to destroy them.

Of the corporations angered by the actions of Arbenz, the most important was the United Fruit Company. This firm began as a Boston-based banana-trading operation in the 1870s and was famous a century later for its Chiquita brand of bananas. In the twentieth century, United Fruit gained a monopoly over many agricultural products in Central America. During the Arbenz regime, the company's multimillion-dollar operations in Guatemala controlled ocean shipping, railroads, and communications as well.

Arbenz regarded agrarian reform as crucial for the Guatemalan population. He began expropriating United Fruit real estate in February 1953, using interest-bearing twenty-five-year bonds to pay for the land. United Fruit complained that the compensation was far too low, but like Castro's expropriations later in Cuba, the price was based on the value the company had provided for tax collection. This dispute occurred during the McCarthy hysteria in the United States, and Americans were suddenly informed that a Red menace had appeared. "Few Americans are aware that less than 2 hours' flying time from the Panama Canal and 3 hours from the vital oil fields and industries of Texas there is a country whose government for all practical purposes is dominated by the Communists"—so warned Theodore Geiger, who authored a study on Guatemala for the National Planning Association.[9] That think tank issued an official policy statement in 1953: "It is imperative that the situation in Guatemala be recognized for what it is—a typical example of Communist tactics and an increasingly successful Communist conspiracy to subvert that country in the interests not of its people but of the worldwide ambitions of Soviet imperialism. . . . In our judgment, Communist infiltration in Guatemala constitutes a threat not only to the freedom of that country but to the security of all Western Hemisphere nations."[10] United Fruit itself published a 235-page book declaring that Guatemala had turned Communist.

Despite alarmist talk from the United States about Guatemala becoming a Russian toehold in the New World, the Soviets actually paid little attention to developments there. They were delighted by the consternation Guatemala caused in the United States; but while Stalin ruled and afterward, the Soviets made no effort to push things along. They felt the United States would never tolerate a leftist regime in Latin America and were not willing to risk the humiliation of backing a doomed cause.[11] Guatemala stood absolutely independent of the Soviet Union.

Complaints such as this one, from Theodore Geiger's National Planning Association study on Guatemala, were typical: "The Government is now rushing to completion a highway, started under the old regime, which parallels the main line of the IRCA [International Railways of Central America, a United Fruit–dominated company] from coast to coast. Such a highway has long been needed, but the Government has also announced its intention of diverting as much traffic as possible from the railroad once the highway has been opened, and thereby rendering its operation uneconomic."[12] This was so-called Communist activity? A much needed and long-planned highway was under construction; it would provide shippers an opportunity to use trucks and avoid the United Fruit railroad. It seems that anything that reduced United Fruit profits was labeled Communist.

The Arbenz regime also encouraged the formation of labor unions. Organized banana workers pried concessions from United Fruit in Guatemala, and the government publicized this success throughout other Central American states. The rulers of those countries, men whose power depended on companies such as United Fruit, W. R. Grace, the Texas Oil Company, and Coca-Cola rather than the people, were disgruntled by Arbenz's success.

By the autumn of 1953 the U.S. Department of State was issuing warnings about Guatemala. Assistant Secretary of State for Inter-American Affairs John M. Cabot (who was also a United Fruit stockholder) said that "activities of the international Communist conspiracy" in Guatemala would be intolerable to governments of the Western Hemisphere.[13] In January 1954 the U.S. ambassador to Guatemala, John E. Puerifoy, declared that American public opinion might create an irresistible demand for steps "to prevent Guatemala from falling into the lap of international Communism."[14]

Guatemala posed no military threat to the United States, and suggestions to the contrary are a commentary on the remarkable atmosphere in America during Senator Joseph McCarthy's heyday. Nor was Guatemala a military threat to its neighbors. Inaccurate claims were made that Communists "have already converted Guatemala into a base for supplying cadres, funds, arms, and advice to the Communist movements in other Latin America countries."[15] Indeed, rather than exporting arms, the Arbenz government was desperately trying to import weapons from any available supplier as a protection against feared attacks by American-supported exiles. Arbenz tried to buy from the United States, but was refused. He tried other Western Hemisphere sources with equal futility.

Finally in 1954 he managed to buy a couple thousand tons of Czechoslovakian arms; President Eisenhower called this action further proof of Arbenz's Communist leanings. In the end, the Czech matériel was irrelevant.

Time ran out for Arbenz in June 1954. In the summer of the previous year, after expropriations of United Fruit Company land had begun, the company began discussions with U.S. government officials about retaliatory action. The company was well connected with the highest echelons of the government. The Sullivan and Cromwell law firm of CIA Director Allen Dulles had negotiated the original agreements by which United Fruit operated in Central America. He was a former president of United Fruit, and his brother and law partner, Secretary of State John Foster Dulles, is credited with having personally written the agreements.[16] In the summer of 1953 a senior United Fruit attorney, Thomas G. Corcoran, discussed the company's grievances in a meeting with Undersecretary of State Walter Bedell Smith. Smith had been Truman's CIA director and would later join United Fruit's board of directors. CIA officers said that Smith's conversation with Corcoran was the start of a plan to overthrow Arbenz with an invading army of Guatemalan exiles.[17] Years afterward Thomas P. McCann, who had been a United Fruit official, wrote that "United Fruit was involved at every level. I was told that the CIA even shipped down the weapons by Fruit Company boats."[18]

In 1953 the CIA recruited a few dozen Guatemalan exiles and trained them in Honduras and Nicaragua for an overthrow of the Arbenz government, which President Eisenhower then (and later) explicitly described as Communist. Although the delivery of Czech arms was later cited as justification for the invasion of Guatemala and overthrow of Arbenz, plans for that action were underway long before the arms deal was arranged and long before the matériel was delivered.

On June 16, 1954, Eisenhower declared in a White House meeting of the invasion planners: "I'm prepared to take any steps that are necessary to see that it succeeds. For if it succeeds, it's the people of Guatemala throwing off the yoke of Communism. If it fails, the flag of the United States has failed."[19]

The attack began on June 18. The invading force led by Colonel Carlos Castillo Armas numbered about 150 men and a few World War II surplus fighter airplanes piloted by American citizens. The invasion force was insignificant, but the Guatemalan military made little effort to resist. The officer corps had been loyal to Arbenz formerly but felt the loyalty was not reciprocated. The officers were particularly alarmed when Arbenz agreed to the formation of a workers' militia, since this could have been the first step toward elimination of the army. Some officers opposed his social reforms, and few were willing to fight in defense of them. Arbenz resigned, and a right-wing junta led by Castillo Armas took over.

America solemnly assured the United Nations that the United States was not responsible for the invasion.

The easy overthrow of the Arbenz government in June 1954 did not mean that Guatemalans opposed the regime, however. If that were the case, they would have aided the invaders. Rather, Guatemalans responded as most populations do in a coup—they did not see the outcome making a big difference to them and simply tried to stay out of the way. They certainly did not act as if they were being liberated.

Indeed, the ensuing Castillo Armas regime was hardly democratic. It instantly outlawed voting by illiterates, eliminating most Indians from the electorate. The right-wing junta also set up a government agency responsible for identifying Communists. The agency's secret proceedings had no appeal process, and any person so identified could be imprisoned for six months. Whether or not such a "Communist" was incarcerated, he suffered other penalties automatically—he was prohibited from serving in public office or even from owning a radio. Previous agrarian reforms were cancelled, with hundreds of thousands of acres seized from peasants who had received them from the Arbenz government. Labor unions were restricted.

Nor did democracy make much headway in the years to come. General Enrique Peralta Azurdia seized power through a military coup in 1963. Under him death squads freely roamed the countryside, murdering suspected Communists. U.S. officials in Guatemala became targets for assassination by the left. By the 1970s the right-wing Guatemalan regime was not only firmly antidemocratic, it was a military threat to neighboring Belize. Guatemala had a long-standing claim to that British colonial territory, formerly known as British Honduras, and disputed Britain's decision to grant independence to the colony rather than give it to Guatemala. Guatemala broke diplomatic relations with England and seemed ready to enforce its claim by military means when Belize became independent, but apparently was deterred by vague pledges of British defense and by the united support Belize received from other nations of the region. The issue continued to simmer in the 1980s, however, because the Reagan administration claimed that

Belize could become a Communist foothold. The Reagan attitude stiffened Guatemala's intransigence.

The United States saw to the overthrow of a Guatemalan government that tried to improve life for the average citizen and posed no military threat to its neighbors. In its place the United States established a rightist dictatorship that immediately stripped most of the population of their voting rights and became feared as a military threat by neighboring countries.

The historical record indicates that the American government was less concerned about defending freedom than defending corporations operating in Guatemala. United Fruit sold its Guatemalan plantations in 1972, but dozens of other corporations continued to thrive under the right-wing dictatorship there. American business finds such an environment profitable and desirable.

CHILE

Like Guatemala, Chile had been exploited as a Spanish colony for hundreds of years before achieving independence in 1818. The constitution adopted in 1833 was designed to assure that wealthy interests would control the government. The document remained in force for almost a century. As late as 1925, less than 8 percent of the population was registered to vote. Assuming a 100 percent voter turnout, a landslide victory might represent the will of only five percent of the population—hardly a mandate. Chile's national emblem contains the motto "By Reason or by Force."

The United States has been involved with Chile since the 1800s. In one sixty-year period, the mineral resources removed from Chile by United States corporations had a dollar value greater than Chile's gross national product over a 400-year span. Such profitability gave these corporations an intense interest in policies promoted by the government of Chile. John Schofield, secretary of war under Andrew Johnson, became General-in-Chief of the U.S. Army in 1888. In his memoirs Schofield wrote:

> I was asked to make an estimate of the military force which would be necessary to occupy and hold a vital point in Chilean territory until the demands of the United States were complied with. It was assumed, of course, that the navy could easily do all the rest. Pending the consideration of this subject, so disagreeable to me, I had a dream which I repeated at the time to a few intimate friends. I saw in the public street a man holding a mangy-looking dog by the neck, and beating him with a great club, while a crowd of people

assembled to witness the "sport." Some one asked the man why he was beating the poor dog. He replied: "Oh just to make him yelp." But the dog did not "yelp." He bore his cruel punishment without a whine. Then he was transformed into a splendid animal, one of the noblest of his species, and the entire crowd of bystanders, with one accord, rushed in and compelled the man to desist from beating him.[20]

The tremendous profits that flowed from Chile to American corporations were jealously resented by Chilean politicians, as was American control over the economy. Nationalism was characteristic of Chilean political parties, and none was more nationalistic than the Socialist party founded in 1933. The party had no firm ideology other than patriotism. Those who loved their country right or wrong and believed in Chile for Chileans were likely to be comfortable with the Socialists. They did not maintain a steady leftist ideology; over the years they had been anti-Communist, pro-fascist, and Communist-allied. This history has been characterized as opportunistic, but it can also be viewed as flexible promotion of nationalism—which was the core of Chilean Socialist philosophy.

This nationalism meant that Socialists viewed the influence of some great American corporations in Chile as a threat to national sovereignty. The copper mining firms Anaconda Company, the Kennecott corporation, and Cerro Corporation were particularly resented by Socialists. Moreover, the Socialists were interested in increasing the political power of ordinary workers—which naturally would be opposed by employers and other interests whose wealth depended on exploitation of the lower classes.

In Salvador Allende Gossens, the Socialists had a superb candidate. Trained as a physician, he eventually became president of the country's medical association. He was from a well-to-do family, but his medical practice among public welfare patients helped convince him that revolutionary social change was needed in Chile. He rejected Communist dogmatism, however, and became one of the founders of the Socialist party. He was a member of the president's cabinet in the 1930s and 1940s, and through his calls for government programs in housing, health, and welfare, Allende became known as an advocate for the lower classes. He began running for president in 1952 and became a perennial Socialist candidate every six years. He was a well-known figure in 1970, having participated in public life for decades. Despite his outspoken advocacy of socialism, he was not antibusiness; he himself was a director of several business firms. He had a genial and reassuring personality, much like that of the stereotypical ideal family physician. Allende's personality diminished the effect of fear tactics by opponents; he was "cultured, urbane, witty and elegantly dressed: to wavering non-Marxists, an almost reassuringly bourgeois figure."[21] Despite dire warnings from Allende's right-wing foes, it was hard to believe this unthreatening man could do anything frightening.

In the 1958 election, President Carlos Ibáñez del Campo, a conservative military man, supported Allende as his successor. In another campaign twelve years later, Chile's conservative former president Jorge Alessandri Rodríguez praised Allende's "long and proven democratic conviction, reflected in attitudes of constant respect for the constitution and the laws."[22] Such endorsements demonstrated Allende's position in the mainstream of Chilean politics despite his Socialist affiliation. Allende lost in 1958, having received almost a third of the votes after making an electoral alliance with the Communist party. This alliance continued in subsequent campaigns. In 1964 Allende received almost 40 percent of the vote. In past elections this number of votes would have swept him into office, but this time the rightist forces were allied and achieved an absolute majority—nearly unheard of in Chile's multi-party politics. In the 1970 election, his opposition was divided, and he received a plurality. Allende was the choice of just over a third of the electorate, a total representing perhaps 15 percent of the population. Allende's main support came from the working class. After tense political maneuverings, Chile's congress declared him the winner.

After a tough campaign and fair election, Chile had democratically elected a Communist-allied Marxist president who promised to lead the country into socialism. As in the Kerala state elections in India, this outcome was distinctly embarrassing to those who argued that free men would never choose such a government. Now it had happened again.

Allende did not underestimate the task ahead of him. During the election his coalition had stated that Chile's problems were "clearly the result of class privilege which will never be given up voluntarily."[23] The tenacious attitude of the privileged class meant that financial and agrarian reform could only be achieved through expropriation. The possible consequences were clear to Allende, who said, "The lesson of Guatemala has been learnt."[24]

Popular enthusiasm existed for Allende's goals: nationalization of large mining, banking, and communications companies; reform of the judicial and legislative branches of government; land reform;

and social programs such as assuring milk for all children. Milk for children seems to have been uncontroversial. Judicial reform was another question, as it was intended to make the system more responsive to the people's needs, such as through establishment of municipal courts to hear minor cases locally. Even that modest change was defeated by defenders of the status quo. Allende's proposals for legislative reform would have given even more power to the people—one aspect would have permitted a proposed law to be introduced by the public upon collection of 5,000 signatures. The legislative reforms were blocked by those whose power depended on privileged access to the system.

Of all the interests arrayed against Allende, however, the most deadly were those that opposed his nationalization program. They orchestrated the forces that brought about his downfall.

Nationalization had formerly been uncontroversial. Allende's immediate predecessor, Eduardo Frei Montalva, had nationalized large portions of the American-owned Anaconda copper-mining company. Anaconda was paid in promissory notes, not cash, but the nationalization was not characterized as communistic or even hostile to American business. Frei had also moved to nationalize electric-power facilities owned by America's Boise Cascade Corporation.

Although Allende pursued nationalization as part of his socialist philosophy, his program received support from every major non-leftist political party. This support indicated that the ruling elite of Chile was unoffended and perhaps even pleased by Allende's expropriations of American companies. The company profits, after all, would be used to promote Chile's economy. Other foreign capitalists even found ways to take advantage of Allende's program: Fiat representatives offered to help operate the Ford Motor Company plant after the government takeover.

If companies proved that compensation from the expropriating government was inadequate, the firms picked up the difference from expropriation insurance provided by a federal agency known as Overseas Private Investment Corporation (OPIC). They were not losing their investments under Allende, merely the profits they would have enjoyed from continued exploitation of Chilean resources and people. The fury of American reaction indicates how lucrative those profits were and suggests that the revenue could have allowed the Allende regime to finance tremendous social reforms if the United States had refrained from waging economic war against Chile.

Complaints about nationalization came from Anaconda Company, International Telephone and Telegraph (ITT), Kennecott copper, and other U.S. firms that claimed they were not receiving fair compensation from Allende's government. They had an arguable case because Chile's ingenious accounting methods drastically reduced the value of properties, but the issue was certainly not clear-cut. This ambiguity was demonstrated when the companies tried to collect on their OPIC expropriation insurance policies. According to OPIC most of the property that Anaconda claimed had been seized by Allende had actually been nationalized by Frei, and OPIC paid less than 10 percent of what Anaconda said was owed by Allende. So even the U.S. government disputed Anaconda's figures. And not every American company found Allende difficult. The Cerro mining company not only reached agreement on compensation but helped Chile to run the company's old property.

There is compelling evidence that nothing in Allende's actions prompted the alliance of the multinational business community and Richard Nixon's administration that worked to bring Allende's downfall. Their effort was, after all, already underway before Allende's inauguration as president.[25] Instead it was more probably Allende's socialist philosophy that generated fear and hate among American government and business leaders; for ideological and economic reasons, they decided that a freely elected Marxist government could not be allowed to succeed. On October 13, 1970—three weeks before Allende's inauguration—the American ambassador to Chile, Edward Korry, and National Security Adviser Henry Kissinger met with Nixon in the Oval Office. Nixon was "pounding his fist into the palm of his hand and saying, 'That sonofabitch, that sonofabitch! . . . That bastard Allende.' "[26] Minutes made at a meeting of the National Security Council before Allende's election recorded Kissinger as saying, "I don't see why we need to stand by and watch a country go Communist due to the irresponsibility of its own people."[27]

Although Allende had Communist support, he was not a Communist himself—indeed, he had helped found the Socialist party because of his opposition to the Communists. His regime arrested leftist extremists and respected Chile's multiparty heritage—Allende's opponents expressed themselves vocally in congress and in the streets. Allende did occasionally restrict freedom of the press in moments of crisis, but the measures were temporary and legal. Allende did not impose a totalitarian state, and certainly nothing in his record or in the record of Chilean communism indicated that Chile would become a military threat to anyone.

The record did indicate that Allende was fiercely patriotic and believed that economic dominance by U.S. corporations compromised Chilean sovereignty and impoverished its people. He unquestionably intended to change that. And U.S. corporations unquestionably found this prospect frightening. For if Allende were allowed to succeed in Chile, a model would be established for the rest of the Third World to follow. Allende was therefore perceived as a threat to American business interests around the world. Billions of dollars were at stake. Like Arbenz and Castro, Allende became a marked man.

The ITT director who promoted the U.S. government-business alliance against Allende was former CIA director John McCone, whose virulent anti-Communism in that position under John F. Kennedy caused even Kennedy to question his analysis of events. ITT had limited success in recruiting assistance from other companies, but received a sympathetic hearing from the Nixon administration. A decade earlier Nixon had urged a military overthrow of Castro long before the new Cuban regime had expropriated a single American property. Secretary of State William P. Rogers told a closed meeting of corporation executives with interests in Chile, "The Nixon Administration is a business Administration. Its mission is to protect business."[28]

The multinational business community's activity against Allende, along with that of the CIA, Nixon, and Kissinger, is a well-known story. They hoped to cause turmoil in Chile's economy by stifling international loans and breaking local banks, thereby sending Chilean businessmen into a panic that would pressure Chile's congress to refuse to certify Allende as winner of the election. He took office despite the disruption, which then continued throughout his presidency. Notes taken by CIA Director Richard Helms during a September 15, 1970, anti-Allende strategy meeting with Nixon contain the phrase "make the economy scream."[29]

The Nixon administration convinced American banks to refuse new loans to Chile. Since about 80 percent of Chile's short-term credits had been from the United States, this halt devastated the economy under Allende. U.S. military aid to Chile, however, increased to seven times the pre-Allende level. This may sound paradoxical, like strengthening Castro's army, but in Chile the military opposed Allende, a fact well known in the United States. ITT vice-president William R. Merriam told Nixon aide Peter Peterson that economic warfare should persuade the Chilean military to "step in and restore order."[30] The United States equipped the armed forces for the coup in which Allende was killed.

The economic warfare proved Allende's contention that U.S. business interests held Chile in their grip. Moreover, the United States was clearly willing to harm Chile's businessmen by attacking that nation's economy. The situation was not one of capitalist solidarity, but rather of foreign capitalists seeking to maintain their dominance by destroying Chilean capitalists and Allende both, leaving the foreigners in an even stronger position than before Allende.[31]

The chaos that developed in the Chilean economy was encouraged by the United States, but disruption by Chilean businessmen themselves would surely have occurred anyway, although their motives were not necessarily malevolent. Contrary to popular impression, the business community can do quite well in both capitalist and socialist economies. The key to success in the latter is timing: set up business in a mature socialist state, such as the Soviet Union or the People's Republic of China, which has established niches in which private enterprise is welcome. These countries experience less labor unrest and fewer elections to cause abrupt changes of government policy. In addition, the property is far safer from expropriation in an established socialist nation than in a country that is just starting to convert to socialism.

The problem with business confidence in Chile was more than socialism per se. The problem was that Chilean socialism was in its infancy, and no one knew what the rules would be. How many and what sorts of firms would Allende expropriate? Would government-run industries have strong competitive advantages over remaining private ones? What loan policies would be adopted by government-run financial institutions? Such questions were legitimate. Until answers came, businessmen would be unsure how to direct their resources. In the meantime many liquidated their holdings, which reduced production, created shortages, and raised prices. In addition, investors began withdrawing money from productive enterprises while investing in foreign currencies. This reduced production further, at the same time as it reduced tax receipts and the price of government securities. Thus, government revenue declined.

The result was nasty inflation, which climbed to an annual rate of 300 percent in 1973. Wages did not keep up, and the working person was worse off economically after Allende's attempts to improve the average person's lot.

This disaster did not occur, however, until after the economic war conducted by the United States took hold. Left to his own devices, Allende managed to cut inflation to 7.5 percent in mid-

1971. At the same time, he presided over a 40 percent increase in wages, accompanied by booming manufacturing of consumer goods. If the United States had provided friendly help, or at least benign neglect, perhaps he could have achieved a long-term improvement in living standards.

The economic downslide became obvious in 1972. Despite a rise in demand, industrial production declined and was accompanied by roaring inflation. Nationwide strikes were called in 1972 and again in 1973 by owner-operators of trucks. This breakdown in the transportation system affected commerce throughout the country and was accompanied by regional stoppages by shopowners, taxi and bus owners, physicians, nurses, dentists, druggists, lawyers, engineers, and pilots. These self-employed and professional workers had legitimate economic grievances: creation of a competing government trucking operation, nationalization of a wholesale company owned by small business operators, shortages of spare parts, shortages of medicine, size of salaries. But strike leaders openly stated that the stoppages were intended to hurt the Allende regime. Indeed, the United States helped finance the truck driver strikes.[32] In 1972 the organizers demanded that Allende appoint military officers to his cabinet, and the next year, when Allende was overthrown in a military coup, strike leaders congratulated their own followers and the junta for eliminating the Allende regime.

These strikes, however, were by entrepreneurs and members of professions that normally are not associated with labor unrest. Blue-collar workers did not participate. Indeed, in the March 1973 congressional elections, Allende's coalition achieved a higher percentage of votes than in 1970 and gained seats in the national legislature. Despite all the turmoil, the last democratic expression of the electorate before the American-supported military coup indicated that Allende had gained support among the electorate of Chile. One day ordinary citizens filled a street curb to curb as they paraded by him. The sun set, and into the night the throng still passed by, carrying torches and continuing the chant they had shouted during the day, "Allende, Allende, the people will protect you!"

In 1986 such popular support from Filipinos enabled Corazon Aquino to triumph over dictator Ferdinand Marcos and was called the glory of the Philippines, proof that no tyrant could endure. In 1973 such support caused agony in Chile, the people unable to save the democratically elected man they hailed as their champion.

In each case, perhaps the power of the people was less significant than the power of the U.S. government.

Allende spouted tough revolutionary rhetoric without ruthlessly undercutting the frightened interests who had the power to destroy him. But just because a more ruthless revolutionary leader, such as a Castro, prevailed against American opposition does not mean a more ruthless Allende would have succeeded. The circumstances in Chile were far different from those in Cuba. Allende's opponents were so strong, and their hatred so implacable, that it is hard to see how he could have succeeded with a different approach. He might have escaped with his life, but nothing more.

In September 1973 rebels among the Chilean officer corps mounted a sharp, quick coup in which Allende died. The military junta headed by General Augusto Pinochet Ugarte vowed to exterminate Marxism, and instituted a reign of terror, arresting so many suspected Communist sympathizers that a large athletic stadium in the capital city of Santiago was needed to hold them all. Tortures and killings there and elsewhere in the country were widely reported. Up to the time this book was written, Pinochet's regime continued to mete out horrifying punishments summarily, such as dousing protesters with flammable liquid and setting them afire. In contrast to arrests of suspected Communists, the junta immediately freed neofascist terrorists who had been arrested during the Allende regime. The Pinochet junta banned political parties and dozens of newspapers and magazines. Junta member General Gustavo Leigh Guzmán explained, "This is not a time for discussions, dialogues, meetings, forums, or Congressional debates."[33] A junta decree prohibited "elections of any type—be they in unions, economic associations, politics, schools or any other groups."[34] The junta shut down Allende's local medical clinics in low-income districts and closed the Allende government warehouses that had made inexpensive food and household items available in poor urban areas. The country's largest labor union was abolished, and government employees were ordered to work "in a real spirit of discipline."[35]

The Pinochet regime ordered an end to agrarian reform and began returning nationalized companies to former owners. In 1974 Anaconda announced that all its disputes with the Chilean government had been resolved. Soon after the coup, American banks resumed granting large commercial loans to Chile, and the U.S. government offered tens of millions of dollars of credits to the junta.

Allende's government was neither totalitarian at home nor a

military threat abroad. It was voted into power democratically by the people of Chile and was not installed by a foreign invasion or domestic coup, nor did it receive military aid from the Communist bloc. The new right-wing junta's policies were good for business, but by any objective standard, the freedoms of the Chilean people were far fewer under the American-backed military regime than under Allende. In helping to overthrow him, the American government proved it was less concerned about communism or liberty than about corporate profits.

THE SITUATION ELSEWHERE IN LATIN AMERICA

Throughout Latin America the cry of Communist aggression has been raised by government officials in the United States and in right-wing dictatorships of the region. Again and again, however, the facts have failed to support the rhetoric. For example, during the 1960s Castro did try to promote a revolution in Bolivia. But the native Bolivian Communist party rejected Castro's plans and declined to help. Brazil is notable for having hosted the only serious armed revolt by Latin American Communists—in 1935. The country's harsh right-wing president Getúlio Dornelles Vargas easily defeated the rebels and used the outbreak to persuade the legislature to provide him with dictatorial powers. Other than that single anomaly, Brazil's Communists have a record of seeking power through peaceful means. Hotheads are shunned by the party and must form their own factions. When in 1964 the military overthrew the João Goulart regime, which had come to power through the democratic process, the much-feared Communists mounted no resistance. Little was heard from them afterward.

Through their moderate policies, leaders of the weak Colombian Communist party acted in the 1970s as if they were attempting to prevent violent revolution rather than promote it. The same was true in Peru. And historically, it has been the same throughout Latin America. Communist parties are among the most law-abiding political organizations in that part of the world. Ironically the party of world revolution has no revolutionary heritage whatsoever in Latin America. This is one reason why Castro has trouble promoting revolution. Indeed, one observer has noted, "There is probably no conservative or liberal party in all of Latin America that has not staged more insurrections and incited more civil wars than the communists."[36]

In that region the Communists operate like any other political party, with all the compromises and deals required in political life. Remember how well the Communists got along with Batista in Cuba, for example. The same happened with the oppressive rightists Anastasio Somoza in Nicaragua and Rafael Trujillo in the Dominican Republic. Revolutionaries such as Castro learned to expect no help from the Communists. Americans, who are used to viewing Communists as ruthless totalitarians using every form of deceit and brutality to seize power, may be surprised that Latin American Communists have followed the normal rules of political life for many decades. Non-Communist politicans routinely join with the Communists for one election and spurn them for the next. Real-life experience has shown Latin American politicians that Communists are competitors but not threats.

The historical record demonstrates that the greatest threat to governments in Latin America has been neither the Soviet Union nor Cuba nor native Communists. Instead, the United States, again and again, has helped to overthrow democratically elected governments that have sought to improve their people's lives by reducing American power in their countries. Guatemala, El Salvador, Argentina, Peru, Ecuador, Brazil, Dominican Republic, Chile—in each of those countries, the United States worked to replace democratically elected governments with military dictatorships. A book about that meddling would be far thicker than one documenting Communist aggression. One could easily see why Latin American peoples might regard United States as the greater threat to their freedom.

But a tit-for-tat evaluation—the United States in Guatemala, Russia in Latvia—misses the point. Too often the United States seemingly discourages democratic alternatives to right-wing dictatorship in Latin America. In such circumstances the only successful alternative, by default, is Communist revolution. Instead of encouraging the growth of democracy as a challenge to Communism, the United States has at times encouraged the growth of Communism as a challenge to right-wing dictatorships.

XIX.

Africa

The history of Communist activity in Africa differs in several aspects from that elsewhere. Unlike Europe, centuries of political inseparability did not bind the African states with Russia, nor was there any history of military conflict between them. Unlike Latin America, no single predominant colonial power imposed a common language and promoted a common culture in Africa. Unlike Asian countries in their gradual realization of nationalist aspirations, the European colonies in Africa achieved their independence quickly over roughly a fifteen-year period starting around 1960. Such a sudden change in governance throughout a continent might have caused turmoil in any era, let alone at the height of cold war hostility.

Since Russia had never possessed an African colony, the Soviets were able to greet African revolutionaries with clean hands. This pristine colonial record was of some importance. In theory, Western democracy might sound better than Russian communism. But Africans judged the situation by deeds. Western Europe, not Russia, had oppressed African peoples. The Soviet Union, not Western Europe, offered tangible help in achieving and defending national independence. And since Western free enterprise powered colonialism, African leaders were understandably interested in alternative economic structures for their newly independent states. Thus, the Soviet Union had an advantage in dealing with the emerging African states of the 1960s, not achieved by trickery or caused because African tyrants recognized kindred spirits there.

Rather, the West had always been the enemy of African nationalism, whereas the Russians had been friends.

The Belgian Congo is a good example of how the impact of sudden independence created cold war conflict in Africa. An examination of that experience will be followed by a brief scan of Soviet involvement with the rest of the continent.

CONGO (ZAIRE)

Europe had long been aware of Africa's physical existence and of its civilizations near the seacoast, but not until the Congo explorations of Sir Henry Morton Stanley in the late nineteenth century did Europe become aware of the economic potential in the continent's interior. The European discovery of the Congo prompted a scramble for African colonies. The competition for colonies became so intense that military conflict seemed possible among the contestants in Europe. A diplomatic conference was called in Berlin, where in 1885 the European powers reached an agreement on how to divide Africa peacefully among themselves.

Belgium received the Congo. There King Leopold II instituted "forced labour on a scale unknown in modern times until the advent of Hitler. Under his rule thousands of victims were to be massacred every year."[1] After witnessing the conditions, novelist Joseph Conrad wrote "Heart of Darkness" and said of the story, "It is experience pushed a little (and only a little) beyond the actual facts of the case."[2] The wealth extracted so brutally from the Congo's plantations and mines was so enormous that during the first half of the twentieth century no one with any influence in Belgium entertained the slightest thought of freeing the colony.

Nonetheless, nationalist aspirations had grown in the Congo, as elsewhere in colonial Africa. Belgium had largely disregarded the native leadership, but that did not mean the leadership was uninfluential among the native population, which resented being treated as ignorant children and dumb work animals. The peoples of the Congo were beginning to realize that the region had enough natural wealth to be a self-sustaining independent state in the modern world. To Western eyes the expression of this realization would appear chaotic, since the African political heritage was very different from that of Western Europe. Moreover, the areas of traditional tribal power had little to do with the colonial boundary lines drawn on a map in Berlin in 1885, yet those boundary lines would become the borders of modern African states.

In 1959 rioting broke out in the Belgian Congo's capital, Léopoldville (Kinshasa). The disorder was characterized by vehement expressions of hatred for white men. The Belgians seemed surprised and began discussions with native leaders. The emotions released by the rioting and by the discussions became intense, so intense that Belgian possession of the Congo could not continue without military action of a size and ferocity beyond Belgium's capacity to sustain. In January 1960 Belgium saw no other choice but to announce that the colony would be freed in six months. The Belgians hoped to continue profiting from the Congo nonetheless—the Congo Central Bank, a key to financing business operations in the country, was to remain under Belgian control, as was the civil service.

The Belgian Congo became the Republic of the Congo on June 30, 1960. Gala festivities were attended by Baudouin, king of the Belgians, who was told by the Congo's new premier, Patrice Lumumba, "We are no longer your monkeys."[3] Lumumba was clever, having made a fortune while embezzling from the Belgian colonial government and selling beer. He became a leader of the independence movement and at first expressed a generous attitude toward Belgians, inviting those in the Congo to stay and prosper along with the rest of the country's population. His attitude changed in the spring of 1960 as the Belgian government negotiated details of the changeover to independence. The exact details of the disagreement are unclear, but probably involved Lumumba's extreme sensitivity to paternalism. He would become furious at the slightest implication, real or imagined, that the peoples of the Congo must accede to the wishes of some foreign authority. In the June 1960 parliamentary elections Lumumba gained a plurality of seats for his Mouvement National Congolais party. He felt keenly the racist exploitation endured by his countrymen and cried out, "We have known ironies and insults; we remember the blows that we had to submit to morning, noon, and night because we were Negroes!"[4]

He became feared by the Belgians. In the final days before independence, Belgium sabotaged Lumumba's efforts to create a parliamentary coalition that would make him the ruler of the new state. Only one Congolese political figure, Joseph Kasavubu, had refused to negotiate with Lumumba, and in its last gasp of colonial power, Belgium invited Lumumba's opponent Kasavubu to form the government that would rule the new state. Kasavubu's record of hostility toward Belgium was, if anything, stronger than Lumumba's. They disagreed, however, over the form of national organization for the Congo. Lumumba wanted a strong unitary state, and Kasavubu wanted a looser confederation based on traditional tribal divisions (an arrangement that would also make it easier for Belgian business to operate as it always had in the Congo). Neither man was strong enough to triumph over the other, so the two agreed that Kasavubu would be president and Lumumba would be prime minister. With the two top governmental leaders disputing the basic nature of the country, it did not take long for conflict to arise after the Congo became independent.

In early July, only a few days after independence was proclaimed, the Congo's army mutinied. This was the old Force Publique composed of black enlisted men and white Belgian officers. The Force Publique, raised by conscription and voluntary enlistment, was notorious for its low pay and vicious behavior. The Belgian officers remained after independence and had taken pains to assert that independence would make no difference in the harsh treatment that enlisted men endured. The men decided otherwise and mutinied. The unrest spread through units nationwide, and soldiers threatened white civilians as well as officers. Eyewitness reports differ as to the seriousness of the threat. Whatever the truth, Belgians began to flee the Congo. The loss of these businessmen and technicians was an economic blow to the new country, followed by a military blow on July 11 as Belgian paratroops arrived in Léopoldville and moved out across the country on the excuse of protecting Europeans.

Also on July 11, Moise Tshombe declared that the Congo's Katanga province (Shaba) had seceded and become an independent state. Tshombe was a prominent political figure, but his reputation was as a servant of Belgian interests. Katanga province was the key to the Congo's viability. In 1960 the province had 80 percent of the world's industrial diamonds, over 70 percent of the global supply of cobalt, 60 percent of the West's uranium, and astonishing amounts of other minerals as well. Operations of the gigantic Belgian monopolistic mining company Union Miniere du Haut Katanga were based in the province. Tshombe's declaration, simultaneous with the arrival of Belgian troops, was supported by Union Miniere and created a strong international impression that Belgium was attempting to cancel the economic losses it suffered because of the Congo's independence by instigating the establishment of a separate Katanga nation with a government friendly to Belgian commercial interests.

In retrospect this impression is open to question. In negotiations leading to the Congo's independence, Belgium had insisted that

Katanga must remain part of the Congo, and Belgium never granted diplomatic recognition to Tshombe's regime (nor did Great Britain or the United States). While it was both presumptuous and a violation of national sovereignty for Belgium to send troops into the Congo, it may have been a genuine attempt to protect Belgian citizens during the Force Publique mutiny. There seems to be no reason to think that Belgium would have sent its troops without the mutiny; and the outbreak was not caused by foreign or domestic political disputes but was rather a rebellion against continuing colonial conditions in the army.

Nonetheless, the Belgian military came without invitation and refused to leave upon the Congo government's demand. Whatever Belgium's motives, there was no question that it had invaded a sovereign state. Nor was there any doubt that Tshombe's pretensions of Katanga statehood were possible only because of the Belgian military presence there.

Premier Lumumba asked the United States to intervene militarily in defense of the republic against Belgian aggression. The United States refused, vowing to operate strictly through the United Nations.

He next turned to the United Nations for military aid to repel Belgian aggression. A general consensus of Western and Communist bloc powers supported action but not on Lumumba's terms. United Nations secretary general Dag Hammarskjöld saw the primary task as restoring order to the republic's military and civilian agencies, not as fighting Belgian aggression. United Nations forces eventually numbered 19,000 soldiers from thirty countries and began arriving July 15, but as peacekeepers rather than as Congo allies.

Lumumba then asked the Soviet Union if it would be willing to send unilateral help specifically for the republic. The Soviets had a strong and well-known ideological commitment to preserving the independence of former colonies from the European masters. Although Nikita Khrushchev's reply was strong on rhetorical support, it was vague about actual specifics.

On July 16 Lumumba announced an ultimatum, saying that if Belgian forces were not removed from the Congo before July 19, the republic would seek Soviet help. Tremendous world pressure was brought to bear on Belgium, pressure resented so bitterly by the Belgians that they threatened to leave the NATO alliance. Belgian forces withdrew from five provinces of the Congo by July 23, but instead of leaving the country, they concentrated themselves in Katanga, in defiance of the United Nations.

The United Nations Security Council immediately passed a tougher resolution against Belgium but failed to see the situation as Lumumba did. He felt the mutiny and civil turmoil in the republic were promoted by Katanga rebels. That rebellion, in turn, appeared to be engineered by Belgian interests. Lumumba therefore felt that Katanga forces were agents of Belgian aggression. The Security Council chose to view the Katanga rebellion as strictly an internal civil war in which the United Nations could take no sides. The republic would thus receive no help from the United Nations in fighting the Katanga secession. Indeed, the United Nations appeared bent on cleaning up the original mutiny in the Force Publique by disarming it, leaving the republic without any defense of its own against Katanga and Belgium.

On July 20 Lumumba requested Russian aid. Soviet technicians began arriving shortly thereafter. Within a month Russian troop-transport aircraft and trucks had also arrived, along with some food, weapons, and communications equipment. It was a modest quantity of strictly defensive matériel.

In mid-August Belgium finally removed its forces from Katanga and officially left the Congo, although an unofficial presence remained in the form of Belgian officers and sergeants who were transferred to the Katanga rebel army. Following the official Belgian withdrawal, United Nations troops immediately crossed into Katanga to preserve order. This frustrated Lumumba because the United Nations forbade his forces from entering Katanga to put down the rebellion. From Lumumba's viewpoint, instead of defending the Congo, the United Nations was helping to preserve the loss of Katanga province.

Barred from Katanga, at the end of August Lumumba used reconstituted elements of the Force Publique to attack and defeat a rebel stronghold in the province of Kasai, adjacent to Katanga. The only foreign forces involved in this operation were a few Russian pilots for the transport planes. Those few pilots, however, fatally tainted Lumumba in the West. England, the United States, and the United Nations decided that Lumumba was giving the Soviet Union an opening in Africa. And this could not be tolerated.

The Russian aid also brought to a climax the simmering dispute between Prime Minister Lumumba and President Kasavubu over a unitary state versus a confederation. Lumumba's ability to obtain Soviet assistance in his fight against the rebels gave him added prestige and strength in Congo politics. His opponents feared that his vision of a unitary state might be unstoppable if they failed to move against him soon. On September 5 Kasavubu dismissed

Lumumba as prime minister and replaced him with Joseph Ileo. The United Nations immediately accepted Ileo as the legitimate prime minister. The Congo parliament, however, refused to ratify Lumumba's dismissal. Lumumba declared that he had dismissed Kasavubu as president, but as Lumumba had no authority to do so, parliament refused to accept his action. The result was two competing regimes, Ileo's and Lumumba's, each claiming to be the legitimate Congo government.

After the United Nations high command closed airfields to prevent the arrival of Lumumba loyalist troops by airlift, Colonel Joseph Mobutu used the Force Publique to seize the government. Mobutu had been "cultivated for weeks by American diplomats and CIA officers."[5] He placed Lumumba under arrest with the help of United Nations soldiers and expelled the Communist bloc diplomats and aid advisers. Mobutu's forces were so brutal that the United Nations' chief representative in the Congo recommended that the United Nations disarm them.

Lumumba escaped custody once, was captured, escaped again, and was recaptured. Mobutu's government turned Lumumba over to Katanga province officials—his deadly enemies—who in early 1961 announced that "villagers" had killed him during an escape attempt.

The West looked with disfavor upon Communist penetration into the heart of Africa. Journalist Dan Kurzman later listed the physical evidence of Soviet support: seventeen transport airplanes, perhaps a hundred trucks, and thirty jeeps.[6] What Dwight Eisenhower's memoirs described as a "Soviet invasion"[7] was particularly notable for its lack of troops. No Soviet combat personnel were in the Congo, although seven Soviet officers were discovered there.

Because Lumumba sought help from wherever it was available, the West immediately decried him as a Communist. He emphatically rejected the label: "We are not communists, and never will be!"[8] His deeds supported that contention: throughout the crisis he not only refrained from expressing any disapproval of American actions, he actively worked to achieve a large natural-resource exploitation partnership with the American-run Congo International Management Corporation. Given the circumstances, the Russian aid to the Republic of the Congo can hardly be called aggression. Soviet advisers and equipment arrived in response to urgent request by the internationally recognized Congo government. The Soviets did not invade, subvert, or infiltrate the Congo. Western countries could have chosen to answer the Congo's appeal.

One chronicler of the 1960 Congo events described "the smell of world war."[9] It is scarcely believable that rational men would regard thirty jeeps as evidence that World War III loomed and that they would gird the military might of the West in readiness.

In this context, it is interesting to note a collection of essays edited three years later by Zbigniew Brzezinski, one of the toughest cold warriors and head of the National Security Council under President Jimmy Carter. One essay declared that "Soviet support for Lumumba was overwhelmingly verbal" and stated that, despite Russian propaganda gains from the Congo crisis, it "exposed the U.S.S.R. to the African peoples as a power claiming to be their friend in words, . . . but ultimately failing to act on behalf of the African revolution it claimed to champion."[10] A situation widely portrayed at the time as Soviet aggression was later considered proof of Soviet unwillingness to intervene.

In 1961 the United Nations command convinced Secretary General Hammarskjöld that an attack against Katanga was necessary. The same request by Lumumba had incurred Hammarskjöld's wrath, but now the Secretary General saw his own forces endangered by Katanga. The United Nations invaded Katanga in September 1961. At first this seemed to be a successful lightning operation, putting down the Katanga rebellion once and for all. But Belgian officers and white mercenaries fighting for Katanga soon began pressing back United Nations forces. Both sides agreed to a ceasefire. Although Secretary General Hammarskjöld died in a plane crash en route to handle negotiations personally, a truce was signed. The United Nations then broke the truce a couple of months later, justifying the attack with a claim that Katanga was plotting military action against United Nations forces. England and France opposed this second incursion into Katanga, but the United States supported it. The Katanga rebels were finally defeated in January 1963, and the province remained part of the Congo.

Colonel Mobutu professed loyalty to President Kasavubu and had allowed the president to resume power in 1961 along with Cyrille Adoula as prime minister. Adoula was followed in 1964 by Prime Minister Tshombe as the head of a so-called "government of national reconciliation."[11] The next year Mobutu overthrow both Tshombe and Kasavubu. He instituted a repressive regime that defied description in terms of Western ideology but was allied with the West. In 1971 Mobutu renamed the country Zaire. Into the 1980s he and Zaire followed a policy of staunch anti-Communism. His son-in-law Holden Roberto would play a major role in the Angolan struggle described later in this book.

THE CONTINENTAL PICTURE

The events in Zaire are a good example of the nature of East-West conflict in Africa. The conflict is an overlay, distorting African struggles that have nothing to do with communism or democracy. This is true in the sub-Sahara region and in the Mediterranean Arab civilizations. Developments in Angola and Ethiopia are important enough to merit examination in a later chapter, but in terms of East-West conflict they do not differ in essence from events elsewhere on the continent. Even a brief glance at claims of Communist aggression or influence in various African countries can show that the allegations have little merit.

The charges are based for the most part on the presence of Communist bloc arms in a country: Egypt, Guinea, Libya, Nigeria, Tanzania, and even Zaire. Weapons shipments requested by an internationally recognized government cannot fit any reasonable definition of military aggression even if the weapons are used to attack a neighbor. If that were otherwise, the international arms trade conducted by the United States and the nations of Western Europe might be considered major aggression throughout the Third World.

The circumstances by which Communist arms are acquired should be evaluated. In Zaire the source of supply seems to have been other African states sharing their equipment. In other instances, such as Egypt in 1955 and Nigeria in 1967, the governments first unsuccessfully sought weapons from the United States before turning to the Communist bloc. A country with Communist tendencies would not turn first to the United States for national security needs; nor is a country's willingness to accept Communist aid after requests for help are rejected by the West evidence of Communist leanings. Accusations of pro-Communist sympathies are particularly questionable when the Communist arms are supplied in a cash sales transaction, as in the case of Libya, rather than as a gift.

Often the amount and quality of such weapons are modest. And, although the scale of fighting in African wars has also been modest, so that a little bit of matériel can make a big difference, the Communist-supplied arsenals tend to be small. John K. Cooley's account of a 1964 parade in Tanzania noted that the government "proudly displayed Soviet weapons: submachine guns, eighteen trucks, six heavy machine guns and four each of heavy mortars, anti-aircraft and anti-tank artillery."[12] University scholar Christopher Stevens compiled a list of Communist arms possessed by Guinea in 1960: "eight MIG-17's, six transports, small arms, and many armoured vehicles, including T-34 tanks."[13] Around 1965 Kenya refused similar Soviet arms as worthless.

The possession of Communist-bloc weapons does not mean that a country is under foreign or domestic Communist control, and even the amount of influence is questionable. After the Soviet Union extended the Conakry airport runway to accommodate Soviet jets, Guinea refused to refuel Russian aircraft headed for Cuba during the missile crisis in 1962. Egypt expelled its Russian military advisers in 1972. The Communist party of Sudan was once feared as the strongest on the continent. Yet by the 1980s President Ja'far an-Numayri had virtually destroyed it.

Accusations of Communist involvement in African warfare are so prevalent that they are often accepted without careful examination. The label Communist, however, is applied rather loosely to African leaders and fighters. The label also tends to obscure the fact that the Communists are generally Africans rather than Soviets. The Soviets appear to be very cautious about getting ensnared by African conflicts. In the Brzezinski book on Africa, Cameroon was called "perhaps the outstanding instance of Soviet failure to support African movements engaged in armed struggle."[14] Even if willingness existed, the capability of foreign Communists to control African events is doubtful. Fidel Castro staunchly supported Equatorial Guinea's horrific ruler Francisco Macías Nguema but was unable to prevent the 1979 military coup that overthrew the dictator and established a government friendly to the West.

There is little evidence that the African nations that began to emerge around 1960 have much interest in either communism or democracy. They are willing to play the Free World and the Communist bloc against each other in hopes of gain, but the ideological competition that seems to motivate so much Western and Eastern involvement in Africa seems to have little inherent interest there. Fears of communism and hopes for democracy in Africa are probably both exaggerated.

Africa has seen the underbelly of Western society, not its glory. Africa leaders question whether the glory can be desirable if it requires the kind of payment extracted from their continent. If Western values are to prevail in Africa, the West has much work ahead. Even if the West fails in this task, however, Soviet ideals might not dominate the continent. Africa has its own history, its own way of life, its own values. Just because Africans take help from where they can get it, that does not mean they intend to imitate the benefactor's way of life.

The time for missionaries is over. Western ideals, the good ones, can prevail in Africa if the West is an example that Africans want to emulate. If the West lives as free and caring peoples should, Africa may then decide to adopt democratic ways.

XX.

Czechoslovakia

The Third World did not have a monopoly on turmoil in the 1960s. In 1968 Czechoslovakia made headlines in the West. The "Czech spring" heralded a colorful blossoming of personal freedom in the Communist regime, only to be followed immediately by a killing frost and a Soviet winter.

CZECHOSLOVAKIA 1948

Czechoslovakia has generally viewed Russia amiably. There is no heritage of fear or antagonism stretching over centuries. In the 1930s the two countries even signed a military alliance requiring the U.S.S.R. to defend Czechoslovakia—but only if France joined the defense as well. In the Czechoslovak republic, Communists were considered just another political party, in no way disloyal to the government.

Relations with Russia were cordial during World War II. Hitler took over Czechoslovakia, but a government in exile in London continued to exist and pledged to never form a military alliance that the Soviet Union disapproved. President Edvard Beneš hailed this pledge as "one of the links in the postwar system of security."[1] The Soviet Red Army withdrew from the country after liberating it from the Nazis, and elections were soon held.

The balloting in May 1946 was considered fair.[2] The Communist party received 38 percent of the vote, an excellent showing in a multiparty contest. The Communists achieved a plurality of votes and even received an absolute majority in some regions. The combined national totals for all Marxist parties gave them a majority of all ballots cast. As a result of this election, a Communist named Klement Gottwald became premier, and the Communists allied themselves with Social Democrats to form the government.

In considering subsequent events, it is important to remember that when given a choice free of coercion, more Czechoslovakians chose Communism than any other alternative. It is also important to remember that a mainstream political party, and its followers, chose to cooperate with the Communists in a coalition government. A majority of voters and politicians viewed the Communists as either preferable or acceptable.

Over a period of months, opinion polls showed that electoral support for the Communist government was declining in 1947. This did not necessarily mean that the Czechs were now rejecting the Communists—most governments decline in popularity during their term in office, and they are then replaced in elections.

This normal political process was occurring in Czechoslovakia. In September 1947 the Communists lost a cabinet vote and soon lost on a couple of issues in parliament. Scenting a change in the wind, the Social Democrats switched from helping the Communists to hindering them. This was normal political maneuvering designed to increase Social Democrat votes in the 1948 election and had nothing to do with attitudes about Communism per se. The Social Democrat goal was to force their Communist competitors out of the government.

The Communists, however, did not view this as part of the normal ebb and flow of politics. This was 1948 and Eastern Europe. Communists in Czechoslovakia felt they had a civilizing mission to perform, just like their comrades elsewhere in Eastern Europe. For them politics was simply a means to an end—control of the government. If electoral politics threatened that goal, electoral politics would have to be abandoned. Events in France and Italy also affected their perspective, as anti-Communists in those countries had successfully conspired to eliminate Communists from their governments despite electoral support the Communists had received. As 1948 began, neither European Communists nor their opponents were necessarily committed to the electoral process.

The Communists turned to one of the oldest tools of government influence, bribery. They offered top government jobs to politicians in opposition parties contingent on their support for the Communists in any political showdown. These friends in opposition camps also kept the Communists informed of developments there, so the Communists could be forewarned and take countermeasures in time.

The ease with which the Communists recruited politicians from other parties is a telling commentary on the caliber of opposition—both in personal integrity and commitment to a political philosophy. The Czechoslovakian experience is a somber warning of what can happen when such opportunists are welcomed into a political party.

Discussions of the Communist seizure of power also tend to ignore that opponents delivered their own heads on a platter. In February 1948 the National Socialist party (no relation to the Nazis) decided to have all its cabinet members resign. This was to be a signal for other non-Communists to resign, thus causing the government to fall, necessitating new elections in which the Communists were expected to do poorly. Unfortunately, the National Socialists apparently had failed to tell the other political parties of the plan;[3] after their resignations, ministers from those other parties stayed on, leaving the Communist premier Gottwald with a quorum to continue doing business. He seized this opportunity and filled vacant cabinet posts with opportunists who had been cultivated from other parties. This gave the appearance of a cabinet shuffle merely involving names rather than parties. On paper it was no Communist takeover, but in fact the Communists now had overwhelming control of government ministries.

The ineptly planned effort to pull down the Communist government had instead given it an unshakeable foundation. The new cabinet legally rubber-stamped Communist desires. No more free elections were held. This was the Communist takeover of Czechoslovakia.

The actual events were not as calm as this account has suggested. People in Czechoslovakia quickly realized the anti-Communist blunder and the Communist opportunity, and several days of high excitement ensued. Rallies were held, soviets sprang up around the country, a workers' militia appeared, and the Communists implied they were ready to use violence if the premier's cabinet nominees were rejected by the republic's president, Beneš. But no riots erupted, nor terrorism, nor labor strikes. Certainly the Soviet Red Army was not involved.

When the Communists declared that they were going to run the government, no implacable opposition appeared. Perhaps many people were displeased, but no one seemed to think it was worth fighting about.

We hear rhetoric about how the Communists crushed Czechoslovakian freedom in 1948, but we rarely hear that the freely elected government was already headed by a Communist. Or that the Communists pretty closely followed the letter, if not the spirit, of the law in seizing permanent power. Or that the citizenry never put up a fight. The absence of fighting does not prove that the population was indifferent to the Red takeover, but the absence of anger or grief is compelling evidence. In contrast, there had been general public lamentation over the Nazi takeover. The difference may have been the loss of national independence under Hitler, rather than loss of political freedoms. Writers have referred to the traditional Czechoslovakian love for democracy, but they do not mention that this so-called tradition lasted only twenty years, from 1918 to 1938; prior to that, Czechoslovakia had been part of the Austro-Hungarian empire, ruled by feudal monarchs. A few leaders such as Tomáš Masaryk may have promoted Western parliamentary democracy, but their dedication to the principle does not seem to have been shared by the population as a whole.

There was no outpouring of grief in Czechoslovakia following the Communist takeover; there was even substantial support for it among intellectuals. Nor was there much fear that the next step would lead to Russian domination. There had always been Russian influence in Czechoslovakia; it was a fact of life. Moreover, Czechoslovakians in 1948 tended to regard the Soviets as liberators from the Nazis, rather than as oppressors. It was Britain and France that had given Czechoslovakia to Hitler in the Munich Pact of 1938, and their troops had been absent in the Czechoslovak struggle against Nazi tyranny. So closer ties to the Soviet Union were not a fearsome prospect.

CZECHOSLOVAKIA 1968

The two decades following the Communist seizure of power were neither happy nor prosperous for Czechoslovakia. A Stalinist economic development policy, neglecting agriculture and emphasizing heavy industry regardless of market demand, had ended the country's economic growth by 1961. Inflation and worker productivity became concerns. In the 1960s management of the economy was critiqued by academic specialists whose expertise could not be ridiculed by the government. Their university colleagues in science, sociology, and agriculture began to argue for increased access to the West and its knowledge in order to improve conditions at home. Writers and students began to demand fewer restrictions on their activities and more sensitivity to their needs. By 1968 a cascade of demands, seeming to grow one from another, squeezed the Communist state.

First Secretary Gottwald had died in 1953 and was replaced by a harsh Stalinist named Antonín Novotný. In the early 1960s Novotný began feeling criticism from colleagues in the Czechoslovak Communist party. Although the critics were disappointed with various government programs and policies, they had no basic philosophical differences with Novotný. Nonetheless, his Stalinist background became a liability as the Soviet Union spurned the memory of the great dictator. This change in Russian attitude gave an opening to Novotný's reformist enemies, who took full advantage of it. Cultural journals in Czechoslovakia began carrying harsh articles about Novotný, something that could not happen without substantial support in the party hierarchy. In 1962 party reformers forced an investigation of Stalinist misdeeds in Czechoslovakia. The results were kept secret, but in April 1963 two important associates of Novotný were fired, and later that same year Stalinist premier Viliam Široký was replaced. Novotný, however, was a master at manipulating the party machinery through a blend of patronage and punishment; he survived the turmoil and remained in power.

For another four years, Novotný exercised command over the country's affairs while he resisted ever-growing calls for change. Part of his success must be credited to the strong support he received from Nikita Khrushchev. In 1967 Novotný faced down a challenge by Central Committee member Ota Šik. Novotný's leadership style had caused so much resentment that Šik emerged as spokesman for forces that desired, essentially, a legalization of factions within the Communist party. Novotný's opponents wanted the right to agitate against him within the party and to advocate alternatives to his policies. Although that sort of thing was going on anyway, Šik and his supporters wanted guarantees that they would not be punished for challenging Novotný. This touchy issue affected party discipline and would determine whether leaders or the rank and file gave the orders. The Soviet Union long before had established that Communist leaders give the orders, and the East European parties were organized on that principle.

Demonstrating his political wiliness, Novotný transformed his weakness within the Czechoslovak party into a strength. He made sure that the Soviet Union was aware of the factional dispute, so he could be portrayed as the man holding back wild-eyed reformers. Russian support for him thereby increased, since faction reform in Czechoslovakia could spread to parties elsewhere, including the Soviet Union. It would be no threat to the Communist party itself, but it could threaten the job status of current party leaders.

Novotný succeeded almost too well, inspiring a plot among Czechoslovak hard-liners to use military action to prevent party reform.[4] At one point Novotný may have been friendly to the plan, but he soon realized army action could be disastrous, inciting the population while raising Soviet questions about his ability to control events. He gave orders that prevented the military operation.

In the short run, Novotný had been clever to play his Soviet card as he lost influence in the Czechoslovak party. But to defend his leadership position, he had convinced the Soviet Union that Czechoslovak party reformers were dangerous to Russia. As a result, relations between the two countries could sour if Czechoslovak reformers ever gained the upper hand. Eventually the wily Novotný, like so many other dictators, could no longer withstand the opposition arrayed against him.

The reformers won in January 1968 when Alexander Dubček replaced the weakened Novotný as party first secretary; Ota Šik became a deputy prime minister soon thereafter. At forty-six, Dubček was a young Communist star whose career demonstrated upward mobility and fresh ideas. "The chief method of Party guidance is, and must be, persuasion," he said. "We must resist attempts to assert the influence of the Party in society by means of methods which society might regard as authoritative or as forceful."[5]

Although Dubček was considered a daring innovator among Communists, he was hardly a democrat, and his beliefs were actually in the mainstream of Communist thought. A person does not ascend to the top of an East European Communist party by causing trouble.

The reformers in control of the Czechoslovakian party proceeded to hand down decisions as Communist bosses always had, but with the important innovation of "socialist democratization." This was not democracy. The party leaders still gave the orders, and the rank and file still had to obey. The change was that the feelings of party members were considered important and an effort was made to explain decisions and generate support for them, so implementation would be more effective. A government that operates in this way is still a dictatorship. Dubček provided no method of making leaders accountable to the people—just a way of making leaders more popular. Dubček's ideas were a step toward democracy, rather than away from it, but they were not democratic, nor is there any reason to believe that this lifelong Communist had any intention of nurturing democracy.

Czechoslovakian citizens were encouraged to state their views freely without fear of reprisal. Newspapers and magazines no longer had to submit articles to censors. Although advance censorship was officially abolished in June 1968, looser control did not signal that Dubček instituted freedom of the press. Editors were still held accountable for the contents of their publications, although a lapse in self-censorship was punishable by loss of job rather than by arrest and imprisonment. Dubček explicitly stated that the press was supposed to promote government policy and to avoid conduct that would hinder the government's goals.

The Dubček regime also emphasized a separation of powers between party and government administration. The distinction between the two hinged on whether an official exercised authority by virtue of position in government or position in the party. Dubček's view was that authority came from position in government; theoretically that meant continuation of the Communist party was irrelevant to the continuation of the state. Perhaps this notion shocked traditionalists, but Dubček was merely promoting a policy that had recently been advocated in the Soviet Union itself.

Soon after Dubček took office he met with Soviet leaders in Moscow and discussed his plans. After the Russian invasion, *Pravda* would say that he was warned about his actions at this January 1968 meeting, but no warning was noticed by the Czechoslovak leadership at the time.[6] The next month Dubček made a major address extolling the Czechoslovakian reforms. Soviet general secretary Leonid Brezhnev himself attended the speech, which could be interpreted as a stamp of approval—just as high-ranking politicians in the West publicly meet less prominent colleagues in order to demonstrate solidarity. The content of a major speech such as Dubček's is known in advance in high party circles, and it is unlikely that Brezhnev would have traveled to Prague to share the stage with Dubček if the Russian leader disagreed with the proceedings.

Although Dubček's program was within the mainstream of Communist philosophy, the reforms encouraged other developments that were not. For instance, students established a student union and other organizations independent of the Communist party. Adults established the K 231 club to rehabilitate victims of the Stalinist years, the Club of Engaged Non-Party People to promote political activism among persons who did not hold party membership, and the Society for Human Rights. These activities were contrary to the doctrine that all such groups must be answerable to the party. Hard-liners worried that non-Communist activities could readily become anti-Communist.[7] Yet viewed in the context of Dubček's program, the establishment of such groups portended no great change. The Communist party still unquestionably had the last word about policies in Czechoslovakia, even if there was no longer an obsession with saying *everything* on a subject.

Nonetheless, the Western press hailed the Dubček reforms as steps toward democracy. A *New York Times* editorial said, "Forces of freedom and personal dignity seem to be experiencing a rebirth in a land that spiritually has always belonged to the West."[8] Such attention was damaging to the reformers. This unintended injury occurred because, ironically, hopeful anti-Communists in the West and fearful Stalinists in the East were both sniffing for evidence of Czechoslovakian democracy and for evidence of its spread elsewhere in the Soviet bloc.[9]

Hard-line Communists viewed the Western praise for Czechoslovakian developments as damning. Bulgaria's Communist party newspaper warned that the "threat to socialism in Czechoslovakia is growing every day."[10] In May 1968 Poland sent a stiff diplomatic note to Prague: "In no case can we accept that counterrevolution should gain the upper hand in Czechoslovakia."[11] On July 15 the Warsaw Pact dispatched an equally strong warning: "We cannot agree to have hostile forces push your country from the road of Socialism."[12] Nothing of the kind was happening, however.

Dubček took great care to avoid the errors Imre Nagy had made in Hungary a dozen years earlier. Czechoslovakia reiterated its support of the Warsaw Pact in both word and deed.[13] Dubček was careful to maintain correct politeness in diplomatic relations with the West, especially with Russia's bete noire, West Germany. Dubček also kept the growing friendship with Yugoslavia and Romania within normal bounds, avoiding any attempt to reestablish the Little Entente—an alliance that had existed before World War II among the three countries, when Czechoslovakia was considered a French satellite. Nonetheless, the regimes in Yugoslavia and Romania expressed strong support for the Dubček program. Marshal Tito of Yugoslavia and President Nicolae Ceauşescu of

Romania each traveled to Prague at the height of tension in August 1968 to reiterate their support. Romania and Czechoslovakia signed a formal treaty of friendship at this time. Yugoslavia and Romania had both broken away from Soviet dominance. A triumvirate comprising the countries of the old Little Entente could be a formidable challenge to the accomplishment of any unpopular Soviet desires in the region. Despite Dubček's caution, in the summer of 1968 such an alliance appeared to be emerging. A Soviet desire to forestall it may have helped prompt the Soviet invasion of Czechoslovakia.

Nonetheless, almost every aspect of the Dubček program found support from members of the Soviet leadership. Not everyone liked everything Dubček was doing, but some important Russian official could be found to vouch for particular items.[14] Soviet economists Yevsey Liberman and A. Birman, along with political leaders such as Boris Ponomarev and politburo members Aleksandr Shelepin, Dimitri Poliansky, Mikhail Suslov, and Premier Aleksey Kosygin were all on record as tolerating and even supporting particular aspects of the Dubček program.[15] On a piecemeal basis, everything in the Dubček program may have been within the mainstream of Communist thinking, but he had combined the ideas in an unprecedented package, and the combined effect made some traditionalists uneasy.[16]

Fear that Czechoslavak reform might spread through Eastern Europe was a powerful motive for savage pressure and even military intervention. In addition, the sudden Western discovery of Czechoslovakian "democracy" raised questions about the seduction of the country away from its Eastern bloc orientation. In May 1968 Soviet president Nikolay Podgorny declared that Russia was ready to defeat "imperialist intrigues"[17] in Czechoslovakia. The Soviet Union's basic goal in World War II had been to assure that no more Western daggers would be pointed at Russia from Eastern Europe. Any possibility of change in that region's pro-Soviet postwar status quo would be viewed with gravity and alarm in the Kremlin.

As with Hungary and Poland in 1956, the 1968 Czechoslovak tensions were intertwined with disputes among Soviet leaders. In some regards Khrushchev's reforms in Russia had gone further than Dubček's program in Czechoslovakia,[18] but controversy over Khrushchev's reforms had contributed to his downfall. Dubček's activity reopened old arguments in the Kremlin that had festered since Khrushchev's time. In turn, the effect of these arguments on the power of individual Russian leaders affected Moscow's attitude toward Dubček. A striking example is provided by the competition between Premier Kosygin and General Secretary Brezhnev.[19] Kosygin's prestige was rising because of his success in arms control negotiations with the Americans. He was also tolerant of Dubček's program, opposed Russian pressure against Dubček, and questioned whether any threat to Russian national security was arising in central Europe. Brezhnev was unfriendly toward the Czechoslovakian reforms but refused to support action against Dubček until Kosygin convinced the United States to agree to a nuclear nonproliferation treaty in July 1968. Brezhnev felt threatened by the premier's growing status, and in self-protection began to ally himself with Kosygin's opponents. Unfortunately for Czechoslovakia, Kosygin's opponents favored harsh action against Dubček. This Brezhnev-Kosygin competition is better known than other Kremlin power struggles of that time, but we may be confident it was not unique and that Czechoslovakia was caught in the middle of others as well.

The flow of these Kremlin debates began to run against Dubček by May 1968. In that month a Soviet military delegation headed by Marshal Andrey Grechko went to Czechoslovakia. He had succeeded Marshal Rodion Malinovsky as defense minister upon the latter's death in 1967. In American terms this would be like a general on active duty serving as secretary of defense and therefore indicated that the professional officer corps continued to intrude on civilian control of the military in Russia. This intrusion was not unprecedented and did not mean that the civilians in government, let alone the party, had no control over the military. It did mean, however, that there was a power-sharing arrangement between civilians and military officers. The officer corps had significant influence on defense decisions.

The Soviet military seemed to view the developments in Czechoslovakia as a threat to Russian security.[20] General Aleksey Yepishev was a member of the Grechko delegation and was known to favor intervention to eliminate the threat. The delegation had gone to Prague to demand that Warsaw Pact forces be stationed on the country's border with West Germany. Czechoslovakia's record of friendship toward the U.S.S.R. was so strong that Soviet troops had never been stationed there after World War II; the unprecedented May 1968 demand indicated that the Russian military believed Czechoslovakia could no longer be trusted.

Premier Kosygin quickly followed the generals to Prague and achieved a compromise that abandoned the permanent stationing of foreign forces in Czechoslovakia; temporary Warsaw Pact joint exercises would, however, begin in the country during June. This action briefly mollified Kremlin hard-liners who felt a need to send Soviet troops into Czechoslovakia. It also gave the Dubček regime a strong warning about the depth of Soviet concern.

This concern was reiterated at an extraordinary joint meeting of the Soviet and Czechoslovak politburos held in the border town of Čierná, Czechoslovakia, at the end of July. Soviet critics accused the Dubček regime of not only abandoning the cause of communism but of working with Western anti-Communists. The Russian hard-liners expressed particular concern that Dubček had loosened censorship controls, arguing that through this step the party had surrendered its leadership of the country. If this were the case, there could be little doubt that the Soviets would invade to protect the socialist order, as in Hungary twelve years earlier. Dubček and his men vigorously defended their actions and convinced enough of the Russian politburo to win approval of the Czechoslovak program. In early August the two groups signed an agreement in Bratislava, Czechoslovakia, that explicitly recognized the Dubček regime's right to pursue its reform program.

The Bratislava agreement, however, signaled a reopening of the argument in Moscow. Back in the Kremlin, the Russian politburo came under pressures that had been muted in far-off Čierná and Bratislava. The KGB secret police, under the leadership of Yury Andropov, had been dismayed when the Dubček regime expelled it from Czechoslovakia earlier in the year. The KGB was disturbed when the politburo accepted that act as final at Bratislava. Andropov was already on record as believing that a KGB absence from Eastern Europe could encourage the growth of anti-Communism there. The military believed that Czechoslovakia could no longer be depended upon as an effective member of the Warsaw Pact and was alarmed at the politburo's agreement to end the exercises in Czechoslovakia and withdraw forces. Politburo member Petr Shelest, head of the Ukrainian party organization, had been vocal about the related question of the Dubček program's effect on Ruthenia, which had been taken from Czechoslovakia at the end of World War II and incorporated into the Soviet Ukraine. At the Čierná conference, Shelest had accused Czechoslovakia outright of producing leaflets calling for rebellion against the Soviet Union in Ruthenia—an accusation angrily denied by Czechoslovak officials. Romania's defiance of Russia and support for Dubček also raised questions about possible encouragement of dissidents in Transcarpathia, which had been taken from Romania at the end of World War II and also made part of the Soviet Ukraine. Latvian party leader Arvid Pelshe worried about Czechoslovakia's effect in his region. Polish party chief Wladyslaw Gomulka and East German chairman Walter Ulbricht also objected to the Bratislava accord, saying that it threatened political stability in their countries.

The resumption of the argument in Moscow was distorted by a decision that had been made in late July. At that time Russia called up military reserves and announced major maneuvers along its western boundary. This activity was unaffected by the end of Warsaw Pact exercises in Czechoslovakia, so it was a way for Kremlin moderates to compromise with hard-liners about using troops for intimidation. The decision may have been viewed as a way to procrastinate and to keep options open—the massed forces would pressure Dubček without crossing into his country, as they would be easily available for instant invasion of Czechoslovakia. Instead of preserving options, however, the border maneuvers in this threatening atmosphere had a built-in momentum toward war. The United States, in contrast, beginning in July 1968, took extreme care to limit its army operations along West Germany's boundary with Czechoslovakia. The peril of large border maneuvers in a time of tension is so well known, as illustrated by the sequence of events that led to the opening of hostilities in World War I, that it has been abandoned in the modern practice of diplomacy. In a tense confrontation with another state, the mere presence of a battle-ready army on the border begins to generate arguments for the army's use. Instead of preserving options, the Russian maneuvers began to eliminate options before they could be used. This was not Soviet deviousness.[21] It was an authentic and serious error in crisis management.

The Soviet politburo had not voted unanimously for the Čierná-Bratislava accord, and back in Moscow the hard-liners managed to tip the decision the other way. The circumstances of the reversal are ambiguous and reflect a continued division in the Soviet leadership. Brezhnev and other top Soviet officials had gone on holiday after completing the Bratislava work. Jiri Valenta, a careful student of these events, believes that Petr Shelest may have been left in charge of party business.[22] All along Shelest had been a leader of Kremlin hard-liners on the Dubček question. On August 14 and 15, some of Dubček's opponents in the Czechoslovak party hierarchy informed Moscow that Dubček and his followers were planning to remove hard-liners, who were also staunchly pro-Russian, from the Czechoslovak party leadership. Shelest may have called a politburo meeting on August 15 and 16, at which the decision was made to invade Czechoslovakia to protect continuation of the Communist state there.²³ The decision was not unanimous, and it is unclear whether Brezhnev, Kosygin, or Podgorny were even present when the vote was taken. These three top leaders were summoned from their vacations to a Central Committee meeting in Moscow just hours before the invasion. The meeting does not appear to have been called by any of the three top men.

Evidence of serious division in the Soviet leadership and intense controversy over the invasion can be found in the Russian news media. Normally major announcements are published in a joint statement made by the party first secretary (Brezhnev), the Soviet president (Podgorny), and the chairman of the council of ministers (Kosygin). No such statement announced the invasion. The absence of a proclamation with even one of those three signatures demonstrates not only the division on this issue among the Soviet leadership, but that events may have gotten out of hand. The lack of coordination in the Soviet news media also indicates high-level disputes about the invasion. *Izvestia* reported Czechoslovakian gratitude over liberation, whereas the KGB-associated newspaper *Trud* reported enmity.

The Soviet invasion of Czechoslovakia should have come as no surprise. It was preceded by weeks of military intimidation via extended Warsaw Pact maneuvers that filled Czechoslovakia with Soviet forces. The slow exit of Soviet troops who had been conducting Warsaw Pact maneuvers, the arrival of Soviet reserve forces on the border, a *Pravda* declaration that the situation in Czechoslovakia was becoming similar to what had happened in Hungary a decade earlier—all made it clear that the Soviet Union was contemplating an invasion.

Five Warsaw Pact countries—Russia, East Germany, Poland, Hungary, and Bulgaria—invaded during the night of August 20–21. The East German contingent must have caused particular resentment in Czechoslovakia, recalling memories of German seizure of the country thirty years earlier. The Dubček government immediately instructed its citizens and armed forces to offer no violent resistance. Few casualties occurred. The prevalent spirit centered on survival, in the hopes of regrouping another day. The prevalent emotion was sorrow, as much as anger, a feeling of betrayal by fraternal Communist states.²⁴ On the night of the invasion, Dubček wept at a presidium meeting, crying out, "I have devoted my entire life to cooperation with the Soviet Union, and they have done this to me."²⁵

The Soviet invasion lacked even a veneer of legality. No group with any standing in Czechoslovakia could be found to make the standard request for fraternal assistance. The country was actively assisting the Warsaw Pact, so no imminent military threat could be used as an excuse either. Russian critics had failed to win the debates on Czechoslovakian Communist orthodoxy. Nonetheless, the Russians invaded. The lack of even a paper excuse demonstrates how jittery the Soviets were—normally they are fastidious about having a document purportedly authorizing their actions.

The Kremlin lost standing among Communists around the world. Yugoslavia and Romania condemned the invasion. The latter frankly labeled it as illegal. In the face of Bulgarian military maneuvers on the Romanian and Yugoslav borders, plainly intended as intimidation, Romanian head of state and general secretary Ceauşescu told a cheering crowd that Romania's leadership backed Dubček 100 percent. To protest the invasion, Albania formally withdrew from the Warsaw Pact, and Romania refused to take part in Pact exercises thereafter. Not only did the Warsaw Pact break up, but Communist parties around the globe declared their support for Czechoslovakia. The restiveness held out the prospect of a Czechoslovakian government in exile on the territory of a fellow Communist state, enjoying its full protection.

The result, in combination with unrelenting firmness from Czechoslovakian leaders, was that Dubček and his associates retained their positions. They did not suffer the fate of Nagy in Hungary, and no Soviet minions were able to take over. Kremlin hard-liners invaded Czechoslovakia to overthrow Dubček, yet failed to accomplish this elementary goal despite a military victory. Instead, the Russians achieved a political catastrophe.

It is true that Dubček and his fellow reformers moderated their actions as desired by the Soviet Union hard-liners. But the Czechoslovakians had always demonstrated willingness to acquiesce to Soviet desires. Dubček had never done anything in the face of implacable Soviet opposition. Members of the Soviet leadership stood behind his innovations.

In this context, the invasion should not be considered an example of Russian perfidy. Rather, it demonstrated how confused the Soviet leadership was. Apparently some voices said that everything was fine. Some said there was a crisis. And there was every gradation in between. The friendly voices heard by Dubček had just as much authority as the disgruntled ones. He was not being tricked. His Kremlin friends simply lost the argument to his Kremlin adversaries.

Even after the invasion, Moscow officials remained divided about what to do, and Czechoslovakia exploited these divisions.

No police terror appeared in the country. People who had voiced criticisms still walked the streets unpunished. Despite the Russian military occupation, which soon took a very low profile, the Czechoslovakian government remained the least oppressive regime in Eastern Europe. Dubček and his colleagues performed an astounding salvage job.

In the West various attempts have been made to draw lessons from the 1968 events in Czechoslovakia. Probably the most important, and least recognized, lesson is that the Soviet dictatorship is not a monolith. Stress tends to heighten the bickering among Soviet leaders, and in a time of acute crisis, serious question can arise about who is in charge. The available evidence suggests that the invasion of Czechoslovakia occurred not because the Soviet leadership had concluded that Czechoslovak developments were dangerous, but because the Soviet leadership was confused and uncertain about what was happening.

The Russian military aggression against Czechoslovakia in 1968 has been cited as evidence of Soviet intolerance for political freedoms and even as evidence of a Russian plan of world conquest threatening the Free World. In reality Czechoslovakia in 1968 was still a Communist dictatorship despite reforms that loosened the omnipresent feeling of party control. Russia did not invade a democratic country, but rather sent its forces into a state long regarded as a Soviet satellite. This fact does not make the Russian action less objectionable, but it does mean that the invasion should not be viewed as an act that was directed against a democracy or the Free World.

XXI.

French Indochina

The Vietnam War, as it was called by Americans, was really a war that extended throughout and beyond the area once known as French Indochina—Vietnam, Laos, and Cambodia. The struggle began after World War II as France attempted to retain its colonies in that region. When the French abandoned that fight in 1954, the United States then stepped in and transformed the conflict into a battle against communism. France and the United States both fought the same opponents in Indochina. Those opponents did not change, but the perception of them underwent a transformation from anticolonial freedom fighters to agents of Communist world conquest. Tracing this metamorphosis may help to explain the American war in Indochina. The path is a winding one, shaped by communism and nationalism and twisted by the backgrounds of the Asian combatants and Western decision makers.

VIETNAM

During the nineteenth century, France gradually increased its influence east of Burma in the Indochina peninsula and incorporated much of that area into the French empire. Among those colonial peoples were the inhabitants of Vietnam. They shared in the great reemergence of Asian nationalism in the early twentieth century, and one of their anticolonial agitators was Ho Chi Minh, a man with many names and a murky background. His father was a minor government official in Vietnam. Ho Chi Minh traveled to Europe, and after World War I he attempted to argue Vietnam's case for statehood with diplomats preparing the Treaty of Versailles. During the war President Woodrow Wilson had inspired idealists around the world with his calls for national self-determination of oppressed peoples, but European diplomats applied his call only to the extinct empires of defeated Germany and Austria-Hungary, as well as czarist Russia. The Versailles diplomats refused to deal with either Ho Chi Minh or the question of Vietnamese independence, but Ho remained in Paris. In 1920 he was a founder of the French Communist party.

He soon became frustrated with European comrades who believed freedom for colonies could come only after proletarian revolution in Europe. Ho contended that the argument of India's M. N. Roy was correct—that revolution in the colonies had to occur before workers could rise in Europe. Because the French Communist party rejected Roy's theory and remained indifferent to Vietnam and the rest of French Indochina, Ho had to turn elsewhere for support.

He turned to the Comintern, the ineffective Moscow-based agency that was supposed to promote Communist revolution around the world. During the 1920s he became a Comintern official operating out of Shanghai. He proved to be a ruthless man willing to betray anyone if he thought that would promote his cause, as demonstrated by his role as a French double agent. For many years he eliminated competitors to his revolutionary leadership—and received reward money—by reporting nationalist revolutionaries and independent-minded Communists to French colonial security agencies.[1]

Because Ho Chi Minh was an agent of the Comintern, naturally enough the Vietnamese Communists closely cooperated with Soviet desires right up to World War II, when the Comintern disbanded. While it is fair to describe Ho and his associates as Russian agents, it is also fair to describe them as Vietnamese nationals who were using any available assistance to promote their own goals. Just because the Vietnamese Communists cooperated with the Comintern, that does not mean the Soviet Union directed them—Joseph Stalin, after all, took an unfriendly attitude toward the Comintern. Russian and Vietnamese Communist desires simply coincided for the time being. During World War II, the Vietnamese Communists began using peasant-based tactics of social agitation and guerrilla warfare similar to those advocated by Mao Tse-tung.

When the French government surrendered to Hitler in 1940, it also agreed to admit Japanese forces into Vietnam. In return for being allowed to continue administering government functions in French Indochina, the French actively cooperated with Japan in hunting down Vietnamese resistance fighters. As long as French officials recognized Japanese sovereignty, Japan let them operate pretty much as they wished in Vietnam.

In contrast, Vietnamese resistance fighters were supported by Chiang Kai-shek and the United States. Nationalist China funded Ho Chi Minh's operations. The Chinese interest was not entirely altruistic, as the Chinese hoped that Ho's group could be bought and used to help push the Chinese border southward.[2] The United States provided supplies to Ho, who was careful not to squander resources on fighting Japan when they might be needed for fighting the French later. He never had much of a resistance force anyway: Vo Nguyen Giap's famed "army" mustered thirty-four members and had only two pistols, seventeen rifles, and one light machine gun. Ho Chi Minh did, however, act as a U.S. spy and helped American aviators who crashed in Vietnam.

At the end of the war in 1945, Ho and his associates declared Vietnam an independent state. Incoming British occupation troops, however, refused to recognize Vietnamese independence. They quickly turned the administration of Vietnam back to the defeated Japanese colonial units until the French could arrive in force to resume control. The United States, which had backed Ho's anti-Japanese activities in the war, now abandoned him and supported France's colonial claims.

It should be emphasized that when Ho called for a free and independent Vietnam in 1945, he was speaking of national sovereignty, not democracy. A dictatorship can be free and independent if it has diplomatic recognition. Ho Chi Minh was dedicated to creating a Communist state in Vietnam. Unlike such leaders as Fidel Castro, Ho Chi Minh did not turn to the Communists as a last resort after being spurned by the West. Ho wanted a Communist Vietnam all along. To him, non-Communist nationalists were as big an enemy as the French.

As in his days as a double agent, Ho Chi Minh cooperated with the French in ferreting out and killing non-Communist nationalist revolutionaries. Ho's Communist military organization, known as the Viet Minh, and French forces conducted joint operations to track down Vietnamese patriots. Ho's Communists soon became the only significant revolutionary force in Vietnam.

In March 1946 he attempted a negotiated settlement with the French, agreeing to tolerate 15,000 French troops north of the 16th parallel (essentially the area that became North Vietnam), with the understanding that they would be gradually withdrawn. In exchange the French agreed to give the colony its freedom. When Ho traveled to Paris to complete the arrangement, he discovered new conditions. France insisted on determining Vietnam's foreign policy and dominating Vietnam's armed forces. In addition France sought to retain the territory that later became South Vietnam. The talks dragged on, not so much because either side thought a diplomatic solution possible, but because both sides found the months useful for building their military arsenals.

As 1946 progressed, an increasing number of violent outbreaks in Vietnam indicated that the Vietnamese would resort to force. In November France attacked the port of Haiphong, killing thousands of citizens. The Viet Minh retaliated with unsuccessful attacks on French positions at Hanoi. The Vietnam War had begun.

The French Communist party was part of the French government at that time—the party general secretary was vice-president of the council of ministers, and a Communist soon became French minister of defense—so, in a very real sense, the war against Ho Chi Minh was started by the Communists of France.

East-West geopolitics were not at the root of the Vietnam War. The conflict was between France and Vietnam, the old story of Europeans against the Third World.

THE UNITED STATES ENTERS THE ABYSS

In 1954 an international conference at Geneva agreed on terms of a French withdrawal from the entire Indochina peninsula. The accord was endorsed by France, England, Communist China, Russia, Cambodia, Laos, and Ho Chi Minh's Viet Minh army. The United States and the old French-supported regime in Vietnam participated in the conference but did not endorse the settlement.

One of the most important aspects of the agreement was its declaration that Vietnam was one country. The Communists in the north and the French-supported regime in the south both claimed to be the legitimate government. They consented to suspend military operations and have the dispute settled by a nationwide election. As part of the Geneva agreement, Ho Chi Minh's forces agreed to stay north of the 17th parallel until elections were held.

With backing from the United States, the regime in South Vietnam refused to hold the elections required by the Geneva settlement. Both sides knew that Ho Chi Minh was certain to win a majority of the vote, although he would not be a unanimous choice—serious unrest appears to have occurred within North Vietnam itself in late 1956. But, overall, Ho seems to have been the choice of the people.

Since the South Vietnamese regime broke the Geneva agreement, Ho no longer felt obligated to observe the military armistice contingent on holding of elections, and he resumed the war. Instead of fighting France, this time the enemy was a South Vietnamese government supported by the United States. The United States labeled the conflict as aggression against South Vietnam. This was a change in definitions. At Geneva it had been agreed that Vietnam was one country; therefore any fighting among Vietnamese was a civil war. The United States subsequently helped create the state of South Vietnam and then argued that Ho Chi Minh was attacking a neighboring country, and that South Vietnam was entitled to receive aid in repelling the aggression. Ho maintained that the United States was interfering in the internal affairs of Vietnam; the United States argued that Ho was violating the integrity of South Vietnam. Admittedly, both the United States and the old French-supported regime in South Vietnam had stood aloof from the Geneva accord. Yet, even though they were not obligated to abide by it, their repudiation of the agreement was the immediate cause of the resumption of hostilities. It is also important to recognize that the identification of the aggressor, if any, in this war is an arguable question. Whatever the answer to that question, the historical record certainly fails to support any charge that the war was inspired or directed by Russia or Communist China.

In September 1954 U.S. secretary of state John Foster Dulles engineered the South-East Asia Treaty Organization (SEATO) to frustrate the accord reached in Geneva during July. Only three Asian nations joined: Thailand, the Philippines, and Pakistan. The other members were France, the United States, Britain, Australia, and New Zealand. Modeled upon the NATO alliance, SEATO offered American protection to "the free territory under the jurisdiction of the State of Vietnam," that is, the politicians in southern Vietnam supported by France and the United States. This protection was accepted and helped solidify South Vietnam as a sovereign state—although the Geneva agreement had specified that the area was not a sovereign state and was to be united with the north as one country. SEATO had several other intriguing aspects. In one provision the United States noted that its obligations in response to "aggression and armed attack . . . apply only to communist aggression." The treaty also declared the right of military intervention against aggression, whether or not the victim was a member of SEATO. The treaty said that such intervention would not happen without the victim's permission, but in 1962 the United States government proclaimed that it was entitled to act under the SEATO treaty regardless of what the other signatories desired; members had signed a blank check authorizing the United States to do anything it claimed was on their behalf, whether they wanted it or not.[3] If the United States was willing to disregard the treaty provisions requiring joint decisions, it was unlikely to be very concerned about whether a country desired intervention by SEATO. Since the treaty had an elastic clause calling for SEATO action in response to "any fact or situation which might endanger the peace of the area," the treaty gave the United States ample freedom of action. SEATO was less a military defense pact than a legal defense for anything the United States wanted to do in the region.

Secretary of State Dulles maintained that the document allowed the United States to send whatever aid South Vietnam needed to assure its existence as a non-Communist state. Vice-President Richard Nixon had already urged American military intervention to help France in the late winter of 1954. U.S. Army Chief of Staff Matthew Ridgway was appalled at the suggestion. He described South Vietnam as "a land of rice paddy and jungle—particularly adapted to the guerrilla-type warfare. . . . Every little detachment, every individual, that tried to move about that country, would have to be protected by riflemen. . . . Every rear-area aid station would have to be under armed guard or they would be shot at around the clock."[4] Ridgway believed that heat and disease would devastate American soldiers and that major engineering and construction would be needed for harbors and communications and transport. He predicted that an American military response in Vietnam would become larger than that in the Korean War. Ridgway's report on the military prospects went to President Dwight Eisenhower, who forbade the project so fervently endorsed by Nixon. Soon thereafter General Ridgway wrote in satisfaction, "When the day comes for me to face my Maker and account for my actions, the thing I would be most humbly proud of was the fact that I fought against, and perhaps contributed to preventing, the carrying out of some hare-brained tactical schemes which would have cost the lives of thousands of men. To that list of tragic accidents that fortunately never happened I would add the Indo-China intervention."[5]

Senator John F. Kennedy agreed that sending an American military force to Vietnam would be a mistake: "For the United States to intervene unilaterally and to send troops into the most difficult terrain in the world . . . would mean that we would face a situation which would be far more difficult than even that we encountered in Korea. It seems to me it would be a hopeless situation."[6] When Kennedy was elected president in 1960, there were only 800 American military personnel in Vietnam, fewer than in many countries where no hostilities existed. He treated the Vietnam conflict as just a routine excitement, one among dozens of others in the world. Vietnam was not a major commitment, but it needed more men to get the job done. In 1961 Kennedy increased the American military contingent in Vietnam to 1,364 and in 1962 to 9,865.

Kennedy was astonished by a visit he received in 1962 from Jean-Jacques Servan-Schreiber, a prominent French intellectual who had been an aide to the French prime minister Pierre Mendès-France during the 1954 Geneva conference. "We in Paris knew that a really explosive danger lay in the shadowy, covert escalation of the American military expedition into the well-known, to us, swamps of Vietnam. We imagined with horror the profound consequences of this new 'march of folly,' following our own path, leading also to final humiliation and defeat—only in much larger dimension, both in the world and at home. I reported that to John Kennedy, as the simple message of my visit."[7] Servan-Schreiber watched Kennedy act with "total surprise and disbelief" as the former French official delivered his solemn warning about Vietnam. Kennedy made an appointment for Servan-Schreiber to see Secretary of Defense Robert McNamara the next day. McNamara dismissed the warning: "You see, it is not conceivable that an American force in Vietnam would meet, as you imagine, the sad fate of the French army. It is not a question of bravery but of technology. We have something your generals did not have and left them so vulnerable: thousands of helicopters. We can saturate the skies in Vietnam."[8] When Kennedy died in 1963, there were 15,500 American military personnel in Vietnam.

His successor, Lyndon Johnson, was a long-time advocate of American assistance to South Vietnam. "What is American policy on Indochina?" he asked in 1954. "We have been caught bluffing by our enemies. Our friends and allies are frightened and wondering, as we do, where we are headed." He complained of "this picture of our country needlessly weakened in the world."[9] In 1961 Johnson told Kennedy that a failure to preserve South Vietnam "would say to the world in this case that we don't live up to our treaties and don't stand by our friends. This is not my concept. I recommend that we move forward promptly with a major effort."[10] When Johnson made that recommendation he was referring to supplying South Vietnam with military goods and training, not American combat troops. When he became president, however, he soon decided that American soldiers were the answer after all.

In 1964 he decided that the level of involvement approved by Kennedy was ineffective, because the South Vietnamese regime had so little support among the Vietnamese people that it would collapse under Ho Chi Minh's pressure. Johnson believed that a large aerial bombardment of North Vietnam, accompanied by enough American ground troops to clear out remaining Communists from the south, was necessary to force Ho from the field. But first, in the face of growing congressional and voter opposition to the Vietnam War, Johnson recognized that he would need a reason to escalate the war. The so-called domino theory—contending that if South Vietnam fell to Communist aggression so would Laos, Cambodia, Thailand, Malaysia, the Philippines, and all other countries of the region—was highly touted but proved insufficient to galvanize the American public. In August 1964 Johnson announced that North Vietnam had made unprovoked attacks upon American naval vessels on the high seas in the Gulf of Tonkin, and Johnson asked Congress for a resolution approving any steps deemed necessary by the president. In a flush of patriotic drum-beating, Congress passed the so-called Gulf of Tonkin resolution authorizing Johnson to do anything. Long afterward it was learned that the "unprovoked attacks on the high seas" had not occurred. Johnson had manufactured the incident to win approval for the escalation he had desired for months. In 1965 he boosted the United States military contingent in Vietnam to 200,000; in 1966, 400,000; in 1968, 500,000.

In the United States, the war ignited passions not seen since the Civil War of the 1860s, with debates in the press, riots in the streets, and arguments even around family dinner tables. People watched the evening television news in disbelief, seeing films of villages being destroyed and their residents slaughtered in order to save them from the Communists. The Vietnamese Communists were no less brutal; even children were trained to kill American soldiers. U.S. officials reported good "body counts" and "kill ratios" after battles, that the war was being won, that there was "light at the end of the tunnel," but every day more young men were sucked into the war's hungry maw. When in 1968 the army asked Johnson to send another 200,000 troops in addition to the half-million already in Vietnam, even Johnson shrank back. He never admitted defeat, but he refused the army and announced he would not run for reelection that year.

His successor was former vice-president Richard Nixon, who had long advocated an American military answer to Ho Chi Minh. As a candidate for president in 1968, Nixon implied he had a secret plan to end the war, but after he entered the White House, the secret plan never emerged. Nixon did reduce the number of American ground troops in Vietnam, but he intensified the aerial bombardments throughout North and South Vietnam. An estimated 20 million bombs fell on Vietnam, nearly 500 pounds of explosives for every man, woman, and child in the country. Far from ending the Vietnam War, Nixon expanded it into Cambodia.

CAMBODIA

The French colonial administration in Cambodia and Laos had ruled with a lighter hand than in neighboring Vietnam and had depended on the willing collaboration of native leaders. By 1950 France had granted substantial local autonomy to Cambodia and Laos, and they achieved independent statehood in 1954 as part of the Geneva proceedings that provided for an orderly withdrawal of French forces from Vietnam after the Vietnamese military victory at Dien Bien Phu.

By 1953 Viet Minh forces had entered the two countries as part of the struggle to expel France from Indochina. This Vietnamese Communist military presence in Cambodia and Laos was different from the Chinese aid to Vietnam. An argument could be made that Ho's Vietnam was a sovereign state soliciting and accepting foreign aid. This could not be said of the Communist Khmer Rouge insurgents fighting the French-supported monarchy in Cambodia or the Communist-allied Pathet Lao fighting the French-supported monarchy in Laos. Perhaps the guerrillas welcomed Viet Minh assistance, but there can be little doubt that Ho's forces were committing aggression against their neighbors. Whether that aggression was inherently Communist or inherently Vietnamese is another question. Historically Vietnam has felt a manifest destiny to control Cambodia. This feeling was not a Communist phenomenon, but was shared by the anti-Communist regime in South Vietnam as well.

Communist influence fluctuated dramatically in Cambodia. At

the 1954 Geneva conference, Ho Chi Minh's forces agreed to leave Cambodia. Elections were held there, and the resulting Cambodian government proceeded to eliminate most native Communists by 1960. Rightly or wrongly, the Khmer Rouge blamed the Vietnamese for this persecution, a blame which created considerable hostility between the two Communist camps.

Secretary of State John Foster Dulles and his brother, CIA Director Allen Dulles, each tried to convince Cambodia's leader, Prince Norodom Sihanouk, to have Cambodia join SEATO. Sihanouk was committed to a policy of neutrality, reinforced by the 1954 Geneva agreement which arguably prohibited Cambodian membership in an organization such as SEATO. Sihanouk's refusal to bring Cambodia into SEATO prompted the United States to suspect him of pro-Communist sympathies, a suspicion heightened in the 1960s by his willingness to tolerate a Vietnamese Communist supply route through Cambodia. Sihanouk nonetheless showed a vigorous hostility to Cambodian leftists. They were purged from official positions of responsibility, which ironically fostered Communist guerrilla activity because the Communists had no legal way to promote their goals politically.

In 1966 right-wing general Lon Nol became Sihanouk's premier. Lon Nol pursued a stiff antiguerrilla campaign: "The pacification of the disturbed region was undertaken with the rude vigor peculiar to a soldiery who had been promised a monetary reward for each severed head they might forward to the military headquarters."[11]

By 1970 Cambodia's rightists had become implacable enemies of Sihanouk because of his refusal to go to war against the Vietnamese Communists. The rightists received sympathy and encouragement from the Nixon administration; and while Sihanouk was out of the country in March 1970, trying to persuade the Soviet Union to pressure the North Vietnamese to respect Cambodian neutrality, General Lon Nol staged a coup. The monarchy was abolished, and Lon Nol declared the establishment of the Khmer Republic, which immediately received diplomatic recognition and military aid from the Nixon Administration.

Neither Nixon nor his predecessor Lyndon Johnson had respected Cambodian neutrality in the Vietnam conflict. They routinely permitted joint United States-South Vietnamese attacks against Communists in Cambodia. Nixon, however, carried the effort much further. He secretly ordered massive B-52 bomber raids over regions of Cambodia where Communist forces might be located. From 1970 to 1973 United States aircraft bombarded Cambodia with three times the amount of explosives that were dropped on Japan in all of World War II. Nixon also ordered a full-scale invasion of Cambodia in April 1970. This act generated widespread protests in the United States, particularly by college students (the infamous killing of protestors and bystanders at Kent State University occurred at that time). The invasion failed to uncover any significant Communist forces and instead drove them deep into the interior of the Khmer Republic, where they became a menace to Lon Nol's regime instead of a threat to South Vietnam. North Vietnamese units, which had merely passed through Cambodia when Sihanouk had declared it neutral, now entered the country in force to help Cambodian Communists fight the United States.

The large-scale American aid to Lon Nol might have been more effective if so much of it had not been siphoned off and sold by his corrupt officials. They sold American food to the Communists and collected salaries of nonexistent troops from padded payrolls. The effort invested in corruption was so staggering that officials had scarcely any time left to defend the country against Communists. Ordinary Cambodians gave so little backing to the regime that it would have collapsed quickly without the massive support provided by Nixon. In defense of that type of government, Nixon helped kill one million Cambodians—for no greater crime than living where he thought there might be Communists.

Interestingly, Lon Nol also received armament shipments from Communist China and the Soviet Union, presumably to reward him for tolerating North Vietnamese and Viet Cong activity in Cambodia. The Chinese and Soviet matériel assisted Lon Nol's campaign against native Communist guerrillas fighting the Cambodian regime. North Vietnam stood aloof from those guerrillas in the late 1960s, hoping to keep Prince Sihanouk and his premier Lon Nol from entering the Vietnam War on the American side. The North Vietnamese did provide crucial help to Cambodian Communists when they came under American attack in the 1970s. In January 1973, however, a diplomatic accord between the United States and North Vietnam halted American air strikes against that country. This understanding allowed Nixon to divert those American bombers for use over Cambodia, and the agreement therefore incensed the Khmer Rouge. They decided that fraternal Communist states could not be trusted, ordered Vietnamese Communists out of the country, and thenceforward operated in isolation from the rest of the world.

When, under the leadership of Pol Pot, the Khmer Rouge triumphed in 1975, they established a regime like nothing ever seen in modern times. Even Hitler limited himself to atrocities against minorities. Cambodian Communists took on the majority. The entire population of three million in the capital city of Phnom Penh disappeared in three days. Many residents later turned up alive; many did not. In the end, over one million Cambodians were executed or killed by enforced hardship. A certain Comrade Tek explained how to execute someone by making a cut in the abdomen and squeezing until the liver popped out in one piece. He emphasized the importance of good technique: "I would have [to] put my foot in the cut to get the right pressure—otherwise the liver never comes out properly."[12] Salman Rushdie asked, "How can men become like Comrade Tek? I don't know the answer, either. But the terrible lesson of our century is that *it isn't difficult.*"[13]

Even other Communist states were horrified. The Soviet Union, in contrast to its usual hearty encouragement of new Communist governments, looked the other way. China tried to reason with the Pol Pot regime, without success. The North Vietnamese decided to put an end to the madness in Cambodia, now officially called Kampuchea. Hostility had been simmering between Vietnam and Cambodian Communists for years. During the struggle against Lon Nol, it was reported that Cambodian Communists would shoot North Vietnamese advisers in the heat of combat. In 1977 Cambodian forces attacked Vietnam in earnest, and Vietnam responded with a vigorous counterattack. In January 1978 both sides claimed victory, and Vietnam began pulling out of Cambodia. The Vietnamese invaded again in December, and when they finished in 1979 there was little doubt they had won.

In 1982 Prince Norodom Sihanouk reemerged, this time as the leader of a coalition of resistance groups attempting to overthrow the Vietnamese-dominated Communist government in Cambodia. In 1985 the U.S. House Foreign Affairs Committee approved $5 million worth of aid to arm Sihanouk's coalition.

The ongoing war between Cambodia (aided by China) and Vietnam (aided by the Soviet Union) is little noted by persons who argue that a world Communist conspiracy is run smoothly from Kremlin headquarters. A war between two Communist states does not support the idea that the Kremlin presses buttons that make things happen. Nor does it support the argument that Communist regimes are all the same, or that they all cooperate, or that they even have the same goals.

The reality is that Communist states can hate and fear one another, even go to war with another. This suggests there is nothing special, let alone magical, about Communist governments. If they fuss and fume and fight one another, then perhaps it is wrong to look upon them as a bloc. Perhaps they should be viewed as individuals, having different needs and wants, requiring individual consideration in dealings with them.

LAOS

In addition to Vietnam and Cambodia, the Indochina war also embroiled the former French colony of Laos, which became a constitutional monarchy in 1949. Two brothers, Prince Souphanouvong and Prince Souvanna Phouma, competed for and shared power into the 1970s.

Souphanouvong had attempted to use the 1941 Japanese occupation as an opportunity to eliminate French rule. After the war French troops reentered Laos, and Souphanouvong was badly injured while fighting them. He became embittered against England and the United States for their support of French colonialism and in 1951 founded a resistance group called the Pathet Lao. Some question exists about who made up the Pathet Lao; the term is generally used as a synonym for Communist forces, but the Pathet Lao may have been more cosmopolitan. At any rate, they welcomed support from Ho Chi Minh's Viet Minh, and Souphanouvong thereby earned the nickname "Red Prince." During 1953 and 1954 Viet Minh forces entered Laos in large numbers, with the Red Prince's blessing. The Pathet Lao in turn used camps in Vietnamese territory. The two groups were separate but cooperated closely.

After the Geneva conference of 1954, Souphanouvong entered a coalition government headed by his neutralist brother Prince Souvanna Phouma. Elections held in 1958 gave Souphanouvong and the Pathet Lao's political arm, Neo Lao Hak Xat, a majority. Soon afterward, the Pathet Lao began to integrate with the Royal Lao Armed Forces, giving the Communists even more influence in the government. This development provoked Laotian rightists, particularly the business-allied Committee for the Defense of National Interests, a group with a staunch friendship for the United States—a stance influenced no doubt by support the group received from the CIA.

Souvanna's neutralist coalition government fell and was followed by several rightist regimes that disregarded the 1958 election results. A civil war broke out between the Pathet Lao and these governments.

In August 1960 Laotian paratroop captain Kong Le took power through a military coup. The United States suspected him of being a leftist, a suspicion that was not allayed by his choice of neutralist Souvanna Phouma as premier—the Eisenhower administration viewed neutralism as virtually a pro-Communist policy. In autumn 1960 the United States backed right-wing General Phoumi Nosavan in a military revolt against the neutralist government. Since Phoumi was minister of defense, the United States had been able to arm his revolt with little suspicion. Indeed, Souvanna Phouma had looked forward to using this improved military capability against the Pathet Lao.

Rather than achieving a definitive result, Phoumi's revolt confused and intensified the civil war. In an ironic turn of events, the Kong Le-Souvanna Phouma loyalist troops now joined with the Pathet Lao in common cause against the American-supported Phoumi. The American-sponsored overthrow of the neutralist government had made the Communists stronger than ever. Souvanna Phouma and his brother Souphanouvong, the Pathet Lao leader, established a competing regime that requested and received military aid from the Soviet Union.

The war festered until President Kennedy decided to halt American support of Phoumi. A diplomatic settlement was then reached in 1962, creating a neutralist coalition government, similar to what had existed in Laos before Phoumi and the United States became involved.

The North Vietnamese and the Pathet Lao remained powerful in Laos. The United States violated Laotian neutrality with a massive aerial bombardment of Communist supply routes. In addition, the CIA secretly armed a large fighting force comprised of Laotian Meo tribesmen and Thai mercenaries, which did not support the neutralist government of Laos. The United States was supplying an army that resisted not only Communists but the authority of the central government. The Communists, too, were seeking victory in Laos. Under attack from both the United States and the Communists, the neutralist government was doomed. The only question was whether the successor would be allied with the Communists or the West.

A cease-fire was arranged in 1973. Souvanna Phouma once again became prime minister of a coalition government, with his brother Souphanouvong also holding a senior position as chairman of the National Political Council. Despite the cease-fire, Communist-held territory expanded over the next two years, as did Pathet Lao influence in the government. The coalition government resigned in 1975, and the Lao People's Democratic Republic was proclaimed with Souphanouvong as president. Members of the bourgeois and professional classes fled the country as a program was instituted that rivaled Pol Pot's Cambodia in political extremity, though the scale of brutality was nothing like the Cambodian atrocity. The economy declined, and Laos was soon unable to meet even its own basic food needs.

The government was heavily influenced by Communist Vietnam. Ties with the West were severed, and even Chinese representatives and aid programs were expelled. In the 1980s China appeared to be helping resistance groups fighting the Laotian Communist government. This Chinese activity may have resulted from the close relations between Laos and Vietnam—an interpretation strengthened by training that the resistance fighters received from Vietnam's deadly enemy, the Chinese-supported Khmer Rouge of Cambodia. Laotians themselves showed signs of resentment against arrogant treatment from Vietnam and put out feelers toward better relations with the United States. In the mid-1980s the Laotian government decided to reintroduce capitalist profit incentives into the economy, which began to improve.

A SUMMING UP

The war in Vietnam ended with a Communist victory in 1975. A Communist triumph had been expected through elections after the 1954 Geneva conference. Military intervention by the United States had delayed a Communist victory for twenty years, but the Communists won on the field of battle what America would not permit them to win by the ballot box. North and South Vietnam were united at last.

All along the United States had claimed that the war was a Vietnamese affair, that the South Vietnamese would have to win or lose it on their own. Yet as the South Vietnamese steadily lost, the United States refused to tolerate their defeat. Instead, the conflict gradually became an American war. After the debacle Americans accused one another in the United States and ignored the role of the South Vietnamese regime. Yet perhaps the crucial factor in the Communist victory was that the Vietnamese people found the corrupt dictatorship in the south less attractive than rule by Ho Chi Minh. The Communists did not defeat a democracy.

U.S. leaders entered the Vietnamese civil war on the side they knew was overwhelmingly rejected by the Vietnamese people. That side could not prevail unless the population was eradicated—and such an outcome could hardly be considered victory. From the very start of American involvement, the Vietnam War was unwinnable. Defeat would not have been averted by stronger willpower, by more guns, by more troops, by better diplomacy. The United States went down to the seashore and commanded the tide not to come in. Afterward, Americans sat around a fire trying to dry off and angrily pointed fingers at one another, saying that someone should have done more. But the fault was not in anyone's performance of assigned tasks. The fault was in the basic policy flaws that permitted such a project to be mounted.

In Vietnam, the United States confused defending democracy with fighting Communism—the two are not synonymous. Fighting Communism is relatively easy—even Adolf Hitler succeeded in doing it. But defending democracy presupposes a democratic alternative exists, and such was not the case in South Vietnam. Establishing a democracy by force is a contradiction in terms, as democracy, by its very definition, is chosen by the people. And, even if a true democracy had existed in South Vietnam, the method chosen to fight Communism to preserve it was ill considered, for when the goal is to defend democracy, the method chosen to fight Communism becomes all-important. "Every bomb that falls on helpless peasants destroys the clearest claim upon humanity's allegiance that Western democracy once could make: that it was no terrorist society, that for all its defects it was a way of solving problems peacefully, and for that reason well worth defending."[14]

The Vietnam War starkly demonstrated what the American government had become after twenty years of cold war: a land of law that disregarded liberty. Some observers had trouble seeing vestiges of Jefferson or Lincoln.

THE LESSON OF VIETNAM

How could intelligent men, controlling the mightiest military machine the world has ever known, achieve such a dismal result? The key problem was the misapplication of a lesson provided by historical experience.

In reviewing the rationale that American leaders gave for their behavior, their concern with the "lesson of Munich" stands out. At a meeting in Munich during 1938, Adolf Hitler convinced

Western leaders to stand aside as he took over Czechoslovakia. In later days Western compliance with Hitler's demand was portrayed as cowardice in the face of danger, but actually the Western diplomats hoped to encourage the growth of a strong Germany that would attack the Soviet Union. Nonetheless the lesson of Munich, derived from the myth of cowardice, is that compromise is impossible with a leader bent on conquest, and that diplomatic accommodation of an aggressor leads only to more aggression. Therefore, one must take a firm stand at the first inroad and either restrain or destroy the perpetrator by military means before the problem worsens. Some hailed Truman's stance in Korea as vindication of that attitude.

Such was the view that American leaders took of the situation in French Indochina. In their single-minded stubbornness, they succeeded in finding a pattern of aggression regardless of reality and responded as Munich had taught them. The Communists fighting the French were seen not as nationalists seeking independence but as agents in a plot of world conquest. Because the actions of the United States were based on a misreading of the situation, it is not surprising that American leaders failed to achieve their goal of avoiding another Munich. There was no plan of world conquest. All the killing, all the destruction, all the horror, was conjured up as America battled a phantom. The Vietnam War was one particular example of what can happen when a lesson of history is misapplied.

Afterward, the "lesson of Vietnam" was invoked in response to one crisis after another, invoked in so many ways that the real lesson became lost in the confusion of warnings against open-ended commitments, warnings against making commitments without intending to win, against failure of nerve, against hindering the military, against abuse of presidential power, against the peril of a hostile population at home or in the region in question.

Most important of all were warnings against the catastrophe of imagining a local and limited conflict to be an expression of some grand scheme of aggression. This admonishment was seared into a generation that was just beginning to enter positions of power as this book was written.

The true lesson of Vietnam, however, is the danger of misapplying the experience of history. An earlier generation was seared by Munich and responded to events as Munich had taught. Just as that older generation was determined to avoid another Munich, a new generation is determined to avoid another Vietnam. What if, in their passion to achieve that goal, they are faced by incidents that really do express a plan of world conquest? Will the new generation exhibit single-minded stubbornness that ignores a pattern of aggression regardless of reality, or will the new generation have wisdom that the older one lacked? Will the new leaders be able to understand events that do not fit into their preconceived pattern of the world? Will they avoid misapplying the experience of history and thereby prove they have learned the lesson of Vietnam?

XXII.

The Fate of Empires

Empires fall. The process can be slowed, but it has never been avoided.

This chapter deals with the fate of two empires in Africa, one imposed by Europeans, the Portuguese in Angola; the other created by native Africans, the Ethiopians under Haile Selassie.

When the British saw the demand for political freedom increase within their empire, they graciously granted what could not be withheld. As the 1980s began, not one of the former British colonies in Africa could properly be called Communist. When Portugal and Haile Selassie faced the upswelling demand for political freedom, each fought against it bitterly, refusing to yield until overthrown by their own people. The result in Angola and Ethiopia was a strong Communist foothold. To contrast the British experience with the two experiences featured in this chapter is to contrast a generous acceptance of reality with pigheaded refusal to face facts.

ANGOLA

At about the time Christopher Columbus discovered America, Portugal was already fighting native populations in Africa. Angolan unrest continued for almost 500 years, as did staunch and uncompromising Portuguese resistance. Portugal, which became a fascist dictatorship under Antonio de Oliveira Salazar, granted its citizens few rights, and colonial subjects fewer still. In the 1960s the Salazar dictatorship made 800,000 Angolans available for forced labor. The colonial government arrested and executed Angolans at will. When cotton workers protested labor conditions in early 1961, the Portuguese responded by bombing villages. An armed rebellion erupted, and Angolans demanded independence.

The conflict continued into the 1970s. Portuguese military officers recognized that the colonial war created an incredible drain on Portugal's resources. Portugal was neither big nor powerful nor wealthy. It had 100,000 military personnel committed to fighting African guerrillas. The Portuguese dictatorship began to founder under Salazar's successor, Marcello Caetano, and a military coup overthrew the regime in 1974. The new junta, determined to abandon the former diehard colonial policy before the whole country collapsed, relinquished its African colonies. Angola will be the focus of our attention here.

Neither the United States nor the Soviet Union had considered the Angolan situation important before the Portuguese coup of 1974. But when it became clear that the Portuguese were going to give up Angola and that the status quo in the heart of Africa was consequently going to change, both the United States and the Soviet Union wanted to benefit.

Three prominent resistance movements were active in Angola, but they spent as much time fighting one another as they did fighting the Portuguese. UNITA (União Nacional para a Independência Total de Angola—National Union for the Total Independence of Angola), led by Jonas Savimbi, forged close ties with the Republic of South Africa's racist regime. The urban-based MPLA (Movimento Popular de Libertação de Angola—Popular Movement for the Liberation of Angola) was founded by intellectual Angolans who moved freely in the Portuguese culture. MPLA leader António Agostinho Neto was a Methodist comfortable with communist ideology, and MPLA viewed the economic class system as more important than race or tribe. FNLA (Frente Nacional de Libertação de Angola, also called Frente Nacional para a Libertação de Angola—National Front for the Liberation of Angola) had less of an urban identity and less of an intellectual flavor. It was anti-Communist and—unlike MPLA—worked within traditional Angolan racial and tribal boundaries. FNLA leader Holden Roberto married the sister-in-law of Zaire's president, Joseph Mobuto. The ups and downs of FNLA seem at least somewhat linked to its relationship with the Zaire government.

UNITA received backing from the fanatical Communist North

Korean regime and from the equally fanatical anti-Communist Republic of South Africa. Communist China helped the anti-Communist FNLA, while various other Communist states aided MPLA. On the other hand, both FNLA and MPLA were also funded by the World Council of Churches. Both were armed by Algeria and received assistance from sources in Morocco. And although FNLA received help from the Ford Foundation, the United States government sent Portugal military assistance for use against Angolan rebels. Stereotyping the resistance movements and the Angolan struggle in terms of East-West geopolitics is therefore almost impossible.

When Portugal granted independence to Angola on November 11, 1975, the pro-Communist MPLA had a strong claim as Angola's true government since it already controlled most provincial capitals and had served in the national transitional government, which preceded independence.[1] MPLA was quickly recognized as the legitimate Angolan government by many Communist states. Significantly, no state anywhere in the world recognized FNLA or UNITA as the government. Even in the mid-1980s, the United States supported UNITA as a rebel group, not as the legitimate government.

Agostinho Neto was no longer merely the leader of MPLA; he was now the leader of Angola. This outcome must have been particularly offensive to Holden Roberto, whose movement had received recognition from the Organization of African Unity's Liberation Committee as Angola's government in exile a dozen years earlier.

The United States and South Africa had been supporting attacks against MPLA, and this activity continued when MPLA took control of the Angolan government. Portugal had disregarded South African incursions into the colony, supposedly to protect various economic interests. The new Angolan government, however, was distinctly unfriendly about such violations of its territory. As the November 11, 1975, Independence Day approached, the character of South African attacks changed from quick in-and-out border raids to a full-scale invasion. Fears arose that South Africa intended to detach a section of Angola, reminiscent of the Katanga situation when the Congo became independent.

Since the legitimate Angolan government was under attack from forces supported by the United States, it is not surprising that Angola turned elsewhere for military aid. It requested aid from Cuba and the Soviet Union.

MPLA soldiers had already received some Cuban training in the mid-1960s, conducted in the Congo and in Cuba itself. Cubans were already in Angola weeks before November 11, 1975. Their aid to the Angolan government began modestly, but quickly escalated in response to South Africa's attacks. The increase of Cuban aid was an apparent response to events rather than preplanned, and seemed to grow far beyond Castro's original intention.[2] This interpretation seems reasonable since Castro made several attempts to reduce Cuban military personnel in Angola, but each withdrawal was abandoned when South African attacks resumed. Soviet aid was given in accordance with United Nations and Organization of African Unity resolutions. In Angola, the Soviets obeyed internationally recognized standards of conduct; the United States did not. Even the CIA's Angola task force director, John Stockwell, admitted, "What our propaganda was churning out was that the Soviets intervened with massive arms shipments and the Cubans went in with their regular army units. . . . Each major escalation was initiated by our side, by the United States and our allies."[3]

Cuban military personnel were a godsend in saving Angola from South African conquest. Not only were the Cubans valuable in sheer numbers, but they were intimately familiar with the Soviet heavy weapons provided to Angola by Russia. Cuban troops were ready to go into action as soon as they arrived; no time or efficiency was lost in training.

At the same time that Cubans were holding back the South African advance into Angola, they were also repelling an American-supported attack from FNLA and Zairian units, as well as fighting UNITA forces. There seems little question that the government of Angola would have been defeated if Cuba had not provided help.

After the U.S. Senate cut off covert American aid to anti-Angolan forces in December 1975, Saudi Arabia furnished UNITA with $50 million. As with UNITA's South Africa ally, Saudi Arabia's commitment to democracy was undemonstrated.

With military action failing, the United States tried economic warfare against Angola, blocking delivery of American goods, which had already been paid for—a breach of contract that would have angered the United States had it been the victim rather than the perpetrator. The American government also ordered Gulf Oil, which maintained friendly relations with Angola (so friendly that Cuban troops protected Gulf Oil facilities from attack by South Africa and UNITA), to cease operations there. Petroleum represented almost all of Angola's exports, and the Gulf enterprise generated a substantial amount of Angolan government revenue.

Without firing a shot, the United States government thereby eliminated a major element of Angolan economic productivity.

The United States abandoned these steps in 1976 after NATO allies including England, France, and West Germany recognized the MPLA regime as the legitimate Angolan government. Nonetheless, the United States continued to withhold diplomatic recognition and continued to encourage guerrilla warfare against the Angolan regime.

Cuban forces remained in Angola to provide vital help in defending the regime against continuing attacks from UNITA and its South African ally. As with the United States in Vietnam, Cuba became ever more bogged down in Angolan politics. The climax was a coup attempt in 1977 in which Cubans apparently helped both sides.

And like the United States in Vietnam, Cuba began to learn the limits of power—the weak country receiving help was able to bully the strong ally. For instance, in 1978 Cuba strongly opposed Angolan sponsorship of an invasion of Zaire by Zairian exiles in Angola. FNLA opponents of the Angolan government had close relations with Zaire, which had trained FNLA guerillas during the struggle against Portugal. When FNLA's competitor MPLA gained control of the government of Angola, relations between Zaire and Angola soured. Zaire had fought MPLA forces before Angolan independence and continued the attacks afterward. Zaire provided facilities for South African fighter bombers in the war against Angola, and U.S. aircraft flew arms to UNITA from Zaire. So the Angolan government had plenty of motives for encouraging an invasion by Zairian exiles. Castro, however, did not relish the prospect. He was already committed to defending Angola against attacks from UNITA and South Africa and was also in the middle of helping Ethiopia in its war with Somalia. He feared the prospect of a third simultaneous war in Zaire, particularly since it might involve confronting French forces helping to defend that country. Nonetheless, despite Cuba's crucial role in preservation of the Angolan government, Angola proceeded with the Zaire adventure, knowing that Castro could not afford to desert Angola, no matter how displeased he was. Angola was clearly not completely a Cuban pawn and could even ensnare Cuba in a situation that risked a war Castro did not want. Fortunately for him, the invasion of Zaire turned out to be a small operation of little consequence; on two occasions Zairian exiles crossed the border and were quickly defeated.

In the 1980s the Reagan administration complained about Cubans in Angola. Yet the ostensible reason for Cuban presence—attacks from South Africa and its UNITA ally—remained. Angola's fellow African states, which certainly had strong motivation to compare the potential of aggression from Cuba and South Africa, raised little complaint about the Cuban aid to Angola.

Some American Congressmen and Reagan administration officials promoted UNITA as a Free World force fighting Communism in Angola. While obtaining funding for UNITA, these officials tended to downplay UNITA's earlier backing by the North Koreans. And little was said of the Communist origins of UNITA's leader, Jonas Savimbi, who had trained as a guerrilla in China. To the Reagan administration, UNITA's alliance with South Africa was proof enough of Savimbi's credentials as a freedom fighter, an evaluation shared by few African states.

UNITA demonstrated a dedication to terrorism rather than standard military actions. Unarmed civilians were typical targets. Villages in government territory were shot up, and their inhabitants were murdered. UNITA was credited with setting land mines that killed and maimed peasants and even attacked a Red Cross artificial-leg factory. The Institute of Agronomical Research in Huambo was attacked, and a UNITA car bomb in that city killed thirty-five persons. UNITA kidnapped foreign workers such as agronomists and civil engineers, although they were usually released after being marched hundreds of miles. Such tactics, which appeared in other conflicts as well, became known as "low-intensity" warfare. The purpose was not to defeat a government's military forces but rather to make a country uninhabitable, so the government would collapse. UNITA certainly achieved the former goal at least. By 1986 the country's economy was crippled, and 600,000 refugees had been thrown from their homes. A decade of this strategy did not tarnish UNITA among its U.S. congressional supporters, who simultaneously urged worldwide war against terrorists.

ETHIOPIA

In the 1860s construction of the Suez Canal provided the Russian czar with a strategic challenge and an opportunity. The challenge was to protect his sea routes to Korea, China, and eastern Siberia. The opportunity was to worry England about the possibility of disrupting its sea routes to India, thus creating a bargaining chip to promote a more generous English view of Russian interests in

Asia. Both situations called for some sort of Russian presence at the Red Sea. Thus, a vigorous Russian interest in Ethiopia developed in the 1800s and continued through the next century.

Ras Taffari Makoñnen took the name Haile Selassie when he became regent of Ethiopia in 1928. Two years later he was proclaimed emperor. In 1936 he received worldwide sympathy when he was driven into exile after his country was conquered by the Italian fascist dictator Benito Mussolini. The sympathy was misplaced. Throughout Haile Selassie's rule, before and after World War II, he ran a one-party state with no political opposition permitted. Most of the population had no rights, and big landlords—many of them operating on the emperor's behalf—owned most of the land.

Beginning in 1970 a drought devastated the country. Although the government denied the severity of the problem, the situation steadily worsened. Anger and unrest grew into revolution, and in 1974 Haile Selassie was overthrown.

He was replaced by a military junta-parliament called the dergue, which, after some vicious factional infighting, turned Ethiopia into a Communist state. The Communists dealt no better with the drought than the emperor had. What they did instead was put more effort into fighting the segments of Haile Selassie's empire that sought to detach themselves.

One part of the empire seeking freedom was the former Italian colony of Eritrea, put under the emperor's sovereignty by the United Nations in 1950. Dissatisfied with Eritrean autonomy, Haile Selassie formally annexed it to Ethiopia in 1962. This immediately sparked a rebellion. For years the United States trained the emperor's army for the fight against Eritrea and, after his fall, continued supplying military aid to the dergue for a couple of years despite the regime's steady transformation of Ethiopia into a Communist state.

If such assistance to the dergue seems peculiar, remember that the United States was still dealing with the same Ethiopian military that had existed under Haile Selassie, only now it was running the country. The United States had a long relationship with these officers even though they now had Communist leadership. It should also be recognized that the United States was concerned about Soviet aid to the Communist government next door in Somalia, which the United States hoped to counterbalance with Free World aid to Communists in Ethiopia. Such an American policy obviously had to be a boon for communism in the region, but that effect apparently escaped the notice of U.S. officials who designed the policy.

They may have been more concerned about the strategic implications of Soviet friendship with Somalia. Although the czars had wanted a presence in the Red Sea, Russia had no strategic interest in the Indian Ocean until the 1960s, when U.S. missile-carrying submarines could strike key areas of the Soviet Union from the Indian Ocean. Similarly, the Soviets suddenly developed an interest in the Mediterranean when the United States could deploy submarine missiles able to reach the Soviet Union from there.

The United States feared that Soviet aid to Somalia would facilitate a Russian presence in the Indian Ocean. Nonetheless, despite loose talk about Russian naval bases in Somalia, until the 1980s Russia had none. A base is a location where ships can be refitted and repaired in physical security, available at all times regardless of diplomatic tensions. In the 1970s the Soviets did have Somali berthing stations, but those are not bases: "A berthing station is little more than a fancy title for a mooring buoy."[4]

In addition to helping Somalia, the Soviets also sent Ethiopia massive arms shipments devoted to suppressing the Eritrean revolt, in which civilians were prime targets of the Ethiopian regime. The rebellion continued, unabated, into the late 1980s, perhaps partly because the Eritreans were tough and partly because the Ethiopian regime did not make the best possible use of its resources. Cuba also entered the picture with military aid to strengthen the fraternal state of Ethiopia, which ironically hurt the Eritrean revolt, with which Cuba sympathized on the principle of anti-imperialism. Cuba provided less help than the Ethiopian government requested and certainly did not control the regime.

The Communist Ethiopian regime also battled Communist Somalia. Somalia was an independent state melded from an Italian colony and a British colony in 1960. The new country immediately sought arms to protect itself and to pursue its territorial claims against Ethiopia in the Ogaden region. Somalia received a few weapons culled from Egyptian arsenals. A Czech offer was declined in 1961, but the next year an arms deal was accepted from Britain and Italy. Other NATO allies, including the United States, then tried to change the terms of the arrangement. This seems to have reflected Ethiopia's concerns that it might be Somalia's target. The United States offered to increase the dollar amount of weaponry to $10 million if it would be used solely for internal security and engineering projects and if Somalia would refuse all other arms offers.

Negotiations continued for a year, and Somalia eventually announced it had accepted an alternative Soviet proposal. The Soviets had offered more than the United States, oriented it toward combat needs, attached no strings to it, and made most of it an outright gift. As always, the United States grumbled about a country turning to the Communists for help, but Somalia had first turned to the Free World and had even refused a Czech offer.

In the 1970s Somalia acquired a Soviet-supplied military force of formidable strength, on paper at least, including hundreds of tanks and armored personnel carriers, along with powerful aircraft. Fortunately for Ethiopia, maintenance problems considerably reduced the striking power of this force. Airplanes that will not fly and vehicles that cannot move simply do not count for much.

The long-expected war between Ethiopia and Somalia finally broke out in the summer of 1977. This put the Soviet Union in a difficult position, since it supported the governments of both countries. Although Soviet military aid to Somalia had no strings attached when it began in the 1960s, the Soviets later apparently tried to discourage Somali military adventures by withholding ammunition and other supplies needed to use the Soviet-furnished arsenal effectively. When war broke out nonetheless, the Soviets decided to help the greater African state, Ethiopia, even though the choice cost them the Indian Ocean access they had coveted in Somalia. This appears to be an exception to the standard Soviet practice of putting military interests above everything else, but the Somali facilities were more a convenience than a necessity. Perhaps the Soviets were even taking a long-range view, hoping to secure Indian Ocean facilities as a reward from other African states that disapproved of Somalia's war against Ethiopia. Moreover, once the passions of the day had cooled, the West's relative lack of interest in Somalia could lead to a resumption of ties with the Soviets.

At any rate, the Soviet Union began a massive increase of arms assistance to Ethiopia; and Castro transferred thousands of Cubans from Angola in order to help Ethiopia as well. Nonetheless, the Somalis had the better of the contest at first. Then the Soviets became serious. In less than a year, they provided Ethiopia with at least four times the dollar amount of weaponry that the United States had furnished in twenty-five years.

There was some talk of the United States arming the Somalis—perhaps on the geopolitical grounds that the Russians had switched sides, so Americans had to respond and switch sides also. Somali leader Muhammad Siyad Barre encouraged such talk with fierce speeches about the Cuban-Russian threat in the region.

This supposed advocate of Free World interests had seized power in a coup that killed his predecessor, and he had formerly promoted Cuban-Russian activity by accepting their largesse and by providing berthing stations to facilitate Soviet naval operations in the Indian Ocean.

Fortunately the United States remembered that Somalia had started the war in the first place, and with a Soviet-supplied arsenal. The United States refused to supply weapons to Somalia unless it withdrew its forces from Ethiopia. Since Somalia was losing, this was an easy condition to fulfill. Both sides announced an end to the war in early 1978. Somalia, however, continued to back guerrilla action in Ethiopia for years afterward. The United States vacillated on arms deals, but nonetheless improved relations with Somalia and obtained access to the Indian Ocean naval facilities that Russia had wanted.

The experiences in Angola and Ethiopia demonstrate that oppressive regimes promote, rather than prevent, the establishment of Communist governments. Too often, American support for Third World dictators only delays a Communist succession to power and does not not halt it. A more productive approach might be to encourage the well-being of populations. This might be a greater challenge than strengthening a regime's military forces, because an oppressive government will not want to cooperate. If the United States finds that a government opposes the well-being of the people it rules, perhaps it should be unconcerned about such a regime's fate. Rather than stand with the powers of the past, perhaps the United States should stand aside and eagerly await the opportunity to deal with the powers of the future.

New rulers may reject American offers of friendship, but that need not be a bad thing. A true friend does not insist on control of someone else's destiny and does not use personal gain as the measure of a friendship's value. There is something to be said for a world in which countries are free to choose the kind of internal society they desire. Occasionally such a choice may be so heinous as to cry out for remedy, but there is no reason for the United States alone to make that judgment and take on the burden of intervention.

Empires fall. Perhaps the United States should profit from their example and abandon imperialistic pretensions.

XXIII.

The Challenge of Islam

In the 1980s concern about Soviet activities prompted American participation in wars involving the Muslim nations Afghanistan and Iran. The former country was a land of little inherent interest to the United States, where only extensive Soviet involvement attracted American attention. In contrast, Iran involved strategic and economic factors of such importance to the United States that minuscule Soviet activity brought swift American intervention. In neither case did the United States action demonstrate a clear purpose or a sensitivity for the history of Russian interests in those two countries.

AFGHANISTAN

In the 1800s Afghanistan was a desolate area that would have been of little interest to anyone other than its native inhabitants had it not been located between the czarist empire expanding from the northwest and the British colonial empire in India to the southeast. Throughout the nineteenth century these two empires competed for influence in Afghanistan. England invaded Afghanistan in 1839, overthrew the ruling prince, Dōst Moḥammad, and replaced him with Shāh Shojā. Fierce resistance drove the British out of the country with heavy losses, and Dōst Moḥammad was restored as ruler. England invaded again in 1878 but once more failed to gain control of the country. Also in the nineteenth century, Russia helped Iran make two unsuccessful attempts to conquer the western Afghanistan town of Herāt, only to be repelled by native defenders who had British assistance. Neighboring Iran and Afghanistan had long been rivals for territory and dominance. In the eighteenth century, eastern Iran had been part of an Afghan empire; in ancient times Afghanistan had been within the Persian empire. Even in the twentieth century, Iranian nationalists considered Afganistan to be rightfully Iran's.[1]

The indomitable Afghan opposition to foreign conquest may have been fueled by hatred of any sort of government rather than by hatred of a foreign oppressor. Although there was a ruling prince, Afghanistan was not so much a national state as a geographical area inhabited by autonomous tribes and clans. In 1875 British Major-General Sir Henry Rawlinson declared, "The feeling of patriotism, as known in Europe, cannot exist among the Afghans, for there is no common country. In its place is found a strong, turbulent love of individual liberty, which naturally rebels against authority, and would be equally impatient of control, whether exercised by English or Russians or Persians, or even Durranis [the dominant native ethnic group]."[2] The characteristic was still obvious to historian Anthony Hyman in the latter twentieth century, who noted that Afghans demonstrated a "genius for anarchy of a particularly destructive kind."[3]

Russians moved into Afghanistan in the 1880s and succeeded in incorporating the Merv (Mary) region into Russia. At the same time, Britain was hard pressed in Sudan; General Charles George Gordon's famed debacle at Khartoum occurred the year after Russia acquired Merv. The British decided to abandon Sudan to enable those forces to be used to halt Russian expansion toward India. A war between Russia and England suddenly appeared possible; such a war had been fought once before, thirty years earlier. As a rear-guard action, England encouraged Italy to seize Eritrea so a power friendly to Britain would dominate the Indian Ocean approach to the Suez Canal. This in turn attracted Russian attention to Ethiopia as a way of threatening British India.

Thus, we see the interplay of Russian expansion, rebellion in Eritrea, and war in Afghanistan—an interplay that was already in progress a century ago. Although Communists became players, they did not start the game. German chancellor Otto von Bismarck once commmented that events in Poland determined Russian activity in Afghanistan.

Just before World War I, England and Russia agreed to treat Afghanistan as a buffer zone that neither would seek to acquire.

As part of the agreement, however, Afghanistan's ruling prince, Habībollāh Khān, agreed that England could direct his country's foreign policy. His son Amānollah Khān repudiated that agreement soon after he assumed power in 1919 and even attacked British India. He was soundly defeated, but in the course of the conflict, he approached Bolshevik Russia and suggested an exchange of diplomats. Lenin praised Afghanistan as "the only independent Muslim state in the world"[4] (Iran and Turkey were British-occupied) but gave no particular aid to the zealous prince other than diplomatic recognition. Russia was worried that stirring up Islamic rebellion could backfire in the Muslim portions of the Soviet Union.[5]

In 1920 Jemal Pasha, a Turk who had been residing in Moscow, traveled to Afghanistan on invitation of Amānollah and became the ruler's political adviser, much to the dismay of Great Britain, which in 1921 formally relinquished its right to direct Afghanistan's foreign affairs. The country was a sovereign state at last, but it continued to generate minor issues over which England and Russia vexed each other for years.

Amānollah, who styled himself king from 1922 onward, initiated a program of radical social reform—radical in the context of the country's ultraconservative Muslim society—that included emancipation of women, compulsory free education, selection of students for education in Europe, and adoption of Western technology and customs throughout the country. Such steps attracted the friendly support of the Soviet Union, including help from Russian aircraft to suppress a rebellion in 1924. Amānollah's innovations provoked a stiffer rebellion in 1929, and Soviet forces once again entered the country to defend the government. In the middle of the fight, however, Amānollah gave up and fled to India. The Russians quickly abandoned the contest and returned home. A strict and conservative Islamic regime was then reinstituted in Afghanistan by King Nāder Khān and his brothers.

Afghanistan is another country that has never known democracy. Freedom of the press did not appear until 1951, and dissidents were jailed after free speech was banned again the next year. A so-called free press law was enacted in 1965, but the freedom was constricted enough to ban politically offensive newspapers.

Seeking to pursue a nonaligned stand in the cold war, the dictatorial Afghan monarchy of King Mohammed Zahir Shah refused to join the Baghdad Pact, later known as the Central Treaty Organization (CENTO). This military alliance was begun in 1955 by U.S. secretary of state John Foster Dulles. In conjunction with

SEATO and NATO, it completed an encirclement designed to make the Soviet Union feel hemmed in and trapped by enemies. How this was supposed to ease world tension is unclear. The United States was not a formal member of CENTO but was a very interested and influential observer.

CENTO members included England, Turkey, Iraq, Iran, and Pakistan. This lineup disturbed several nations in the region other than the Soviet Union. India became uneasy about the arms sent to Pakistan and so diverted money from internal development to weapons. The arming of Iraq offended both Israel and Saudi Arabia, and the Arab world in general was annoyed that Britain's CENTO membership invited it back into a region where it had already caused much grief.

In addition, Iran and Pakistan had quarrels with Afghanistan, and the Afghans were uneasy about the "anti-Communist" weaponry provided to their two opponents by the United States. These concerns grew after Afghanistan unsuccessfully sought weapons from the United States as well. The United States did not wish to offend CENTO member Pakistan and insisted that Afghanistan first give up claims in what it called the Pashtunistan region of Pakistan. Afghanistan refused to do so and therefore received no American arms.

Afghanistan then turned to the Soviet Union for arms as it had in Amānollah's time. Starting in 1956 and continuing through the next decade, Afghanistan was one of the Soviet Union's prime foreign-aid clients. The Soviet Union and other Communist countries not only provided a bountiful supply of weaponry, they also accepted a trade balance grossly favoring Afghanistan in the arms deals. The Soviets moreover accepted the unreliable Afghan currency as payment in the growing trade relations between the two countries, a favor that capitalist merchants would never grant. The Afghan government ran up a large debt to the Soviet Union as a result of generous loan terms. This, too, was a Soviet favor because international debts can be collected only if the debtor is willing to pay. For the creditor such loans buy friendship, not power over the debtor.

Thus, although Afghanistan stayed formally neutral in the cold war, a friendly relationship was cemented with the Soviet Union during the 1960s. In addition, Russia gained influence within the Afghan military because of intimate professional relations that evolved in the course of training the Afghans in Soviet weapons and tactics.

In 1965 an Afghan Communist party was organized, headed by

Nur Mohammad Taraki. A dozen years earlier, Taraki had been a low-level diplomat assigned to the United States, where he publicly denounced the Afghan government and sought political asylum. The United States refused and forced him to return to his homeland, to whatever fate was in store. He turned out to be a tough character who survived, and in 1965 he became a leader of Afghan Communist opposition to the government.

The Communist party soon splintered into various competing factions, a development that was not surprising given the Afghan tradition of anarchy and resistance to authority. The two main factions were headed by Taraki and Babrak Karmal. The Soviet Communist party frowns upon factions as evidence that a party is undisciplined and unworthy of support, and so apparently the Soviets ignored the Afghan Communists as insignificant.

Soviet involvement with the Afghan military had encouraged a leftist trend among officers. In 1973 the military overthrew the monarchy in a coup and installed Mohammad Daud Khan, a member of the royal family, as president of the republic. Five years later the military staged another coup, killed Daud and assorted relatives, and installed Communist party chief Taraki as the new president.

As might be expected, the United States had little influence with Taraki or his government. A dramatic example occurred in February 1979, when United States ambassador Adolph Dubs was abducted by ultraleftist Setem-i-Meli terrorists. This Maoist group advocated that ethnic minorities use violence against the government to defend their rights and sought to trade Dubs for imprisoned members of their group. The ambassador died when, over American protests, Afghan police shot up the hotel room where the kidnappers were holding him. The Afghan government never offered condolences, let alone an apology.

When Afghanistan's Communist regime was installed in 1978, it immediately set out to liberate the country from Islamic customs they considered backward. King Amānollah had been run out of the country when he had tried such modernization a half-century earlier. Communist zealots found that the attitude of the Muslim population had not changed since then. Rather than seeking reform, the people demanded retention of old ways. The population even rejected land reform as antireligious; in frustration the government then made it a crime to refuse the land.

In 1978 and 1979, the Taraki regime treated the Muslim peasantry with calculated brutality. Afghan Communism was an urban phenomenon, mainly limited to citizens with enough education to regard themselves as superior to those with lesser learning and ruder life-styles.[6] Communist gangs from the cities roamed the countryside, killing anyone who was believed resistant to abandoning Islamic customs. This conduct not only generated conflict between Muslims and Communists, but between city residents and the rural peasantry.

The domestic unrest also created a problem with the Taraki regime's Soviet relations. His government had outsmarted itself in 1978 by sending Karmal and key men of his rival Communist faction overseas as ambassadors—and then dismissing them. This ploy removed the rivals from the country, but the defeated faction had always been friendly to the Soviet Union. With Soviet approval the ex-ambassadors gathered together in Eastern Europe and plotted a return. In essence they formed a Soviet-sponsored shadow government ready to step in if Taraki faltered.

Taraki could see what was happening and tried to impress the Soviet Union by fanatically attacking Muslim "superstition" in the countryside. The idea was to transform the population and thereby show that the Afghan government was successful in creating a Communist society. Taraki hoped the Soviets would then abandon support for Karmal and his exiles. Indeed, Taraki's insensitivity to the desires of the Afghans demonstrated to the Soviets how ineffective his group was: "A small elite of incompetent urban ideologues with no practical experience in governing and with little tolerance for native customs attempted by force to introduce alien and ill-conceived reforms, even though the regime had few capable administrators and little popular support."[7] Taraki's faction responded to lack of support from the people by declaring that the Communist party itself was the people. In contrast to the Afghan government, the Soviets took a more realistic view and recognized the possibility that an Islamic anti-Communist war could arise in an area deemed vital to Soviet military security—Communist Afghanistan was, after all, as much a Russian border state as Poland, and the Islamic element of an anti-Communist Afghan rebellion could incite Muslim populations in Asiatic Soviet republics.

Soviet concerns heightened in mid-1979 when anti-Communist Muslim tribesmen in Afghanistan began a large insurrection against the oppressive Taraki Communist regime. The rebels singled out Soviet advisers and their families for brutal torture, sometimes climaxed by decapitations with triumphal display of the heads on pikes. Even as loyal units of the Afghan armed forces struck the insurgents from land and air, other elements of the

Afghan armed forces deserted to the rebels. A question arose about the Afghan government's authority in the country. The Soviet Union was not about to permit the overthrow of a Communist state on its border; the Taraki regime could see the Soviets' distress and knew that the exiled Karmal faction of native Afghan Communists might well return under Soviet auspices and take power. Tension within the Afghan government was dramatized by quarreling between Taraki and his rival, Hafizullah Amin. Their bickering peaked in a September 1979 gun battle fought within the former royal palace. The two rivals survived without injury; but Taraki was killed soon thereafter, and Amin became president. He failed to make any progress in quelling the rebellion.

The Soviet Union gave up on Amin's ability to preserve the Afghan Communist state. In December 1979 several thousand airborne Soviet troops descended with lightning speed on the capital city, Kabul. They captured the Afghan government's leaders and installed a new government under Babrak Karmal. Amin was executed within hours of his arrest. In the historical context of Soviet-Afghan relations, the Russian decision to intervene had none of the portent of invading Hungary or Czechoslovakia. It was like the United States sending marines to the Dominican Republic or Grenada. It was not a major decision, scarcely more than deciding to hold live manuevers. Soviet invaders overwhelmed the Afghan military in December 1979, but desertions and mutinies had already demonstrated the military's lack of allegiance to the government. Resistance to the Russians was not futile; it was nonexistent.

Although the U.S. government protested loudly about the Soviet invasion crushing Afghan freedom, the country already had a vicious homegrown Communist dictatorship that had been killing its people wholesale, one that had killed the American ambassador. The Afghan government lost its liberty in the sense that the Soviet Union now dominated the Karmal regime, but the invasion took nothing from the Afghan people that they had not already lost long before.

The civil war that started under the first Communist government continued in the mid-1980s. There seemed little doubt that the Karmal government survived only because of enormous Soviet military assistance. As with the United States in South Vietnam, the Russian presence permeated the Afghan government so thoroughly as to destroy its credibility as an independent state. Apparently with Soviet instigation, Karmal was forced to resign in 1986 and was replaced by Sayid Mohammed Najibullah. In 1987 Russia and the deposed reactionary king Mohammed Zahir Shah, who was exiled to Italy, were negotiating the possibility of his return to Afghanistan as a republican head of state, with Najibullah remaining as head of a coalition Communist government that tolerated a traditional Islamic way of life. As this book went to press, Soviet leader Mikhail Gorbachev claimed that his country's forces would leave Afghanistan in 1988.

Without question a wide range of national elements, known collectively as the mujahedin, were fighting the Soviet-backed regime. They were so diverse that they scarcely had anything in common other than opposition to the government. Perhaps this was a sudden expression of new-found Afghan patriotism—or perhaps it was merely a repetition of traditional anarchical resistance to any sort of government.

Although the Reagan administration called the mujahedin "freedom fighters," it is unclear whether they sought the political and social freedoms that Americans enjoy. It is certain only that they were fighting Soviet domination of Afghanistan. The question arises as to whether the United States was seeking democracy in Afghanistan or merely an opportunity to harass the Soviet Union.

IRAN

In contrast to the marginal American strategic interest in Afghanistan during the 1980s, the United States had a vital stake in Iran because of its key role in Western oil supplies and its commanding strategic position in an area of the world threatened by military conflict. The American interest was so great that an innocuous and tangential appearance of Soviet naval power in the area brought a massive U.S. naval task force hurrying to the Persian Gulf in 1987. In the excitement of the moment, Reagan administration policymakers appeared to ignore the Russian interest in Iran that long predated the interest of the United States.

In the early 1700s the czar invaded Iran with a 100,000-man army and seized territory to the south of the Caspian Sea, but Russia gave it all back in the next decade to promote a friendly Iranian attitude in controversies that Russia had with Turkey. Around 1800 Russia once again forced Iran to cede territory, this time in Georgia and along the Kura River. In the next quarter-century Russia gained more Iranian territory to the west of the Caspian Sea, including Persian Armenia. This Russian expansion into Iran carried a potential of conflict with British India and generated the same tensions as did the Afghanistan controversies between the two imperial powers. A few years before World War I, they established formal spheres of influence in Iran, with Russia to dominate the northwest and England the southeast, divided by a neutral zone playing the same sort of buffer role as Afghanistan did. The two great powers ruthlessly grabbed Iran's oil resources in the assigned spheres. During the First World War, Russia, England, France, and Italy all agreed that the czar could take a section of northern Iran after the war and would also hold sway over a wider region of ostensibly independent Iran. The West cancelled the arrangement when the Communists took over Russia, but neither the Soviet Union nor Iran has forgotten that the West had agreed that Russia was entitled to northern Iran.

After the war Iran went to the Versailles peace conference to protest the long-time theft of its mineral wealth by the West. England kept the Iranians out of the conference, and they returned home to watch great foreign corporations take both the oil and the profits. In 1919 Britain took advantage of the postwar confusion to force a treaty on Iran by which the country would, for all practical purposes, be annexed to the British empire.

This act apparently prompted a revolt in the Gīlān area of Iran, on the Caspian Sea—details were murky, but the unrest seemed directed against England. Britain had also occupied Russian oil fields north of Iran, giving the Soviets a grievance that helped prompt their entry into the Gīlān rebellion in 1920. A number of Russian troops were already in the area, having been stranded there when the czarist regime collapsed. A Soviet force took Enzeli by sea, ostensibly to secure naval craft of the Caspian fleet that General Anton Ivanovich Denikin had abandoned in the Russian civil war. A ground force entered the area from Azerbaijan—supposedly a native Azeri operation, but possibly conducted by the Soviet Red Army. In spring 1920 the outcome was the Communist independent Republic of Gīlān.

The Russian effort was limited to the rebellious Gīlān area on the Caspian. This probably had more to do with the pressing military challenge of the Russian civil war than with protests from the feeble Iranian government—the last shah of the decadent Qājār dynasty would soon abandon his country for the pleasures of Paris. Whatever the cause for Bolshevik caution in Iran, no attempt was made to encroach southward. The Soviets were attracted to a trouble spot and appeared ready to profit from circumstances, but did not try to expand the trouble.

The Republic of Gīlān was felled partly by its decision to attack

Muslim "religious superstition" in a program that closed mosques, banned the teaching of Islam, and required women to forgo veils. Unrest grew, just as it did in response to Amānollah's simultaneous social reforms in neighboring Afghanistan, and was encouraged by Shiite clergy.

In 1921 the Russians promised to pull the Red Army out of Gīlān if English forces departed from southern Iran. After the British left, the Russians remained long enough to assist the Republic of Gīlān with a march against the central Iranian government in Teheran. The campaign was an utter failure, and the Soviets shamefacedly denied their participation. The Red Army withdrew from Iran, leaving native Iranians to settle the fate of Gīlān. The Republic of Gīlān was soon conquered by Reza Khan. A few years later he deposed the last Qājār shah and founded a new dynasty.

About this time the Soviet Union and Iran signed a treaty giving the Soviets the right to enter Iran whenever the government was unable to resist a third party that attacked Iran or that attempted to use Iran as a base for aggression against the Soviet Union. It is likely the Iranian government was not altogether displeased about this, since the provision was obviously aimed at England, whose corporations had been draining Iranian oil sources. At the time, a Soviet commentator frankly stated that Russia was concerned about a possible British attack through Iran,[8] understandable enough considering England's record in the Russian civil war. No one imagined that the Soviets would instead use this treaty in response to Hitler.

Between the two world wars, Iran showed less irritation over Soviet conduct than over American behavior. In late 1921 U.S. corporations sought oil concessions that would be intertwined with loans requested by the Iranian regime. Russia, resented American pursuit of oil in northern Iran. In 1922 *Pravda* said, "These concessions are not utilizable without transit through Russia. The Russian Government cannot admit on the Russo-Persian frontier the organization of a capitalist centre capable at the right moment of transforming the concession into a purely military base which would be a menace for Russia."[9] These sentiments are easily understood if it is recalled that the United States had participated in an invasion of the Soviet Union a few years earlier, and if the record of U.S. military conduct in Latin America and the Philippines is considered. *Pravda* was expressing Russian realism, not paranoia.

In 1941 Britain and the Soviet Union jointly conquered Iran, explaining they had to seize Iranian territory before Hitler did. Iran asked the United States to use its influence to stop the invasion, but America stood aside. Reza Shah Pahlavi refused to surrender, and the invaders forced him to relinquish his crown to his son, Mohammad Reza Pahlavi, who served as a figurehead while Russia and England ruled Iran during World War II.

After the war, as after the previous global conflict, the Soviet Union once again took interest in splitting northern Iran from the rest of the country. The Autonomous Republic of Azerbaijan[10] and the Kurdish People's Republic were proclaimed in December 1945 with active Russian encouragement.

Soviet involvement in these two states does not mean that these were puppet regimes with little popular support. Indeed, some Iranians actively sought Russian help against the central government, which was dominated by great landlords. *New York Times* reporter Clifton Daniel verified that Iran resembled a medieval feudal society rather than a Western democracy.[11] Inspired by the great changes sweeping the globe after World War II, Iranian activists called not only for land reform but for revolution to free peasants from the great landlords.

Although the Autonomous Republic of Azerbaijan was led by a Comintern veteran of the old Gīlān republic, it boasted an armed force 10,000 strong, with at least 70,000 and perhaps 100,000 men in reserve. This was not a mere handful of conspirators. The Kurdish People's Republic traced its origins to a secret non-Communist nationalist group formed in 1943. The republic's president was a well-known religious leader with important family connections, Qazi Muhammad. The Soviet Union nurtured these regimes, but did not invent them.

The Truman administration later made much of Soviet garrison troops blocking Iranian government forces from moving into northern Iran, claiming their actions were an "at least indirect" violation of the 1943 joint U.S.-British-Russian-Iranian declaration of support for Iran's territorial integrity.[12]

Less was said about the illegality of the postwar Iranian government, a rightist cabinet that operated without the required vote of confidence. A coalition of leftists and center-oriented politicians had stalled the vote in protest over the cabinet's right-wing actions. These politicians felt that the rebellious areas had legitimate complaints that should be rectified and that the rightist Iranian government had avoided opportunities to build better relations with the Soviet Union.

After a summer of illegal rule, the landlord-dominated central government dispatched troops to suppress a Communist-oriented political party in the north. Angry citizens rose in protest, occupying factories, disrupting rail transit, and taking over towns throughout the north. This was the context in which the Russian garrison troops interfered with movement of Iranian units in the area. The Soviets gave the same explanation that occupiers always give—they were acting to prevent violence that might endanger their forces. In this case the Russians were acting within the normal military rights exercised by an occupation military command.

Although these actions may have furthered a Soviet political goal of weakening the Iranian government in the north (this was some months before the Azeri and Kurdish republics appeared), the United States could hardly ask its wartime ally to expose its forces to danger from native unrest. The Russians thereby had the United States in an awkward diplomatic position. This is probably one reason that the Truman administration got so angry. The United States could see what was happening but legally had a weak case. And there was yet another quirk to the situation.

The Soviet Union and England each had military forces in Iran at the close of the war. The Iranian government was no more pleased about this than it had been when the same two powers had their troops in Iran after World War I. This time the Americans were there as well, providing further irritation. Iran demanded that all foreign troops leave the country in 1946. They did.

Those who point to Russian postwar aggression against Iran rarely mention that exit. When the Soviets were asked to leave, they did. And they did not return during the ensuing months of diplomatic tension—not when Iran scrapped an oil deal it had made with the Russians, nor even when Iran crushed the Azeri and Kurdish Communist republics. The Truman administration claimed that the Soviets did not leave and called this a violation of the United Nations charter, but the claim was incorrect. There has been speculation that the Russians abandoned the Azeri regime because of second thoughts about the effect of an independent Azeri republic on Russian Azerbaijan. If so, this would be evidence that Kremlin decisions are not as carefully thought out in advance as opponents believe.

The abandonment of Communist republics on Russia's border suggests that the Soviets were not intent on increasing their territory, nor were they willing to stand behind foreign movements in the name of world revolution. This refusal to expand into neighboring Iran is also further evidence that the Communist regimes of Eastern Europe resulted from the 1944 Churchill-Stalin deal, in which the two leaders agreed on the postwar political make-up of Europe, rather than from an insatiable Soviet desire to conquer the world.

Over the next three decades Shah Mohammad Reza Pahlavi became a major world figure, in part because of the mighty military force he built in that strategic area of the globe and in part because of his influence on world oil supplies and prices. His tough dictatorship made enemies among liberal reformers while his efforts to modernize Iran with Western customs and technology made enemies among the conservative Shiite Muslim clergy and their followers. The latter opponents became so strong that even the shah's harsh regime was unable to suppress them effectively, and in 1979 he was deposed in a revolution conducted by Islamic reactionaries.

Soon afterward the Muslim seizure of the American embassy and its personnel raised the ire of the United States. The hostages were released after months of exasperating negotiations, but the incident provoked an American rage against Iran that continued up to the time this book was written.

In the 1980s, while U.S. officials worked to isolate Iran from the world diplomatic and economic communities, a bizarre arms supply operation was run directly out of the Reagan White House, selling sophisticated weapons to Iran. The arms were a bribe to obtain help in releasing American hostages taken by the Iranian regime's terrorist allies in Lebanon. The income received from the arms shipments was intended to fund the contra rebels in Nicaragua after the U.S. Congress forbade such aid. When the White House operation was revealed in 1986, America's friends and enemies alike interpreted it as meaning that the word of the Reagan administration could not be trusted, since the president had been calling on other nations to refuse military aid to Iran while the United States secretly provided such aid.

This distrust soon generated an ominous development. In 1986 Iraq had been fighting a war against Iran for several years. The war included attacks on merchant shipping in the Persian Gulf, and Kuwait was uneasy about the safety of its oil tankers. Kuwait had been seeking American naval protection against Iran, but the United States had been slow about taking any action on Kuwait's request. The revelation of American arms shipments to Iran raised questions about whether the slowness was prompted by bureaucratic inertia or by an American tilt toward Iran. Uncertain of American reliability, Kuwait appealed to the Soviet Union for naval protection and received prompt cooperation. This modest, solicited, and nonaggressive Russian naval operation on the high seas supported the oft-stated American policy of resisting Iranian military activity in the region.

Nonetheless, the Reagan administration announced that a Russian naval presence in the Persian Gulf was undesirable and immediately declared that the U.S. Navy would also shield Kuwait's tankers against Iran. This decision resulted from an obsession with opposing the Soviet Union and treated the Iraq-Iran war as a minor background issue. It quickly came to the foreground when an Iraqi jet attacked a United States warship without any provocation, causing severe damage and many casualties. This was followed by Iranian mine explosions against oil tankers receiving American protection. After years of a gigantic buildup demanded by President Reagan, the navy's unreadiness for action in a combat zone was inexplicable. Even more inexplicable was the bewildered admission by Reagan officials that they never thought Iran would dare to strike merchant shipping that the United States was pledged to defend.

At the time this book was written, the United States was rejecting calls for a joint United Nations naval force to protect navigation in the Persian Gulf. Instead, the Reagan administration preferred an open-ended military commitment, arguing that American prestige could permit no retreat once the American naval operation was begun, no matter how faulty the decision might have been. An escalating series of tit-for-tat combat incidents was underway between the United States and Iran, the same type of measured response that proved so unsuccessful in Vietnam, in a confrontation that had no direct bearing on either American interests or the Iraq-Iran war. American commitment nonetheless grew deeper every day, prompted by Reagan's sudden discovery of Soviet activity in a region where the Russians have been active for centuries. Reagan's concern about the Soviet Union drew the United States ever closer to war against Iran, a country with millions of people ready to die in defense of their homeland, and thousands of terrorists ready to take the battle to the cities of the United States.

Islam has challenged the West for world dominance previously, and the Western leaders who took up that challenge so confidently centuries ago found the battle to be a sobering if not humbling experience. The non-Muslim world is once again confident of its superiority and seems almost to relish the prospect of another opportunity to chastise an Islamic society whose reawakening inconveniences Western habits.

The two most recent contests, however, suggest that careful reflection is needed before embarking on a new crusade against the Moslem world. In Iran one of the strongest Free World governments, in possession of a powerful war machine using the most modern technology available, crumpled before Muslim clerics and their followers. In Afghanistan, after having spent almost a decade in ruthless warfare using its best weapons, the Soviet Union appeared to be seeking retreat with honor. The Communist regime in Afghanistan was abandoning its fight against Islamic traditions, and even seemed ready to accept a return of the deposed Muslim monarch as a republican head of state.

If the forces of Islam can not only prevail over a strong Free World regime but thwart the will of the most powerful Communist state on this planet, prudence may dictate a postponement of any challenge the West—or the East—may wish to throw at the Muslim world. The Reagan administration seemed to view the rise of Islam as a background issue to the all-encompassing rivalry between communism and democracy. Muslim clerics seemed to view the cold war as the side issue. This difference in perceptions may have a significant effect on the outcome of both struggles.

XXIV.

Poland in the 1980s

Not long after the Soviet invasion of Afghanistan in December 1979, unrest became acute in Poland. As might be expected, the Soviet Union took an active interest in Polish events. In 1956 the Russians crossed the border of Hungary to crush the unrest there. A dozen years later, in 1968 they crossed the Czech border to do the same. But as in 1956, when the Poles gathered in protests during 1980 and 1981, the Soviet Red Army stayed home. Why was Poland again spared?

POLAND UNDER GOMULKA

When Wladyslaw Gomulka became first secretary of the Polish Communist party in 1956, he was expected to be a liberal reformer. Quite the opposite happened. Having achieved power, Gomulka moderated and then reversed liberal reforms that had already been made. Police terror never returned, but he discouraged criticism of his regime and surrounded himself with yes-men.

His dictatorial actions puzzled observers familiar with his reputation as a reformer. The explanation is that his reputation was unjustified. He favored toleration of dissent when his views were unpopular, but that did not mean he was a democrat. He stood up to Joseph Stalin, but so did Lenin. He defied the Soviet state itself, but so did Adolf Hitler and Mao Tse-tung. Gomulka rejected mindless imitation of Soviet economic policies but insisted on mindless acceptance of his own. If one postulates that Gomulka's primary goal in life was to have his own way, his actions can be viewed as always consistent with that goal.

Under Gomulka the Polish economy made good progress up to 1958, progress which the general population shared through a rising standard of living. In the 1960s, however, Gomulka embraced the Stalinist type of economic development that he had criticized in the 1950s, emphasizing industrialization to the detriment of agriculture and consumer goods. By 1970 a newly married couple typically had to wait seven years before an apartment of their own became available. A two-year wage freeze was scheduled to begin in 1971, and just before Christmas 1970, the Gomulka regime announced a 40 percent increase in food prices. The price raise was intended to increase production and eliminate shortages, but the impact was explosive.

Within four days a man named Lech Walesa helped organize protests in Gdańsk. Apparently on Gomulka's orders, the police began shooting the demonstrators. Unrest grew, and two days later Polish army units were needed to suppress the outbreaks in Gdańsk.

Gomulka was harshly criticized by both the public and the party for his handling of the situation. The party complained that he had not presented the matters to its governing Central Committee even though it had been meeting at the time. He did not call the politburo (the executive committee that made day-to-day party decisions) into session. The politburo believed that circumstances requiring Polish army intervention merited full discussion, and the politburo held a meeting highlighted by savage attacks on Gomulka. He suffered a stroke shortly afterward, and his critics seized this affliction as an excuse to depose him. Edward Gierek, who had argued against the food price increase, became first secretary.

POLAND UNDER GIEREK

In the 1970s Gierek financed a Polish economic expansion with huge loans from Western banks, but too often the products made by newly constructed factories had no market, and the expansion did not noticeably improve the average person's standard of living. Food and housing shortages continued. Under Gierek a newly married couple might have to wait ten years for an apartment of their own (fifteen years in Warsaw). The police even complained of inadequate facilities causing a shortage of arrests! The economic expansion masterminded by Gierek failed to increase productivity. By 1980 Poland's inability to repay Western bank loans reduced the availability of further loans. Since Gierek relied on Western financing to keep the Polish economy going, this portended a day of reckoning.

In July 1980 Polish authorities announced plans to raise the price of meat. The action was less draconian than previous instances that had provoked unrest. Nonetheless the 1980 price increase compounded other domestic shortages, and protests erupted again.

Labor strikes spread through the country in the ensuing weeks. Lech Walesa was again a leader of strikers in Gdańsk. Even though worker grievances at his shipyard were satisfied by management in August, he boldly continued the shipyard strike in solidarity with striking workers at other plants. He became chairman of the Interfactory Strike Committee coordinating the action. This group evolved into a nationwide labor organization called Solidarity (Solidarność).

The strikes in Gdańsk and elsewhere had immediate causes, but the deeper cause was the lack of any means of institutional communication from citizens to the Polish regime. The government and the Communist Party could use finely tuned methods to disseminate directives rapidly to each citizen, but there was no return path of communication. A person who expressed complaints or concerns was silenced and labeled a malcontent or troublemaker. Thus, problems were seldom dealt with until they became crises. Although Gierek's rhetoric indicated an awareness of the situation and of the need for a remedy, his actions led to no improvement.

Solidarity rapidly filled the function of an institutional method of communication from citizens to the regime. This development could have been the blossoming of an era of national renewal, particularly since Solidarity not only supported but called for an expansion of state socialism in Poland.

For several reasons Solidarity's potential as a valuable partner in Polish Communism was never realized. One reason was that statements of support from influential foreigners such as Ronald Reagan allowed Solidarity's opponents to incorrectly label it as a counterrevolutionary force taking orders from abroad. Such a label received further credibility because labor strikes were anti-communist by definition in a state where in theory workers had achieved equality and all economic gains were equally distributed.

Solidarity's rough-and-ready nature also hampered its credibility in Poland. It was a nonauthoritarian confederation of a wide range of labor groups. Miners in Silesia no doubt had a different outlook from university personnel in Warsaw. Solidarity was characterized by churning debates that invigorated the soul but hampered the expression of coherent policies.

The most important reason for Solidarity's failure to achieve its beneficial potential was the Polish Communist party's chronic refusal to accept advice from below or to let any other group participate in decisions affecting the nation. The latter condition is hardly unusual in a Communist state, but often there is some mechanism for the leadership to gauge reactions from ordinary members who know the public mood. A prudent leadership then adjusts its policies upon receipt of such information. The Polish Communist leadership, however, was uninterested in what party members thought.

The Polish Communist regime did have an understanding with the Roman Catholic Church, whose hierarchy had great prestige among the people, whereby the Church could circumspectly express its views and thus indirectly affect the regime's policies. This, however, was an uneasy relationship between two hostile competitors, not a venture in cooperative formulation of public policy.

Unlike the Church, Solidarity had no tradition of influence that predated the Communist party by hundreds of years. And even though many of Solidarity's members and some of its leaders were Communist party members, the party leadership viewed it as a dangerous rival rather than a potential partner in progress. Because of the regime's stubbornness, Solidarity could get results only by threatening and sometimes conducting strikes in one place after another all over the country. What could have become a means of providing citizen input to avert crises instead became an institutionalized process of creating crises.

The regime granted Solidarity recognition as a legal organization. The same step had been taken with the workers' councils that had sprung up as Gomulka came to power twenty-five years earlier; Gomulka then shunted them aside. Solidarity's members were determined to avoid a similar fate, and this attitude contributed to their militancy. Militancy was also heightened by the regime's continual violation of agreements reached with Solidarity.

In addition to Solidarity, various other independent social organizations sprang up, particularly among students and youths.

These sucked membership away from the official party-sponsored groups.

Traditionally, the absence of such independent public organizations was evidence of a Communist state's strength. Elsewhere in Eastern Europe the Soviet Union had interpreted the emergence of such groups as a sign that a country's Communist government was weakening. When the Polish government tried to mollify unrest by tolerating such organizations, Russia could have interpreted such action as a sign of weakness.

In December 1980 Polish officials tried to reassure Moscow by promising to call for fraternal help if Polish Communism seemed endangered; Polish officials were worried about Soviet attitudes toward Polish events. In the spring of 1981, Solidarity demanded that government officials instigating harassment of Solidarity be punished, that top police officials be fired, and that all charges against political dissidents be dropped. Solidarity threatened a general strike until these demands were met and conducted a half-day general strike to prove its resolve. Such a demonstration of government impotence, particularly in a challenge to police prerogatives, was the sort of thing that had provoked a Soviet military invasion of Hungary. The Polish government and Solidarity reached a compromise in this instance, but one assumes the affair must have made a bad impression on the Kremlin.

About this time Solidarity had a membership of 9.5 million, out of a socialist-sector work force of 12.5 million. The official government unions had a membership of only 3.5 million (some persons belonged to both organizations). From April 1980 to May 1981, Communist party membership declined by 300,000. Such a drop was unheard of in a vigorous Communist society and was yet another reason for Soviet alarm.

THE POLISH MILITARY TAKES COMMAND

In September 1980, First Secretary Gierek resigned after suffering a heart attack and was replaced by Stanislaw Kania. Kania worked on internal party reforms but failed to deal with the public's lack of confidence in the party. Solidarity's strength and influence continued to increase.

In contrast to the party's declining prestige, the Polish army's status was growing, partly because the army symbolized past national glory and partly because it was an institution aloof from the political bickering of recent years. The military mind tends to be contemptuous of politicians even in the best of times, and Polish generals decided that the civilian government was behaving too weakly. Military officers began planning to take over the regime and institute a style of rule forceful enough to assure the Soviet Union that conditions in Poland were well in hand. After all, the military's job was to assure the security of the state against threats, both foreign and domestic. (Moreover, the fate of the Polish officer corps after the Russian invasion in 1939 was well remembered, and the Polish military certainly wanted to avoid another such massacre by the Soviets.)

In 1981 the military began demanding, and getting, more influence in governmental affairs. Generals began replacing civilians as cabinet ministers, and retired officers began to appear in lower civilian positions. The party was not only comfortable with this development but even seemed to welcome it as a way for the regime to share in the public's respect for the army.

In February General Wojciech Jaruzelski, a career army man who had spent time in the Soviet Union, became defense minister and prime minister simultaneously, thus eliminating civilian control of the military. Whether motivated by fondness or fear, Prime Minister Jaruzelski's actions demonstrated exquisite sensitivity to Soviet feelings.

These feelings continued to be ruffled. In December 1980 the Soviet news agency Tass had implied that Solidarity was promoting a counterrevolution against the Polish regime. The Polish party newspaper quickly and carefully contested the Tass interpretation of events, but the Soviet attitude created a sense of unease in Poland: the Soviets seemed to be constructing a case to justify military intervention. In the spring of 1981, Soviet statements condemned Solidarity and implied that the Polish Communist party should stand firm against Solidarity. In the summer the Soviet Union supported Polish party hard-liners who claimed that Kania's softness on revisionist elements in the party promoted the possibility of counterrevolution. In June the Kremlin told the Polish party Central Committee that Polish Communists were retreating before the pressure of counterrevolutionaries who seemed to be succeeding in a takeover of Poland. The Kremlin complained that Polish party leaders were ignoring their advice and condemned Kania's party reforms as encouraging eventual elimination of Marxist-Leninists from the Polish Communist party—an extraordinary claim.

An emergency meeting of the Polish Central Committee was called to discuss the Kremlin's June message. The Poles split between those who felt Solidarity must be suppressed and those who felt the regime had to accept change in order to survive. After an emotional debate, Kania retained his post as first secretary, but Soviet pressure made the party become less willing to seek cooperation with Solidarity.

This firmness increased tension in Poland, and in October Kania warned that anti-Soviet elements were growing so strong as to endanger Poland. He followed this virtual invitation for a Soviet invasion by resigning as first secretary.

His replacement was General Jaruzelski. The Polish military now controlled both the party and the government. Under Jaruzelski the regime emphasized the most radical aspects of Solidarity, regardless of the fact that they did not represent the movement. The point was to portray Solidarity as irresponsible and to diminish its esteem, but this tactic could alarm the Soviet Union even more.

On December 10 the Soviet news agency Tass announced that Polish anti-Communists under the leadership of Solidarity were planning a revolution against the Polish government. Given the history of events in Hungary and Czechoslovakia, this was a transparent warning that the Soviet Union was considering a military invasion of Poland.

Jaruzelski moved swiftly. He proclaimed a state of emergency on December 12. Martial law was declared, and the Polish military took over administration of the country. Most Solidarity leaders were arrested within hours. The whole operation went so smoothly that contingency plans must have been made well in advance. The participation of Warsaw Pact forces stationed within Poland suggests that the Soviet Union approved the plans.

Poland was now a military dictatorship, but a Soviet invasion had been deterred.

For the Soviet Union, the Hungarian and Czechoslovakian invasions in 1956 and 1968 had been military successes but diplomatic disasters, disrupting the Communist bloc and costing the Soviet Union dearly throughout the world. In contrast, the 1981 Polish outcome was a triumph. The Soviet Union obtained the desired results without being condemned. The outcome was not only a triumph for the Soviet Union, it was a victory for Kremlin civilians, who demonstrated an ability to prevail over the Soviet Red Army command that had promoted the previous two interventions. In Poland during 1980 and 1981, Soviet crisis management worked superbly.

A key factor was that, unlike the earlier situations in Hungary and Czechoslovakia, the situation in Poland was in the hands of a government pursuing a staid and stolid ideological course, holding to traditional orthodoxy, and attempting to break no new ideological ground. No dangerous ideas existed that could infect other East European regimes. So despite the civil unrest, the situation was inherently less frightening to the Soviet Union.

Some people, including the Polish generals, argued that no military coup had occurred and no military dictatorship prevailed. The latter assertion has pretty strong evidence against it. The military gave orders, and the Polish people had to obey. In addition, military commissars were assigned to monitor government operations from top to bottom, including various factories. Admittedly, the ruling military council's authority was formally derived from a legally constituted government committee that had civilian members. The question, however, is who controls the committee, not who the members are. Furthermore, formal authority is not necessarily practical authority. England's monarch has formal authority to veto any act of parliament, but the monarch lets parliament do as it pleases. And even though the Polish council of ministers and the party politburo remained in place, military officers held key posts in those organizations. Perhaps the army did not tell the council of ministers what to do, but army members of the council made the decisions. The distinction is meaningful to political scientists, but the net effect in Poland was a military dictatorship.

The issue of whether a military coup occurred is nebulous only because the country had become so militarized before December. If generals gradually replace civilians in key government posts, at some point the military controls the government. By definition a coup is a lightning stroke, so a gradual months-long process is not, strictly speaking, a coup. On the other hand, the declaration of martial law was a lightning stroke that was followed by a dramatic increase of military power in all aspects of the country's life. This included a carefully worded announcement that civilian rule was suspended until conditions became normal again. In the light of all this, it is fair to say a coup took place.

The most onerous outward aspects of military control, such as military courts and the omnipresence of uniformed soldiers, were lifted in late 1982, but military influence remained powerful in Poland. Within a few years the once legal independent trade union Solidarity was gasping for survival as an outlaw organization, and other independent social organizations were fast becoming memories as well.

Cries of protest have arisen about the Soviets "crushing Polish freedom" in 1981. Certainly the events must bring sadness to anyone who cherishes democracy. On the other hand, the Polish government was already a Communist dictatorship and had been one for decades. In 1981 the people of Poland did not have political freedoms. Their liberty was not taken away by the military coup.

Nonetheless, although freedom did not exist in Poland, the emergence of independent social organizations was a firm step in the direction of democracy. With luck they may gradually reemerge in a context that will be less frightening to the Communist regime—though that is perhaps a forlorn hope.

XXV.

Central America in the 1980s

Despite loose talk about Soviet and Cuban designs on Central America in the 1980s, the evidence indicates both regimes have been cautious in their activities. As one senior official in the Soviet foreign ministry said in 1981, "If the Americans invaded Nicaragua, what would we do? What could we do? Nothing."[1]

The impetus for revolutionary activity in Central America does not come from agents of the Soviet Union, but rather is generated by decades of history within the region itself. The examples of Nicaragua and El Salvador are excellent case studies.

NICARAGUA

For hundreds of years, Nicaragua was part of a Spanish colony called the Captaincy General of Guatemala. It gained its freedom as a consequence of the Mexican war of independence in the 1820s. The colony became the United Provinces of Central America but soon broke into five separate countries: Guatemala, Honduras, Nicaragua, El Salvador, and Costa Rica. Throughout the region politics became dominated by two groups known as the Conservatives and the Liberals, labels that lacked the connotations implied by those terms in the latter twentieth century and referred instead to sections of the business community competing for government help.

In the nineteenth century, Nicaragua was a key transit point for travel between the east and west coasts of the United States. Boat and stagecoach lines run by the Accessory Transit Company in Nicaragua made a fortune for the American Cornelius Vanderbilt. In the 1850s his competitors offered to help the Liberals seize the government from the Conservatives in return for commercial advantages. A private American force led by William Walker invaded the country and overthrew the Conservative government. Walker and the Americans, however, not only dominated the new Liberal government, but attempted to annex Nicaragua to the United States as a new slave territory. Other Central American states became alarmed at the thought that they might be Walker's next targets. They went to war and defeated him in 1857. The campaign promoted a resurgence of regional identity, and the victory against the military aggression of U.S. capitalists provided a sense of pride. The experience also generated decades of anti-American hostility from the Conservatives, who resumed power in Nicaragua and controlled the government until the Liberal José Santos Zelaya became president in the 1890s.

Oppressive labor policies were a hallmark of Nicaragua regardless of who ran the government. Spain had been notorious for exploiting colonial peoples. The Walker regime outlawed vagrancy, and violators were forced to work on plantations. The Conservatives continued the same policy, directed especially toward peasants and Indians, and moreover abolished communal holding of Indian land so it could be converted to private tracts for coffee plantations. Zelaya expanded the Conservative precedent by allowing plantation owners to conscript peasants for labor. Such policies could be enforced only through violence and cruelty. The average person led a miserable life under a harsh government that served the interests of wealthy businessmen who wanted cheap labor.

In the early twentieth century, Zelaya became angry when the United States decided to build a transcontinental canal in Panama rather than Nicaragua. He retaliated by approaching Germany and Japan for construction of a Nicaraguan canal and by harassing a mining concession owned by American interests. In 1909 the U.S. government responded by supporting a Conservative rebellion, support that included dispatch of U.S. Marines to Nicaragua. Zelaya was overthrown.

U.S. Marines intervened repeatedly as Nicaraguan politics disintegrated in the next quarter-century. In the 1920s and early 1930s warlords and their private armies battled for power, with U.S. military forces supporting Conservatives who claimed to be the

Nicaraguan government. Two Liberal generals emerged whose legacies would affect events for decades to come: Anastasio Somoza García and Augusto César Sandino.

General Sandino called upon the United States to take over the Nicaraguan government, and thereby remove the Conservatives from power, until the 1928 election was held. The United States did not take such a drastic step, but it did supervise the election, in which Liberal general José María Moncada won the presidency. Most Liberals were satisfied; but Sandino became angry that U.S. troops remained in the country after the election, and he conducted a relentless guerrilla war against them and against the American-commanded Nicaraguan National Guard. The United States found the struggle more trouble than it was worth and announced that American forces would withdraw after the 1932 Nicaraguan presidential election.

The winner of that balloting was the Liberal Juan Bautista Sacasa. He appointed his nephew, General Anastasio Somoza García, to command the National Guard when the Americans left in January 1933. Somoza was well liked by American diplomats, but was viewed with suspicion by the National Guard because he replaced professionally trained officers with men known for their Liberal loyalties rather than military expertise. This made an especially poor impression among guard members because they had been fighting a difficult campaign against the Liberal Sandino, and now it appeared that the guard was to become a military arm of the Liberals. Somoza quieted these concerns by meeting personally with Sandino to discuss terms of a cease-fire. As Sandino left one of the negotiating sessions, he was murdered on Somoza's orders. This destruction of the guard's long-time enemy earned Somoza respect and popularity among guard units. They proceeded to descend on Sandino's encampment and slaughtered the inhabitants, including women and children.

Somoza consolidated his position in the National Guard, and in 1936 he overthrew Sacasa. Somoza ruled as a dictator for twenty years. His government was characterized by corruption, friendliness to businessmen, and macabre creativity in repression of opponents. One expects a dictatorship to carry out jailings and torture, but Somoza had special refinements such as a private zoo on the presidential palace grounds. Some of his opponents were thrown into cages with lions and panthers, as Somoza and his family watched the gruesome results. Such measures muted criticism and made Somoza overconfident about his position. He became careless about his personal security and fell to an assassin in 1956.

Somoza was succeeded by his son Luis Somoza Debayle who served as president while his brother Anastasio Somoza Debayle commanded the National Guard. Luis Somoza retired in 1963 and died of natural causes in 1967. His brother Anastasio was the president or strong man behind figurehead presidents almost continuously from 1963 until 1979. Somoza's friendliness to the desires of American corporations earned him support from the U.S. government, and as a graduate of the U.S. military academy at West Point, he had prestige among American military officers. He was a cruel man who personally tortured opponents. The scale of his corruption was staggering; one example will give an idea. In 1972 one of his companies purchased some land for $30,000. The company then sold it to a Nicaraguan government agency for $3,000,000. Upon the agency's pledge to build housing on the land, the United States provided foreign aid that reimbursed the $3,000,000, but the agency never constructed the housing. Perhaps the U.S. government considered such expenditures to be good investments: the Somozas had allowed the United States to use Nicaragua as a base for the American-sponsored overthrow of the Guatemalan government in 1954 and for the Bay of Pigs invasion against Cuba in 1961.

In the 1960s a revolutionary group known as the Sandinista National Liberation Front arose. Its name paid homage to the murdered Liberal general Augusto César Sandino, and the first Sandinista guerrillas even received survival training from a man who had been a young member of the original Sandino army. The Sandinistas viewed themselves as a third force separate from the traditional Liberal-Conservative rivalry. The new group contained a sweeping coalition of dissidents, from Christian social reformers and middle-class protestors to Communist ideologues. Leftists dominated the leadership, but the Sandinista coalition was not a Communist organization.

According to some authorities, Fidel Castro provided rhetoric and little else to the Sandinistas before they overthrew Somoza. Other sources claim that major quantities of Cuban arms were supplied. The different perceptions may relate to disagreement about what constitutes major aid.[2] Whatever the extent of Cuban help, the Sandinistas were also aided by the governments of Venezuela (which apparently provided ammunition and some sort of air transport or support) and Panama (which was a source of weapons and air transport and used its good offices to ask Castro to help the Sandinistas). Costa Rica allowed the Sandinistas to operate from camps in that country and served as a front for weapons delivery—Venezuela sent rifles to the Costa Rican government, and Costa Rica agreed to pass a portion to the Sandinistas. Honduras tolerated Sandinista activity involving its territory. So whatever the extent of Castro's involvement with the Sandinistas, Free World governments were keeping him company.

The Sandinista struggle was notable for frequent battles and skirmishes with a National Guard force that remained vigorous up to the very end. In part this vigor could be ascribed to military supplies and advice from the United States. Because of the strong American backing for the Somoza dictatorship, anyone who challenged Somoza also challenged the United States. Despite unease about the Communist presence in the Sandinistas, President Jimmy Carter refused to order a direct American military intervention in the struggle. When the Sandinistas were on the verge of victory in 1979, the United States did try to convince the Organization of American States to intervene with a joint military peacekeeping force. But other members refused to go along with the proposal; they did not see the Sandinistas as a compelling threat to the hemisphere. Some Sandinista leaders had received training in various Communist countries (Russia, Cuba, North Korea), but the leaders' dedication to Communism was unclear. Their rhetoric was fluent with Communist jargon, but Latin American countries were not convinced that the Sandinista leaders intended to make Nicaragua a totalitarian Communist state, let alone a base for territorial expansion of a Communist empire. Certainly most of the Sandinista followers were less concerned about political theory than about ending the Somoza dictatorship's ability to exploit their economic status and suppress their human rights.

The Sandinistas defeated Somoza in July 1979, and he fled to Paraguay, where he was assassinated the next year. His death was so unlamented that little effort was made to pinpoint responsibility for the act.

After the Sandinistas won the revolution, the United States and the rest of the world recognized them as the legitimate government of Nicaragua. The Sandinistas unsuccessfully sought military aid from the United States and then turned elsewhere. In 1981 the arrival of thirty Soviet tanks generated controversy. The furor seemed to ignore that, although the tanks were made in the Soviet Union, they actually were secondhand merchandise from Algeria. Into the mid-1980s Soviet military aid was modest. Cuba provided direct assistance and tried to keep its support low-profile.

Much has been written about a Sandinista Communist dictatorship, and just as much has been written about Nicaraguans being free at last. As ever, the same data can mean different things to different people. For instance, it is true that the Sandinistas censored and eventually closed the Conservative newspaper *La Prensa*. But Somoza not only censored *La Prensa* intermittently over the years, in 1979 he even blew up the office with tank fire and destroyed the printing plant by aerial bombardment after the newspaper continued to vex him. *La Prensa* battled the government whether it was led by Somoza or the Sandinistas, and the government's suppression of the paper had more to do with standard Nicaraguan practice than the regime's politics. In 1987 the Sandinistas allowed the newspaper to resume publication, a move highly uncharacteristic of classic Communist totalitarian dictatorship, although as this book went to press President Reagan reported that *La Prensa* had been closed yet again. At the same time that reports appeared about the Sandinista government oppressing the Roman Catholic Church, Roman Catholic priests were part of the government. The Sandinista government jailed Communist labor union leaders. In 1984 it held elections in which opposition parties participated and that were judged satisfactory by observers such as Lord Kennet, foreign affairs spokesman for Britain's Social Democrat Party.[3] West Germany's ex-chancellor Willy Brandt said the Nicaraguan elections were more democratic than the El Salvador balloting hailed by the Reagan administration.[4]

None of this means that the Sandinista regime was a model democracy and that human rights violations were imaginary. It does mean that the situation was not as clear-cut as claimed by either the government's opponents or supporters.

One of the most significant changes in Nicaragua under the Sandinistas was the emphasis on improving the lot of ordinary citizens. Massive public health campaigns were instituted to eradicate disease and reduce infant mortality, along with expansion of basic education programs and agricultural assistance. Such efforts built tremendous public support for the Sandinista government.

American president Ronald Reagan in 1981 set out to destroy the Sandinista government with military steps such as the mining of Nicaraguan harbors, attacks on harbor facilities and oil storage areas, and support of so-called contra armies that comprised an unlikely combination of old Somoza National Guardsmen and Somoza opponents tenuously united in a desire to overthrow the Sandinistas. How such enemies intended to sort out their differences afterward was unclear. Their call for support from the United

States was consistent with many previous calls by other Nicaraguan rebel groups who had sought U.S. aid to overthrow regimes. In each era the arguments were tailored to American desires—in the 1980s the call for aid was put in terms of anti-Communism. It is doubtful that the contras could have operated without massive American assistance.

The contras apparently planned to seize a portion of Nicaraguan territory and establish a provisional government that would seek international diplomatic recognition. In Nicaragua, however, popular support for the Sandinista program was so great, and support for the contras so minuscule, that such a goal remained elusive into the latter 1980s. Instead, the contras attacked Sandinista soldiers and ordinary civilians, and they conducted sabotage such as demolition of bridges. Those types of tactics are called "low-level" or "low-intensity" warfare, a term that evokes pictures of occasional skirmishes by patrols. That is not the situation, however. Low-intensity fighting strikes civilian and economic targets in an effort to throw a country into such chaos that the government will collapse. What this meant in Nicaragua every day during the 1980s is exemplified in the words of a visitor: "In my first week in Nicaragua the contras assassinated seven children, all under the age of eleven." The visitor continued, "I chatted with Laura Sanchez, a daughter of one of the Co-operative workers who explained how her uncle, aunt and four cousins were massacred. Each had their eyes pulled out, ears cut off, and intestines smeared against the walls of their farm. Laura is seventeen years of age, a catechist in the Catholic Church, and a member of the women's militia." The visitor also reported, "An eighteen-year-old had been castrated and his genitals stuffed in his throat. His eyes had been burned with battery acid, most of his teeth removed by a bayonet, and his tongue cut out. They left him that way to die."[5]

Reagan was fond of describing the contras as "freedom fighters" and likened them to the leaders of the American revolution of 1776. If the Reagan administration was composed of policy makers who believed that the United States was founded on contra values, that was an ominous portent for the preservation of American democracy.

In response to the American-sponsored contra activity, the Nicaraguan government declared a state of wartime emergency that limited various civil liberties. The United States called this proof of Sandinista totalitarianism.

Although Reagan claimed Nicaragua was a military threat to its neighbors, neither the size of the Sandinista armed forces nor their activities supported this assertion. It was true that they occasionally chased the contras in Honduras, but that did not constitute Nicaraguan aggression against Honduras any more than the contra incursions could be called Honduran aggression against Nicaragua.

The Hondurans, however, became concerned that the contra activity might provoke a real invasion by Nicaragua. In self-defense Honduras began interfering with the contras. The Reagan administration then threatened to cut off aid to Honduras unless the contras were left undisturbed. The United States insisted that friendly Honduras cooperate in a project that Hondurans feared would harm their country; otherwise the United States would harm them. The Hondurans yielded to American pressure.

The American threat may have indicated a desire to set up Honduras for an invasion that could be used as an American excuse to attack and destroy the Nicaraguan government, but it surely demonstrated no respect for Honduran independence. Nor did the Reagan administration's quiet establishment of major military facilities in Honduras, which could be used for operations against Nicaragua. Lengthy and large-scale American war games have been conducted from Honduras to rehearse the logistics and tactics.

As 1987 began, Nicaragua was not attacking or invading anyone. The United States, on the other hand, was supporting armed attacks against Nicaragua and had intimidated Honduras into permitting activity that might provoke an invasion from Nicaragua. The Reagan administration's actions apparently violated article 15 of the charter of the Organization of American States: "No State or group of States has the right to intervene, directly or indirectly, for any reason whatever, in the internal or external affairs of any other State. The foregoing principle prohibits not only armed force but also any other form of interference or attempted threat against the personality of the State or against the political, economic and cultural elements." Reagan's actions also disregarded the 1986 verdict of the International Court of Justice, which ordered the United States to stop attacking Nicaragua. Previously the United States had obeyed the court's directives.

At the end of 1987 Reagan's stance had isolated the United States in the world diplomatic community, and the governments of Central America were rejecting the unsolicited defense against Nicaragua that the United States was ostensibly mounting on their behalf. Despite Reagan's lack of legal or military justification for continuance of his policy, he continued to advocate further support for the contras.

EL SALVADOR

The 1979 Sandinista victory in Nicaragua increased American concern about a guerrilla war occurring in El Salvador, a conflict that the United States viewed in terms of East-West competition in the cold war. As in Nicaragua, however, the struggle in El Salvador had origins far removed from global geopolitics.

Both countries shared the same Spanish colonial heritage, had been part of the United Provinces of Central America during the 1820s and 1830s, and had resisted William Walker in the 1850s. Both saw the growth of Liberal and Conservative political factions. In El Salvador, as in Nicaragua, the government aided the interests of businesses that depended on the easy availability of cheap land and cheap labor.

In El Salvador the victims of these government policies were predominantly Indians. The Nicaraguan government did not treat Indians with respect either, whether in the 1880s or in the 1980s. But persecution was especially severe in El Salvador. In that country wealthy coffee growers formed a shadow government. They achieved abolition of Indian communal land holdings in order to facilitate the expansion of coffee plantations. Without land the Indians had no place to live and no crops to raise. For food and shelter, the Indians were forced to seek work in the capitalist economy. They became a plentiful supply of inexpensive field hands for plantation owners. If a worker tried to leave a plantation before completing his work contract, he would be hunted down by government security forces and returned to the plantation. In the best of times coffee workers were ill treated and poorly paid. In 1931 coffee prices were falling in the world economic depression, and the decline was reflected in daily wages of less than ten cents.

In that year Major A. R. Harris, U.S. military attaché for Central American affairs, wrote an analysis of the situation for Washington. He found that "roughly ninety percent of the wealth of the country is held by about one half of one percent of the population. Thirty or forty families own nearly everything in the country. They live in almost regal splendor with many attendants . . . and spend money lavishly (on themselves). The rest of the population has practically nothing. . . . A socialistic or communistic revolution in

El Salvador may be delayed for several years, ten or even twenty, but when it comes it will be a bloody one."[6]

Although the Reagan administration has accused Cuba of instigating Communist activity in El Salvador, the Castro regime clearly was not a factor when the Harris analysis was written in 1931. In fact, Communist activity in El Salvador was originally inspired and organized in the 1920s by revolutionaries from Mexico and Guatemala. The Guatemalans largely controlled Salvadoran Communists until 1929, when Americans took over. So, while it is true that Communist activity in El Salvador was at that time directed from a great power across the sea, the orchestrators were in the United States. New Yorkers, not Muscovites, sponsored Communist subversion in El Salvador through a Communist secretariat of the Caribbean in New York City. Ironically, Americans dominated both the government and the revolutionaries—a stark example of the extent of American control in Latin America.

The New Yorkers made little headway in El Salvador until the native Agustín Farabundo Martí exploded onto the scene in the 1930s. He was a hot-headed young man from a family with enough wealth to send him to the national university. There he began reading leftist writings on revolution and social justice and decided they were so obviously correct that he was wasting his time at the university, so he dropped out to organize a revolution. He first traveled to Nicaragua where he fought with Sandino in the late 1920s. Martí returned home in 1930 and became the leader of a vibrant chapter of Socorro Rojo International. This organization provided members with fellowship and aid such as health care and emergency funds. Allied with the Communist party, it nevertheless was not a branch of the party itself, and most Socorro Rojo members probably were not Communists. Nonetheless, the benevolent organization did much to counteract propaganda that portrayed Communists as gargoyles, and it made communism seem less threatening to the average person. Popular support grew, as shown by a parade of 80,000 held on May Day, 1930.

Martí's work soon made him the unofficial head of Communist activity in El Salvador. He decided to schedule a nationwide armed revolution for January 1932. Earlier he grandly proclaimed, "When one cannot write with the pen one must write with the sword."[7] Such statements were untempered by thoughtful reflection (he once challenged his philosophy professor to a duel), and in 1932 Martí demonstrated the hazard of calling for violence when the other side has overwhelming firepower.

He had no trouble finding recruits among exploited coffee

workers; many of them were Indians eager for a chance to strike back at plantation owners and supervisors. The night of the revolt was accompanied by volcanic eruptions throughout Central America, including El Salvador. The Indians had a distinct cultural identity and had retained old customs and beliefs, and the eruptions were seen as proof of the earth's support for the uprising. The skies filled with choking ash, and molten lava flowed down the slopes, illuminating grim Indians as they set about their work with machetes. The insurrection lasted long enough for the Indians to kill about three dozen wealthy people and government officials before the revolt fell apart in confusion. The army retaliated by killing several thousand Indians, making no effort to determine which, if any, individuals were connected with the revolt. Martí was executed. Communism in El Salvador was set back for quite awhile.

For almost two decades, from 1913 to 1931, the Melendez Quiñónez family controlled the country's presidency. A coup in 1931 established a military dictatorship that continued to rule into the 1980s, with civilian politicians as figureheads. The military's power in government was not surprising in a country where an oligarchy had long ruled the population through physical coercion rather than political consensus.

In growing numbers, landless and jobless Salvadoreans crossed into neighboring Honduras in hopes of finding a better life. By the 1960s this refugee population had grown to perhaps 300,000 and was putting a strain on Honduras, which was not a wealthy country filled with opportunity for the impoverished. The Honduran regime was more moderate than El Salvador's and realized the importance of agrarian reform in promoting a peaceful and stable society. The easiest way to obtain land for distribution was to confiscate it from Salvadoran refugees, leaving big Honduran landowners undisturbed while satisfying the needs of Honduran peasants. The only losers were the refugees forced back into El Salvador. Their return disturbed the Salvadoran oligarchy because Honduras had been a convenient escape for those who could no longer bear conditions in El Salvador. With no place to go, pressure for revolutionary social change would build in El Salvador and threaten the oligarchy. The returning refugees were a particular danger because, unlike El Salvador, Honduras permitted peasants to organize politically and to form labor unions. This experience was being brought back into the Salvadoran countryside.

The situation provoked a brief war between El Salvador and Honduras in 1969. The result was a return of about 130,000 Salvadoran refugees to their native country. There was no place for them in the economy, and the discontent became as explosive as the oligarchy had feared. At the time of the war, the average Salvadoran led a hard life. Most of the population was rural. The increasing use of machinery on coffee, sugar, and cotton plantations constricted the number of agricultural jobs. Peasants who could find work endured a level of poverty nearly incomprehensible in the United States—coffee workers and their families typically lived in dwellings constructed of large cardboard boxes and suffered from malnutrition. Labor or political organizing in the countryside was illegal. Plantation owners and their private security forces held absolute sway over a peasant's life. Many people were willing to consider an alternative offered by leftist revolutionaries. What was there to lose?

These revolutionaries were frowned upon by the El Salvador Communist party. Like most Latin American Communist parties, the Salvadoran Communists emphasized working within the political system to bring change—certainly a hopeless strategy against the Salvadoran military dictatorship. In the 1960s the regime experimented with elections involving genuine opposition parties, although the experiment was cautiously limited—for example, rural voters did not cast secret ballots. Nonetheless, opposition candidates began to score victories, and the oligarchy ended the experiment in the 1970s.

Frustrated by the El Salvador Communist party's refusal to engage in armed struggle against the oligarchic government, leftist extremists in the 1970s began to form guerrilla groups to conduct a revolution. They took potshots at soldiers and buildings, killed suspected informers, and kidnapped anyone who seemed likely to generate ransom money to finance these activities.

It is important to note that the Communist party had opposed this activity. Warfare had been begun by splinter groups that rejected party control.[8] This lack of party control meant that the guerrillas could not be influenced by pressuring Moscow or Havana or even El Salvador party leaders. The violence was not directed from a central headquarters.

During the 1970s vicious feuding among leftist guerrillas weakened their effectiveness, as splinter groups began splintering. The feuding climaxed in 1975 when one faction murdered guerrilla leader Roque Dalton García, claiming that he was a Soviet-Cuban-CIA agent. That improbable combination demonstrates that Communist guerrillas in El Salvador did not necessarily view Moscow or Havana as friends, a consideration rarely emphasized.

Some persons are surprised to learn that prominent Communist guerrilla leaders in El Salvador have devout Christian backgrounds. One had been a Roman Catholic seminary student, and two were Baptist ministers. The United States may decry atheistic communism, but that concept is alien to Latin America, where liberation theology originated as an attempt to combine the teachings of Karl Marx and Jesus of Nazareth. Father Gustavo Gutiérrez, a Peruvian supporter of liberation theology, defended it by saying, "Those who routinely brand as Communists persons who speak of social justice and the rights of the poor must have a very lofty idea of Marxism. They believe only the Communists can treat these subjects."[9] It was in such a context that Baptists and Roman Catholics could fight together for Communist victory, as bewildering as that may seem to some Americans.

In 1980 quarreling Salvadoran leftists announced they had put their differences aside to unite in a joint struggle against the repressive oligarchy. Groups such as the Popular Revolutionary Bloc, the United Popular Action Front, the Popular Leagues—28th of February, and the Democratic Nationalist Union formed the Movement for National Unity, which operated under the leadership of the Revolutionary Coordination of the Masses (Coordinadora). The new coalition held a press conference to announce its existence, a meeting highlighted by patriotic displays in which speakers said they were tired of the Salvadoran flag being the exclusive property of right-wing militarists. The leftists said they loved their country, and literally waved the flag and sang the national anthem. A few weeks later the leftists staged a huge parade—200,000 strong—to demonstrate popular support. The well-organized marchers were peaceful. Spectators were not. Some began shooting into the crowd and were joined by police and National Guardsmen. Dozens of marchers were killed. The parade broke up in confusion.

The Coordinadora quickly grew to include more and more organizations of Salvadoran citizens: the Popular Social Christian Movement, the National University of El Salvador, and even the Association of Bus Companies of El Salvador. This expanded alliance became known as the Democratic Revolutionary Front. Even the Roman Catholic hierarchy began to demand an end to the military oligarchy. A political dividing line had been drawn as never before, the oligarchy versus the rest of the nation.

The opposition political alliance was supplemented by a newly unified military insurgency. In 1980 the Armed Forces of National Resistance, the Popular Forces of Liberation—Farabundo Martí, the

Popular Revolutionary Army, the Revolutionary Party of Central American Workers, and even—at long last—the El Salvador Communist party allied together in the Farabundo Martí National Liberation Front to wage guerrilla war against the oligarchy.

In 1980 several factors combined to provoke a civil war of unprecedented ferocity in El Salvador. One element was that the two opposing sides were each united as never before. Another was the realization that one side or the other was likely to achieve a decisive victory; the alternatives were survival or eradication. Perhaps the most important factor of all was the Sandinista victory that had just occurred in Nicaragua. The United States considered the new Nicaraguan government to be a Communist totalitarian dictatorship and was appalled. Moreover, 1980 was a presidential election year in the United States, with candidate Ronald Reagan challenging President Jimmy Carter to demonstrate American resolve to prevent yet another Communist regime in Latin America. The Salvadoran oligarchy argued that its opponents were Communists. Carter accepted the argument and provided substantial military aid to the oligarchy, help that dramatically intensified the civil war. In June 1980 Carter's National Security Adviser, Zbigniew Brzezinski, stated, "The United States could never permit another Nicaragua, even if preventing it meant employing the most reprehensible measures."[10]

Such were the measures that were used. One refugee said, "The killings by the army have traumatized the Salvadorean people. One is very cautious about rising up against the government when one has seen the bodies of people sawed in half, bodies placed alive in battery acid or bodies with every bone broken. I saw all those things last year [1980]."[11] Private paramilitary groups and death squads also took stern measures against persons identified as opponents of the oligarchy, including Roman Catholic priests who called for social justice. The White Warriors Union, one of many paramilitary groups allied with the oligarchy, announced that all Jesuits and all students at San Salvador Jesuit schools were military targets. A number of priests were gunned down across the country, climaxing with the murder of Archbishop Oscar Arnulfo Romero in March 1980, one day after he challenged military discipline by declaring that "no soldier is obliged to obey an order to kill if it runs contrary to his conscience."[12] The day after the assassination, the United States announced the granting of another $55 million of aid for the oligarchy. Three days later government soldiers attacked the archbishop's funeral procession and left forty mourners dead. The judge assigned to investigate the archbishop's murder fled the country, and responsibility for the crime was never officially determined, although unofficially the crime was attributed to agents of Robert D'Aubuisson, who later became president of El Salvador's legislature.[13]

When Ronald Reagan took office in 1981, he emphasized a need to help the El Salvador government fight rebels. With verbal encouragement and millions of dollars from the Reagan administration, the oligarchy stepped up its campaign. The Reagan-supported Salvadoran forces seemed to have a free hand in suppressing unrest. One news report of a raid on Monte Carmelos, a lower-class district near San Salvador, said that "men in uniform and civilian clothes . . . pulled 23 from their homes and shot them dead in the street. . . . Bodies ripped by automatic weapons fire were strewn for 100 yards. Two homes were burned, apparently by fires started by bazooka rounds."[14] Another mission was reported in the January 27, 1982, *Washington Post:* "All of the buildings, including the three in which body parts could be seen, appeared to have been set on fire, and the remains of the people were as charred as the remaining beams. . . . In the cornfields behind the houses were more bodies, those unburned by fire but baked by the sun. In one grouping in a clearing in a field were 10 bodies: two elderly people, two children, one infant—a bullet hole in the head—in the arms of a woman, and the rest adults."[15] The day after this report was published, Reagan verified that the oligarchy was respecting human rights, a verification required by Congress in order to release another $25 million of military assistance. Two days later twenty persons, described as guerrillas by the oligarchy, were killed in a raid by the National Guard in San Salvador. Foreign news media arrived rapidly and found witnesses whose stories were uncontested. They reported that no fighting had occurred; the guard had simply rounded up the alleged guerrillas and shot them. Most were young people: "one ten-year-old 'guerrilla' was said to have been raped ten times."[16] Nevertheless, a few days after the January 1982 National Guard roundup in San Salvador, Secretary of State Alexander Haig declared that the United States "would do whatever is necessary to prevent a guerrilla victory"[17] and said that another $55 million of military aid had been earmarked for the oligarchy.

Although the Reagan State Department claimed that the guerrillas depended on a foreign supply of weapons, Salvadoran president José Napoleón Duarte said that the guerrillas simply purchased most of them on the black market. This may explain why they had U.S. arms such as M-16 rifles—perhaps the guerrillas simply bought them from corrupt Salvadoran officials. The insurgents openly claimed this. Certainly the technique was used by Communist guerrillas elsewhere in the world. When faced with the reality of guerrilla camps containing few Soviet weapons but a plentiful supply of American-made ones, the previous contention that the insurgents received massive shipments from the Communist bloc was modified to say that the foreign supplies were U.S. weapons captured by the Communists in Vietnam. This source had not been postulated, however, until the old explanation had been weakened by an absence of Communist-made arms. Belgian FAL rifles, however, were also present in the guerrilla camps. Cuba was known to export its supply of FALs, but it was hardly the world's only source of such weapons.

Nonetheless, the Reagan administration named Cuba as the primary supplier of guerrilla weapons, and to prove it the State Department issued a white paper in early 1981.[18] It was, however, filled with contradictions. The white paper said that the insurgents had received 200 tons of Communist-bloc weapons, but its supporting documents indicated that the deliveries were only 5 percent of what had been claimed. When James Dunkerley analyzed the white paper he discovered that the nineteen accompanying documents had been heavily edited.[19] Only 100 sets of the full documents were released to the press and public; the State Department declined to provide more to meet the demand and would not even produce photocopies when payment was offered. The document collection demonstrated that Cuba, Nicaragua, and the Soviet Union were interested in Salvadoran developments, but it offered no proof that any Communist regime was arming the rebels. The only verified aid from the Soviet Union was one airline ticket.[20]

Jon Glassman, who wrote the white paper, later admitted to the *Wall Street Journal* that it contained guesswork and outright errors.[21] Guesses and errors hardly constitute proof, nor do they form a solid basis for a nation's foreign policy. After releasing the white paper, Secretary of State Haig said, "We consider what is happening [in El Salvador] is part of the global Communist campaign coordinated by Havana and Moscow to support the Marxist insurgency." Haig said the Soviet Union was behind events in Central America—"risk-taking," he called it, in a 1981 statement to NATO representatives.[22] The Reagan administration saw the war in El Salvador as an opportunity to punish Russia and Cuba. The only apparent victims were the people of El Salvador. By 1985 more than 50,000 had been killed since 1980, and still the resistance movement thrived. The rebels were not fighting for Russia and Cuba. They were fighting to free the population from the military oligarchy that had ruled it for the past half-century.

At the time this book was written, the outcome in El Salvador was uncertain. The United States regarded José Napoleón Duarte as El Salvador's best hope for peace and prosperity, although most of the civil war atrocities mentioned in this chapter occurred during Duarte's rule. As a leader of the opposition Christian Democrat party, he had apparently won the presidential election in 1972, but the final vote count by the military dictatorship gave its candidate the victory. Duarte supported an abortive coup to gain his rightful place and afterward was arrested and tortured by the dictatorship. Despite his background as an authentic opposition leader, he was chosen in 1980 by the oligarchy as the civilian president of the country's ruling military junta. He had no apparent power to influence events, and prominent members of his Christian Democratic party left the party because they felt it was being used to provide a legitimate veneer to the oligarchy's actions. In 1982 Duarte won an election held to choose the nation's president—an election with no voter registration (and thus no limit to ballot-box stuffing), intimidation of voters by security forces, and death threats that convinced Duarte's reformist opponents to decline any candidacy. In 1984 he won a similar election. This time there was voter registration, but thousands of the names were fake. Dozens of towns in guerrilla-controlled districts held no balloting. The election results were first announced by U.S. ambassador Thomas Pickering, not by the government of El Salvador.

In late 1984 Duarte met personally with guerrilla leaders and rejected all their demands—a stance that did not leave much room for further negotiation. The rejected demands included a call for the arrest and trial of persons responsible for the murder of Archbishop Romero, legalization of labor strikes, legalization of government employee labor unions (government workers who joined a union had been drafted into the army and assigned to work at their old jobs), a bigger budget for the national university, freedom of the press, and minimum pay equivalent to $4.80 *a day* for plantation workers.

In the latter 1980s, the civil war continued with neither side assured of success.

In the 1980s the United States's stance in Central America was characterized by support of the ruling oligarchy in El Salvador and opposition to the government in Nicaragua. It may be useful to conclude by summarizing the nature of these regimes.

The rulers of El Salvador murdered the Roman Catholic archbishop when he called for peace, murdered the chief of the agrarian reform program Rodolfo Viera when he demonstrated that he took his job seriously, presided over a country where the majority of children suffered from malnutrition, where rural education and health care was nearly unknown, and where ordinary citizens were routinely killed with impunity if they were suspected of opposing the status quo. The Reagan administration claimed this government was a democracy and sent tens of millions of dollars of military aid to fight opponents of the Salvadoran regime who called for freedom of the press, a minimum wage, labor unions, aid to education, and punishment of the murderers of Archbishop Romero. The Reagan administration said that people who made such demands were Communists.

The rulers of Nicaragua asked the archbishop there to help mediate a peace settlement, invited Roman Catholic priests into the government, promoted land reform, worked to reduce infant mortality, provided rural education and health care, and won elections that were viewed as fair by knowledgeable observers from the Free World. The Reagan administration said this was communism and sent contra armies into Nicaragua, where they attacked farms, schools, and health centers while killing and mutilating civilians of all ages as warnings of what happened when impoverished people cooperated with government programs. The Reagan administration said this behavior promoted democracy, gave the contras tens of millions of dollars in aid, and even found ways to continue such help after Congress outlawed it.

In the 1980s the United States had sharply defined the difference between communism and democracy in Central America. It was not hard to figure out which alternative would be chosen by the peoples of that region.

XXVI.

With Their Backs to the Wall

> How poor we all are, even the Communists, at knowing what is a victory and what is a defeat.
>
> —GEORGE F. KENNAN
> *On Dealing with the Communist World*

This book has examined the historical record of Communist military aggression. The popular rhetoric on this topic warns of great danger from an on-rushing Red juggernaut that plans to crush Western democracy. The historical record is far less frightening. Indeed, the following summary can even be considered reassuring.

COMMUNIST FAILURES

We often hear a litany of never-ending leftist triumphs. Perhaps we should pause to recollect some of the failures. The list below may not be comprehensive, but it indicates the sweep of Communist failure across decades and continents.

1917	Latvia	Communist government overthrown
1917	Estonia	Communist government overthrown
1918	Finland	Communist government overthrown
1918	Germany	Communist revolution failed
1918	Holland	Communist revolt defeated

1918	Norway	Workers' revolution prevented
1918	Turkey	Communist Russia returns territory
1919	Estonia	New Communist government overthrown
1919	Latvia	New Communist government overthrown
1919	Hungary	Communist government crushed
1919	Czechoslovakia	Communist regime crushed
1919	Austria	Communist revolt prevented
1919	England	Communist general strike failed
1919	Germany	Communist revolt crushed
1920	Poland	Communist revolution prevented
1921	Iran	Communist regional government crushed
1921	Germany	Communist revolt crushed
1923	Germany	Communist revolt crushed
1924	Bulgaria	Communist revolt crushed
1924	Estonia	Communist revolt failed
1925	Indonesia	Communist revolt failed
1925	Bulgaria	Communist revolt failed
1926	Afghanistan	Communist invasion repelled
1927	China	Communist revolt crushed
1929	Afghanistan	Communist invasion abandoned
1932	El Salvador	Communist revolt failed
1935	Brazil	Communist revolt failed
1936	France	Communist revolt thwarted
1936	Spain	Communist government crushed
1946	Iran	Communist regional government crushed
1947	France	Communists expelled from government
1947	Italy	Communists expelled from government
1948	Finland	Communists expelled from government
1948	India	Communist insurgency failed
1948	Indonesia	Communist coup failed
1949	Greece	Communist revolution crushed
1950s	Burma	Communist rebellion stalemated
1953	Korea	Communist invasion repelled
1954	Guatemala	Communist government overthrown
1955	Austria	Soviet troops abandoned occupation
1955	Finland	Soviet Union abandoned naval base
1956	Philippines	Communist insurgency failed
1957	San Marino	Communist government defeated
1959	India	Communist state government dissolved
1960s	Congo	Communist government overthrown
1960s	Venezuela	Communist insurgency failed
1960s	Argentina	Communist insurgency failed
1960s	Guatemala	Communist insurgency failed

1960s	Peru	Communist insurgency failed
1960	Malaya	Communist insurgency failed
1962	India	Communist invasion failed
1964	Brazil	Communist government overthrown
1965	Indonesia	Communist coup failed
1965	Dominican Republic	Communist revolution thwarted
1965	Algeria	Communist government overthrown
1965	Ghana	Pro-Communist government overthrown
1967	Bolivia	Communist insurgency failed
1970s	Colombia	Communist insurgency failed
1970s	India	Communist rebellion defeated
1971	Sri Lanka	Communist insurgency crushed
1972	Egypt	Soviet military advisers expelled
1973	Chile	Communist government overthrown
1978	Somalia	Soviets and Cubans expelled
1980	Jamaica	Communist government defeated
1983	Grenada	Communist government overthrown

In this list of Communist failures, notice that several Communist governments were overthrown. Clearly it is not true that once a country goes Communist it never turns back. Even after the 1968 declaration of the Brezhnev Doctrine, under which the Soviet Union vowed to defend any Communist state, such governments have been overthrown. Communism is not forever.

Moreover, the list of Communist triumphs includes victories that can only be described as Pyrrhic—victories gained at excessive cost.

Korea is one example of a situation that went worse for the Communists than normal portrayal indicates. The West views that war as a stalemate at best. Nonetheless, the North Koreans obtained no more than they had originally. More important, the conflict provoked the establishment of a permanent war economy in the United States and the formation of alliances among the United States and likely candidates for Communist aggression throughout the globe. Militarily, the Free World became a far more formidable foe as a result of the Korean War. It was a tremendous setback for Communists everywhere.

Another example is the suppression of rebels and reformers in Eastern Europe. The Soviet Union did impose its will on Hungary, Czechoslovakia, and Poland—but the price was the breakup of the Warsaw Pact, accompanied by a setback for the Soviet Union in relations with other governments, Communist or otherwise. Moreover the Soviet actions provoked resentment in the East Europeans and encouraged the growth of patriotic nationalism rather than fraternal socialist solidarity. Seeds of a troublesome harvest were sown.

Such problematic "successes" are not limited to Soviet actions. The West considers Angola a great success for Fidel Castro, but he may not share that opinion. Cuban troops have preserved the government there, but at a substantial cost to Cuba. Moreover, against Castro's wishes, Angola took actions that could have brought Cuba into a war it did not want against Zaire.

Kremlin leaders may be hopeful that communism will ultimately prevail throughout the world, but they see challenging and even frightening conditions for now. In this sense they and American officials share the same view of the world, each side feeling it is slipping behind.

THE DECLINE AND FALL OF THE EVIL EMPIRE

Empires fall. And the view from the Kremlin wall shows that process well underway, with Communist countries in disarray throughout the world. The Soviet Union does not head a monolithic Communist empire. Rather, Communist countries are bickering and fragmented.

First, there is a great philosophical battle between the Soviet Union and China for leadership of the Communist movement. The dispute began over the question of priorities in the 1920s. The Soviets felt Communist revolution had to occur in European countries before their colonies could be freed. China argued that Communist revolutions had to occur in the colonies before Europe could turn Communist. This evolved into a question of war or peace.

For the past three decades, the Soviet Union has advocated peaceful coexistence with non-Communist countries, calmly believing that the future belongs to communism. The Soviets contend that capitalist nations need not be defeated in war; rather, because of their inherent flaws, they are doomed to collapse, and Communists need only be patient as the world becomes theirs. Gains may have to be defended, but military conflicts need not be sought.

In contrast, China has advocated wars of liberation, arguing that only violence can spread Communism. Both the Soviet Union and China have sent military aid to Communists fighting brushfire wars. The difference is that the Soviets feel such wars should only be encouraged if they have no likelihood of escalating into a nuclear conflict. The Chinese deny that such a risk can ever exist, arguing that the West will always back down when intimidated. The Soviets do not share that confidence. The Chinese attacked India during the Cuban Missile Crisis. It is difficult to imagine the Kremlin choosing such a moment to launch a military offensive against a non-Communist nation.

The Soviet Union believes that nuclear war would be disastrous, and therefore views the Sino-Soviet dispute as determining the survival of the Soviet nation and its people. The Soviet Union opposes China and its allies as vigorously as it opposes the capitalist world. It is correct to label both the Soviet Union and China as Communist, but that does not mean they are partners any more than the capitalists Winston Churchill and Adolf Hitler were.

The Sino-Soviet conflict has divided Communist forces and weakened them. In addition, various Communist regimes have chosen sides in this dispute, causing further argument among the lesser powers and further division of Communist resources.

Far from being united in solidarity against the common capitalist enemy, Communist states have engaged in military struggles against one another around the world. This has ranged from a few shots exchanged on the Sino-Soviet border to full-scale invasions such as elements of the Warsaw Pact against Hungary and Czechoslovakia, and the substantial fights Vietnam has had with Cambodia and China.

Moreover, Communist states have been torn by dissension from within. To an outsider a Communist government may appear to operate seamlessly, but in reality the government leaders can quarrel viciously, pulling government policy first one way and then another as factions gain and lose ascendancy. The bickering within the Kremlin is well known, as are the convulsions experienced by China. The same thing goes on in the governments of lesser powers. Perhaps even more significant are the growing calls for more political power made by populations in China, Eastern Europe, and the Soviet Union itself.

Not only is it a mistake to treat the Communist world as a united entity directed from Moscow, it is a mistake to assume the Communist party is unchanging. The Soviets, Chinese, and the rest have altered their rhetoric, their theories, and their leadership many times; and these changes continue in the 1980s. Does the current Soviet leadership understand Lenin any better than prominent American officials understand Jefferson? Lenin had different beliefs and goals than Joseph Stalin did, and Mikhail Gorbachev is as different from Stalin as Ronald Reagan is from Franklin Roosevelt. There are similarities, but the differences are perhaps more important.

Indeed, Communist governments are so dissimilar from one another in the 1980s that responding to their needs and challenges can be as complicated as dealing with those presented by Free World governments in all their diversity. Treating all Communist governments alike is therefore a mistake because it gives dissident governments no incentive to resist Soviet domination.

A regime using Marxist-Leninist rhetoric is not necessarily Communist, any more than a regime using Free World rhetoric is necessarily democratic—Chiang Kai-shek provided a classic example of both. Nor does Cuban training mean a fighter is Communist any more than Fort Leavenworth training means a fighter is a democrat.

The so-called Communist conspiracy was never well organized even in its Comintern days of the 1920s and 1930s. People came and went as they pleased, "obeyed" only if they chose to, and went off on tangents. Few members had extraordinary intelligence or exceptional insights.

One of the most interesting aspects of fraternal turmoil among Communists is the conflict between civilian and military officials. Bulgarian generals were thwarted when they attempted a coup in 1965. There was a possible conspiracy by Czechoslovakian officers a few years later, and a successful coup by Polish generals in 1981. And there is evidence of Soviet Red Army restiveness in 1956 and 1968, which suggests that the Soviet military might be willing to take over the government from civilian control, particularly in a time of crisis.

The struggle for control between civilian and military elements is normally portrayed as afflicting only the non-Communist world, but it poses a conflict in Communist regimes as well. Given the tendency of armed forces to gain control of governments, whether right or left, the question arises as to whether the capitalist-communist fight is hiding a more significant development of world militarization. Is the world being taken over by the military and being organized to promote values important to a common military culture?

THE ULTIMATE VICTOR

A list of Communist successes reveals a startling fact: as of 1987, not a single democracy has ever fallen to Communist military aggression—not one. Every country that turned Communist through violence was already a dictatorship. A democracy has even less chance of falling to Communism through military attack than through the ballot box.

It is unnerving to compare the number of Communist countries in 1941 to the number in 1988, yet it is comforting to recognize that only dictatorships have fallen to Communist attack. History reveals that dictatorships are weak and true democracies are strong.

That historical truth contains a reassuring promise. If democracy is stronger than dictatorship, then democracy will prevail over communism. For the present, various dictatorships may turn Communist, but the future belongs to democracy.

Some implications of that heartening promise will be examined in the next two chapters.

XXVII.

A State of Siege from Within

> There is, let me assure you, nothing in nature more egocentrical than the embattled democracy. It soon becomes the victim of its own war propaganda. It then tends to attach to its own cause an absolute value which distorts its own vision on everything else. *Its* enemy becomes the embodiment of all evil. *Its* own side, on the other hand, is the center of all virtue. The contest comes to be viewed as having a final, apocalyptic quality. If *we* lose, all is lost; life will no longer be worth living; there will be nothing to be salvaged. If we win, then everything will be possible; all problems will become soluble; the one great source of evil—*our* enemy—will have been crushed; the forces of good will then sweep forward unimpeded; all worthy aspirations will be satisfied.
>
> —George F. Kennan
> *Russia and the West under Lenin and Stalin*

Real dangers to the Free World exist, but to what extent are they self-generated?

Despite the alleged peril from Communist Russia, American businessmen have never hesitated to do business there. American exports to Russia in the mid-1920s were more than twice the value exported shortly before World War I. And American sales to Russia in the mid-1920s were double that of any other country. This commerce went on without U.S. diplomatic recognition of the Soviet Union, without any guarantee of government assistance if the Communists violated a contract (which they never did).

American corporations provided crucial aid in the industrialization of the Soviet Union during Joseph Stalin's era. The U.S.

government raised no objections—on the contrary, even a staunch anti-Communist such as Herbert Hoover actively promoted such trade. Although politicians warned of the threat posed by Communist Russia, at the same time the business community was working to strengthen the Soviet state. International Harvester, General Electric, Westinghouse, Ford Motor Company, RCA, Sperry Gyroscope, Chase National Bank, Western Electric, DuPont, and other firms made money by trading with the Soviet Union before World War II.

Although the Soviet Union was portrayed as a threat to the United States at this time, the threat was presented in very different terms from those used by Harry Truman and his successors. Before World War II, the claim was that the Soviets sought to overthrow the United States government by means of propaganda. Short pamphlets and poorly printed leaflets constituted Soviet aggression. Although such "peril" may have been widely feared by the public, it is hard to believe that American leaders took it very seriously.

The ostensible reason for the American government's hostility to the Soviet Union in the 1920s and 1930s was the Communists' refusal to pay the czar's debts. The Bolsheviks had a good argument that they were not responsible for debts other than their own, but the United States capitalized on this issue for years, pointing to the Soviet refusal to stand behind the czar's debts as proof that Communists were untrustworthy. But certainly the American corporations who did business with Stalin were undeterred by any fears that Communists could not be trusted to honor commercial agreements. Perhaps the explanation of U.S. government hostility in this era is found in financial losses suffered by businesses and by upper-class government officials and their friends when czarist paper became worthless.

During the Great Depression of the 1930s, the American business community regarded trade with the Soviet Union as crucial. Over half of the American machine-tool exports were sold to the Soviets. Thus, Soviet-American trade was not a one-way street helping only Stalin; it generated mutual benefits. Private companies doing business in the Soviet Union introduced the federal Reconstruction Finance Corporation to the Soviet trade as well. The U.S. government thereby helped fund the Soviet economy.

In the United States, many businesses feeling the pressure of the depression called for better relations with the Soviet Union. Franklin Roosevelt stressed this angle when he announced diplomatic recognition of the Soviet Union in November 1933. Morality had little to do with the belated diplomatic recognition. Lenin's regime, which the United States refused to recognize in 1917, had taken power with little bloodshed. Stalin's regime recognized in 1933 had engaged in wholesale internal violence. Money was the motivating force in the recognition of the Soviet government.

THE POSTWAR MILITARY THREAT

It is important to realize that the American government did not regard or portray Russia as a military threat before World War II. Indeed, as early as 1921, the Soviet Union was buying munitions in the United States. The situation changed because of World War II.

Before the war the West regarded the Soviet Union as a weak nation of little account, as reflected by an August 1941 agreement (after the Nazi attack on Russia, but before the United States entered the war) between Roosevelt and Winston Churchill that their two nations would determine the postwar situation for the entire world. No thought was given to Soviet participation, even though the Soviet Union was easing Nazi pressure on England. As the war progressed, the importance of the Russian front became evident to all parties. The West became concerned about the possibility of Stalin reaching a separate peace with Hitler to get out of the war. The West tried hard to convince Stalin that it stood behind him and that Russia's best interest was served by continued absorption of Nazi attacks. To convince Stalin, Churchill made the famous deal turning over Eastern Europe to the Soviet Union, an arrangement broadly confirmed at Yalta. This promise had much to do with the Soviets' resolve to continue fighting Hitler.

Hitler's conquest of Eastern Europe had left the territory open to liberation by the Soviet Red Army. Never forget that the Soviets were defeating Nazi regimes in Eastern Europe, not democracies or even independent nations. Unlike the diplomats who negotiated the Treaty of Versailles after World War I, Churchill and Roosevelt graciously accepted the traditional Russian dominance in that area, since they were in no position to contest it. Stalin in turn agreed that the Soviets would attack Japan after a specified time following the Nazi surrender, a commitment the U.S. Joint Chiefs of Staff urgently wanted. These understandings generated goodwill among the Big Three.

After Roosevelt died and Harry Truman became president, the relationship between the United States and the Soviet Union changed. Truman had a long-standing hatred of the Soviet Union, which he regarded as a godless nation. He tried to rush the atomic bomb in order to defeat Japan before Stalin entered the Pacific war, thus keeping the Soviets from laying claim to Pacific territory. This scheme backfired when, after the bombs were dropped, Japan remained in the war, past the date on which Stalin had promised to intervene. Stalin carried out his agreement and swept over exhausted Japanese forces in the final hours of the war, occupying territories Truman had wanted to save for American occupation.

Once the war was over, Truman tried to betray the Eastern Europe understanding. There was a practical difficulty in this because the agreement reflected over a century of military and diplomatic reality. Overturning the Churchill-Stalin deal would require a military force strong enough to reverse the powerful tide of events in that part of the world.

Therefore, shortly after the war ended, Truman urged expansion of the military draft. Much to his annoyance, his fellow citizens saw no need to expand the military once the war had ended. And Truman could hardly argue that the United States had to boost its firepower in order to break an agreement made with the Soviet Union when help was needed to defeat Hitler.

Instead, Truman sought to portray the Soviet Union as a military threat to the United States, hoping to scare the American people into expanding the military machine. The policy of frightening the American people in order to create support for a massive military machine was based on lies about Soviet intentions—these were not honest evaluations that were disproved by later events, but deliberate falsehoods. In 1946 few U.S. government officials regarded the Soviet Union as a military threat. The country had suffered a loss equivalent to the United States losing everything east of Chicago. Deaths in the Leningrad siege were twenty times the losses in London during the blitz. Throughout Russia as a whole, from fifteen to twenty million men had been killed, in addition to deaths among women and children. The Soviet Union had no atomic weapons, its productive capacity lay shattered, famine stalked the land, and the country lacked the money and labor needed to recover even its underdeveloped prewar status.

Few American officials thought that the Soviet Union even *desired* war with the West. A belief in Russia's peaceful intentions was shared by generals such as Dwight Eisenhower and Lucius Clay, cabinet officers such as Commerce Secretary W. Averell Harriman (who had conducted private business dealings with the Soviet government), and even by such an intense anti-Communist as Secretary of the Navy James Forrestal. Nonetheless, the men around Truman were willing to follow his lead. Some, such as Secretary of State James F. Byrnes and Defense Secretary Louis Johnson, were more than willing.

The Truman administration initiated the so-called containment policy designed to force Russia back from Eastern Europe. There was even grumbling in some circles about the Soviet Union retaining the Baltic States, talk that astonished Churchill and angered Stalin. Neither could understand why the Soviet Union should lose territory that it possessed when Hitler attacked: the Soviet Union was one of the victors, not one of the vanquished. Stalin was particularly irked at American complaints about Russian dominance in Romania after he had silently watched Churchill crush the Communists in Greece during 1944. The Greek and Romanian situations were part of the Churchill-Stalin deal, and Truman was trying to welsh after the West had succeeded in Greece. Truman portrayed Soviet dominance of Eastern Europe as muscle-flexing by a powerful foe. In reality, the Soviets were adamant about Eastern Europe because of their own military weakness: they needed an East European buffer zone to reduce Soviet vulnerability. The military angle heightened Soviet suspicions about the motive behind Western objections to Communist control of Eastern Europe.

Although some extremists in the Truman administration, such as secretary of the navy Francis Matthews and secretary of defense Louis Johnson, advocated destroying the Soviet Union while it was exhausted, the president's idea was to confront the Soviets with such an overwhelming military force that they would back away. The only alternative for the Soviets would be an attempt to match the American arms buildup. White House experts demonstrated that the financial requirements of such an effort would cripple the Soviet economy, delaying postwar recovery for years. Indeed, experts showed that the Soviets would have to spend themselves into the ground to match the American military capability.

No one at the White House dreamed that the Soviets would choose to catch up to the United States militarily rather than lose Eastern Europe, for which they had sacrificed so much. No one dreamed that the Soviet state would find the necessary resources by forgoing recovery of the civilian economy shattered by the Nazis. Alas, the only dreamers in the Truman White House were those who thought the Russians would abandon vital national policies in response to military intimidation from the United States.

The United States has never relinquished its national interests in the face of a powerful foe's military activity; why would the Soviets?

To apply additional pressure to the Soviet Union, Truman cut off Lend Lease aid crucial to Soviet postwar recovery. Stoppage of this foreign aid program's assistance did not violate any agreements, but the manner in which Truman ordered the halt clearly communicated that he intended it as a hostile act. Stalin replied that the U.S. attitude toward the Soviet Union seemed to have changed drastically once Soviet help was no longer needed to defeat Hitler and Hirohito, and he maintained that Truman's pressure tactics would cause no change in Soviet policies.

This was in 1945. It did not take long to discover that Truman's tactics were backfiring as cordial relations with the Soviet Union evaporated and Soviet resolve stiffened. Yet more of the same continued in ensuing years.

This antagonism toward the Soviet Union soured even benign actions. For instance, the United States portrayed the Marshall Plan as a selfless act of American generosity, a foreign-aid program designed to rebuild Europe after World War II. But the Soviets perceived it, in the context of Truman's hostility, as a plot to harm them. They noted the lack of any such recovery assistance for them from their wartime ally, and also noted that Marshall aid offers to East European governments could serve to weaken their loyalty to the Soviet Union and thus weaken Soviet military security. Marshall Plan help to Western Europe could also be viewed as a way of shutting out the Soviet Union from influence there.

The formation of NATO sealed a divided Europe. The inclusion and rearming of West Germany particularly concerned the Soviets. Senior officers from the Hitler era became top men in NATO; they had served Hitler, but they were anti-Communists.

Although Americans generally hail the Marshall Plan and NATO as steps thwarting Soviet expansion in Europe, which never extended beyond the nations covered in the Churchill-Stalin deal, less is said about the amount of Marshall Plan and NATO aid that was devoted to defending the colonial empires of England, France, Belgium, and Portugal. In theory, these countries received weapons for protection against the imaginary Soviet advance in Europe; in reality, these supposedly anti-Soviet weapons were used only against Third World peoples. By 1965 the NATO countries had killed four million Third World residents.

ALARMIST RHETORIC

The Truman and Eisenhower administrations used a crisis atmosphere to promote the formation of regional defense pacts to justify military aid to undemocratic Free World regimes that were oppressive but anti-Communist, to expand dramatically government spending on defense industry contracts, and to constrict civil liberties lest Communists take advantage of them. Some Americans questioned the veracity of the cries of alarm, and not all those questioners could be dismissed as Communist sympathizers. In 1957 General Douglas MacArthur was board chairman of Sperry Rand and told the company's stockholders, "Our government has kept us in a perpetual state of fear—kept us in a continuous stampede of patriotic fervor—with the cry of grave national emergency. Always there has been some terrible evil at home or some monstrous foreign power that was going to gobble us up if we did not blindly rally behind it by furnishing the exorbitant funds demanded. Yet, in retrospect, these disasters seem never to have happened, seem never to have been quite real."[1]

Consistent with a growing realization that the Truman and Eisenhower administrations had lied about the extent and peril of Communist aggression, by 1960 the Communist failures enumerated in the previous chapter were plain to see. Few Third World revolutions were Communist, still fewer succeeded, and most that had were friendlier to China than to the Soviet Union. The Chinese, despite their insistence on the need for violent confrontation with the capitalist world, maintained a military force inadequate for prolonged aggression (as demonstrated in India). Soviet influence in Far Eastern Communist regimes had declined, and Eastern Europe was seething. Soviet influence in the Balkan region was but a faint shadow, and Finland had expelled a Soviet navy base. Communist parties had little influence on events in Western Europe, mainly serving as straw men in election speeches. And still the list of Communist failures continued in the next decades.

Despite these setbacks, during the 1970s the Soviet Union held the growth of its defense budget below the level of NATO's and the United States's. During the Carter presidency the defense posture in the West grew increasingly stronger against the Soviet Union.[2] At the same time, Communist states collided with one another in war: Vietnam and Cambodia, China and Vietnam, Somalia and Ethiopia, and the Soviets mired in coup and guerrilla war in Afghanistan.

Yet from every direction in the United States came cries that the

Commies were coming. For decades the United States had declared a state of siege from within, originated by Truman's lies and maintained afterward with fierce indifference to what was really happening outside the fortress walls. Russian boundaries were more constricted in 1986 than in 1886. Only occasionally did a glimmer of the truth escape from officials' statements, such as this one by Assistant Secretary of Defense Richard Perle in 1983: "Democracies will not sacrifice to protect their security in the absence of a sense of danger. And every time we create the impression that we and the Soviets are cooperating and moderating the competition, we diminish that sense of apprehension."[3]

Journalist John Gittings posed a rhetorical question about the effect of alarmist rhetoric. He asked his readers what the proper reaction should be to remarks made by the Soviet foreign minister, in which he told the Supreme Soviet that "what he described as 'Western imperialistic encroachments' should be resisted with Soviet aid 'directly on the ground.' He [the minister] went on to comment pointedly that 'the aspiration for socialism' would not be so easy to suppress in El Salvador, Pakistan, Thailand, or Sudan." Gittings also asked what should be thought of an endorsement of these remarks by the Russian defense minister, "calling for 'a powerful military hand within the glove of diplomacy.'"[4]

Gittings was particularly interested in the response because Soviet officials had not said those things. The remarks (with suitable political and geographical alteration) were made to the U.S. Congress by Ronald Reagan's secretaries of State and Defense, George Shultz and Caspar Weinberger.

The point is that tough rhetoric can work in two directions. It can bolster sacrifice in a population that believes it is in danger of attack. Yet the rhetoric can also frighten the country identified as the potential attacker. The Soviets know that John F. Kennedy was willing to threaten them with nuclear bombardment during the Cuban Missile Crisis although he later said the Cuban missiles had no military significance. This awareness was heightened by Reagan's rhetoric that caused unneeded and harmful tension. According to former Soviet KGB official Oleg Gordiyevsky, in 1981 the Soviet Union feared that Reagan intended to launch a military attack against the Soviet Union.

The shooting down of a Korean commercial airliner by the Soviets in 1983 should be examined in the context of Reagan's rhetoric. For him the horrifying Korean airliner incident was a godsend. He portrayed the destruction of this harmless civilian aircraft and the loss of innocent lives as an example of Soviet ruthlessness, illustrating the kind of monster that supposedly continually seeks to kill defenseless people. The incident was used to argue that the United States must further strengthen its defenses lest the fate of the airline passengers descend on all Americans. Congress approved more nuclear missiles, though American possession of tens of thousands of H-bombs had failed to prevent the loss of the airliner. The justified anguish and revulsion over the Soviet act was orchestrated into almost a war frenzy.

The Soviets have a reputation for shooting down aircraft violating their airspace. Professional aviators flying anywhere near the Soviet Union are well aware of the hazard and know they must take care to avoid Soviet territory. Clearly the crew of the Korean airliner was careless, and their incompetence initiated the tragedy. If they had exercised elementary care, nothing would have happened—the Soviets did nothing until the airliner violated their airspace.

The lesson of this incident is that at times the Soviet air defense system is unable to differentiate a civilian airliner from a United States military aircraft. The Soviets have warned that Reagan's actions may no longer permit them to wait for fail-safe confirmation·of attack before responding. What if an airliner strays during a time of acute crisis, such as the Cuban missile affair? Would the Soviets be tempted to release their bombers lest they be caught on the ground? Would the United States then send its bombers, just to be "safe"? Would attempts to resolve the confusion before tragedy struck be successful?[5]

NUCLEAR ARMS CONTROL

American government promotion of an East-West crisis atmosphere has had a debilitating effect on arms control negotiations. After all, if the Soviets are thought to be seeking conquest of the Free World, they must be presumed to lack a willingness to reduce armaments. From this it is assumed that the Soviets intend to use arms control agreements as a means of tricking the United States into publicly disarming while the Soviets secretly violate the agreements by maintaining or increasing their level of armament.

The Soviets do interpret the terms of treaties so as to squeeze the maximum advantage from them, but it is untrue that they routinely violate treaties. In reality their record is no worse than that of the United States. Lenin once said Communist Russia had violated a treaty with the Kaiser dozens of times, but those violations had to do with a promise to refrain from propaganda activities. Lenin's statement has been cited as proof that Communists do not believe in obeying treaties, but no one made such an observation about Germany when it repeatedly violated the Treaty of Versailles. By the 1920s Soviet regard for international law was virtually indistinguishable from that of the rest of the world.

In particular the Russians have a good record on arms treaties. During the 1920s the Soviet Union even furnished the League of Nations with reports on Russian naval activity in the Black Sea although such information was not obligatory. When the Soviet Union joined the league in 1934, it was one of the staunchest defenders of international obligations. The Truman administration admitted that the Soviets had abided by their military agreements during World War II, even when the agreements were oral. The Soviets have strictly conformed to the treaty banning atmospheric tests of nuclear weapons, and (given the ambiguity of some treaty provisions) apparently have made a forthright effort to obey arms control agreements made in the 1970s.

The United States knows the Russians have a good record on abiding by arms control treaties because, using space-age technology, it closely monitors what is going on in the Soviet Union twenty-four hours a day. A variety of high-tech surveillance techniques can reveal what sorts of weapons are being designed and tested in the Soviet Union and exactly where they are deployed—even mobile missile systems.

Warnings thundered from the Reagan administration during the 1984 election about the Soviets pushing the SALT II accord to its limit, if not outright violating it. In fact, the Soviets had only about half as many nuclear warheads on missiles as SALT II allowed. Conversely, in 1986 the Reagan administration exceeded the SALT II arms limits and unilaterally abrogated the agreement because the Star Wars program could not proceed if America kept its word.

As if to pound home the policy of duplicity, Reagan reported that he personally assured Mikhail Gorbachev that the Strategic Defense Initiative would not use nuclear weapons. Such a palpably false promise would surely leave Gorbachev with the impression that the United States is untruthful, playing a political game with arms control talks.

Amid the arcane and time-consuming diplomatic negotiations about the possibility of limited arms control accords, odd facts appear and disappear with little notice. In 1984 the United States government acknowledged that engine failure had made at least one-third of its Trident C-4 missile force inoperable, and that the entire 700-plus Trident C-4 arsenal might be unusable. Almost simultaneously word arrived that U.S. cruise missiles in England and Pershing Two missiles in West Germany might contain faulty microchips. Yet the Reagan administration accepted that news with equanimity—no cries about windows of vulnerability, no emergency program to replace the weapons, no alerts that the Soviets might be ready to attack while American defenses were diminished. In the spring of 1985, NATO announced that it would unilaterally scrap 2,000 battlefield nuclear weapons, one-third of its arsenal, without any reciprocal Soviet reduction. There were no shouts of alarm, although a peace advocate who proposed such a step would be dismissed as naive, if not Communist. In 1987 the control systems of all U.S. air-launched cruise missiles were discovered to be so faulty that the rockets could not hit their targets. The responsible civilian vendors and Pentagon quality-control personnel came under criticism, but no alarm was raised about a military peril in the situation. At the same time, one-third of the MX missile force could not be launched because of guidance system problems.

These incidents are examples of drastic, overnight, unilateral slashing of the American nuclear strike force. No officials of any government claimed that such losses created any threat to the United States, nor was there any apparent public perception of increased danger. No reciprocal reduction in Soviet forces occurred—each time the net result was to make the Soviets stronger. Yet the situation was accepted without public alarm.

Since, in fact, the United States nuclear strike force has more than once been reduced unilaterally without any perceptible ill effect, there would seem to be no military barrier to arms reduction. The mighty protestations about the difficult complexities of arms reduction begin to seem artificial, invented for political mileage back home.

Indeed, if the United States were really worried about Communist nuclear weapons, it would not supply the Communists with nuclear materials and technology. The Reagan administration approved such sales to the Communist bloc. Such behavior recognizes the historical reality that the rhetoric of every administration since Truman has tried to hide—that the Soviet Union has never demonstrated a desire to attack the United States.

Nor is attack feared from other Warsaw Pact members or China, as demonstrated by the attendance of Communist military officers at arms shows in the United States where, under strict security that excludes ordinary members of the public, Communists are allowed to examine the latest developments in American weapons technology. This suggests that American leaders actually view Communist military forces as potential customers, not as threats.

The nuclear arms reduction agreement reached by the United States and the Soviet Union in late 1987 generated hope that a new era of realism might emerge in the relations of those two powers.

THE WISDOM OF NUCLEAR PROLIFERATION

The broader question is not arms control but whether nuclear weapons are even relevant to national security. Harry Truman's decision to develop the hydrogen bomb had nothing to do with national security. The Atomic Energy Commission's nuclear weapons advisers had concluded that even if the Soviets invented a hydrogen bomb and had a monopoly on the weapon, the United States could adequately protect itself with atomic bombs. Atomic Energy Commission Chairman David Lilienthal fumed about arguments that the hydrogen bomb would be an unanswerable weapon providing ultimate security. He had heard the same thing about the atomic bomb and warned that a decision based on that argument would be fundamentally flawed. Nonetheless, Truman, who believed in military force as the ultimate answer to international controversies, ordered production to proceed. As predicted, hydrogen bombs failed to make the United States a secure fortress. Quite the contrary, Americans quivered in fear behind their bombs, able to destroy an attacker but unable to survive the attack.

In the 1980s Reagan approved yet another ultimate answer, the Strategic Defense Initiative, popularly known as the Star Wars program. He repeatedly made exaggerated statements that the system would shield the United States from nuclear attack. In fact, the shield, if it worked perfectly, would deflect only a percentage of one type of nuclear weapons delivery system. The Strategic Defense Initiative has been aptly described as "a leaky roof on a house with no walls."[6]

It has been openly stated that America cannot lose by proceeding with the Strategic Defense Initiative because the Soviets would not choose to keep up with it, lest they cripple their economy and ruin their productivity and standard of living for decades. This same reasoning, however, had been disproved forty years earlier when the Truman administration used it to argue for the containment policy.

The most disturbing aspect of Reagan's decision is that it will put computers in charge of deciding whether to use the nuclear arsenal. Always until now human beings have evaluated the data produced by defense computers and have decided whether a situation warranted a nuclear response. Reagan has decided to give up that power in reference to nuclear war. This is not a theoretical concern. In June 1980 the North American Aerospace Defense Command (NORAD) computer system detected two missiles fired at the United States by a Soviet submarine. These were followed by more from the sea, indicating that this was no accidental launch from a single submarine. As the B-52 force scrambled, NORAD computers detected an all-out Soviet attack and reported the grim news.[7]

As we all know, having survived that day, the only thing wrong was in the computer system. The human overseers diagnosed the problem in minutes, and no harm was done.[8] But the Strategic Defense Initiative will have no human supervisors to analyze attack warnings, because the decision to activate the system must be made within seconds after the first launch is detected. Can anyone doubt that our fate will be sealed if Reagan's system becomes operational?

Rudyard Kipling provided an uncanny foreshadowing of the situation in his poem, "The Secret of the Machines," in which he says:

> But remember, please, the Law by which we live,
>   We are not built to comprehend a lie,
> We can neither love nor pity nor forgive.
>   If you make a slip in handling us you die!

Many people think that U.S. nuclear weapons are strictly guarded by highly trained and motivated officers, and that the weapons can be used only upon a direct order of the president via a sophisticated fail-safe communications system. The facts, however, are contrary to popular impression. U.S. military officers around the world have the necessary codes and commands to fire nuclear weapons. The president's role is to veto a nuclear attack, not to order one. If lower officers believe conditions for nuclear action are met and their decision is not countermanded, the missiles fly. A news item on April 7, 1985, revealed "the United States Congress had reported that 5,000 service personnel a year were removed from nuclear weapons duties because of alcohol or drug abuse, criminal activities, negligence, or mental problems."[9] So much for the dedicated personnel manning nuclear weapons.

Regarding the sophisticated communications system, General Paul Wagoner, head of NORAD combat operations, attempted to demonstrate it to visiting nuclear expert Daniel Ford. Much to the general's embarrassment, he could not reach anyone on the telephone that was supposed to connect with the president or on a second phone that provided a direct line to the Joint Chiefs at the Pentagon. The general did not know that the Joint Chiefs line was for incoming calls only. Nor did he know that he was supposed to dial "O" for "Operator" in order to use the Missile Attack Conference phone. The general explained that he had had this assignment for only a few months.[10]

If any of this is disquieting, consider what the attack alert technology and communications must be like on the Russian end.

CONVENTIONAL FORCES VERSUS NUCLEAR WEAPONS

A seldom discussed but powerful appeal of nuclear weapons is that, in terms of destructiveness, they are generally considered far cheaper than conventional military forces. The price of manufacturing and storing a hydrogen bomb to destroy a city is far less than the cost of forming and equipping an air/ground/sea invasion force to do the same job, plus maintaining that force in combat readiness twenty-four hours a day, year after year. The European members of NATO have embraced the theory of nuclear deterrence because it allows those countries to avoid the expense of maintaining conventional forces comparable to the Soviet conventional capability. Monetary rather than military considerations are the basis of NATO's defense posture.

Arguments about the deterrence value of nuclear weapons should be evaluated with the knowledge that proponents may be less concerned about military deterrence per se than about budgets. Citizens are justified in asking whether the use of nuclear instead of conventional weapons in a time of crisis may involve costs that cannot be measured in money alone.

Perhaps Americans should be concerned less about military superiority than about military sufficiency. The question should not be whether the United States has more nuclear bombs than the Soviets do, but whether it has enough. What is needed is a definition of national security that extends beyond weapons. After all, cities normally do not define their greatness by the size of their police departments. Perhaps things such as plentiful food and shelter, excellent schools, affordable health care, and a robust job market also affect national security. The United States has only a certain amount of resources. How much can go into building fortress walls before achieving an impregnable defense guarding nothing?

THE COST OF THE COLD WAR

President Harry Truman, who prided himself on his knowledge of history, rejected the values that inspired his nation's founders. His predecessor John Quincy Adams forthrightly declared, "America goes not abroad in search of monsters to destroy. . . . She well knows that by once enlisting under other banners than her own, were they even the banners of foreign independence, she would involve herself, beyond the power of extrication, in all the wars of interest and intrigue, of individual avarice, envy, and ambition, which assume the colors and usurp the standard of freedom. . . . She might become the dictatress of the world; she would no longer be the ruler of her own spirit." John Quincy Adams declared that such a course would "change the very foundations of our own government from *liberty* to *power*."[11]

Enough time has passed that a judgment can be reached as to who was right. Did Truman, a man who loved politics but despised democracy, bring forth a blossoming of freedom by militarizing American society and defending any foreign rascal who claimed to fight Communism? Or did such a course turn out as John Quincy Adams predicted, embroiling the United States in routine power struggles among foreign despots who falsely claimed to be freedom fighters, while extinguishing freedoms at home lest they endanger national security?

Such developments inspired cold war historian John Lukacs to ask, "May we not see the emergence of totalitarian democracies? By this I mean democracies where universal popular suffrage exists but where the essential and earlier basic conditions of political freedoms, of freedom of speech, of the press, of assembly, are hardly more than theoretical benefits to the average citizen, whose life and ideas, whose rights to privacy, to family autonomy, and to possessions are regimented by the state and rigidly molded by mass production and by mass communications."[12]

This can happen because many people find freedom uncomfortable. They do not want to take responsibility for what they do with their lives and for what goes on around them. Such people feel safer and more content when someone tells them what they should do and takes responsibility for what happens. It is possible to live in a dictatorship and feel perfectly free. Many citizens of Nazi Germany who supported the regime never noticed any intrusions on their freedoms or else disregarded the limitations. This is because those people's activities, desires, and dreams were so limited that they never reached the walls of their cage. So the complacent Germans never felt the limitations clamped on their society. Dictatorships have millions of happy and enthusiastic supporters. Only the victims experience the terror.

More and more often since World War II, Americans have heard their leaders insist that various liberties must be limited or relinquished in order to protect the United States. In reality such a path imperils national security, for only by adhering to democratic ideals can a democratic society hope to retain its inherent strength over communism.

If the Soviet Union has ever had any intention of attacking the United States, it has had long enough to act. After all, from the time Hitler took power, he needed only eight years to attack Russia. The Bolsheviks have had seventy years to attack the United States.

If the historical record can reassure us, the question arises as to why anyone would want to distort that record to frighten us. Perhaps there are more votes in frightening people with lies than in reassuring them with truth. But the answer is deeper than that.

The harsher a government's internal policies, the more urgent the need to portray national danger to justify harshness. Thus the Truman administration and its successors had a need to portray Russia as threatening, not only to divert government revenue to weapon and defense material suppliers, but sometimes to subvert civil liberties and to mute protests about the destruction of barriers that hindered the exploitation of citizens by wealthy individuals and corporations.

Instead of heeding malevolent counsels of despair, can we not take assurance from the historical record of failed Communist aggression? In facing the Soviet Union, perhaps we should have the courage to admit that we need not be afraid.

XXVIII.

The Cheated Generation

The sources of national strength are many. America's monetary wealth alone, administered by banks and other financial institutions, exerts such power that the will of the United States has often been imposed without calling upon armed force. Since World War II, however, military compulsion has been necessary again and again as the United States faced Third World foes who disregarded the economic costs of defiance.

Such American willingness—or, more precisely, desire—to use armed force did not exist before World War II. After two full generations of dependence on the military to enforce national goals, however, patriotism has become equated with support for war. The American flag, once the symbol of aspirations of all the nation's people, has become the exclusive property of those who support decisions to commit military personnel to combat. Citizens who cherish the lives of fighting men and ask whether the talents and bravery demonstrated in battle could be put to better use in other endeavors are called cowards and traitors. Patriotism is defined as support of war, right or wrong—a definition almost unheard of before World War II. The competence of lawyers, physicians, and congressmen can be questioned today. But anyone who questions the wisdom of generals or admirals is suspected of stupidity, cowardice, or treason. Seemingly the past forty years have turned respect for the military into servitude, causing the United States to imitate some aspects of what it fought against in World War II.

The militarization of American society, in turn, has been promoted by a postwar U.S. foreign policy that requires a worldwide military presence. The determination of U.S. foreign policy is based more on financial profitability for major corporations than on freedom or democracy. The United States supports dictators if they provide a climate that benefits major corporations. The United States opposes, with money and blood, governments that fail to provide such a climate.

Because the slant of such a foreign policy is in itself insufficient to inspire the kind of support and sacrifice necessary to implement it, after World War II the foreign policy establishment cynically manufactured a myth that America was threatened by Communist military aggression around the world. Admittedly, even the wisest statesman can make mistakes. It is, however, difficult to understand how hundreds of government officials with a keen grasp of the worlds of commerce and jurisprudence could, decade after decade, consistently misread the power and intentions of Communist leaders. Perhaps it was mass delusion. Although no national defense justification existed for the decisions to seek the destruction of Communist regimes, such decisions always promoted profit-making opportunities for American corporations abroad. Perhaps it was all coincidence. But the decision makers did not climb to the highest reaches of business, law, and politics by leaving things to chance.

The myth of Communist aggression was, and still is, a very powerful one, supported by enough arguments to make it sound plausible. It grew, however, not from the reality of Communist actions but rather from the need to make these actions appear threatening. Only such a threat would convince the American public to tolerate the postwar conduct of its government, a policy of lies and militarism and provocations and support for dictatorships around the world.

This is not to say that Soviet actions have always been friendly. The Soviets are, after all, competing with Americans for influence throughout the world. But competitive behavior is not necessarily hostile or threatening—vigorous competitors are not necessarily trying to destroy one another. Just as the United States has no wish to destroy the Soviet Union and its people, so the Soviets have no desire to annihilate the United States.

The fear of Soviet conquest powered a massive American military presence in Europe for decades, with the United States spending great sums on NATO forces. Yet wealthy European NATO countries have been strangely reluctant to pay their share of NATO costs. If they feel no need to defend themselves from the Soviet Union, perhaps the United States should not bother to take on the task either. How convenient for American allies and commercial rivals to demand that the United States accept the burden of policing the world; these same countries, freed of paying for expensive defense matériel, bleed the United States white as its creativity is diverted from competitive civilian technology in order to fulfill military needs.

Various cold war incidents were used as excuses to promote American defense spending. These incidents demonstrated Soviet hostility, but not a single one of them has contained a military threat against the United States. As with most propaganda, the reality of the Soviet military threat does not live up to the hype about it. This does not mean the United States should throw down its guns and retire its military personnel. But more guns will not reduce the peril it faces. American policies fighting the trend of Communist expansion in the past forty years have failed. If the United States pursues these policies more vigorously, the result will only be more failure. The Communist threat is something other than military. And thus if America hopes to survive and prosper, that "something other" must be dealt with, namely, the Communist promise to provide mundane but crucial aspects of life—such as food, shelter, health, control of one's own labor. When such things are already present, Communists make little headway.

In deciding upon appropriate military action, the United States assumes that war is an enterprise in which the risks and benefits are rationally calculated. Not all war is like this. Sometimes wars are caused by hatreds and madness that are unaffected by rational calculation. Such conflict can break out even when the troublemaker knows he is outnumbered and outgunned. These kinds of wars cannot be prevented with guns. All that can be done is try to minimize the damage if they occur.

Wars also occur for idealistic reasons, unfashionable as that notion is today. Oppressed peoples, even when outgunned, are willing to engage in hopeless battles. Military superiority therefore does not guarantee peace—people are willing to fight even when the odds are against them.

Nor would unfavorable odds deter a nation from striking at an overwhelming military power that threatened it. Nuclear superiority would not protect the United States if the Soviet Union wrongfully felt imminent danger from the United States.

We hear about the dangers of "miscalculation," as if the United States and the Soviet Union were carefully adding up the pros and cons of unleashing nuclear weapons. We hear less about whether communist and democratic governments base their calculations on the same philosophical values, and less still about whether people and nations make decisions using rational criteria or through madness, idealism, or fear. Rational calculations would have meaning only if one military power wished to conquer the other; there is no available evidence that the Soviet Union intends to conquer the United States.

Indeed, if the Soviet Union wanted to conquer the United States, it could do so without firing a shot; the Communist bloc could simply default on the huge loans given by United States bankers. The same bankers who warn about the dangers of communism are only too happy to finance Communists if there is potential for profit. Unfortunately, the Communists often refinance rather than repay, and this is one cause of inflation—American workers must carry the burden of financing Communist countries through these unpaid bank loans. A few phone calls from the Kremlin to the big United States banks to announce a default would collapse the monetary system, halt industry, and impoverish the American people almost overnight. The Soviets do not need missiles to destroy America.

Strategically, the United States and the Soviet Union each acts as a giant mirror, bouncing back every new weapons system and provocation that the other side throws up in defiance. The Soviet military buildup is only a reflection of that in the United States, and vice versa. By facing each other, they have created an infinite number of reflections; the stockpile of weapons will not decrease until the two countries angle away from a direct face-off.

Military power should not be regarded as an answer in itself, but merely as a means of buying time: time to touch the minds of opponents and achieve victory not by destroying them but by helping them to understand the survival value of facing reality; time to provide for basic health, nutrition, and shelter needs for everyone in the Third World; time to comprehend the discontent in the Third World and transform that powerful energy into a force that can guarantee peace and prosperity and American national security.

So why not pursue a policy intended to save civilization and make a little money? Surely there is a fortune to be made from promoting peace, assuring good health, cleansing the environment, and all the other things that will enrich Americans' lives.

Some may argue that these goals are too expensive, but the cost is now simply shifted to our planet and to future generations. No one can speak for future generations, but clearly our planet is throwing the cost back at us via climatic and atmospheric changes, caused by pollution, that will eventually destroy human life.

Beyond strengthening American national security, such a program would boost the economy, not only with profits for new companies but by increasing Third World productivity, enabling those nations to ease their burden of debt and thereby reduce the inflation that their debt causes in the United States.

If the United States were to liberate the Third World from the oppression of hunger, disease, and inadequate shelter, Americans would also gradually liberate themselves from the burden of military spending, freeing that money and talent to attack problems afflicting their own nation at home, and thereby improving their own lives as they improve those in the Third World. Moreover, every ruble that the Soviets spend on their military that Americans refuse to match is a ruble taken from the Soviet economy. If the Soviets spend more and the Americans spend less on national defense, the United States may grow stronger yet.

And perhaps most important of all, such a new foreign policy would liberate us from the great fear of destruction by enemies looming just beyond the horizon.

In that regard let this book close with a personal message from the author to readers in the United States.

In the movie *Thirty Seconds over Tokyo,* one of the aviators' wives says something like, "Won't it be wonderful when the war is over, and we won't have to be afraid any more?" Yet who among us has not known fear and anxiety since World War II? My father and his friends went overseas and risked their lives to defeat Hitler and Hirohito. My father and a million guys like him did this so their children, my friends and I, could know peace. But my generation has never known peace. Waiting for the bomb is not peace. We have been cheated.

By cheated, I mean that the postwar tension between the United States and the Soviet Union was not inevitable. It was brought about by old knaves and young fools. Some were European professors enamored with Old World conflicts but entrusted with the future of the United States, men such as Henry Kissinger from Germany, Edward Teller from Hungary, and Zbigniew Brzezinski from Poland. Others were attorneys and businessmen who served temporarily in government but put fortune ahead of all else.

We Americans hear much about the cost of defense spending.

That is nothing. The cost of freedom is *buried in the ground*. That is a debt we can never repay, a debt we can only try to be worthy of owing. For our own sake, and for respect for our brothers who died for us in Vietnam, our parents who died for us in Korea and in World War II, our grandparents who died for us in World War I, *their* parents who died in the Civil War, and their forebears who died in the American Revolution, we must abandon failing policies that are leading the United States to doom. We must instead find courage to face the future, saving ourselves and the world with policies based on reality instead of on greed and lies.

The idea that each person's happiness is equally important is the basis of majority rule. Elitists complain that elections don't necessarily produce the wisest decisions, that an equal vote for all assumes that everyone is equally wise. But that's not the assumption that really drives democracy. The assumption is that each person has equal worth as a human being and therefore an equal right to happiness. Therefore, the most ethical way of deciding an issue is to let everyone have an equal vote—the procedure may not produce the best decision, but it allows people to do what they want to do on an issue. People have a right to be wrong.

In a democracy, because there is recognition that everyone has an equal right to happiness, there will be respect for minority rights by the majority. The minority's feelings won't be disregarded, and there are barriers beyond which the majority can never trespass against the minority. The minority's equal right to happiness doesn't mean they get to have their way; it means the majority proceeds with humility, seeking to minimize the intrusion on the minority's happiness.

I don't argue that everyone's needs and desires are equal and should be met equally—some people need more food and shelter than others or different types of these necessities. And desires are as diverse as individuals. Just as immutable and exact mathematics can be used to understand the ever-changing fuzziness of nature, the diversity of human want and need can be treated by a democratic recognition of one unchanging element in the diversity—the right to happiness.

Harry Truman and his successors convinced us to put our faith in guns, and communism immediately swept the world. Can we not put our faith in ourselves? Can we not find the courage to abandon forty years of failure that have brought us to the verge of destroying civilization and perhaps humanity itself?

I believe we can. As a historian I have tried to aid that process by writing this book. I have tried to tell the truth, to help my fellow citizens understand that we have nothing to fear from the Soviet Union, that what we see when we look at the Soviets is but a mirror reflecting our own needless anxieties.

The future belongs to democracy, if only we have the courage to practice it and to believe in it.

This book, then, has been a story for the cheated generation, my generation, the sons and daughters of Americans who risked all they had to win World War II. This sacrifice was made so we would know peace and contentment. This birthright was stolen, but we are now old enough and numerous enough and powerful enough to seize back our birthright if we want it. And our parents and children will help us if only we ask.

Notes

Chapter I.
The First Communists

1. V. I. Lenin, "Frederick Engels," *Collected Works*, vol. 2, in *Karl Marx and Frederick Engels: Selected Works*, p. 16.
2. Karl Marx and Friedrich Engels, "The Communist Manifesto," in *Karl Marx and Frederick Engels*, pp. 52–53.
3. Karl Marx and Friedrich Engels, "Communist Manifesto," p. 34.
4. Friedrich Engels, introduction to *Dialectics of Nature, Karl Marx and Frederick Engels*, p. 356.

Chapter II.
Communists and World War I

1. Russell, *Bolshevism and the United States*, pp. 5–7; Feuer, *Conflict of Generations*, pp. 93–95, 134–35. Engels himself recognized the danger posed by student radicals such as Lenin: "How awful for the world . . . that there are 40,000 revolutionary students in Russia, without a proletariat or even a Russian peasantry behind them and with no career before them except the dilemma: Siberia or abroad—to Western Europe. If there is anything which might ruin the Western European movement, then it would have been this import of 40,000 more or less educated, ambitious, hungry Russian nihilists: all of them officer candidates without an army" (quoted in Feuer, *Conflict of Generations*, p. 163).
2. Quoted in Williams, *American-Russian Relations*, p. 92.
3. Williams, *American-Russian Relations*, pp. 100–101.
4. Quoted in Williams, *American-Russian Relations*, pp. 116–17.
5. Wilson was also interested in White General Grigori Semenov, but he turned out to promote Japanese interests over American. His violent actions against American troops became notorious.
6. Quoted in Williams, *American-Russian Relations*, p. 123.
7. Williams, *American-Russian Relations*, pp. 131–35, 140.
8. Quoted in Williams, *American-Russian Relations*, p. 153.

9. Quoted in Horowitz, *Empire and Revolution*, p. 65 n. 26.
10. Hoover, *Ordeal of Woodrow Wilson*, pp. 118–19.
11. Quoted in Williams, *American-Russian Relations*, p. 127.
12. Russell, *Bolshevism and the United States*, pp. 313–14. The same point is made by Bilmanis, *History of Latvia*, p. 328; see also Lampe, *Bulgarian Economy*, p. 61.
13. Williams, *American-Russian Relations*, p. 170.
14. Fleming, *Cold War and Its Origins*, pp. 19–20.

Chapter III.
Europe after the War

1. Werner T. Angress, "The Takeover That Remained in Limbo: The German Experience, 1918-1923," *Anatomy of Communist Takeovers*, ed. Hammond p. 174; Fowkes, *Communism in Germany*, p. 33; Grunberger, *Red Rising in Bavaria*, pp. 142–45. The major and the sign are quoted in Grunberger, which also has the photograph of the White vehicle opposite p. 81.
2. Quoted in Carr, *History of Soviet Russia: Bolshevik Revolution*, vol. 3, p. 105.
3. Hoover, *American Epic*, pp. 358–59.
4. Quoted in Tökés, *Béla Kun*, pp. 203–4. See also Borkenau, *World Communism*, p. 132.
5. Quoted in Lord, *Second Partition of Poland*, p. 450.
6. Quoted in Lord, *Second Partition of Poland*, p. 442.
7. Hoover, *American Epic*, pp. 62, 67.
8. Hoover, *American Epic*, pp. 63, 66.

Chapter IV.
Toilers of the East

1. Quoted in Feuer, *Conflict of Generations*, p. 190.
2. Quoted in Feuer, *Conflict of Generations*, p. 187.
3. Quoted in Feuer, *Conflict of Generations*, p. 182.
4. Quoted in Claudin, *Communist Movement*, pp. 555–56.
5. Quoted in Carr, *History of Soviet Russia: Bolshevik Revolution*, vol. 3, p. 538.
6. Quoted in Carr, *History of Soviet Russia: Socialism*, vol. 3, p. 722.
7. Quoted in Carr, *History of Soviet Russia: Socialism*, vol. 3, pp. 716–17.
8. Quoted in Carr, *History of Soviet Russia: Bolshevik Revolution*, vol. 3, p. 541.
9. Quoted in Gottfried-Karl Kindermann, "The Attempted Revo-

lution in China: The First Sino-Soviet Alliance, 1924-1927," in *Anatomy of Communist Takeovers*, ed. Hammond, p. 211.
10. Gruber, *Soviet Russia Masters the Comintern*, p. 441.

Chapter V.
Soviet-German Amity

1. Kennan, *Russia and the West*, pp. 243–44.
2. Quoted in Carr, *History of Soviet Russia: Interregnum*, pp. 258, 263.
3. Quoted in Carr, *History of Soviet Russia: Interregnum*, p. 155.
4. Quotation from Russian official in Carr, *History of Soviet Russia: Socialism*, vol. 3, p. 433. See also Carr, *German-Soviet Relations*, pp. 93–94.
5. Horowitz, *Empire and Revolution*, pp. 68–69.
6. Quoted in Bolloten, *Grand Camouflage*, p. 92 n. 13.
7. Quoted in Carr, *Twilight of Comintern*, p. 97.
8. Quoted in Bolloten, *Grand Camouflage*, pp. 92–93.
9. Carr, *German-Soviet Relations*, pp. 123, 135–37; Carr, *Spanish Civil War*, p. 15; Borkenau, *World Communism*, p. 407; Horowitz, *Empire and Revolution*, pp. 171–72; Goldston, *Civil War in Spain*, p. 75; Claudin, *Communist Movement*, p. 242; Fleming, *Cold War and Its Origins*, pp. 85, 87, 89, 1036.

Chapter VI.
Republican Communists and the Spanish Civil War

1. Quoted in Carr, *Spanish Civil War*, p. 12.
2. Bolloten, *Grand Camouflage*, pp. 110–111.
3. Bolloten, *Grand Camouflage*, p. 273.

Chapter VII.
The Baltic Region

1. Hoover, *Ordeal of Woodrow Wilson*, p. 128.
2. Hoover, *Ordeal of Woodrow Wilson*, pp. 132–33; Hoover, *American Epic*, p. 43.
3. Borkenau, *World Communism*, p. 106.
4. Hoover, *American Epic*, p. 27.
5. Quoted in Williams, *American-Russian Relations*, p. 254.
6. Hodgson, *Communism in Finland*, pp. 194–95. For Finland's cooperation with Nazi Germany, see Ohto Manninen, "Oper-

ation Barbarosa and the Nordic Countries," ed. Nissen, in *Scandinavia in Second World War*, pp. 139–181.
7. Hodgson, *Communism in Finland*, p. 196.

Chapter VIII.
Poland in World War II

1. Quoted in Carr, *History of Soviet Russia: Bolshevik Revolution*, vol. 3, p. 364.
2. Quoted in Fleming, *Cold War and Its Origins*, p. 25.
3. Quoted in Carr, *History of Soviet Russia: Interregnum*, p. 166.
4. Fleming, *Cold War and Its Origins*, pp. 87–88.
5. Fleming, p. 228.
6. Quoted in Williams, *American-Russian Relations*, p. 268.
7. Rings, *Life with the Enemy*, p. 262; Fleming, *Cold War and Its Origins*, p. 236.
8. Quoted in Polonsky and Drukier, *Communist Rule in Poland*, p. 15.
9. Fleming, *Cold War and Its Origins*, p. 267.
10. Quoted in Polonsky and Drukier, *Communist Rule in Poland*, p. 126.
11. Quoted in Fleming, *Cold War and Its Origins*, p. 1052.

Chapter IX.
The Balkans

1. Churchill, *Second World War*, vol. 6, p. 227. A photograph of the document is in Sulzberger, *Long Row of Candles*.
2. Quoted in Koliopoulos, *Greece and the British*, pp. 7–8.
3. Quoted in Fleming, *Cold War and Its Origins*, p. 183.
4. Quoted in O'Ballance, *Greek Civil War*, p. 78n.
5. Horowitz, *Empire and Revolution*, p. 184.
6. Kenneth Matthews, *Mountain War Greece*, pp. 94, 100.
7. Laqueur, *Guerrilla*, p. 284.
9. Engels quoted in Lendvai, *Eagles in Cobwebs*, pp. 314–15.
10. Hoover, *American Epic*, p. 140.
11. Borkenau, *World Communism*, pp. 99–100.
12. Quoted in Sulzberger, *Long Row of Candles*, p. 99.
13. Ibid., pp. 79–80.
14. Snow, *Pattern of Soviet Power*, p. 34.
15. Quoted in Fleming, *Cold War and Its Origins*, p. 1043.
16. Quoted in Carr, *History of Soviet Russia-Socialism*, vol. 3, p. 397n.

17. Lendvai, *Eagles in Cobwebs*, p. 216.
18. Fleming, *Cold War and Its Origins*, p. 1043.
19. Sulzberger, *Long Row of Candles*, p. 64.
20. Brown, *Bulgaria under Communist Rule*, pp. 8–10.
21. Lendvai, *Eagles in Cobwebs*, p. 72.
22. Lendvai, *Eagles in Cobwebs*, p. 70.
23. Laqueur, *Guerrilla*, p. 215.
24. Quoted in Lendvai, *Eagles in Cobwebs*, p. 78.
25. Quoted in Lendvai, *Eagles in Cobwebs*, p. 41.
26. Lendvai, *Eagles in Cobwebs*, p. 41.

Chapter X.
Three Governments That Fought the Future

1. Sulzberger, *Long Row of Candles*, pp. 48–49.
2. Roucek, *Politics of the Balkans*, p. 93.
3. Jon Halliday, "The Bandit Who Made His Revolution Stick," *Manchester Guardian Weekly*, 21 April 1985. "Bandit" in this context refers to a victim striking back at oppressors, in the manner of Robin Hood, rather than a self-serving criminal.
4. Editorial, *Manchester Guardian Weekly*, 21 April 1985.
5. Hamm, *Albania*, p. 80.
6. Lendvai, *Eagles in Cobwebs*, pp. 185–86.
7. Seton-Watson, *East European Revolution*, pp. 265–66.
8. Quoted in Fleming, *Cold War and Its Origins*, p. 260.
9. Quoted in Fleming, *Cold War and Its Origins*, p. 462n.
10. Fleming, *Cold War and Its Origins*, p. 462n.
11. Martin Gilbert, "Don't Forget the Suffering—and Don't Forget the Aid," *Manchester Guardian Weekly*, 19 May 1985.
12. Snow, *Pattern of Soviet Power*, pp. 59–60.
13. Quoted in Snow, *Pattern of Soviet Power*, p. 59.

Chapter XI.
Communist Triumph in China

1. Laqueur, *Guerrilla*, p. 241.
2. Carr, *Twilight of Comintern*, pp. 351–52, 360. See also Chong-Sik Lee, *Struggle in Manchuria*, p. 160.
3. Bergamini, *Japan's Imperial Conspiracy*, p. 750; Toland, *Rising Sun*, p. 694. See also Boyle, *China and Japan at War*, pp. 319–21.
4. Lukacs, *Cold War*, p. 91n.
5. Snow, *Pattern of Soviet Power*, p. 133.

Chapter XII.
Communist Failure in Korea

1. Quoted in Williams, *American-Russian Relations*, p. 21.
2. Quoted in Williams, *American-Russian Relations*, p. 21.
3. Quoted in Morris, "Korean Trusteeship," p. 201 n. 42.
4. Chung, "United States in Korea," p. 39.
5. Suh, *Korean Communist Movement*, p. 296.
6. Truman, *Trial and Hope*, p. 329.
7. Quoted in Smith, *MacArthur in Korea*, p. 43.
8. Quoted in Chung, "United States in Korea," p. 243.
9. Quoted in Smith, *MacArthur in Korea*, p. 44.
10. Morris, "Korean Trusteeship," p. 194; U-Gene Lee, "American Policy toward Korea," p. 367.
11. Morris, "Korean Trusteeship," p. 201.
12. In 1952, in the midst of the Korean War, the United States did consider waging war against Rhee. Rhee was up for reelection by the National Assembly and his opponents there seemed on the verge of ending his presidency. Rhee told the assembly to amend the constitution so that the people elect the president. It refused, and Rhee arrested a group of opposition members on trumped-up charges, characterizing the South Korean legislature as Communist-controlled. When the United States looked askance, Rhee organized huge anti-American demonstrations. The Truman administration responded with plans to inspire a coup overthrowing Rhee (Goulden, *Korea*, pp. 615–18.). The coup was shelved when the National Assembly agreed to Rhee's demand, and he released the arrested politicians.
13. Truman, *Trial and Hope*, p. 327.
14. Suh, *Korean Communist Movement*, pp. xi, 301, 311–14, 319, 323.
15. James, *Years of MacArthur*, vol. 3, p. 399.
16. Manchester, *American Caesar*, p. 540.
17. Stone, *Korean War*, p. 64.
18. Quoted in Morris, "Korean Trusteeship," p. 224.
19. Morris, "Korean Trusteeship," p. 224.
20. Chung, "United States in Korea," p. 302.
21. Kotch, "Policy toward Korea," p. 227; Manchester, *American Caesar*, p. 540.
22. Kotch, "Policy toward Korea," p. 240.
23. Manchester, *American Caesar*, p. 540.
24. Stueck, *Road to Confrontation*, p. 154.
25. Goulden, *Korea*, p. 31; James, *Years of MacArthur*, vol. 3, p. 401; Manchester, *American Caesar*, p. 542.

26. Goulden, *Korea*, p. 30; Leckie, *Conflict*, p. 31; Manchester, *American Caesar*, p. 541.
27. Leckie, *Conflict*, p. 31; Manchester, *American Caesar*, p. 542; Stone, *Korean War*, p. 12.
28. Khrushchev, *Khrushchev Remembers*, p. 403.
29. Quoted in Khrushchev, *Khrushchev Remembers*, p. 403.
30. Eyre, *Roosevelt-MacArthur Conflict*, pp. 48–49. (Eyre was an adviser to Philippines Commonwealth president Sergio Osmeña).
31. James, *Years of MacArthur*, vol. 2, p. 90.
32. James, *Years of MacArthur*, vol. 2, pp. 89–90, 430, 534; Smith, *MacArthur in Korea*, pp. 79–80, 136, 202–3.
33. Smith, *MacArthur in Korea*, pp. 72–73.
34. James, *Years of MacArthur*, vol. 2, pp. 405ff; Mattern, "Dark Horse," 39, 44–45, 48, 52–56, 60, 62, 66, 72–74, 127, 133–35, 278.
35. Manchester, *American Caesar*, pp. 521–25; Mattern, "Dark Horse," pp. iv, 158–60, 167, 243, 251, 265–67.
36. James, *Years of MacArthur*, vol. 3, pp. 408, 410.
37. Manchester, *American Caesar*, p. 556.
38. McGovern, *To the Yalu*, p. 68.
39. Quoted in Manchester, *American Caesar*, p. 567.
40. Stone, *Korean War*, pp. 117–18.
41. Kaufman, *Korean War*, p. 90; Manchester, *American Caesar*, pp. 587–88; Rees, *Korea*, p. 121; Stone, *Korean War*, p. 150.
42. Stone, *Korean War*, p. 184.
43. James, *Years of MacArthur*, vol. 3, pp. 540–41; MacArthur, *Reminiscences*, pp. 422–26; Manchester, *American Caesar*, p. 612.
44. James, *Years of MacArthur*, vol. 3, pp. 540–41; Manchester, *American Caesar*, p. 614.
45. Goulden, *Korea*, p. 477.
46. Quoted in Manchester, *American Caesar*, p. 639.
47. MacArthur, *Reminiscences*, p. 440.
48. Quoted in Smith, *MacArthur in Korea*, pp. 159–60.
49. On August 28, 1950, the Joint Chiefs asked MacArthur for details on the planned landing at Inch'ŏn. No reply came. On September 5 they asked again, and MacArthur promised to send details via courier by September 11. But he missed this deadline. "MacArthur had carefully arranged that the Joint Chiefs have no grounds for disapproving his plans simply by not delivering them into their hands until literally hours before the troops began assaulting the beaches" (Alexander, *Korea*, p. 190). The Joint Chiefs received the plans at 11:00 A.M. on

September 14, Washington time; the landing was to occur less than six hours later.
50. James, *Years of MacArthur*, vol. 3, p. 576; Smith, *MacArthur in Korea*, pp. 125–26.
51. Quoted in Manchester, *American Caesar*, p. 651.
52. Goulden, *Korea*, pp. 635–36.

Chapter XIII.
Southeast Asia

1. Philippe Pons, "Under Aquino or Marcos, Sugar Still Tastes Bitter," *Manchester Guardian Weekly*, 6 April 1986, *Le Monde* section.
2. Quoted in Philippe Pons, "Under Aquino or Marcos."
3. Quoted in Philippe Pons, " 'Christian-Communists' Not Ready to Lay Down Their Arms," *Manchester Guardian Weekly*, 30 March 1986, *Le Monde* section.
4. Quoted in Philippe Pons, "Under Aquino or Marcos."
5. Quoted in Komisar, *Corazon Aquino*, p. 130.
6. Komisar, *Corazon Aquino*, p. 181.
7. Quoted in Komisar, *Corazon Aquino*, p. 171.
8. Quoted in Harry Anderson with Richard Vokey, "A Country Between Two Cultures: Filipinos Begin Asking: Is This 'A Sick Nation'?" *Newsweek*, February 1, 1988.
9. Kurzman, *Subversion of the Innocents*, p. 436.
10. Clutterbuck, *Long, Long War*, pp. 4–5.
11. Clutterbuck, *Long, Long War*, pp. 4–5; Miller, *Jungle War in Malaya*, pp. 96, 148, 151.
12. Clutterbuck, *Long, Long War*, pp. 104–11; Short, *Insurrection in Malaya*, pp. 418–19, 422–24; Kurzman, *Subversion of the Innocents*, p. 437.
13. Carr, *History of Soviet Russia: Socialism*, vol. 3, p. 675; Fairbank, Reischauer and Craig, *East Asian Civilization*, vol. 2, p. 736.
14. Quoted in Kurzman, *Subversion of the Innocents*, p. 6.
15. Caldwell, *Terror in Indonesia*, pp. 209ff; De Riencourt, *American Empire*, pp. 113, 162; Marchetti and Marks, *CIA*, pp. 29, 40, 114, 138, 166, 299; Prados, *Presidents' Secret Wars*, pp. 130–44; Schlesinger, *Thousand Days*, p. 532; Southwood and Flanagan, *Indonesia*, pp. 11–15, 32–37; Wise and Ross, *Invisible Government*, pp. 137, 141, 145.
16. Komisar, *Corazon Aquino*, p. 32.
17. Quoted in Wise and Ross, *Invisible Government*, pp. 140–41.
18. Quoted in Guy Pauker, "The Rise and Fall of the Communist

Party in Indonesia," *Revolution in Asia*, ed. Scalapino, pp. 279–80.
19. Pauker, "The Rise and Fall of the Communist Party in Indonesia," p. 285.

Chapter XIV.
The Challenge of India

1. Quoted in Overstreet and Windmiller, *Communism in India*, p. 149.
2. Carr, *History of Soviet Russia: Bolshevik Revolution*, vol. 3, p. 292.
3. Quoted in Overstreet and Windmiller, *Communism in India*, p. 113.
4. The Soviet Union initially supported the Nehru government during this Sino-Indian dispute. The Soviets also encouraged Nehru in his seizure of Portuguese colonial outposts in India. In the end, however, the Kremlin tilted toward Peking on the border issue.

Chapter XV.
Decline of the Stalinist System: Poland and Hungary, 1956

1. Quoted in Meray, *Thirteen Days*, p. 6.
2. Quoted in Bill Lomax, *Hungary 1956*, p. 34.
3. Molnár, *Budapest 1956*, p. 86.
4. Quoted in Bethell, *Gomulka*, p. 214. A similar version is quoted in Gibney, *Frozen Revolution*, p. 11.
5. Fleming, *Cold War and Its Origins*, pp. 798–99; Meray, *Thirteen Days*, p. 110.
6. Meray, *Thirteen Days*, pp. 143–44.
7. Meray, *Thirteen Days*, pp. 199–200.
8. Meray, *Thirteen Days*, pp. 202–3.
9. Kolkowicz, *Soviet Military*, p. 371.
10. Fehér and Heller, *Hungary 1956 Revisited*, pp. 55–56.
11. Khrushchev, *Khrushchev Remembers*, pp. 457–58.
12. Fehér and Heller, *Hungary 1956 Revisited*, p. 10.

Chapter XVI.
Cuba: The Emergence of Castro

1. Quoted in Zeitlin and Scheer, *Cuba*, p. 42.
2. Quoted in Aguilar, *Cuba 1933*, p. 181.

3. Carleton Beals and Clifford Odets, quoted in Taber, *M-26*, p. 25.
4. Quoted in Szulc, *Fidel*, p. 137.
5. Many books recounting the Batista years discuss the brutal activities of his police. One of the most readable is Taber's *M-26*; briefer and more subdued accounts can be found in Herbert Matthews's *Revolution in Cuba* and Thomas's *Cuba*, two books with different slants.
6. Casuso, *Cuba and Castro*, pp. 159–60; Herbert Matthews, *Revolution in Cuba*, pp. 133–35; Szulc, *Fidel*, pp. 483–84; Taber, *M-26*, pp. 308–9; Zeitlin and Scheer, *Cuba*, pp. 66–70. There was a highly publicized exception to normal judicial atmosphere in one trial. Claims of mob justice seem to be based on this single instance, but one example hardly serves to discredit all the other proceedings held with proper decorum. Moreover, the case in question was later retried.
7. Herbert Matthews, *Revolution in Cuba*, pp. 94, 133; Szulc, *Fidel*, p. 482; Zeitlin and Scheer, *Cuba*, p. 70.
8. Casuso, *Cuba and Castro*, p. 100.
9. Senate Judiciary Committee, *Communist Threat to the United States through the Caribbean, Hearings*, 86th Cong., 1st sess., 5 November 1959, pt. 3, pp. 162–64.
10. Quoted in Zeitlin and Scheer, *Cuba*, p. 103.
11. Quoted in Zeitlin and Scheer, *Cuba*, pp. 126–27.
12. Zeitlin and Scheer, *Cuba*, pp. 263–78.
13. Department of State, "Responsibility of the Cuban Government for Increased International Tensions in the Hemisphere" (August 1, 1960), *The Department of State Bulletin*, vol. 43, no. 1105 (August 29, 1960), p. 337.
14. Department of State, "Responsibility of the Cuban Government," p. 320. Capitalization changes in the two versions are given as found in the Department of State document.
15. Department of State, "Responsibility of the Cuban Government," p. 331.
16. Quoted in Zeitlin and Scheer, *Cuba*, p. 272.
17. Department of State, "Responsibility of the Cuban Government," p. 345.
18. Schlesinger, *Thousand Days*, pp. 245–46.
19. Zeitlin and Scheer, *Cuba*, pp. 278–82. See also Maurice Halperin, *Fidel Castro*, p. 95.
20. Department of State, *Cuba*, Dept. State pub. 7171, Inter-American Series 66, April 1961, (S1.26:66), p. 20.
21. Zeitlin and Scheer, *Cuba*, p. 281.

22. Department of State, *Cuba*, p. 5.
23. A less publicized reason for the invasion was that the Kennedy administration feared what the private adventurers might do if they were left stranded in Guatemala. There was concern that they might overthrow one of the Central American governments friendly to the United States. The United States felt it could not control the force it created. During the 1980s similar concerns arose about the contra forces in Nicaragua supported by the Reagan administration.

Chapter XVII.
Communism on One Island

1. Khrushchev, *Khrushchev Remembers*, pp. 546, 548.
2. Maurice Halperin, *Fidel Castro*, p. 168; Karol, *Guerrillas in Power*, pp. 261–63. Castro said many apparently conflicting things about the missiles, and untangling the truth is difficult.
3. See Tatu, *Power in the Kremlin*, for more about these Kremlin intrigues. Tatu was the respected Moscow correspondent of *Le Monde*. Khrushchev's memoirs say that he devised the Cuban missile project while on a trip to Bulgaria (Khrushchev, *Khrushchev Remembers*, p. 546). That was in May 1962, and would therefore weaken Tatu's contention that the April personnel shifts related to the project. Given the uncertainties about the acuteness of the elderly Khrushchev's memory and about the precise dating of Kremlin personnel shifts, the chronological inconsistency may be insignificant. Allison (*Essence of Decision*, pp. 112–13) presents evidence that the military was enthusiastic and may have exceeded the civilian leadership's orders by including intermediate-range rockets in the Cuban project. Military infighting may have occurred, with some officials opposing and some favoring the project; see Allison, pp. 115–16.
4. Abel, *Missile Crisis*, p. 7.; Detzer, *Brink*, pp. 62–63; Allison, *Essence of Decision*, p. 190.
5. Abel, *Missile Crisis*, p. 13; Allison, *Essence of Decision*, p. 122. In government jargon a CIA agent is analogous to an FBI informant and is not an agency professional.
6. Detzer, *Brink*, p. 75; Allison, *Essence of Decision*, p. 122.
7. Wise and Ross, *Invisible Government*, p. 297.
8. Detzer, *Brink*, p. 75.
9. Larry Booda, "U.S. Watches for Possible Cuban IRBMs," *Aviation Week and Space Technology*, 1 October 1962, p. 20. During

the crisis the same journal referred to the missiles as "long-expected" (29 October 1962, p. 26, see also p. 32).
10. Allison, *Essence of Decision*, pp. 236–37.
11. Hilsman, *To Move a Nation*, p. 225.
12. Robert Hotz, "What Was the Threat?" *Aviation Week and Space Technology*, 12 November 1962, p. 21.
13. Horowitz, *Free World Colossus*, pp. 384–85; Abel, *Missile Crisis*, p. 38; Allison, *Essence of Decision*, pp. 195–96; Hilsman, *To Move a Nation*, p. 195; Thomas, *Cuba*, p. 1401.
14. Detzer, *Brink*, p. 73; "Photos Documented Cuban Arms Buildup," *Aviation Week and Space Technology*, October 29, 1962, p. 31.
15. Detzer, *Brink*, p. 73; Hotz, "What Was the Threat?" p. 21.
16. Detzer, *Brink*, p. 73; Hotz, "What Was the Threat?" p. 21.
17. Allison, *Essence of Decision*, p. 56; "Photos Documented Cuban Arms Buildup," p. 34.
18. Allison, *Essence of Decision*, p. 104; Lukacs, *Cold War*, p. 240 n. 15; Thomas, *Cuba*, p. 1401 n. 43; Robert Hotz, "The Cuban Crisis," *Aviation Week and Space Technology*, 29 October 1962, p. 21; "Russia Avoids Early Chance to Test U.S. Determination in Cuban Arms Blockade," *Aviation Week and Space Technology*, 29 October 1962, p. 26. Presumably the intermediate-range rockets were en route at sea when the project was canceled.
19. Abel, *Missile Crisis*, p. 182; Allison, *Essence of Decision*, p. 59; Maurice Halperin, *Fidel Castro*, pp. 194, 322; Karol, *Guerrillas in Power*, p. 255; Lukacs, *Cold War*, p. 239; Thomas, *Cuba*, pp. 1389, 1401.
20. *Public Papers of the Presidents of the United States* (Washington, D.C.: Office of the *Federal Register*, National Archives and Records Service, 1963), John F. Kennedy 1962, "Television and Radio Interview: 'After Two Years—a Conversation with the President,' " 17 December 1962, p. 898. See also Detzer, *Brink*, p. 105; Horowitz, *Free World Colossus*, pp. 385–86; Sorensen, *Kennedy*, p. 678.
21. Detzer, *Brink*, p. 105; Allison, *Essence of Decision*, pp. 193–94.
22. Quoted in Larson, "Cuban Crisis," p. 3.
23. Quoted in Larson, "Cuban Crisis," p. 18.
24. Quoted in Larson, "Cuban Crisis," p. 3.
25. Allison, *Essence of Decision*, p. 231.
26. Thomas, *Cuba*, p. 1387 n. 11.
27. Maurice Halperin, *Fidel Castro*, p. 173; Hyland and Shryock, *Fall of Khrushchev*, pp. 61–62, 67–68; Karol, *Guerrillas in Power*, p. 269.

28. Abel, *Missile Crisis*, pp. 158–59; Allison, *Essence of Decision*, p. 221.
29. Allison, *Essence of Decision*, pp. 221–23; Crankshaw, *Khrushchev*, p. 282; Khrushchev, *Khrushchev Remembers*, pp. 546, 549.
30. Abel, *Missile Crisis*, p. 168; Allison, *Essence of Decision*, pp. 223–24; Hyland and Shryock, *Fall of Khrushchev*, p. 62.
31. Karol, *Guerrillas in Power*, p. 269.
32. Kennedy, *Thirteen Days*, pp. 108–9.
33. Crankshaw, *Khrushchev*, p. 283.
34. Allison, *Essence of Decision*, pp. 104–5, 108, 112.
35. Abel, *Missile Crisis*, p. 190; Karol, *Guerrillas in Power*, p. 277.
36. Hilsman, *To Move a Nation*, pp. 197, 225. Although Hilsman was frank about political concerns, he was also convinced that the missiles were a serious military threat.
37. Detzer, *Brink*, p. 104.
38. Detzer, *Brink*, p. 104.
39. Detzer, *Brink*, p. 133; Allison, *Essence of Decision*, p. 194.
40. Detzer, *Brink*, p. 132.
41. Detzer, *Brink*, pp. 202, 214. Canadian prime minister John Diefenbaker was so suspicious of the circumstances that he initially questioned the authenticity of missile-site photos (Maurice Halperin, *Fidel Castro*, p. 178).
42. Quoted in Herbert Matthews, *Revolution in Cuba*, p. 213.
43. The author's phraseology about isolation is inspired by the words of Senator Gale McGee, quoted in Herbert Matthews, *Revolution in Cuba*, p. 421.

Chapter XVIII.
Communist Failure in Latin America

1. Quoted in Rosenthal, *Guatemala*, p. 115.
2. Rosenthal, *Guatemala*, p. 192.
3. Quoted in Rosenthal, *Guatemala*, p. 201.
4. Quoted in Schneider, *Communism in Guatemala*, p. 192.
5. The military man's contempt for politicians worldwide is thoroughly examined in Finer, *Man on Horseback*.
6. Schneider, *Communism in Guatemala*, p. 197.
7. Quoted in Schneider, *Communism in Guatemala*, p. 194.
8. Quoted in Schneider, *Communism in Guatemala*, p. 192.
9. Geiger, *Communism Versus Progress*, p. 1.
10. Quoted in Geiger, *Communism Versus Progress*, pp. vi–vii.
11. Ronald M. Schneider, in *Anatomy of Communist Takeovers*, ed.

Hammond, pp. 574–75. Nikita Khrushchev's memoirs exuberantly describe many Soviet foreign activities but make no mention of Guatemala.
12. Geiger, *Communism Versus Progress*, pp. 43–44.
13. Quoted in Geiger, *Communism Versus Progress*, p. 61.
14. Quoted in Prados, *Presidents' Secret Wars*, p. 102.
15. Geiger, *Communism Versus Progress*, p. 24.
16. McCann, *American Company*, p. 56.
17. Prados, *Presidents' Secret Wars*, p. 99.
18. McCann, *American Company*, pp. 59–60.
19. Quoted in Wise and Ross, *Invisible Government*, p. 176.
20. Schofield, *46 Years in the Army*, pp. 489–90.
21. Horne, *Small Earthquake in Chile*, p. 112.
22. Quoted in Sobel, *Chile and Allende*, p. 34.
23. Loveman, *Chile*, p. 329.
24. Quoted in Ernst Halperin, *Nationalism and Communism*, p. 139. Allende's remark was made in July 1960, when the lesson was fresh in mind.
25. Boorstein, *Allende's Chile*, pp. 58–59; Davis, *Salvador Allende*, pp. 7–16, 313–19; Hersh, *Price of Power*, pp. 275–94; Powers, *Man Who Kept Secrets*, pp. 234–38; Prados, *Presidents' Secret Wars*, pp. 317–18; Sobel, *Chile and Allende*, pp. 31, 33–34; Senate Committee on Froeign Relations, *Nomination of Hon. Cyrus R. Vance to be Secretary of State*, Hearings, 95th Cong., 1st sess., 11 January 1977 [Y4.F76/2:V27], p. 50; Senate Select Committee to Study Government Operations with Respect to Intelligence Activities, *Covert Action in Chile 1963–73*, Committee Print, Staff Report, 94th Cong., 1st sess., 18 December 1975, pp. 2, 23, 25–26; Senate Select Committee to Study Governmental Operations with Respect to Intelligence Activities, *Alleged Assassination Plots Involving Foreign Leaders*, Interim Report, 94th Cong., 1st sess., 20 November 1975, pp. 225–54.

Additional government documents concerning American relations with Chile under Allende include Senate Committee on Foreign Relations, *The International Telephone and Telegraph Company and Chile, 1970–71*, Committee Print, Report, by the Subcommittee on Multinational Corporations, 93rd Cong., 1st sess., 21 June 1973; Senate Committee on Foreign Relations, *Multinational Corporations and U.S. Foreign Policy*, Hearings, before subcommittee on Multinational Corporations, 93rd Cong., 1st. sess., pt. 1, 20–22 March, 27–29 March, 2 April 1973 [Y4.F76/2:M91/pt.1], and pt. 2 [Y4.F76/2:M91/pt.2].
26. Powers, *Man Who Kept Secrets*, p. 230.

27. Quoted in Prados, *Presidents' Secret Wars*, p. 317.
28. Quoted in Barnet and Müller, *Global Reach*, pp. 81–83.
29. Quoted in Senate Select Committee to Study Governmental Operations with Respect to Intelligence Activities, *Alleged Assassination Plots Involving*, p. 227.
30. Quoted in Sobel, *Chile and Allende*, p. 77.
31. To improve its own position, ITT was even willing to attack other American firms in Chile. ITT suggested that Chile first pay ITT for its property and then seize Anaconda and Kennecott's mining property without compensation, on the grounds that they were an inherent natural resource of Chile. Allende could then point to ITT's compensation as proof that he was not antibusiness. In the midst of these negotiations, Allende learned of ITT's efforts to prevent his election in 1970, and the deal fell through (Sobel, *Chile and Allende*, p. 119.)
32. Senate Select Committee to Study Government Operations with Respect to Intelligence Activities, *Covert Action in Chile*, p. 2; Prados, *Presidents' Secret Wars*, pp. 319–20.
33. Quoted in Sobel, *Chile and Allende*, p. 149.
34. Quoted in Sobel, *Chile and Allende*, p. 163.
35. Quoted in Sobel, *Chile and Allende*, p. 163.
36. Ernst Halperin, *Nationalism and Communism*, p. 13.

Chapter XIX.
Africa

1. Legum, *Congo Disaster*, p. 15.
2. Quoted in Legum, *Congo Disaster*, p. 13.
3. Quoted in Legum, *Congo Disaster*, p. 107.
4. Quoted in Kurzman, *Subversion of the Innocents*, p. 138.
5. Prados, *Presidents' Secret Wars*, p. 234.
6. Kurzman, *Subversion of the Innocents*, p. 146.
7. Eisenhower, *Waging Peace*, p. 575.
8. Kurzman, *Subversion of the Innocents*, p. 145.
9. Kurzman, *Subversion of the Innocents*, p. 144.
10. Alexander Dallin, "The Soviet Union: Political Activity," in *Africa and the Communist World*, ed. Brzezinski, pp. 32–33.
11. Wright, *Zaire since Independence*, p. 6.
12. Cooley, *East Wind over Africa*, p. 48.
13. Stevens, *Soviet Union and Black Africa*, p. 184.
14. Dallin, "Soviet Union: Political," p. 39.

Chapter XX.
Czechoslovakia

1. Staar, *Communist Regimes in Eastern Europe*, p. 63.
2. Hammond, *Anatomy of Communist Takeovers*, p. 28; Mayer, *Art of the Impossible*, p. 9.
3. Pavel Tigrid, "The Prague Coup of 1948: The Elegant Takeover," in *Anatomy of Communist Takeovers*, ed. Hammond, pp. 422–23; Seton-Watson, *From Lenin to Khrushchev*, p. 259.
4. Remington, *Winter in Prague*, pp. 48–50; Salomon, *Prague Notebook*, pp. 56–61; Schwartz, *Prague's 200 Days*, pp. 66–67; Shawcross, *Dubcek*, p. 135; Tigrid, *Why Dubcek Fell*, pp. 34–36; Zeman, *Prague Spring*, pp. 106–7.
5. Schwartz, *Prague's 200 Days*, p. 74.
6. Windsor, "Czechoslovakia, Eastern Europe and Détente," in Windsor and Roberts, *Czechoslovakia 1968*, pp. 18–19, 23.
7. Mayer, *Art of the Impossible*, p. 18; Schwartz, *Prague's 200 Days*, p. 112.
8. Editorial, *New York Times*, 17 February 1968. A glance at the 1968 *New York Times* index demonstrates the intensity of Western press coverage of Czechoslovakia.
9. Ivan Svitak, "The Prague Spring Revisited," in *Czechoslovakia*, ed. Brisch and Volgyes, p. 160; Jan F. Triska, "Czechoslovakia: The Politics of Dependency," in *Czechoslovakia*, ed. Brisch and Volgyes, pp. 173–74; Jiri Valenta, "The USSR and Czechoslovakia's Experiment with Eurocommunism: Reassessment after a Decade," in *Czechoslovakia*, ed. Brisch and Volgyes, pp. 202, 204; Johnson, *Vantage Point*, p. 486; Mayer, *Art of the Impossible*, pp. 9, 18–20; Svitak, *Czechoslovak Experiment*, pp. 133–34, 139; Vernon V. Aspaturian, "The Soviet Union and Eastern Europe: The Aftermath of the Czechoslovak Invasion," in *Czechoslovakia*, ed. Zartman, pp. 32, 34; Andrew M. Scott, "Military Intervention by the Great Powers: The Rules of the Game," in *Czechoslovakia*, ed. Zartman, p. 97; Zeman, *Prague Spring*, pp. 156–57; Windsor, "Czechoslovakia, Eastern Europe and Détente," pp. 10, 60–61, 74; William E. Griffith, "The Prague Spring and the Soviet Intervention in Czechoslovakia," in *Anatomy of Communist Takeovers*, ed. Hammond, pp. 610–11; Schwartz, *Prague's 200 Days*, pp. 104, 114.
10. Quoted in Zeman, *Prague Spring*, p. 156.
11. Quoted in George Gomori, "Hungarian and Polish Attitudes on Czechoslovakia, 1968," in *Soviet Invasion*, ed. Czerwinski and Piekalkiewicz, pp. 113–14.

12. Quoted in Vernon V. Aspaturian, "The Soviet Union and Eastern Europe: The Aftermath of the Czechoslovak Invasion," p. 32.
13. Johnson, *Vantage Point*, p. 486; Windsor, "Czechoslovakia, Eastern Europe and Détente," pp. 3, 19–21, 35, 81; Griffith, "The Prague Spring and the Soviet Intervention in Czechoslovakia," p. 608; Lendvai, *Eagles in Cobwebs*, p. 362; Aspaturian "The Soviet Union and Eastern Europe: The Aftermath of the Czechoslovak Invasion," p. 35.
14. Windsor, "Czechoslovakia, Eastern Europe and Détente," p. 14.
15. Jiri Valenta, "Soviet Decisionmaking and the Czechoslovak Crisis of 1968," *Studies in Comparative Communism*, vol. 8, nos. 1 and 2 (Spring/Summer 1975), pp. 150–51, 153–54, 156, 161.
16. Schwartz, *Prague's 200 Days*, p. 112; Windsor, "Czechoslovakia, Eastern Europe and Détente," pp. 34, 60–61.
17. Quoted in Valenta, "Soviet Decisionmaking," p. 160.
18. Windsor, "Czechoslovakia, Eastern Europe and Détente," p. 34.
19. Valenta, "Soviet Decisionmaking," pp. 151, 158, 162–64.
20. Valenta, "Soviet Decisionmaking," p. 155.
21. Aspaturian, "The Soviet Union and Eastern Europe: The Aftermath of the Czechoslovak Invasion," p. 37; Valenta, "USSR and Czechoslovakia's Experiment," p. 203.
22. Valenta, "Soviet Decisionmaking," p. 170.
23. Valenta, "Soviet Decisionmaking," p. 171.
24. Mayer, *Art of the Impossible*, pp. 8, 13, 17, 23, 25, 27.
25. Quoted in Schwartz, *Prague's 200 Days*, p. 217.

Chapter XXI.
French Indochina

1. Turner, *Vietnamese Communism*, pp. 9, 11.
2. Bernard Fall, "A 'Straight Zigzag': The Road to Socialism in North Viet-Nam," in Barnett, *Communist Strategies in Asia*, p. 202.
3. Louis Lomax, *Thailand*, pp. 153–54, 170–71; Tanham, *Trial in Thailand*, p. 21.
4. Ridgway, *Soldier*, p. 277.
5. Ridgway, *Soldier*, p. 278.
6. Quoted in Schlesinger, *Bitter Heritage*, p. 27.
7. Jean-Jacques Servan-Schreiber, "Shared Research Could End

396 ■ HERITAGE OF FEAR

Soviet-American Hostility," *Manchester Guardian Weekly*, 13 September 1987, *Washington Post* section.
8. Quoted in Servan-Schreiber, "Shared Research."
9. Quoted in Schlesinger, *Bitter Heritage*, pp. 27–28.
10. Quoted in Schlesinger, *Bitter Heritage*, p. 38.
11. Donald Lancaster, "The Decline of Prince Sihanouk's Regime," in *Indochina in Conflict: A Political Assessment*, J. J. Zasloff and A. E. Goodman, ed. (Lexington, Mass.: Lexington Books, 1972), p. 52, quoted in Etcheson, *Democratic Kampuchea*, p. 70.
12. Quoted in Salman Rushdie, "Escaping from One Nightmare into Another," *Manchester Guardian Weekly*, 16 December 1986.
13. Rushdie, "Escaping from One Nightmare."
14. Barrington Moore, Jr., "Why We Fear Peasants in Revolt," *The Nation*, 26 September 1966, p. 274.

Chapter XXII.
The Fate of Empires

1. The control of cities, especially the capital city, is the traditional measure of a group's claim to rule. This is a holdover from the illusion of empire, in which a few officials in towns supposedly control a vast area they never even visit.
2. This conclusion is supported by the analysis of University of California at Los Angeles political science professor Edward Gonzalez in "Complexities of Cuban Foreign Policy," *Problems in Communism*, vol. 26, no. 6 (November-December 1977), pp. 10–11. See also Klinghoffer, *Angola War*, p. 111.
3. Quoted in Wolfers and Bergerol, *Angola in the Frontline*, pp. 6–7. See also Stockwell, *In Search of Enemies*, p. 68, 68n. Stockwell became so disillusioned with the Angola project that he resigned from the CIA and revealed his concerns to the public.
4. Stevens, *Soviet Union and Black Africa*, pp. 176–77.

Chapter XXIII.
The Challenge of Islam

1. Hyman, *Afghanistan under Soviet Domination*, p. 38.
2. Quoted in Hyman, *Afghanistan under Soviet Domination*, p. 6.
3. Hyman, *Afghanistan under Soviet Domination*, p. 43.
4. Carr, *History of Soviet Russia: Bolshevik Revolution*, vol. 3, pp. 238–39.
5. Carr, *History of Soviet Russia: Bolshevik Revolution*, vol. 3, pp. 238–39, 239n.

NOTES ■ 397

6. Hyman, *Afghanistan under Soviet Domination*, pp. 78, 93, 95–96; Hammond, *Red Flag over Afghanistan*, p. 73.
7. Hammond, *Red Flag over Afghanistan*, p. 73.
8. Carr, *History of Soviet Russia: Bolshevik Revolution*, vol. 3, p. 469.
9. Quoted in Carr, *History of Soviet Russia: Bolshevik Revolution*, vol. 3, p. 472.
10. The Soviet Union and Iran had adjoining areas each known as Azerbaijan, with close cultural links.
11. Fleming, *Cold War and Its Origins*, p. 341.
12. Clark Clifford memorandum to Harry S. Truman, September 1946, quoted in Krock, *Memoirs*, p. 421.

Chapter XXV.
Central America in the 1980s

1. Quoted in Dunkerley, *Long War*, p. 183.
2. Christian, *Nicaragua*, pp. 94, 105–6, 112–13; North, *Bitter Grounds*, pp. 133–34, 152–53; Dunkerley, *Long War*, pp. 183–84, 212.
3. Jonathan Steele, "A Revolution That Proved Itself at the Poll," *Manchester Guardian Weekly*, 18 November 1984.
4. Jonathan Steele, "Lies, Damned Lies—and USIA Statistics," *Manchester Guardian Weekly*, 23 December 1984.
5. Paul Laverty, letter to the editor, *Manchester Guardian Weekly*, 7 July 1985.
6. Quoted in Anderson, *Matanza*, pp. 83–84.
7. Quoted in Anderson, *Matanza*, p. 88.
8. Montgomery, *Revolution in El Salvador*, p. 121.
9. Quoted in *Manchester Guardian Weekly*, 17 February 1985, Le Monde section.
10. Quoted in Dunkerley, *Long War*, p. 162.
11. Quoted in North, *Bitter Grounds*, p. 12.
12. Quoted in Dunkerley, *Long War*, p. 156.
13. Rodriguez, *Voices from El Salvador*, p. 78n; Dunkerley, *Long War*, p. 157; North, *Bitter Grounds*, app. 1, p. xi.
14. Quoted in Arnson, *El Salvador*, p. 1.
15. Alma Guillermoprieto, "Salvadoran Peasants Describe Mass Killing," *Washington Post*, 27 January 1982.
16. Dunkerley, *Long War*, p. 186.
17. Quoted in Dunkerley, *Long War*, p. 189.
18. Department of State, *Communist Interference in El Salvador* (1981), [S1.129:80]; Department of State, *Communist Interference*

in El Salvador: Documents Demonstrating Communist Support of the Salvadoran Insurgency (1981), [S1.2:C 73/9].
19. Dunkerley, *Long War*, pp. 179–80.
20. Dunkerley, *Long War*, p. 180; Arnson, *El Salvador*, p. 74; North, *Bitter Grounds*, p. 94; Montgomery, *Revolution in El Salvador*, p. 179.
21. Jonathan Kwitney, "Tarnished Report?; Apparent Errors Cloud U.S. 'White Paper' on Reds in El Salvador; State Department Aide Says Parts May Be Misleading But Defends Conclusions; A Raid on an Art Gallery," *Wall Street Journal*, 8 June 1981.
22. Quoted in *New York Times*, 21 February 1981.

Chapter XXVII.
A State of Siege from Within

1. Quoted in Fleming, *Cold War and Its Origins*, p. 1052.
2. "Taking Stock: The U.S. Military Buildup," *The Defense Monitor*, vol. 13, no. 4 and "U.S.-Soviet Military Facts," *The Defense Monitor*, vol. 13, no. 6.
3. Quoted in "Militarism in America," *The Defense Monitor*, vol. 15, no. 3, p. 2.
4. John Gittings, "Words in Context," *Manchester Guardian Weekly*, 24 March 1985.
5. Allegations that the airliner was on some sort of spy mission were hotly denied. Although it is hard to believe that a regular commercial airline flight would be endangered in such a way, at least one Western military aircraft has pretended to be a civilian airliner in order to conduct espionage missions against Soviet military forces; see Joe Joyce, "Spy Plane Causes Concern," *Manchester Guardian Weekly*, 28 July 1985. Such tactics surely create peril for authentically blundering civilian craft.
6. "Star Wars: Vision and Reality," *The Defense Monitor*, vol. 15, no. 2, p. 1.
7. David Bodanis, "The Catastrophe Program," *Manchester Guardian Weekly*, 7 July 1985.
8. Over 20,000 false-attack alarms were recorded at NORAD from 1977 to 1984. Most were obvious mistakes, but about 1,000 required a so-called Missile Display Conference by senior defense officials, who determined that the warnings were false. Six warnings, however, seemed so credible that a Threat Assessment Conference was held, the last step before a Missile Attack Conference in which the president would be involved. The public record indicates that no presidential decision was

ever requested, and such a conference would be so newsworthy that it surely would become known.
9. Andrew Veitch, "Risk of Nuclear War through Error 'Unacceptably High,' " *Manchester Guardian Weekly*, 7 April 1985.
10. Ford, *Button*, pp. 20–21; Kosta Tsipis, "It's Not Just The President Who Can Release Armageddon," *Manchester Guardian Weekly*, 23 June 1985, *Washington Post* section.
11. Quoted in Williams, *Revolutionary World*, p. 65.
12. Lukacs, *Cold War*, p. 399n.

Sources Cited

At some point in research on a topic, whether the field be biology or physics or history, it is appropriate to sit back and review the findings of investigators. If a consensus has emerged on some points or if odd and little-noticed bits of information take on importance when seen together, such a review can help indicate fruitful directions for further research. A review can also summarize the current state of knowledge for interested persons who find it impractical to keep up with the findings reported by the many investigators in a field.

A review is a tertiary source rather than secondary source, conducted on a higher level of abstraction than raw field research. A benefit of this higher level is that the review thereby puts things in perspective. A drawback is that distance from raw data increases the difficulty of verifying data on which the perspective is based.

In my work as a historian, I have been struck by factual inaccuracies in various books. I discovered these errors while examining actual correspondence, transcripts of meetings, and other raw data produced in connection with events described in the books. I recognize the usefulness of such primary source materials in scholarly research when the goal is a definitive account of exactly what happened.

This does not mean, however, that books and other secondary sources are useless. What would be the point of producing them if readers cannot learn anything from them? If one recognizes their limitations, there is nothing wrong with using them to learn about things. After all, few have the skill to learn the necessary languages, the money to travel around the globe, and the time to spend decades in various archives, trying to piece together the story of civilization from scattered documents. Scientists do not work like that. They depend on the findings of researchers who have gone before them and build upon those findings in new work. They duplicate the research of previous scientists only if new information contradicts earlier findings.

Archives and other repositories of primary source material are crucial if history is to be built on a solid factual basis. Facts *exist*, and history is *built* on those facts. History is manufactured and can have many different appearances based on the same facts, just as different-appearing houses can be constructed from the same bricks.

In physics or in history, it is sometimes appropriate to sit back and review what has been done. And that is what I tried to do in this book. I have examined the work of previous researchers and tried to show a different way of looking at their findings.

Like a scientist, I do not thereby guarantee that the findings of previous researchers are true (though I certainly have presented nothing that I feel to be false). If those findings are true, however, then I believe this book explains them well.

Some readers may frown at my decision to do a review. They may believe that I should have duplicated the research already done by hundreds of historians who have preceded my own study of the cold war. I found, however, that so much data had accumulated that it was time for someone to review it. If someone finds my interpretations and conclusions provocative, that person is welcome to verify the raw data compiled by previous researchers and thereby confirm the facts on which my argument is based.

Although my findings stand on the foundation painstakingly constructed by previous workers, my book is certainly no rehash of cold war history, any more than Einstein's theories were a rehash of physics.

The following list includes only books cited in the notes, not every reference consulted while writing this volume. Traditionally one is supposed to cite only hardback editions of books, but paperbacks are common, even in academic libraries. So I have dispensed with that tradition.

Abel, Elie. *The Missile Crisis*. 1966. Reprint. New York: Bantam Books, 1966.

Aguilar, Luis E. *Cuba 1933: Prologue to Revolution*. Ithaca, N.Y.: Cornell University Press, 1972.

Alexander, Bevin. *Korea: The First War We Lost*. New York: Hippocene Books, 1986.

Allison, Graham T. *Essence of Decision: Explaining the Cuban Missile Crisis*. Boston: Little, Brown and Company, 1971.

Anderson, Thomas P. *Matanza: El Salvador's Communist Revolt of 1932*. Lincoln, Nebr.: University of Nebraska Press, 1971.

Arnson, Cynthia. *El Salvador: A Revolution Confronts the United States*. Washington, D.C.: Institute for Policy Studies, 1982.

Barnet, Richard J., and Ronald E. Müller. *Global Reach*. New York: Simon and Schuster, 1974.

Barnett, A. Doak. *Communist Strategies in Asia: A Comparative Anal-

ysis of Governments and Parties. New York: Frederick A. Praeger, 1963.

Bergamini, David. *Japan's Imperial Conspiracy.* 1971. Reprint. New York: Pocket Books, 1972.

Bethell, Nicholas. *Gomulka: His Poland, His Communism.* New York: Holt, Rinehart and Winston, 1969.

Bilmanis, Alfred. *A History of Latvia.* 1951. Reprint. Westport, Conn.: Greenwood Press, 1970.

Bolloten, Burnett. *The Grand Camouflage: The Spanish Civil War and Revolution, 1936–39.* 1961. Reprint. New York: Frederick A. Praeger, Publishers, 1968.

Boorstein, Edward. *Allende's Chile.* New York: International Publishers, 1977.

Borkenau, Franz. *World Communism: A History of the Communist International.* 1938. Reprint. Ann Arbor, Michigan: University of Michigan Press, 1962.

Boyle, John Hunter. *China and Japan at War 1937–1945: The Politics of Collaboration.* Stanford, Calif.: Stanford University Press, 1972.

Brisch, Hans, and Ivan Volgyes, eds. *Czechoslovakia: The Heritage of Ages Past: Essays in Memory of Josef Korbel.* East European Monographs, no. 51. Boulder, Colo.: East European Quarterly; New York: Columbia University Press, 1979.

Brown, J. F. *Bulgaria under Communist Rule.* New York: Praeger Publishers, 1970.

Brzezinski, Zbigniew, ed. *Africa and the Communist World.* Stanford, Calif.: Stanford University Press, 1963.

Caldwell, Malcolm, ed. *Ten Years' Military Terror in Indonesia.* [Nottingham]: Spokesman Books, 1975.

Carr, Edward Hallett. *The Comintern and the Spanish Civil War.* London: Macmillan and Company, 1984.

———. *German-Soviet Relations between the Two World Wars, 1919–1939.* Baltimore: Johns Hopkins Press, 1951.

———. *A History of Soviet Russia.* Vols. 1-3, *The Bolshevik Revolution 1917–1923.* New York: Macmillan Company, 1950–53.

———. *A History of Soviet Russia. The Interregnum 1923–1924.* New York: Macmillan Company, 1954.

———. *A History of Soviet Russia.* Vols. 1-3, *Socialism in One Country 1924–1926.* New York: Macmillan Company, 1958–64.

———. *The Twilight of Comintern, 1930–1935.* London: Macmillan Press, 1982.

Casuso, Teresa. *Cuba and Castro.* Translated by Elmer Grossberg. New York: Random House, 1961.

Christian, Shirley. *Nicaragua: Revolution in the Family*. 1985. Reprint. New York: Vintage Books, 1986.

Chung, Manduk. "The United States in Korea: A Reluctant Participant, 1945–1948." Ph.D. diss. Michigan State University, 1975.

Churchill, Winston S. *The Second World War*. Vol. 6, *Triumph and Tragedy*. Boston: Houghton Mifflin Company, 1953.

Claudin, Fernando. *The Communist Movement: From Comintern to Cominform*. Translated by Brian Pearce. 1970. Reprint. New York: Monthly Review Press, 1975.

Clutterbuck, Richard L. *The Long, Long War: Counterinsurgency in Malaya and Vietnam*. New York: Frederick A. Praeger, 1966.

Cooley, John K. *East Wind over Africa: Red China's African Offensive*. New York: Walker and Company, 1965.

Crankshaw, Edward. *Khrushchev: A Career*. New York: Viking Press, 1966.

Czerwinski, E. J., and Jaroslaw Piekalkiewicz, eds. *The Soviet Invasion of Czechoslovakia: Its Effects on Eastern Europe*. Praeger Special Studies in International Politics and Public Affairs. New York: Praeger Publishers, 1972.

Davis, Nathaniel. *The Last Two Years of Salvador Allende*. Ithaca, New York: Cornell University Press, 1985.

De Riencourt, Amaury. *The American Empire*. 1968. Reprint. New York: Dell Publishing Company, Delta, 1970.

Detzer, David. *The Brink*. New York: Thomas Y. Crowell, 1979.

Dunkerley, James. *The Long War: Dictatorship and Revolution in El Salvador*. London: Junction Books, 1982.

Eisenhower, Dwight D. *Crusade in Europe*. 1948. Reprint. New York: Avon Books, 1968.

———. *Waging Peace 1956–1961*. Garden City, N.Y.: Doubleday and Company, 1965.

Etcheson, Craig. *The Rise and Demise of Democratic Kampuchea*. Boulder, Colo.: Westview Press, 1984.

Eyre, James K., Jr. *The Roosevelt-MacArthur Conflict*. Chambersburg, Pa.: Self-published, 1950.

Fairbank, John K., Edwin O. Reischauer, and Albert M. Craig. *A History of East Asian Civilization*. Vol. 2, *East Asia: The Modern Transformation*. Boston: Houghton Mifflin Company, 1965.

Fehér, Ferenc, and Agnes Heller. *Hungary 1956 Revisited: The Message of a Revolution—A Quarter of a Century after*. London: George Allen and Unwin, 1983.

Feuer, Lewis S. *The Conflict of Generations: The Character and Significance of Student Movements*. New York: Basic Books, 1969.

Finer, Samuel. *The Man on Horseback: The Role of the Military in Politics.* New York: Frederick A. Praeger, 1962.
Fleming, D. F. *The Cold War and Its Origins: 1917–1960.* Garden City, N.Y.: Doubleday and Company, 1961.
Ford, Daniel. *The Button: The Pentagon's Strategic Command and Control System.* New York: Simon and Schuster, 1985.
Fowkes, Ben. *Communism in Germany under the Weimar Republic.* London: Macmillan Press, 1984.
Geiger, Theodore. *Communism Versus Progress in Guatemala.* Washington, D.C.: National Planning Association, 1953.
Gibney, Frank. *The Frozen Revolution, Poland: A Study in Communist Decay.* New York: Farrar, Straus and Cudahy, 1959.
Goldston, Robert. *The Civil War in Spain.* 1966. Reprint. Greenwich, Conn.: Fawcett Publications, 1969.
Goulden, Joseph C. *Korea: The Untold Story of the War.* New York: McGraw-Hill Book Company, 1982.
Greig, Ian. *The Communist Challenge to Africa: An Analysis of Contemporary Soviet, Chinese and Cuban Policies.* Surrey, England: Foreign Affairs Publishing Company, 1977.
Gruber, Helmut. *Soviet Russia Masters the Comintern: International Communism in the Era of Stalin's Ascendancy.* Garden City, N.Y.: Anchor Books, 1974.
Grunberger, Richard. *Red Rising in Bavaria.* London: Arthur Baker, 1973.
Halperin, Ernst. *Nationalism and Communism in Chile.* Center for International Studies, Massachusetts Institute of Technology. Studies in Communism, Revisionism, and Revolution, no. 5. Cambridge, Mass.: The M.I.T. Press, 1965.
Halperin, Maurice. *The Rise and Decline of Fidel Castro: An Essay in Contemporary History.* Berkeley and Los Angeles: University of California Press, 1972.
Hamm, Harry. *Albania—China's Beachhead in Europe.* Translated by Victor Andersen. New York: Frederick A. Praeger, 1963.
Hammond, Thomas T. *Red Flag over Afghanistan: The Communist Coup, the Soviet Invasion, and the Consequences.* Boulder, Colo.: Westview Press, 1984.
Hammond, Thomas T., ed. *The Anatomy of Communist Takeovers.* New Haven, Conn.: Yale University Press, 1975.
Hersh, Seymour M. *The Price of Power: Kissinger in the Nixon White House.* New York: Summit Books, 1983.
Hilsman, Roger. *To Move a Nation: The Politics of Foreign Policy in the Administration of John F. Kennedy.* Garden City, N.Y.: Doubleday and Company, 1967.

Hodgson, John H. *Communism in Finland: A History and Interpretation*. Princeton, N.J.: Princeton University Press, 1967.

Hoover, Herbert. *An American Epic*. Vol. 3, *Famine in Forty-Five Nations: The Battle on the Front Line 1914–1923*. Chicago: Henry Regnery Company, 1961.

―――. *The Ordeal of Woodrow Wilson*. New York: McGraw-Hill Book Company, 1958.

Horne, Alistair. *Small Earthquake in Chile: Allende's South America*. New York: Viking Press, 1972.

Horowitz, David. *Empire and Revolution: A Radical Interpretation of Contemporary History*. New York: Random House, 1969.

―――. *The Free World Colossus*. New York: Hill and Wang, 1965.

Hua Wu Yin. *Class and Communalism in Malaysia: Politics in a Dependent Capitalist State*. London: Zed Books, 1983.

Hyland, William, and Richard Wallace Shryock. *The Fall of Khrushchev*. New York: Funk and Wagnalls, 1968.

Hyman, Anthony. *Afghanistan under Soviet Domination, 1964–83*. New York: St. Martin's Press, 1984.

Jackson, J. Hampden. *Estonia*. London: George Allen and Unwin, 1941.

James, D. Clayton. *The Years of MacArthur*. Vols. 2 and 3. Boston: Houghton Mifflin Company, 1975, 1985.

Johnson, Lyndon Baines. *The Vantage Point: Perspectives of the Presidency*. New York: Holt, Rinehart and Winston, 1971.

Karl Marx and Frederick Engels: Selected Works. New York: International Publishers, 1968.

Karol, K. S. *Guerrillas in Power: The Course of the Cuban Revolution*. Translated by Arnold Pomerans. New York: Hill and Wang, 1970.

Kaufman, Burton I. *The Korean War: Challenges in Crisis, Credibility, and Command*. Philadelphia: Temple University Press, 1986.

Kennan, George F. *On Dealing with the Communist World*. New York: Harper and Row, 1964.

―――. *Russia and the West under Lenin and Stalin*. Boston: Little, Brown and Company, Atlantic Monthly Press, 1960.

Kennedy, Robert F. *Thirteen Days: A Memoir of the Cuban Missile Crisis*. New York: W. W. Norton and Company, 1969.

[Khrushchev, Nikita S.] *Khrushchev Remembers*. 1970. Reprint. Translated and edited by Strobe Talbott. New York: Bantam Books, 1971.

Klinghoffer, Arthur Jay. *The Angolan War: A Study in Soviet Policy in the Third World*. Westview Special Studies on Africa. Boulder, Colo.: Westview Press, 1980.

Koliopoulos, John S. *Greece and the British Connection 1935–1941*. Oxford: Oxford University Press, 1977.
Kolkowicz, Roman. *The Soviet Military and the Communist Party*. Princeton, N.J.: Princeton University Press, 1967.
Komisar, Lucy. *Corazon Aquino: The Story of a Revolution*. New York: George Braziller, 1987.
Kotch, John Barry. "United States Security Policy toward Korea 1945–1953: The Origins and Evolution of American Involvement and the Emergence of a National Security Commitment." Ph.D. diss., Columbia University, 1976.
Krock, Arthur. *Memoirs: Sixty Years on the Firing Line*. 1968. Reprint. New York: Popular Library, 1968.
Kurzman, Dan. *Subversion of the Innocents: Patterns of Communist Penetration in Africa, the Middle East, and Asia*. New York: Random House, 1963.
Lampe, John R. *The Bulgarian Economy in the Twentieth Century*. Croom Helm Series on the Contemporary Economic History of Europe. London: Croom Helm, 1986.
Laqueur, Walter. *Guerrilla: A Historical and Critical Study*. Boston: Little, Brown and Company, 1976.
Larson, David L., ed. *The "Cuban Crisis" of 1962: Selected Documents and Chronology*. Boston: Houghton Mifflin Company, 1963.
Leckie, Robert. *Conflict: The History of the Korean War, 1950–1953*. New York: Avon Books, 1962.
Lee, Chong-Sik. *Revolutionary Struggle in Manchuria: Chinese Communism and Soviet Interest, 1922–1945*. Berkeley and Los Angeles: University of California Press, 1983.
Lee, U-Gene. "American Policy towards Korea, 1942–1947: Formulation and Execution." Ph.D. diss., Georgetown University, 1973.
Legum, Colin. *Congo Disaster*. Harmondsworth, Middlesex [London]: Penguin Books, 1961.
Lendvai, Paul. *Eagles in Cobwebs: Nationalism and Communism in the Balkans*. Garden City, N.Y.: Doubleday and Company, 1969.
Lomax, Bill. *Hungary 1956*. London: Allen and Busby, 1976.
Lomax, Louis E. *Thailand: The War That Is, the War That Will Be*. New York: Random House, 1967.
Lord, Robert Howard. *The Second Partition of Poland: A Study in Diplomatic History*. Harvard Historical Studies, vol. 23. Cambridge, Mass.: Harvard University Press, 1915.
Loveman, Brian. *Chile: The Legacy of Hispanic Capitalism*. New York: Oxford University Press, 1979.

Lukacs, John. *A New History of the Cold War*. 3rd ed. Garden City, N.Y.: Doubleday and Company, 1966.

MacArthur, Douglas. *Reminiscences*. 1964. Reprint. Greenwich, Conn.: Fawcett Publications, 1965.

McCann, Thomas P. *An American Company: The Tragedy of United Fruit*. Edited by Henry Scammell. New York: Crown Publishers, 1976.

McGovern, James. *To the Yalu: From the Chinese Invasion of Korea to MacArthur's Dismissal*. New York: William Morrow and Company, 1972.

Manchester, William. *American Caesar: Douglas MacArthur 1880–1964*. Boston: Little Brown and Company, 1978.

Marchetti, Victor, and John D. Marks. *The CIA and the Cult of Intelligence*. New York: Alfred A. Knopf, 1974.

Mattern, Carolyn J. "The Man on the Dark Horse: The Presidential Campaigns for General Douglas MacArthur, 1944 and 1948." Ph.D. diss., University of Wisconsin—Madison, 1976.

Matthews, Herbert L. *Revolution in Cuba: An Essay in Understanding*. New York: Charles Scribner's Sons, 1975.

Matthews, Kenneth. *Memories of a Mountain War Greece: 1944–1949*. London: Longman, 1972.

Mayer, Milton. *The Art of the Impossible: A Study of the Czech Resistance*. A Center Occasional Paper, vol. 2, no. 3. Santa Barbara, Calif.: Center for the Study of Democratic Institutions/ Fund for the Republic, 1969.

Meray, Tibor. *Thirteen Days That Shook the Kremlin*. Translated by Howard L. Katzander. New York: Frederick A. Praeger, 1959.

Miller, Harry. *Jungle War in Malaya: The Campaign against Communism 1948–60*. London: Arthur Baker, 1972.

Molnár, Miklós. *Budapest 1956: A History of the Hungarian Revolution*. Translated by Jennetta Ford. London: George Allen and Unwin, 1971.

Montgomery, Tommie Sue. *Revolution in El Salvador: Origins and Evolution*. Boulder, Colo.: Westview Press, 1982.

Morris, William George. "The Korean Trusteeship, 1941–1947: The United States, Russia, and the Cold War." Ph.D. diss., University of Texas at Austin, 1974.

Nissen, Henrik S., ed. *Scandinavia during the Second World War*. Minneapolis: University of Minnesota Press, 1983.

North, Liisa. *Bitter Grounds: Roots of Revolt in El Salvador*. Toronto: Between the Lines, 1981.

O'Ballance, Edgar. *The Greek Civil War 1944–1949*. New York: Frederick A. Praeger, 1966.

Overstreet, Gene D., and Marshall Windmiller. *Communism in India*. Berkeley and Los Angeles: University of California Press, 1959.

Polonsky, Antony and Boleslaw Drukier. *The Beginnings of Communist Rule in Poland*. London: Routledge and Kegan Paul, 1980.

Powers, Thomas. *The Man Who Kept the Secrets: Richard Helms and the CIA*. New York: Alfred A. Knopf, 1979.

Prados, John. *Presidents' Secret Wars: CIA and Pentagon Covert Operations since World War II*. New York: William Morrow and Company, 1986.

Rees, David. *Korea: The Limited War*. New York: St. Martin's Press, 1964.

Remington, Robin Alison, ed. *Winter in Prague: Documents on Czechoslovak Communism in Crisis*. Center for International Studies, Massachusetts Institute of Technology. Studies in Communism, Revisionism, and Revolution, no. 14. Cambridge, Mass.: M.I.T. Press, 1969.

Ridgway, Matthew B. *Soldier: The Memoirs of Matthew B. Ridgway*. New York: Harper and Brothers, 1956.

Rings, Werner. *Life with the Enemy: Collaboration and Resistance in Hitler's Europe 1939–1945*. Translated by J. Maxwell Brownjohn. Garden City, N.Y.: Doubleday and Company, 1982.

Rodriguez, Mario Menendez. *Voices from El Salvador*. San Francisco: Solidarity Publications, 1983.

Rosental, Mario. *Guatemala*. New York: Twayne Publishers, Inc., 1962.

Roucek, Joseph S. *The Politics of the Balkans*. New York: McGraw-Hill Book Company, 1939.

Russell, Charles Edward. *Bolshevism and the United States*. Indianapolis, Indiana: Bobbs-Merrill Company, 1919.

Salomon, Michel. *Prague Notebook: The Strangled Revolution*. Translated by Helen Eustis. Boston: Little, Brown and Company, 1971.

Scalapino, Robert A., ed. *The Communist Revolution in Asia: Tactics, Goals and Achievements*. 2nd ed. Englewood Cliffs, N.J.: Prentice-Hall, 1969.

Schatten, Fritz. *Communism in Africa*. New York: Frederick A. Praeger, 1966.

Schlesinger, Arthur M., Jr. *The Bitter Heritage: Vietnam and American Democracy 1941–1966*. 1966. Reprint. New York: Fawcett World Library, 1967.

———. *A Thousand Days: John F. Kennedy in the White House*. Boston: Houghton Mifflin Company, 1965.

Schneider, Ronald M. *Communism in Guatemala 1944–1954.* New York: Frederick A. Praeger, 1958.
Schofield, John M. *46 Years in the Army.* New York: Century Company, 1897.
Schwartz, Harry. *Prague's 200 Days.* New York: Frederick A. Praeger, 1969.
Seton-Watson, Hugh. *The East European Revolution.* New York: Frederick A. Praeger, 1951.
———. *From Lenin to Khrushchev: The History of World Communism.* New York: Frederick A. Praeger, 1960.
Shawcross, William. *Dubcek.* London: Weidenfeld and Nicolson, 1970.
Short, Anthony. *The Communist Insurrection in Malaya 1948–1960.* London: Frederick Muller, 1975.
Smith, Robert. *MacArthur in Korea: The Naked Emperor.* New York: Simon and Schuster, 1982.
Snow, Edgar. *The Pattern of Soviet Power.* New York: Random House, 1945.
Sobel, Lester A., ed. *Chile and Allende.* New York: Facts on File, 1974.
Sorensen, Theodore C. *Kennedy.* New York: Harper and Row, 1965.
Southwood, Julie, and Patrick Flanagan. *Indonesia: Law, Propaganda and Terror.* London: Zed Press, 1983.
Starr, Richard F. *The Communist Regimes in Eastern Europe.* 2d rev. ed. Stanford, Calif.: Hoover Institution on War, Revolution and Peace, 1971.
Stevens, Christopher. *The Soviet Union and Black Africa.* London: Macmillan Press, 1976.
Stockwell, John. *In Search of Enemies: A CIA Story.* New York: W. W. Norton and Company, 1978.
Stone, I. F. *The Hidden History of the Korean War.* 1952. Reprint. New York: Monthly Review Press, 1971.
Stueck, William Whitney, Jr. *The Road to Confrontation: American Policy toward China and Korea, 1947–1950.* Chapel Hill, N.C.: University of North Carolina Press, 1981.
Suh, Dae-Sook. *The Korean Communist Movement 1918–1948.* Princeton, N.J.: Princeton University Press, 1967.
Sulzberger, Cyrus L. *A Long Row of Candles: Memoirs and Diaries 1934–1954.* New York: Macmillan Company, 1969.
Svitak, Ivan. *The Czechoslovak Experiment 1968–1969.* New York: Columbia University Press, 1971.
Szulc, Tad. *Fidel: A Critical Portrait.* New York: William Morrow and Company, 1986.

Taber, Robert. *M-26: Biography of a Revolution.* New York: Lyle Stuart, 1961.
Tanham, George K. *Trial in Thailand.* New York: Crane, Russak and Company, 1974.
Tatu, Michel. *Power in the Kremlin: Khrushchev to Kosygin.* New York: Viking Press, 1969.
Thomas, Hugh. *Cuba: The Pursuit of Freedom.* New York: Harper and Row, 1971.
Tigrid, Pavel. *Why Dubcek Fell.* Translated by Pavel Tigrid and Lucy Lawrence. London: Macdonald, 1971.
Tökés, Rudolf. *Béla Kun and the Hungarian Soviet Republic: The Origins and Role of the Communist Party of Hungary in the Revolutions of 1918–1919.* New York: Frederick A. Praeger, 1967.
Toland, John. *The Rising Sun: The Decline and Fall of the Japanese Empire.* 1970. Reprint. New York: Bantam Books, 1971.
Truman, Harry S. *Years of Trial and Hope, 1946–1952.* Garden City, N.Y.: Doubleday and Company, 1956.
Turner, Robert F. *Vietnamese Communism: Its Origins and Development.* Hoover Institution Publications, no. 143. Stanford, Calif.: Hoover Institution Press, 1975.
Williams, William Appleman. *America Confronts a Revolutionary World: 1776–1976.* New York: William Morrow and Company, 1976.

———. *American-Russian Relations 1781–1947.* New York: Rinehart and Company, 1952.
Windsor, Philip, and Adam Roberts. *Czechoslovakia 1968: Reform, Repression and Resistance.* New York: Columbia University Press, 1969.
Wise, David, and Thomas B. Ross. *The Invisible Government.* New York: Random House, 1964.
Wolfers, Michael, and Jane Bergerol. *Angola in the Frontline.* London: Zed Press, 1983.
Wright, J. B. *Zaire since Independence.* Conflict Study, no. 153. London: Institute for the Study of Conflict, 1983.
Zartman, William, ed. *Czechoslovakia: Intervention and Impact.* Studies in Peaceful Change, the Center for International Studies, New York University. New York: New York University Press, 1970.
Zeitlin, Maurice, and Robert Scheer. *Cuba: Tragedy In Our Hemisphere.* New York: Grove Press, 1963.
Zeman, Z. A. B. *Prague Spring.* New York: Hill and Wang, 1969.

Index

Accessory Transit Company, 332
Acheson, Dean, 145, 227
Adams, John Quincy, 370
Adoula, Cyrille, 260
Afghanistan, 179, 307–14, 350, 362
Africa, 253–54, 261–63, 297
Aidit, Dipa Nusantara, 173
Albania, 115–18, 277
Albatrosswerke, 46
Algeria, 335, 351
Allende Gossens, Salvador, x, 243–51
Alessandri Rodríguez, Jorge, 244
Alexander II (Russia), 107
Alexander Joseph (Bulgaria), 107
Alexeev, Mikhail, 10
Almond, Edward, 156
Amanollah Khan, 309, 311, 316
American Relief Administration, 12, 23–24
Amin, Hafizullah, 313
Anaconda Company, 243, 245–46, 393 (n. 31)
Anders, Wladyslaw, 87
Andropov, Yury, 199, 274
Anglo-Persian Oil Company, 116
Angola, 231, 297–302, 305, 352, 362
Aquino, Benigno, 172
Aquino, Corazon, 163–65, 172, 249
Arana, Francisco J., 235
Arbenz Guzmán, Jacobo, 235–241, 247
Arciszewski, Tomasz, 87
Arévalo, Juan José, 235
Argentina, 231, 252, 350
Associated Press, 232
Augustus III (Poland), 25
Australia, 283
Austria, 26–27, 113, 121–22, 125, 350

Azerbaijan, Autonomous Republic of, 317–18

Baghdad Pact. *See* Central Treaty Organization
Baker, Newton, 12
Baltic States, 61–80. *See also* specific countries
  absorption by U.S.S.R., 74–75
Barbados, 232
Batista y Zaldívar, Fulgencio, 204–10, 213, 252
Baudouin (Belgium), 255
Bay of Pigs invasion. *See* Cuba, Bay of Pigs
Belgium, 26, 254–258, 361
Belize, 241
Beneš, Edvard, 264, 266
Beria, Lavrenty, 187, 197
Berlin, Treaty of, 101
Bethell, Nicholas, 192
Bethlehem Steel, 213
Bezobrazov, A. M., 138
Birman, A., 272
Bismarck, Otto von, 308
Bloem und Voss, 46
Boehm, Walter, 23
Boise Cascade Corporation, 245
Bolivia, 251, 351
Bonsal, Philip, 210
Borkenau, Franz, 71
Borodin, Mikhail, 36
Boxer Rebellion, 138
Bradley, Omar, 150–51, 155
Brandt, Willy, 336
Braun, Otto, 130–31
Brest-Litovsk, Treaty of, 11–13, 17, 19, 54, 64, 67
Britain. *See* Great Britain
British Honduras. *See* Belize

413

Brazil, 251–52, 350–51
Brezhnev Doctrine, 351
Brezhnev, Leonid, 270, 272–73, 275–76
Brown, J. F., 110
Broz, Josip. *See* Tito
Brzezinski, Zbigniew, 260, 262, 344, 376
Bukharin, Nikolay Ivanovich, 179
Bulganin, Nikolay, 190
Bulgaria, 98, 107–11, 196, 271, 276, 350
  Sofia cathedral bombing, 108
  World War I, 107
  World War II, 108–109
Bundy, McGeorge, 221, 223
Burma, 166–168, 182, 350
Byrnes, James F., 360

Cabell, C. P., 210
Cabot, John M., 239
Caetano, Marcello, 298
Cairo Conference, 140
Caldwell, John, 14
Cambodia, 279, 282, 286–91, 362
Cameroon, 262
Capehart, Homer, 226
Carol II (Romania), 103
Carr, Edward Hallett, 179
Carter, Jimmy, 227, 260, 335, 344, 362
Caspian Sea, 314–15
Castillo Armas, Carlos, 240–41
Castro Ruz, Fidel, 203–04, 207–220, 222, 226, 229–33, 247, 251, 262, 281, 301, 305, 352
Ceaușescu, Nicolae, 103, 271, 277
CENTO. *See* Central Treaty Organization
Central Intelligence Agency
  Burma, 166
  Cambodia, 288
  Chile, 247
  Cuba, 210–13, 215, 217
  Guatemala, 240
  Indonesia, 172
  Laos, 291–92
Central Treaty Organization, 309–10

Cerro Corporation, 243, 246
Céspedes y Quesada, Carlos Manuel de, 204
Chamberlain, Neville, 93
Chang Tso-lin, 39
Chase National Bank, 204, 357
Chernyshevsky, Nikolay, 6
Chiang Kai-shek, 134–36, 178, 354
  Burma, 166–67
  Germany, 130
  Japan, 131
  Korea, 150, 154, 157
  Mongolia, 130
  Tibet, 181–82
  U.S.S.R., 35–40, 132–34
  Vietnam, 281
Chibas, Eduardo, 206
Chile, x, 234, 237, 242–52, 351
China, 34–40, 138, 248, 302, 350, 352–53, 362, 366. *See also* Sino-Soviet split.
  and Burma, 166–68
  Cambodia, 290
  Communists, 34–38, 129–36, 147
  India, 181–84, 387
  Korea, 150–55
  Laos, 293
  nationalists, 35
  Tibet, 181–82
  Vietnam, 281–83
Chinese Eastern Railway, 132
Chomón, Faure, 216
Chu Teh, 34
Churchill, Winston, 126, 358, 360
  and Greece, 93–97, 99–100, 110
  Hitler, 48
  Poland, 85–90
  Romania, 105
Chrysler, 232
CIA. *See* Central Intelligence Agency
Clay, Lucius, 123, 359
Clifford, Clark, 105
Coca-Cola, 239
Collins, J. Lawton, 154
Colombia, 251, 351

Comintern, 110, 178
  Anti-Comintern Pact, 49
  China, 36, 39, 130, 133
  Iran, 317
  Korea, 139
  Germany, 29, 48
  Mexico, 177
  Romania, 103
  Spain, 54
  Vietnam, 280
Communism. *See also* National self-determination; "socialism in one country"
  early, 2–6
  non-monolithic, x, 114
  peaceful coexistence, 114, 118, 125, 352
  "scientific" basis, 4
  varieties, x
  wars of liberation, 113–14, 118, 352–53
  world revolution, ix–x, 17, 30, 43, 45, 50, 230, 232, 295, 349–55
Communist Manifesto, 1–3
Communist parties of Latin America, 205–206, 251–52
Congo, 254–61, 298, 301, 350, 352
Congo International Management Corporation, 259
Congress of Oppressed Nationalities, 178
Congress of Vienna, 26
Connally, Tom, 145
Conrad, Joseph, 254
Constantine I (Greece), 92
Cooley, John K., 261
Coolidge, Calvin, 204
Corcoran, Thomas G., 240
Costa Rica, 331, 335
Counterinsurgency tactics, 161–62, 169–70
Crimean War, 101
Cuba, 203–33, 331
  and Angola, 299–302, 352
  Bay of Pigs invasion, 210, 213, 217–18, 220, 334, 389 (n. 23)
  Communist Party, 205–207, 210–12, 214, 217, 229–30
  El Salvador, 346–47
  Ethiopia, 304–306
  military interventions by, 231
  missile crisis, 218–29, 262, 353, 363–64
  Nicaragua, 334–35
Cuban-American Sugar Company, 204
Cuban Electric Company, 205, 212
Cuban Telephone Company, 212
Curzon Line, 83, 85, 88
Cyrankiewicz, Józef, 189–90
Czechoslovakia, 125, 264–67, 304, 313, 350
  and Germany, 49, 83, 295
  Guatemala, 240
  Hungary, 23
  Poland, 83
  Somalia, 304–305
  Soviet invasion, 264, 267–78, 328, 351

Daniel, Clifton, 317
Daud Khan, Mohammad, 311
Democracy, 165–66, 370, 377
Denikin, Anton Ivanovich, 15, 315
Dewey, Thomas, 149
Dictatorship, 370–71
Dillon, Douglas, 227
Dimitrov, Georgi, 109–10
Diplomatic corps class loyalty, 106
Dobrynin, Anatoly, 225
Dominican Republic, 212, 252, 313, 351
Domino theory, 286
Dorticos Torrado, Osvaldo, 216
Dōst Moḥammad, 307
Droller, Frank, 210
D'Aubuisson, Robert, 345
Duarte, José Napoleón, 345, 347
Dubček, Alexander, 269–78
Dubs, Adolph, 311
Dulles, Allen, 211, 213, 215, 240, 288

Dulles, John Foster, 157, 172, 240, 283–84, 288, 309
Dunkerley, James, 346
DuPont, 357

East Germany. *See* Germany, East
Ecuador, 252
Egypt, 222, 261–62, 304, 351
Eisenhower, Dwight, 215, 236, 359
 Congo, 259
 Cuba, 211, 217
 Guatemala, 240
 Korea, 157
 Vietnam, 284
El Salvador, 237, 252, 331, 339–48, 350
 and Cuba, 232, 340
Elizabeth II (Great Britain), 232
Engels, Friedrich, 19, 34, 122, 379
 biographical, 1–2
 Romania, 101
England. *See* Great Britain
Equatorial Guinea, 262
Estonia, 62, 65–69, 72, 78–79, 81, 349–50
Ethiopia, 297, 302–306, 308, 362
Europe, World War I aftermath, 18–19
Europe, Eastern, 191, 352, 362. *See also* specific countries
 Churchill-Stalin deal, 91–92, 98–99, 101, 105, 111, 114–15, 118, 121, 191, 358–59
 economic exploitation, 106, 111
 Russia and World War I, 17, 126–27
 post-World War II, 51, 125–28

Ferdinand I (Bulgaria), 107
Fiat, 245
Finland, 196, 349–50, 362
 civil war, 70–72
 Continuation War, 75–76
 independence, 69–71, 78–79

Poland, 81
Winter War, 72–74
Fleming, D. F., 15, 89, 120, 201
Ford Foundation, 299
Ford Motor Company, 232, 245, 357
Forrestal, James, 360
Fort Leavenworth, 354
Frachet d'Esperey, Louis-Félix-Marie-François, 21
France, 265, 283, 301, 350, 361
 and Czechoslovakia, 267, 271
 Finland, 73–74
 Germany, 123
 Hungary, 21–23
 Indochina, 279–82, 284–85, 287, 291, 295
 Iran, 315
 Poland, 25–28, 45, 63, 81–83
 Romania, 102
 Spain, 53–54
 U.S.S.R., 11, 83
Franco, Francisco, 52–53, 59, 232
Francis, David, 8–9
Frei Montalva, Eduardo, 245–46
Friedrich Karl (Finland), 71
Fulbright, William, 223

Gandhi, Mohandas, 177–79, 184
Geiger, Theodore, 238–39
General Electric, 357
General Motors, 232
George II (Greece), 92–96
Germany, 26, 28–29, 332, 371
 Berlin, 224
 Berlin blockade, 123—25
 Communist revolts, 20, 29–30
 and Lithuania, 63
 nonaggression pact with U.S.S.R., 47, 49–50, 64, 66, 72–73, 83, 205
 rearmament, 46–47
 U.S.S.R., 19, 41–42, 45–50, 72–73, 82–83
 World War I aftermath, 19–21, 29–30
 World War II aftermath, 121–25

INDEX ■ 417

Germany, East, 125, 185, 192, 224, 276
Germany, West, 123–25, 158, 271, 301
Gerö, Ernö, 188, 193–94, 202
Ghana, 351
Gheorghiu-Dej, Gheorghe, 196
Giap, Vo Nguyen, 281
Gierek, Edward, 323–24, 326
Gīlān, Republic of, 315–16
Gilpatric, Roswell, 222
Gittings, John, 363
Glassman, Jon, 346
Golikov, F. I., 220
Goltz, Rüdiger von der, 65, 67, 71
Gomulka, Wladyslaw, 87, 189–90, 192–93, 196, 202, 275, 322–23, 325
Gorbachev, Mikhail, 314, 354, 365
Gordiyevsky, Oleg, 363
Gordon, Charles George, 308
Gottwald, Klement, 265, 268
Gough, Hubert, 68
Goulart, João, 251
Grace, W. R., company, 239
Grau San Martín, Ramón, 204–206
Great Britain, 108, 121, 123–24, 159, 241, 267, 282–83, 291, 297, 301–302, 304, 307–10, 350, 361
  and Estonia, 67–68
  Finland, 73
  Iran, 315–18
  Poland, 26, 28
  Russian Revolution, 10–11
  U.S.S.R., 83
Grechko, Andrey, 273
Greece, 92, 113, 146
  and Bulgaria, 108
  civil war, 94–101, 350, 360
  World War II, 92–101
Grenada, 313, 351
Grenville, Lord William Wyndham, 26
Grotewohl, Otto, 196
Groves, Leslie, 236

Guatemala, 234–42, 244, 331, 334, 340, 350, 389 (n. 23), 392 (n. 11)
Guevara, Alfredo, 207
Guevara de la Serna, Ernesto "Che," 210
Guinea, 261–62
Guiteras Holmes, Antonio, 205
Gulf of Tonkin, 286
Gulf Oil, 300
Gutiérrez, Gustavo, 343
Guyana, 232

Habībollāh Khan, 309
Haig, Alexander, 345–46
Haile Selassie, 297, 303
Hammarskjöld, Dag, 257, 260
Harriman, W. Averell, 359
Harris, A. R., 349–50
Harsch, Joseph, 120
Havana University, 204–208
Hayden, Stone company, 215
Helms, Richard, 247
Hevia, Carlos, 205–206
Hilsman, Roger, 222, 226
Hirohito (Japan), 361, 376
Hitler, Adolf, 45, 47–50, 53–56, 66, 75–76, 83, 90, 93, 103, 108, 126, 235, 267, 290, 294–95, 316, 322, 361, 371, 376
Ho Chi Minh, 279–83, 286, 288, 291, 293
Hodge, John, 140, 142
Honduras, 331, 335, 338, 341
Hong Kong, 124
Hoover, Herbert, 8, 12, 23–24, 27, 64–65, 71, 102, 357
Hoxha, Enver, 117
Hsü Shu-tseng, 32–33
Hugenberg, Alfred, 48
Hungary, 118, 276, 313, 326, 350
  revolt of 1956, 185–88, 193–202, 271–72, 274, 328
  World War I aftermath, 21—24
  World War II, 118–19
  World War II aftermath, 119–21
Hurley, Patrick, 134

Hussain, Ghulam, 179
Hyman, Anthony, 308

Ibáñez del Campo, Carlos, 244
Ileo, Joseph, 259
India, 177–84, 302, 309–10, 350–51, 362
Indian Ocean, 304–306
Indonesia, 170–75, 222, 350–51
International Court of Justice, 338
International Harvester, 16, 213, 357
International Railways of Central America, 239
International Telephone and Telegraph, 246–47, 393 (n. 31)
Iran, 179, 307–308, 310, 314–20, 350
Iraq, 310, 320
Islam, 170, 320–21
Israel, 29, 231
Italian Railways, 116
Italy, 92–93, 95, 113, 116, 118, 265, 304, 314–15
ITT. *See* International Telephone and Telegraph

Jadwiga (Poland), 61
Jamaica, 232, 351
Japan, 15, 158–60, 171, 220, 281, 332
  and Germany, 49
  Korea, 151
  Mongolia, 32
Jaruzelski, Wojciech, 327
Jefferson, Thomas, 353
Jemal Pasha, 309
Johnson, Andrew, 242
Johnson, Louis, 150, 360
Johnson, Lyndon, 285–88
Junkers, 46

Kádár, János, 194–96, 199–201
Kaledin, Alexei, 10
Kania, Stanislaw, 326–28
Kaganovich, Lazar, 192, 197
Kamenev, Lev Borisovich, 82
Karmal, Babrak, 311–13

Kasavubu, Joseph, 255–56, 258–60
Kashmir, 182
Katyn massacre, 84–85
Kautsky, Karl, 20
Kazan University, 6
Keating, Kenneth, 226
Kennan, George F., 145, 349, 356
Kennecott corporation, 243, 246, 393 (n. 31)
Kennedy, John F., 247
  Cuba, 215, 217–19, 221–29, 363
  Laos, 292
  Vietnam, 285–86
Kennedy, Robert, 225
Kennet, Lord, 336
Kent State University, 289
Kenya, 262
Kerala, 180–81, 183–84, 244
Kerensky, Aleksandr, 7–8, 44, 52, 61–62, 66, 70, 78
KGB secret police, 274, 276, 363
Khrushchev, Nikita, 145–46, 214, 272, 392 (n. 11)
  Congo, 257
  Cuba, 218–20, 223–26, 229
  Czechoslovakia, 268
  Hungary, 186–87, 196–99, 201
  peaceful coexistence, 57, 118
  Poland, 191–92, 196
Kim Il-sung, 143–46
Kipling, Rudyard, 368
Kissinger, Henry, 246–47, 376
Kolchak, Aleksandr, 15–16
Kolkowicz, Roman, 198
Konev, Ivan, 192
Kong Le, 292
Kopp company, 46
Korea, 137–58, 182, 284–85, 295, 302, 350–51, 384 (n. 12)
Korea, North, 298–99, 302, 335
Korry, Edward, 246
Kosygin, Aleksey, 272–73, 276
Krupp, 46
Kun, Béla, 22–24, 29, 119–20, 186
Kuomintang, 34–39, 131–33, 136, 178

Kurdish People's Republic, 317–18
Kurzman, Dan, 259
Kuwait, 319–20

Lansing, Robert, 9–10, 12, 204
Laos, 279, 287, 291–93
Largo Caballero, Francisco, 57–58
Latvia, 62, 64–66, 78–79, 81, 349–50
Leahy, William, 88–89
Lebrun-Tondu, Pierre Henri, 26
Leigh Guzmán, Gustavo, 250
Lend Lease program, 361
Lendvai, Paul, 108
Lenin, Vladimir Ilich, 186, 353, 364–65, 379
  Baltic states, 79
  biographical, 6
  colonies, 177–78
  China, 35–36, 132
  democracy, 5
  Estonia, 68
  Finland, 79
  "German agent," 10, 13
  Poland, 28
  and Stalin, 43
Leopold II (Belgium), 254
Leszczyński, Stanislaw, 25
Liberation theology, 163, 343
Liberman, Yevsey, 272
Libya, 261
Lilienthal, David, 367
Lithuania, 61–64, 78–79, 81, 83
Little Entente, 191, 271
Liu Shao-chi, 34
Lloyd, Lord, 49
Lloyd George, David, 10
Lon Nol, 288–89
Londonderry, Marquess of, 48
Louis XV (France), 25
Lukacs, John, 192, 370
Lumumba, Patrice, 255–60
Luxemburg, Rosa, 20–21
Lvov, Georgy Yevgenyevich, 7–8

MacArthur, Douglas, 144–45, 147–58, 160, 171, 236, 362, 385 (n. 49)

McCann, Thomas P., 240
McCarthy, Joseph, 147, 238–39
McCone, John, 221, 247
Macedonia, 98, 107, 109
Machado y Morales, Gerardo, 204, 207, 209
Macías Nguema, Francisco, 262
McMahon Line, 167, 182
McNamara, Robert, 222, 285
Magsaysay, Ramón, 161–62, 165
Malaya, 168–70, 351
Malaysia, 286
Malenkov, Georgy, 197–98
Malinovsky, Rodion, 273
Mao Tse-tung, 34, 38, 118, 129–36, 144, 178, 182, 280
Marcos, Ferdinand, 162–65, 249
Marinello, Juan, 205
Marshall, George, 144
Marshall Plan, 361
Martí, Agustín Farabundo, 340–41
Martin, Joseph, 155
Marx, Karl, 19, 31, 34, 122, 343
  biographical, 1
  Romania, 101
Masaryk, Tomáš, 267
Matthews, Francis, 360
Matthews, Kenneth, 98
Melendez family, 341
Mendés-France, Pierre, 285
Mendieta, Carlos, 205
Merriam, William R., 247
Metaxas, Ioannis, 92–93
Mexico, 53, 177, 208, 234, 340
Michael (Romania), 105
Mikolajczyk, Stanislaw, 85, 87–88
Mikoyan, Anastas, 192–93, 195–96, 199
Military culture, 191, 197–98, 236–37, 274, 354, 372–73, 391 (n.5)
Mindszenty, József, 120
Mobutu, Joseph, 259–60, 298
Molotov, Vyacheslav, 192, 197
Mohammad Reza Pahlavi, 317, 319
Mohammed Zahir Shah, 309, 314
Molina, Pedro, 234–35

Moncada, José María, 333
Mongolia, 31–34, 36, 129–30
Morocco, 299
Moskalenko, K. S., 220
Munich Pact, 83, 267, 294–95
Mussolini, Benito, 53, 116, 303

Nāder Khān, 309
Nagy, Imre, 186–88, 193–96, 199–202, 271
Najibullah, Sayid Mohammed, 313–14
Napoleon I (France), 26
National Planning Association, 238–39
National Security Council, 145, 246
National self-determination, 10, 76–80
NATO. See North Atlantic Treaty Organization
Ne Win, 167
Negrín, Juan, 58
Nehru, Jawaharlal, 171, 177–80, 184
Netherlands, 159, 170–72, 349
Neto, António Agostinho, 298–99
New Zealand, 283
Nicaragua, 252, 319, 331–39, 344, 348, 389 (n.23)
  and Cuba, 232, 334–35
Nicholas II (Russia), 7, 14, 17, 27, 32–33, 61, 69–70, 78, 127, 181, 315, 357
Nigeria, 261
Nixon, Richard, 156
  Cambodia, 287–89
  Chile, 246–47
  Cuba, 209–11, 213
  Vietnam, 284, 287
Noli, Fan, 116
North American Aerospace Defense Command, 368
North Atlantic Treaty Organization, 257, 283, 301, 304, 310, 361–62, 369, 373
North Korea. See Korea, North
Norway, 350

Novotný, Antonín, 268–69
Nowak, Zenon, 189
Nuclear strategy, 227, 364–70
Numayri, Ja'far an-, 262

O'Donnell, Kenneth, 226
Oil, 106, 116, 213–14, 300, 314–16
Osmeña, Sergio, 385 (n.30)
Organization of African Unity, 299
Organization of American States, 214–15, 232, 335, 338
Ovares, Enrique, 207
Overseas Private Investment Corporation, 245–46

Paderewski, Ignacy, 27, 82
Pakistan, 182, 283, 310
Panama, 332, 334
Panama Canal, 332
Papandreou, Georgios, 95–97
Paraguay, 335
Paul VI, Pope, 232
Pearl Harbor attack, 220
Peking University, 34–35
Pelshe, Arvid, 275
Peralta, Azurdia, Enrique, 241
Perle, Richard, 363
Perón, Juan, 231
Persian Gulf, 319–20
Peru, 251–52, 351
Peter II (Yugoslavia), 112
Peterson, Peter, 247
Philippines, 159–66, 283, 286, 316, 350
Phoumi Nosavan, 292
Pilsudski, Józéf, 27, 82
Pinochet Ugarte, Augusto, 250
Pius XII, Pope, 113
Podgorny, Nikolay, 272, 276
Pol Pot, 289–90, 293
Poland, 25–27, 81–83, 271–72, 276, 308, 350
  aggression by, 27–29, 126
  France, 45, 81
  Germany, 28–29, 49–50, 81
  Lithuania, 63

revolt of 1956, 185, 188–93, 201–202, 351
unrest of 1980s, 322, 324–30
World War I aftermath, 27
World War II, 50, 83–89
World War II aftermath, 88–90
Poliansky, Dimitri, 272
Pompidou, Georges, 232
Ponce Vaides, Federico, 235
Poniatowski, Stanislaw, 25
Ponomarev, Boris, 272
Portugal, 297–99, 361, 387
Prasad, Rajendra, 181
Primo de Rivera y Orbaneja, Miguel, 51
Princeton University, 139
Prío Socarrás, Carlos, 208, 211
Puerifoy, John E., 239

Qazi Muhammad, 317
Quiñónez family, 341
Quirino, Elpidio, 160–62

Radhakrishnan, Sarvepalli, 183
Radio Corporation of America, 357
Rákosi, Mátyás, 119, 121, 185, 187–88, 193, 199
RAND Corporation, 198
Rawlinson, Henry, 308
Reagan, Ronald, 175, 227, 232, 241, 320, 324, 336–38, 344–45, 354, 363, 365, 367
Reconstruction Finance Corporation, 357
Red Sea, 303–304
Reza Shah Pahlavi, 316–17
Rhee, Syngman, 139, 141–46, 151, 157–58, 384 (n.12)
Ridgway, Matthew, 156, 284
Riga, Treaty of, 28, 81
Rio Pact, 209
Roberto, Holden, 298–99
Robins, Raymond, 8
Rodgers, William P., 247
Rodríguez, Carlos Rafael, 205
Roman Catholic Church (*See also* Liberation theology)
Cuba, 208–09
El Salvador, 343–45, 348
Hungary, 119–20
Nicaragua, 336, 348
Philippines, 163
Poland, 26, 81–82, 88, 190, 193, 325
Spain, 51
Yugoslavia, 113
Romania, 101–106, 196, 360
and Bulgaria, 108–109
Czechoslovakia, 271–72, 277
invades Hungary, 24
World War I, 101–102
World War II, 103–105
Romero, Oscar Arnulfo, 344, 348
Roosevelt, Franklin, 97, 126, 134, 191, 204, 354, 357, 358
Poland, 85–87
Roy, Manabendra Nath, 177–79, 184, 280
Roxas, Manuel, 160
Rushdie, Salman, 290
Rusk, Dean, 140, 227
Russell, Charles Edward, 14
Russia. *See* Union of Soviet Socialist Republics
Russo-Japanese War, 138, 181
Russo-Turkish War, 101

Sacasa, Juan Bautista, 333
Salazar, Antonio de Oliveira, 297–98
Salonga, Jovito, 165
San Marino, 350
Sanchez, Laura, 337
Sandino, Augusto César, 333–34
Sarria, Pedro, 208
Saudi Arabia, 300, 310
Savimbi, Jonas, 298, 302
Scheer, Robert, 214, 216
Schlesinger, Arthur, Jr., 215–16
Schofield, John, 242–43
SEATO. *See* South-East Asia Treaty Organization
Seeckt, Hans von, 42, 45–46, 81, 130

Semenov, Grigori, 35, 379 (n.5)
Seton-Watson, Hugh, 102
Shāh Shojā, 307
Shelepin, Aleksandr, 272
Shelest, Petr, 274–75
Shell Oil, 214
Shultz, George, 165, 363
Sihanouk, Norodom, 288–90
Šik, Ota, 268–69
Sikorski, Wladyslaw, 85
Singer Sewing Machine, 16
Sino-Soviet split, 114, 129, 178, 183–84, 219, 352–53
Široký, Viliam, 268
Smith, Howard K., 105
Smith, Walter Bedell, 240
Snow, Edgar, 104, 127, 133, 136
"Socialism in one country," 30, 43–45
Socorro, Rojo, 340
Solidarity labor union, 324–29
Somalia, 303–306, 351, 362
Somoza García, Anastasio, 252, 333–34
Somoza Debayle, Anastasio, 334–35
Somoza Debayle, Luis, 334
Sorensen, Theodore, 226
Sosnkowski, Kazimierz, 87
Souphanouvong, 291–93
South Africa, 298–302
South-East Asia Treaty Organization, 283–84, 288, 310
South Vietnam. *See* Vietnam, South
Souvanna Phouma, 291–92
Spain, 159
  civil war, 50–60, 350
Sperry Gyroscope, 357
Sperry Rand, 362
Sri Lanka, 351
Stalin, Joseph, 80, 126, 178, 185–88, 197, 238, 354, 360–61. *See also* "Socialism in one country"
  biographical, 42–43
  China, 34, 38–39, 134
  Greece, 97–101

Hitler, 49–50, 66, 72, 75, 103
Hoxha, 117
India, 179
Korea, 139, 145–46
Malaya, 168
Mongolia, 129–30
Poland, 28, 84–90, 190
Romania, 105
Spain, 54
terrorism, 108
Tito, 112–13, 118
world revolution, 30, 179, 280
Stanislaw I (Poland), 25
Stanislaw II (Poland), 25
Stimson, Henry, 88–89
Standard Oil, 214
Stanley, Henry Morton, 254
Stepinac, Archbishop, 113
Stevens, Christopher, 261
Stockwell, John, 300
Stone, I. F., 153
Strategic Defense Initiative, 365, 367–68
Sudan, 262
Suez Canal, 302
Suharto, 175
Sukarno, 171–75
Sullivan and Cromwell, 240
Sulzberger, C. L., 103, 110, 115
Summers, Maddin, 8, 10
Sun Yat-sen, 32, 34–37, 132, 181
Suslov, Mikhail, 195–96, 199, 272
Syria, 231

Tai Chi-t'ao, 38
Tanzania, 261
Taraki, Nur Mohammad, 311–13
Taylor, Maxwell, 157
Tek, Comrade, 290
Teller, Edward, 376
Texaco, 214
Thailand, 283, 286, 292
Thatcher, Margaret, 175
Thirty Seconds Over Tokyo, 376
Thompson, William Boyce, 8
Tibet, 181–82

INDEX ■ 423

Tikhonov, General, 193
Tito, 54, 112–14, 117–18, 131, 196
  Czechoslovakia, 271
  Greece, 98–100
Togliatti, Palmiro, 54
Toriello, Jorge, 235
Trinidad and Tobago, 232
Trotsky, Leon, 44
Trujillo, Rafael, 252
Truman Doctrine, 99–100
  and Hungary, 120
Truman, Harry S., 236, 367, 370, 377
  Germany, 121
  Greece, 99
  Korea, 141–42, 146–47, 149, 151–55, 295
  Romania, 105
  U.S.S.R., 357–63, 366
Tsaldaris, Constantine, 99
Tsankov, Aleksandŭr, 107
Tshombe, Moise, 256
Turkey, 92, 225, 310, 314, 350

U-2 affair, 214
Ubico, Jorge, 235
Ulbricht, Walter, 54, 196, 275
Ulmanis, Kārlis, 64–66
Union Miniere du Haut Katanga, 256
Union of Soviet Socialist Republics, 248
  and Afghanistan, 307–14
  Angola, 298–300
  Cambodia, 290
  civil war, 14, 16, 68, 315–16
  El Salvador, 346–47
  Ethiopia, 303–306
  Guinea, 262
  India, 387
  Indian Ocean, 304–306
  invasion by Allies, 12–17
  Iran, 314–20
  Korean airliner destruction, 363–64, 398 (n.5)
  Korean War bombing, 152

Nicaragua, 331, 335
  revolution (1917–18), 7–9
  Somalia, 303–306
  territorial expansionism, 10–11, 62, 75, 314
  treaties, 122, 125, 364–65
  United States policy toward 8–11, 47, 356–78
  Vietnam, 282–83, 290
  World War I, 5, 7, 11–13
  World War II, 126–27
United Fruit Company, 238–40
United Nations
  and Burma, 167
  Congo, 257–60
  Hungary, 199–200
  Korea, 145–47, 151–52, 156–58, 199–200
United Press International, 232
Usmani, Shaukat, 179

Valenta, Jiri, 275
Vandenburg, Hoyt, 154
Vanderbilt, Cornelius, 332
Vargas, Getúlio Dornelles, 251
Velchev, Damyan, 110
Venezuela, 334–35, 350
Versailles, Treaty of, 17, 23, 28–29, 41, 46, 63, 81–82, 139, 280, 358, 365
Veterans of Foreign Wars, 150
Viera, Rodolfo, 348
Vietnam, 279–96, 301, 320, 362
Vietnam, South, 59, 282–83, 286–87, 293–94
Vyshinsky, Andrey, 105

Walesa, Lech, 323–24
Walker, William, 332, 339
Wang Ching-wei, 131
Warsaw Pact, 195, 199, 202, 271, 273–77, 351, 366
Weinberger, Caspar, 363
West Germany. See Germany, West
West Point, 334
Western Electric, 357

Westinghouse, 357
Westinghouse Brake, 16
Wihelm II (Germany), 10–12, 15, 54, 61–62, 64, 364
Williams, William A., 15
Willoughby, Charles, 149
Wilson, Robert, 221
Wilson, Woodrow, 9, 15–16, 64, 139, 204, 280, 379 (n.5)
Wladyslaw II (Poland), 61
Wladyslaw IV (Poland), 25
World Council of Churches, 299
World War I, 111
  and Russia, 5, 11–12
World War II, 358
  anti-fascist alliance proposal, 49, 54, 83, 126
  appeasement, 48–49, 53–54
Wrangel, Pyotr Nikolayevich, 116

Wyszyński, Stefan, 193

Yalta conference, 88–89, 101, 105, 129, 132, 140, 358
Yepishev, Aleksey, 273
Yudenich, Nikolay, 67–68, 72
Yugoslavia, 111–14
  and Albania, 117–18
  Bulgaria, 108
  Czechoslovakia, 271–72, 277

Zaire. *See* Congo
Zápotocký, Antonín, 196
Zeitlin, Maurice, 214, 216
Zelaya, Jos Santos, 332
Zhivkov, Todor, 196
Zhukov, Georgy, 190, 197
Zog (Albania), 116
Zogu, Ahmed. *See* Zog (Albania)